THE 9/11 CONSPIRACY

Other books by James H. Fetzer

AS AUTHOR:

The Evolution of Intelligence: Are Humans the Only Animals with Minds?
Scientific Knowledge: Causation, Explanation, and Corroboration
Artificial Intelligence: Its Scope and Limits
Philosophy and Cognitive Science
Computers and Cognition
Philosophy of Science
Render Unto Darwin

AS CO-AUTHOR:

Glossary of Epistemology/Philosophy of Science
Glossary of Cognitive Science
American Assassination

AS EDITOR:

Foundations of Philosophy of Science: Recent Developments
Principles of Philosophical Reasoning
Science, Explanation, and Rationality
The Philosophy of Carl G. Hempel
Aspects of Artificial Intelligence
Sociobiology and Epistemology
The Great Zapruder Film Hoax
Epistemology and Cognition
Probability and Causality
Consciousness Evolving
Murder in Dealey Plaza
Assassination Science

AS CO-EDITOR:

Program Verification: Fundamental Issues in Computer Science
Philosophy, Language, and Artificial Intelligence
Philosophy, Mind, and Cognitive Inquiry
The New Theory of Reference
Definitions and Definability

THE 9/11 CONSPIRACY
The Scamming of America

Edited by
James H. Fetzer

This book and others from CATFEET PRESS® and Open Court may be ordered by calling toll-free 1-800-815-2280, or from the Open Court website at www.opencourtbooks.com.

First printing 2007

Printed and bound in the United States of America.

Library of Congress Cataloging-in-Publication Data
The 9/11 conspiracy : the scamming of America / edited by James H. Fetzer.
p. cm.
Summary: "Scholars argue that the events of September 11, 2001, could not have happened as the U.S. government claims, and that the Twin Towers could not have been brought down merely by the impact of aircraft and attendant fires"--Provided by publisher.
Includes bibliographical references and index.
ISBN-13: 978-0-8126-9612-7 (trade paper : alk. paper)
ISBN-10: 0-8126-9612-3 (trade paper : alk. paper) 1. September 11 Terrorist Attacks, 2001--Miscellanea. 2. Terrorism--United States. 3. Conspiracies. 4. World Trade Center (New York, N.Y.)--Miscellanea. I. Fetzer, James H., 1940- II. Title: Nine eleven conspiracy. III. Title: September eleven conspiracy.

HV6432.7.A1283 2007
973.931--dc22

2007003612

In honor of those who lost their lives that day,
whose survivors deserve to know how and why they died

in memoriam

. . . America is too democratic at home and too autocratic abroad. This limits the use of America's power, especially its capacity for military intimidation. Never before has a populist democracy attained international supremacy. But the pursuit of power is not a goal that commands popular passion, except in conditions of a sudden threat or challenge to the public's sense of well being. *The economic self-denial (that is, defense spending) and the human sacrifice (casualties even among professional soldiers) required in the effort are uncongenial to democratic instincts. Democracy is inimical to imperial mobilization.*

—Zbigniew Brzezinski, *The Grand Chessboard* (1997)

CONTENTS

Construction on the Twin Towers began in 1966, occupancy in 1970.

Preface

James H Fetzer

As the founder of Scholars for 9/11 Truth, a non-partisan organization of students, experts and scholars, I have been astonished at the public vilification that has been directed at members of this society for pursuing the truth about 9/11. This has taken place at different kinds of institutions and across the country. William Woodward, a professor of psychology at the University of New Hampshire, for example, has been subjected to verbal attacks by the Republican governor of the state and one of its United States Senators. Judy Wood, a professor of mechanical engineering at Clemson University, was not reappointed to her position, which she is convinced was because of her research on 9/11, rsearch I consider to be some of the most important, if not the most important, ever conducted about these events.

Kevin Barrett, a lecturer in the humanities at the University of Wisconsin, Madison, has drawn the ire of members of the state legislature, of the GOP candidate for governor in the election of 2006, and even of the Democratic governor of the state, all of whom have called for him to be fired. In this case, however, the university has supported academic freedom and scholarly research and resisted pressures to which lesser institutions have succumbed. And Steven E. Jones, whom I invited to become co-chair when I founded Scholars, has been eased out of his position as a professor of physics at Brigham Young University, even though he was a long-time faculty member in good standing. The academic administration nudged him into "early retirement," so that his research would no longer be associated with BYU.

There are multiple reasons why these actions and attitudes verge on the absurd. Even according to President George W. Bush, 9/11 was "the pivotal event" of the twenty-first century. Colleges and universities are the institutions best positioned to study significant historical events. It is therefore entirely appropriate that faculty in psychology should be studying the psychological dimensions of these events; in mechanical engineering, the physical properties of the destruction of the World Trade Center; in the humanities, their significance for relations between religions and cultures; and in physics, how the Twin Towers can have been so completely demolished. How are these events to be understood if we do not study them and openly debate our findings?

The primary reason these institutions want to separate themselves from those few scholars who are studying 9/11, however, is that they are supposed to qualify as "conspiracy theorists." Yet, according to the government's "official account," on 9/11, nineteen Islamic fundamentalists hijacked four commercial airliners, then outfoxed the most sophisticated air defense system in the world, and perpetrated these deeds under the control of a man in a cave in Afghanistan. Because it only requires two or more persons who collaborate together to perpetrate an illegal act to qualify as a "conspiracy," the government's own account is a conspiracy theory.

If the faculty at universities and colleges are going to study "the pivotal event" of the twenty-first century, therefore, they are going to have to deal with conspiracy theories. Indeed, even this elementary point seems to defy understanding by the television commentators and newspaper reporters who provide the nation with some ninety percent of its news. And if those who study 9/11 arrive at conclusions that are at variance with the government's "official account," isn't it just possible that they have arrived at those conclusions on the basis of logic and evidence and the standards of research appropriate to their respective fields? And if they should ultimately embrace the opinion that deeper and darker forces were involved here than the government allows, how can we know, apart from studying these events for ourselves, that they are wrong? The faculty, after all, are experts in their fields.

Moreover, most Americans are unaware of the most basic facts about 9/11. During a recent press conference, for example, President Bush acknowledged that Saddam Hussein had nothing to do with 9/11. The Senate Intelligence Committee has now issued its report that Saddam was not only not in cahoots with al-Qaeda but was actively pursuing its leaders to incarcerate and even kill them. And the FBI, our own FBI, has recently acknowledged that it has "no hard evidence" tying Osama bin Laden to the events of 9/11. But if Saddam was not responsible and if Osama was not responsible, then who was responsible for the mass murder of 3,000? It should be apparent that our government has been lying about 9/11 from scratch.

Why Doubt 9/11?

As a philosopher I am committed to truth. As a philosopher of science, I know that science is our most reliable method for discovering truth. And as a former Marine Corps officer, I care about our nation's future. Although Michael Ruppert, *Crossing the Rubicon* (2004), has built an imposing case for the complicity of the American government in the events of 9/11, he foregoes objective, scientific evidence and relies instead upon personal reports and subjective recollections. While I admire his contributions to understanding what may have happened, it should go without saying that objective scientific evidence provides a more reliable foundation for coming to grips with these events, where the most complete account will require integrating those reports and recollections with objective and scientific findings.

That is the approach adopted here. Members of Scholars for 9/11 Truth, building on prior research by earlier students of 9/11, have established more than a dozen refutations of the official government account, the truth of any number of which is enough to show that the government's account—in one or another of its guises—cannot possibly be correct. According to the "official account" presented in *The 9/11 Commission Report* (2004), the Twin Towers were destroyed as the result of the combined effects of airplane impacts and ensuing jet-fuel based fires, which caused the steel in the towers to weaken and the floors to "pancake" collapse.That is a skeleton outline of the government's position and almost exhausts what the 9/11 Commission has to tell us about the physical properties of these events.

Unfortunately, the impact of the planes cannot have caused enough damage to bring the buildings down, since the buildings were designed to withstand them. As Frank DeMartini, the project manager, has observed, the planes that hit the Towers were very similar to those they were designed to withstand, and they continued to stand after those impacts with negligible effects. During an interview he gave not long before his death on 9/11, DeMartini observed that the sophisticated load redistribution capabilities designed into the forty-seven core columns and 240 external columns was such that the impact of a Boeing 707 would be analogous to "sticking a pencil through mosquito netting" and that the buildings could easily withstand multiple hits by aircraft. At least three others involved in the project have said the same thing.

There were 47 core columns and 240 external columns in each tower. This inovative design created open office space which had been previously unavailable.

The melting point of steel at 2,800° F, moreover, is about 1,000° F higher than the maximum burning temperature of jet-fuel-based fires. Jet fuel is kerosene based, and does not exceed 1,800° F when it burns even under optimal conditions, so the fires cannot have caused the steel to melt, which means that melting steel did not bring the buildings down. Moreover, Underwriters Laboratory certified the steel in the buildings for up to 2,000° F for as much as three or four hours before it would even significantly weaken, where these fires burned too low and too briefly at temperatures that were around 500° F—about one hour in the South Tower and one and a half in the North—to have even caused the steel to weaken, much less melt.

If the steel had melted or weakened, then the affected floors would have displayed completely different behavior, with some asymmetrical sagging and tilting, which would have been gradual and slow, not the complete, abrupt, and total demolition that was observed. Since the steel was thicker at the base and tapered off toward the top, even though the towers did not look like the Eiffel Tower, would anyone in their wildest dreams imagine that, if a plane had hit the top of the Eiffel Tower or a fire had broken out far up, it would sustain a complete, abrupt, and total collapse? Well, the situation with the Twin Towers was the same. Apart from these relatively modest fires, the rest of the steel in these 500,000-ton buildings was stone cold.

William Rodriguez, the senior custodian in the North Tower and the last man to leave the building, has reported massive explosions in the sub-basements, which effected extensive destruction, including the demolition of a 50-ton hydraulic press and ripping the skin off a fellow worker, a report corroborated by the testimony of around three dozen other custodians. Willie reported that the explosion occurred prior to the airplane's impact, a claim that has now been substantiated in a new study by Craig Furlong and Gordon Ross, "Seismic Proof: 9/11 was an Inside Job," which is archived at 911scholars.org, demonstrating that these explosions took place as much as 14 and 17 seconds prior to the airplanes' hitting the buildings.

Physical Impossibilities

Heavy steel construction buildings like the Twin Towers, which were built with more than 100,000 tons of steel, are not amenable to "pancake collapse." It can occur with concrete structures of "lift slab" construction as the result of shoddy materials or faulty construction, but could occur in "redundant" welded-steel buildings, such as the towers, only if every supporting column were removed at the same time, as Eric Hufschmid, *Painful Questions* (2002), has observed. That would require the simultaneous failure of hundreds of joints and trusses on each floor. No one can explain how that would be possible on the official account.

According to the government's own sources, the South Tower "collapsed" in ten seconds and the North in comparable time. That is even faster than free fall with only air resistance, which, with a grand piano, for example, would have taken at least 12 seconds, an astounding result that would have been impossible without extremely powerful sources of energy. The towers are exploding from the top, not collapsing to the ground, where the floors do not move, a phenomenon that Judy Wood has likened to two gigantic trees "turning to sawdust from the top down," which, like the pulverization of the concrete, the official account cannot possibly explain.

Not all of the WTC buildings sustained the same kind of destruction. WTC-7, a 47-story building, in particular, came down in a classic controlled demolition at 5:20 pm after Larry Silverstein suggested that the best thing to do might be to "pull it", and a fire department commander made the decision to pull. It displayed all of the characteristics of classic controlled demolitions, including a complete, abrupt, and total collapse into its own footprint, where all of the floors are falling at the same time at about the rate of free fall, an event so embarrassing to the official account that it is not even mentioned in *The 9/11 Commission Report* (2004).

If events in New York were perplexing enough, those at the Pentagon were simply baffling. The hit point at the building, which was about 10 feet high and 15–17 feet wide on the ground floor, was too small to accommodate a 100-ton airliner with a 125-foot wingspan and a tail that stands 44 feet above the ground. The kind and quantity of debris was wrong for a Boeing 757: no engines, no wings, no fuselage, no seats, no bodies, no luggage, no tail! The absence of those effects means that, whatever hit the building, it cannot have been a Boeing 757!

Although there are as many as 84 videos that might be expected to show what happened, the Pentagon has released only three, none of which show a Boeing 757 hitting the building, as even Bill O'Reilly had to admit when one was shown on "The Factor." The claim is made that absence of evidence is not always evidence of absence, which is true. But at 155 feet, the plane was more than twice as long as the Pentagon at 77 feet is high and should have been present and visible; it was not, which means, once again, that the building was not hit by a Boeing 757!

Indeed, Manhattan did not have a monopoly on the alleged occurrence of impossible events. Notably, the aerodynamics of flight would have made the official trajectory—flying at high speed barely above ground level—physically impossible; and if it had come it at an angle instead, it would have created a massive crater. But there is no crater and the government has no way out, which means that, on the official account, it is not even physically possible that the Pentagon was hit by a Boeing 757!

If Flight 93 had come down as advertised in Shanksville, PA, there would have been a debris field of about a city block in size, but in fact the debris is distributed over an area of about eight square miles, which would be explainable if the plane had been shot down in the air but not if it had crashed as required by the official scenario. There are more, especially about the alleged hijackers, including that they were not competent to fly the planes; their names were not on any passenger manifest; they were not subject to any autopsy; several have turned up alive and well and living in the Middle East; the government has never even produced their tickets; on and on. Evidence may be found here and sources at 911scholars.org.

Additional Anomalies

Virtually every aspect of the official account of 9/11 is open to suspicion or even outright refutation. For example, there are nearly as many questions about the alleged aircraft as there are about the alleged hijackers. AA #11 left Logan Airport in Boston with only 92 occupants when it could have carried 351. Similarly, United #175 had only 65, when it could have handled 351. AA #77 departed from Dulles with 64 aboard when it could carry 289. Likewise, United #93 carried only 45 of 289. FAA deregistration of AA #11 and of AA #77 did not occur until 14 January 2002. FAA deregistration of United #93 and of United #175 did not even take place until 28 September 2005 ("FAA Registry: N-Number Inquiry Results").

Although we cannot reconstruct the Twin Towers to test their fire resistance, that was done for us on 13 February 1975, when the 11th floor of the North Tower was enveloped by an intense fire that burned at temperatures around 2,000° F for over three hours and enveloped 65 percent of the floor, including the core. The steel suffered no serious damage; in particular, none of the steel trusses connecting the core columns to the external columns needed to be replaced (*New York Times*, 14–15 February 1975). This counted as a severe test of UL certification, which the building passed effortlessly, and clearly refutes the claim that more modest fires would have done more serious damage.

Even Steve Jones, who has touted conventional explosives, including thermite and thermate, as the crucial ingredients to understand what brought down the Twin Towers, has implicitly acknowledged that more sophisticated devices may have been used:

> Those who wish to preserve fundamental physical laws as inviolate may wish to take a closer look at the collapse of the south tower. We observe that approximately 30 upper floors began to rotate as a block, to the south and east. They began to topple over, as favored by the Law of Increasing Entropy. The torque due to gravity on this block was enormous, as was its angular momentum. But then—and this I am still puzzling over—this block turned mostly to powder in mid-air! (David Ray Griiffin and Peter Dale Scott, eds., *9/11 and American Empire* (2007), pp. 47–48)

This is an important observation by Jones, since it confirms the thesis of Judy Wood that the buildings were pulverized—turned into very fine dust—from the top down.

Having learned that the FBI did not charge Osama bin Laden with offenses related to 9/11 in its wanted poster, Ed Haas, editor of *Muckraker Report*, called the FBI and spoke with Rex Tomb, Chief of Investigative Publicity for the FBI. Asked why there was no such charge, Tomb said, "The reason why 9/11 is not mentioned on Usama bin Laden's Most Wanted page is because the FBI has *no hard evidence* connecting bin Laden to 9/11,"

Muckraker Report (6 June 2006). Stunned when she read this, Carol Brown of INN World Report called Rex Tomb and read him what Ed Haas had published, and Rex Tomb verified that it was right as printed.

Serious questions have arisen about the authenticity of the alleged "confession tape" attributed to bin Laden. Although he initially denied having anything to do with 9/11, in a second tape of dubious authenticity, he allegedly claimed to have been responsible for the attacks. When Ed Haas submitted a formal request for the government to certify the "confession tape" as genuine, the government refused to do that, *Muckraker Report* (11 August 2006), which is consistent with research by Scholars that the "confession tape" appears to be bogus. That an apparently faked video serves as the government's strongest argument speaks volumes about the case.

In their book, *Without Precedent* (2006), former Governor Thomas Kean (R) and Rep. Lee Hamilton (D) expressed their concerns that the Pentagon, especially, had not been forthcoming in testimony about the events of 9/11, particularly in relation to the lack of coordination between the FAA and NORAD. "We still to this day don't know why NORAD [the North American Aerospace Command] told us what they told us", Kean was quoted as saying in *The Washington Post* (2 August 2006). "It was just so far from the truth . . . ." A man with this little comprehension of the motives for lying—to distract from or to distort the truth—may not have been a wise choice to get to the bottom of the events of 9/11.

Are Conspiracy Theorists Paranoid?

William Douglas, an expert on parenting, began investigating media coverage of 9/11 after reading an article in the *Milwaukee Journal Sentinel* (29 June 2006), entitled "Sept. 11 Claim Stirs UW Probe—Instructor Says U.S. Planned the Attacks to Provoke War." He would later write, "Exposing the 9/11 Conspiracy Wing Nuts" Information Clearing House.com), how "This led to (his) discovery of some wild conspiracy theorists that endanger our government and media establishments, with quite frankly insane assertions." He began with a google search and turned up a "Hannity and Colmes" interview with Kevin Barrett, an earlier interview with James Fetzer, and an even earlier appearance on Fox by Mike Berger of 911truth.org.

Some referred to an organization called "Scholars for 9/11 Truth" with a website at www.st911.org, which pointed to the temperatures of the fires in the Twin Towers, the construction of the buildings, and the speed at which they fell, Douglas wrote, as evidence that what we had all observed in Manhattan that day had properties like those of the controlled demolitions used to bring down resorts and casinos in Las Vegas. "Their claim," he said, "was that [what happened to] the WTC buildings could not have been caused solely by the airplanes hitting the WTC buildings that day." Indeed, we maintain that they could not have been brought down as the combined effect of aircraft impacts and jet-fuel based fires.

Douglas contacted the office of Wisconsin State Legislator, Rep. Stephen Nass (R-Whitewater), who had called for Kevin Barrett to be fired from his teaching position at the University of Wisconsin-Madison. He asked if they were familiar with the Scholars website and, when told they had learned of it that week, asked if he or Rep. Nass could address the arguments presented there, including evidence that demolition-type explosives may have been involved. "The gentleman responded that no, they had not looked at this information, and this would not be something they would look at," Douglas wrote, "further indicating that anyone who made such charges was blinded by their hatred of President Bush."

When he reviewed the three programs cited above, Douglas noticed that they were dominated by the themes that, first, those who challenge the official account are "a fringe movement" and, second, that they are of questionable sanity. So he looked at the claim that a majority of Americans disagreed with the program's guests. A CNN viewers poll, which is non-random, on 10 November 2005, asked, "Do you believe there is a US government cover-up surrounding 9/11?" 89% replied "Yes," they did believe there was a cover-up by the US Government (9,441 votes), while only 12% felt there was no cover-up. That motivated him to dig deeper to determine if this result might be derived from a biased sample or a statistical anomaly.

A national Zogby poll of May 2006, for example, which was random, found that 45%, of the American public felt a new 9/11 investigation should be launched because "so many unanswered questions about 9/11 remain that Congress or an International Tribunal should re-investigate the attacks, including whether any US government officials consciously allowed or helped facilitate their success." And an earlier Zogby poll of New York City residents, from August 2004, reported that half (49.3%) of New Yorkers felt that U.S. government officials "knew in advance that attacks were planned on or around September 11, 2001, and that they consciously failed to act." 66% of New Yorkers, Douglas discovered, called for a new probe by Congress or by New York's Attorney General.

The 9/11 Conspiracy Wing-Nuts

When he turned to consider the "questionable sanity" allegation, Douglas found a mass of evidence to the contrary. Among the most outspoken critics of the official account of 9/11 turned out to be prominent Republican and past Chief Economist for the Department of Labor in the administration of George W. Bush, a professor emeritus at Texas A&M, Morgan Reynolds. He discovered that the 9/11 skeptics include "a host of high level Republican administration officials, defense experts, intelligence experts, and respected scholars, as well as well known celebrities who are now adding the spotlight of their names to the issue of 9/11." He listed these:

Robert Bowman, Former Director of Advanced Space Programs Development for the US Air Force, under President Reagan; Ray McGovern, Former CIA Intelligence Advisor to Reagan and George H. W. Bush; Kevin Ryan, former department head at UL (Underwriter Laboratories); Paul Craig Roberts, former assistant secretary of the US Treasury; The Honorable Paul Hellyer; the Canadian National Defense Minister; Michael Meacher, Minister for the Environment, Member of Parliament (UK); Andreas von Bulow, National Minister of Defense (Germany); and General Leonid Ivashov, former Chief of Staff of the Russian armed forces.

He also turned up David Shayler, former MI6 British Counter Intelligence Officer; James Fetzer, Distinguished McKnight University Professor of Philosophy at the University of Minnesota, Duluth; Steven Jones, Professor of Physics, Brigham Young University; David Ray Griffin, Emeritus Professor of Philosophy of Religion and Theology, Claremont Graduate University; A. K Dewdney, Professor of mathematics, University of Western Ontario, and founder of the Scientific Panel Investigating Nine-Eleven (SPINE); USAF Col. (Ret) George Nelson, aircraft crash investigation authority, and USAF Col. (Ret) Don de Grand-Pre, a former chief Pentagon arms negotiator for the Middle East.

Douglas also reported that Actors Charlie Sheen, Ed Asner, and Ed Begley, Jr., were among those speaking out about 9/11. Based upon his research, he was forced to conclude that the main concerns express by television hosts—the "fringe" group and the "sanity" issue—were "very weak arguments, really with no merit at all." There is even more support for that proposition today: a recent New York Times/CBS poll has revealed that 53% of the American people are skeptical about the official 9/11 account and 28% reject it altogether. Only 16% believe it ("Americans Question Bush on 9/11 Intelligence," 14 October 2006). And now more than one hundred academicians have joined their ranks ("Professors Question 9/11").

The biting irony, in Douglas' view, is that, "too many of our media spokespersons on television and radio adhere to a wild conspiracy theory . . . that anyone who looks into the facts of the events of one of the important issues in history is alone, and insane, but yet somehow organized in some united conspiratorial effort. Of course," he observes, "the facts fly in the face of this conspiracy theory, but these media personalities appear unable to grasp reality even when it is pointed out to them." From the perspective of parenting, he believes "it is unhealthy to have insane people in charge of the national information highways our children are taught to watch. We need sane media people who look at facts regarding issues, not ones who launch into insane screeds of paranoia to avoid reality."

He concludes by extending these reflections to Rep. Nass and his staff, who "want to fire a university teacher for presenting facts, many of which were available on (www.st911.org). To fire someone for presenting facts, facts that you dispute, yet have no idea what those facts are, and are unwilling to look at them to find out what they are . . . is also insane." Thus, "These politicians apparently assert some wild conspiracy theory that millions of Americans are questioning the events of 9/11 because they are "Bush haters" according to the aide at Nass' office. This kind of delusional paranoia by our elected officials is of particular concern. Such wild-eyed conspiratorialists should not be allowed in government."

The problem that confronts the nation now is that, even though most Americans are skeptical of what our government has told us, most of our politicians are behind the curve. Rational beliefs, unlike paranoid ones, are responsive to logic and evidence. This book presents, in a lucid and compact volume, what every responsible citizen should know about 9/11. A monstrous hoax of violence and of threats of violence has been used to instill fear into the population of the United States to manipulate us for political purposes. Since that is the classic definition of terrorism, the bottom line is that, since 2001 but almost certainly earlier, the American government has been practicing terrorism on the American people. What you will read here makes this fact apparent beyond any reasonable doubt.

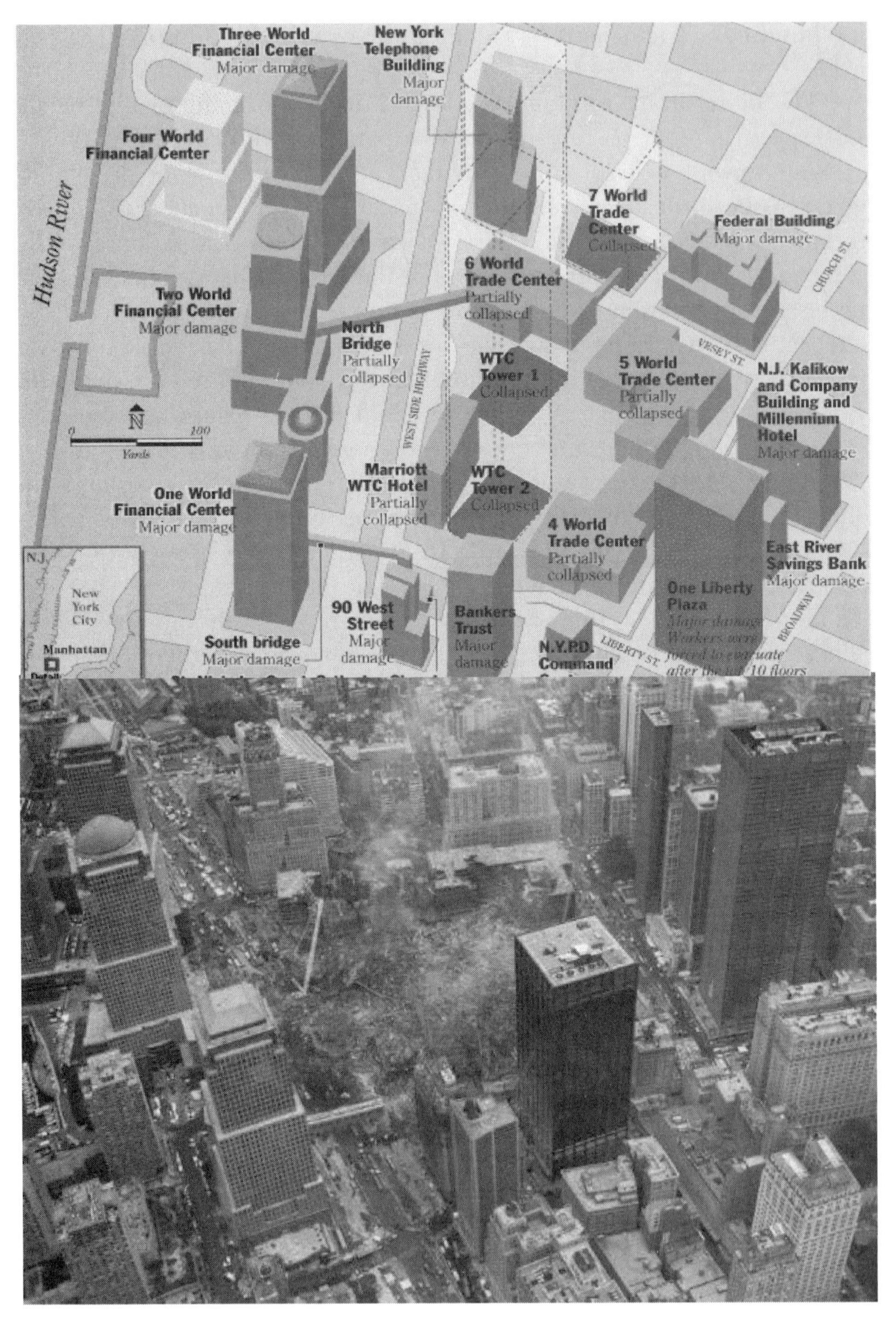

The pattern of destruction was as though the "terrorists" planned to destroy all and only building with "WTC" designations.

Contributors

John C. Austin earned his BA in law and J.D. from William Howard Taft College in Santa Ana, CA. He has had an extensive career in radio, including serving as News Director at KOHI, St. Helens, OR, Staff Announcer at KOMW, Omak, WA, Program Director at KRUZ, Santa Barbara, CA, and other positions in Eugene, OR and Los Angeles, CA, including Placement Director and National Instructor for the Columbia School of Broadcasting. Among his other activities have been forming bands, including "Racoon" in Vancouver, B.C., "Okanogan Smith" in Omak, WA, and "Emmitt & Austin" in Santa Barbara, CA.

Elias Davidsson was born in Palestine in 1942, the child of German Jews forced to emigrate to Palestine to escape Nazi persecution. For more than 20 years, he was a computer programmer and systems engineer, when he decided to change his profession. He has now published 20 volumes of original compositions for musical education. Co-founder of the Association Island-Palestine, he has engaged in intensive research on the compatibility of economic sanctions with human rights. In 2002, Elias began research on 9/11 and founded the Islandic chapter of the 9/11 truth movement.

James H. Fetzer, Distinguished McKnight University Professor Emeritus at the University of Minnesota, Duluth, has published more than 20 books in the philosophy of science and on the theoretical foundations of computer science, artificial intelligence, and cognitive science. A former Marine Corps officer, he edited three books on the assassination of JFK and co-authored another on the crash that took the life of US Senator Paul Wellstone. Apart from 9/11, his most recent area of investigation has been evolution, cognition, and morality.

Joe Firmage is the founder and CEO of ManyOne Networks, and founder of the Digital Universe Foundation. A pioneer in object oriented programming and commercial applications of the World Wide Web, USWeb became the world's largest Internet consulting firm under his leadership. In partnership with Carl Sagan Productions, he has initiated research for a modern "Encyclopedia Galactica", an internet based visual navigation system for scientific knowledge, experience, and exploration. His chapter originally appeared in *The Journal of 9/11 Studies*.

David Ray Griffin is Professor of Religion and Theology, Emeritus, Claremont School of Theology and Claremont Graduate University in Claremont, CA. He is the author or editor of over 30 books, primarily in philosophy and theology, and he has also published six books dealing with 9/11: *The New Pearl Harbor* (2004), *The 9/11 Commission Report: Omissions and Distortions* (2005), *The American Empire and the Commonwealth of God* (2005, co-authored), *Christian Faith and the Truth about 9/11* (2006), *9/11 and American Empire: Intellectuals Speak Out* (2006), co-edited with Peter Dale Scott, and *Debunking 9/11 Debunkers* (2007).

John McMurtry earned his BA in English Literature and his MA in Philosophy from the University of Toronto. He earned his Ph.D. in Philosophy from the University of London in 1975 and became Full Professor of Philosophy at the University of Guelph in 1975. Elected to the Royal Society of Canada in 2001, he is currently a University Professor Emeritus. His articles have been widely translated. In 2004, he was selected to the principal author and editor of the United Nation's only work in philosophy, *Philosophy and World Problems*.

Rick Rajter is currently completing his Ph.D. in Materials Science and Engineering at MIT, where he earned his BS in the same department. Valedictorian of his high school class, he taught himself computer programming. Rick has been studying historical hoaxes by applying his skill as an engineer and scientist to analyze cases. Rick is currently working with other colleagues on the possibility that high-tech weaponry might have been used on the Twin Towers.

Morgan O. Reynolds is Professor of Economics Emeritus at Texas A&M University. A former Chief Economist in the Department of Labor 2001-02, he has also served as the Director of the Criminal Justice Center and as Senior Fellow at the National Center for Policy Analysis, Dallas, TX. He is author or co-author of six books, including *Public Expenditures, Taxes and the Distribution of Income* (1977), *Power and Privilege: Labor Unions in America* (1984), *Crime by Choice* (1985), and *Economics of Labor* (1995).

Peter Dale Scott, is a former Canadian diplomat and professor of English at the University of California, Berkeley. A leading expert on the assassination of JFK, his next book is entitled, *The Road to 9/11: Wealth, Empire, and the Future of America* (2007). He co-edited *9/11 and American Empire: Intellectuals Speak Out* (2006) with David Ray Griffin. He is also noted for his poetry, and received the 2002 Lannan Poetry Award. He maintains a web site at www.peterdalescott.net.

Jack White has an extensive history related to art and photography, where most of his career has been spent in Ft. Worth, TX. He is an expert on the photographs and films associated with the assassination of JFK and served as a consultant to the US House Select Committee on Assassinations during its hearings in 1977-78. He has published two videos of his studies about JFK. His extensive research on films and photographs related to 9/11 may be accessed from 911scholars.org and other sites.

Judy Wood is a former professor of mechanical engineering with research interests in experimental stress analysis, structural mechanics, optical methods, deformation analysis, and the materials characterization of biomaterials and composite materials. She is a member of the Society for Experimental Mechanics (SEM) and co-founder of its Biological Systems and Materials division. She earned her B.S. in civil engineering, her M.S. in engineering mechanics, and her Ph.D. in materials engineering science from the Department of Engineering Science and Mechanics, Virginia Polytechnic Institute and State University, Blacksburg, VA.

PROLOGUE

American Nightmare 2001–?

John C. Austin

Have you ever woken from sleep unsure if you were having a dream or not? You're relieved to find that it was just a dream in most cases. But what if the dream or nightmare becomes real over a longer period of awakening? At what point are you awake?

We have been fortunate in this great experiment of a democratic republic; we've seen the wisdom of a structure created for the benefit and good of the individual—the Constitution. A largely self-correcting document that still continues to inspire most people to preserve human rights in the face of numerous threats against those rights. A worthy plan that has largely kept us from internal threats upon the individual by those in and out of government. Until now.

This book attempts to describe the most recent threat against every American. A threat based on fear of losing our freedoms that, at the same time, takes those very freedoms. A threat that has consciously moved to remove power from the sovereignty of the people, to government and corporate control. A threat based on the simplest and worst of mankind's ideologies—greed and power.

All that was needed was an excuse to begin the process. A way to provide the ingredient of fear. Certainly, the efforts seem to be orchestrated as an entire plan, a plan that accomplishes several goals:

- To position America as the sole superpower in the world;
- To obtain greater control of American society;
- To ensure security of America; and
- To also obtain the natural resources that would power the other efforts.

Is there any evidence of such a plan? Indeed there is.

In 1997, "Project for the New American Century" (PNAC) was formed as a think tank and policy-making organization. The stated goals of the group closely align with the goals stated above. However, PNAC is not just another think tank. Unlike many other organizations, PNAC is full of people who came into the Bush administration. Its members include:

Name	Department	Title	Remarks
Elliott Abrams	National Security Council	Representative for Middle Eastern Affairs	President of the Ethics and Public Policy Center
Richard Armitage	Department of State (2001-2005)	Deputy Secretary of State	
John R. Bolton	Department of State	U.S. Ambassador to the United Nations	Previously served as Undersecretary for Arms Control and International Security Affairs in the first administration of GWB.
Richard Cheney	Bush Administration	Vice President	PNAC Founder
Seth Cropsey	Voice of America	Director of the International Broadcasting Bureau	
Paula Dobriansky	Department of State	Undersecretary of State for Global Affairs	
Francis Fukuyama	President's Council on Bioethics	Council Member	Professor of International Political Economy at Johns Hopkins University
Bruce Jackson	U.S. Committee on NATO	President	
Zalmay Khalilzad	U.S. Embassy Baghdad, Iraq	U.S.Ambassador to Iraq	Previously served as U.S. Ambassador to Afghanistan from November 2003 to June 2005
Lewis Libby	Bush Administration	Chief of Staff for the Vice President	Indicted by Grand Jury on charges of Obstruction of Justice, False Statements and Perjury and resigned October 28, 2005.

Peter W. Rodman	Department of Defense	Assistant Secretary of Defense for International Security	
Donald Rumsfeld	Department of Defense	Secretary of Defense	PNAC founder and previously Chairman of the Board of Gilead Sciences Developer of Tamiflu
Randy Scheunemann	U.S. Committee on NATO, Project on Transitional Democracies, International Republican Institute	Member	Founded the Committee for the Liberation of Iraq.
Paul Wolfowitz	World Bank	President	Deputy Secretary of Defense, 2001-2005
Dov S. Zakheim	Department of Defense	Comptroller	Former V.P. of System Planning Corp.
Robert B. Zoellick	Department of State	Deputy Secretary of State	Office of the United States Trade Representative (2001-2005);

Sources – wikipedia.org and www.newamericancentury.org

As one can see, PNAC members initially virtually controled the Bush administration. Membership includes the Vice-President, Richard Cheney, whom many believe is the real power behind Bush. And almost all the stated members of PNAC are neo-conservatives (or "neocons").

Cheney and Donald Rumsfeld are of particular interest because they are the men in close control of the military and intelligence arms of the Bush administration. But what other evidence ties these members of PNAC to a national plan that is intended to meet the goals stated previously? The evidence lies in the stated goals of PNAC, presented in the following policy statement from a PNAC paper entitled "Rebuilding America's Defenses: Strategies, Forces and Resources for a New Century" (2000):

> The United States has for decades sought to play a more permanent role in Gulf regional security. While the unresolved conflict with Iraq provides the immediate justification, the need for a substantial American force presence in the Gulf transcends the issue of the regime of Saddam Hussein.

But how to accomplish this plan? To get people to agree to massive military build-ups, pre-emptive war, the necessity of America being the sole superpower in the world?

"The process of transformation," the plan said, "is likely to be a long one, absent some catastrophic and catalyzing event—like a new Pearl Harbor."

The majority of that 90-page report outlines plans for increasing military spending to the point where America could "fight and decisively win multiple, simultaneous major theater wars."

This plan flies in the face of America's long history of non-involvement in imperialistic ambitions. There have been some exceptions, many will note, but the vast majority of us have been absolutely against America being an aggressor toward nations that were not a threat.

A "New Pearl Harbor"?

Has the United States accidentally followed the exact plan of PNAC? Have we seen the New Pearl Harbor? The writers of this book believe that is exactly what has happened. And—that it was no accident.

As previously mentioned, we as Americans have had a long streak of good fortune, largely due to our nation's defining principles as described in the Constitution. The first ten Amendments to the Constitution were created to protect the individual from government transgressions. The freedom to speak, to assemble, to petition the government for redress, to be secure in our homes and possessions, to have a fair and speedy trial if accused, and to basic representation—are all under very real and specific attack by the Bush administration. An administration that is full of people who want to make the world itself a satellite of American ambitions, capable of winning simultaneous wars in various theaters. This is a basic shift in who holds sovereignty, from the People . . . to the government that was intended to represent the People.

The nightmare was in the works, but didn't see full expression until 11 September 2001, when the incredible happened. Or perhaps it was December of 2000, when George W. Bush was elected by, to say the least, questionable processes.

11 September 2001. The "official version," released in very short order, was that nineteen hijackers took over four commercial aircraft and crashed them, with only Flight 93 showing some evidence of resistance. Ten days later, 21 September 2001, Secretary of State Condoleezza Rice reiterated that basic explanation, responding to reporters' questions that a

full "white paper" of evidence would be forthcoming. This "white paper" would have all the evidence showing the truth and supporting their early conclusion. We are still waiting for that "white paper".

All we had was nineteen photographs and a verbal story.

The government quickly named Osama bin Laden as the master-mind of the event. This was the same bin Laden that the CIA supported with funds and weapons when he was fighting against the Russian occupation of Afghanistan for many years. In late September, 2001, bin Laden, in a news article in Pakistan that was largely ignored, denied that he was involved in 9/11. In December, a video was released that showed an Osama look-alike taking credit for the attack. The person in that video resembles bin Laden, but is left-handed, wears a gold ring and has quite different facial features. Wearing gold jewelry of any kind is forbidden in the Wahhabi sect.

In the years since, in fact almost immediately, uncomfortable facts began to surface—facts that the government has yet to respond to. As early as 23 September 2001, the BBC reported that four of the alleged hijackers were alive. Their source was the Saudi government. The U.S. explanation was that the "hijackers" had stolen identifications of real people. Later, when even more "hijackers" turned up alive and well in various countries, FBI director Mueller was forced to admit that we "couldn't be sure about any of the identities" of the "hijackers".

It was later learned that there were no Arabic names on any of the passenger lists of the aircraft.

Other facts began to surface, and various people began to look into the official story, sensing something was not quite right. Two of the "hijacked" aircraft were still listed as operational two years after they were destroyed on 9/11. In the meantime, New York firefighters and police were ordered to say nothing about the events of that day. The Federal Aviation Administration likewise, told its employees that 9/11 cannot be discussed. The military, through more conventional means, also ordered public silence about the event.

Meanwhile, researchers began to study the videos and news reports of that date. In short order, the major news outlets, NBC, CBS, ABC, CNN, Fox News, and others, became unwilling to supply video tapes and news reports regarding 9/11. This was indeed curious. Usually, a reporter may purchase a copy of news video and reports, simply paying the outlet for the cost, and giving proper attribution. Not after 9/11.

Fortunately, some of the video had already been obtained, and people who taped the event on their home televisions had a great deal of material to share. These videos invariably had the logo of the news organization at the bottom of their screens. This is important because of the news clamp-down later. A great deal of the video, containing comments about "secondary explosions" was, at first, unobtainable except from individual viewers. Later came the tapes and transcripts of firefighters and police during the event.

Many of these videos have been compiled into DVDs that question the official story. (Many of these are featured on the web site of Scholars for 9/11 Truth, 911scholars.org.)

Perhaps the most important of these videos was taken by the Naudet Brothers, documentary film-makers who fortunately were filming a project about a new Firefighter who had joined the NYFD. Their footage happened to catch the first commercial jet hit Tower I of the World Trade Center. It was the only known film of the first strike.

However, more and more questions arose as to exactly what happened. Why, if no steel-framed building in history had ever collapsed because of fire, did three of them at the World Trade Center collapse by fire on the very same day? What pulverized every bit of the thousands of tons of concrete to fine powder? Why did NORAD fail to intercept any aircraft, even after the first two strikes on the Towers? Why was there no wreckage of a 757 at the Pentagon? Why were their no videos of the Pentagon strike? This, at the United States' premier defense installation?

Surely, the government could provide evidence of its claims. But so far, the only "evidence" is the questionable photos of nineteen "hijackers" and the Rice statement. Nothing further, since 21 September 2001.

To believe that the government has been less than forthcoming may be somewhat difficult for Americans to accept. Yet that is the case. In the matter of the Pentagon, the government belatedly offered five frames of the moments before explosion. None of those frames provide a picture of a Boeing 757. In fact, a Boeing 757 could not possibly hide behind a very small parking box in the first frame. A trail of white smoke is seen, which would contradict it being from a commercial aircraft. White contrails can only be seen at high altitude, and are composed of frozen water vapor. At ground level, the exhaust of commercial jets is faintly black, if visible at all.

As more and more people began to question the evidence, the more peculiar the official story became. WTC-7 was undamaged by any aircraft, having only two small fires on different floors. Yet that building, also steel structured, fell at free-fall speed into its own footprint in six seconds. The landlord of the World Trade Center, Larry Silverstein, said he told firefighters to "pull it", an industry term that means "to demolish". This is unusual, because firefighters are not in that business. Also, do fire trucks carry around high explosives to fire scenes? Lastly, setting up a good demolition requires at least two weeks, according to experts.

Other researchers, carefully examining videos (by reputable news sources) found instances of explosions, and the casting out of huge steel beams hundreds of feet from Towers I and II. And both I and II fell at free-fall speeds—impossible, considering they would have met resistance from the strong structure that was still cool and unburned. Towers I and II were designed, according to their architect, to withstand one or more hits from the largest plane at the time of construction, a fully loaded Boeing 707, approximately the same size as a Boeing 767.

Then contradictory information was found about Flight 93. This flight was confirmed to have landed at Cleveland Airport by United Airlines. The flight allegedly landed there because of a bomb threat on board, according to the Mayor of Cleveland and United Airlines itself. Perhaps the government missed that in all the confusion. After all, some twenty-two aircraft at one point, were on radar screens of the FAA, sowing confusion amongst the traffic controllers as to "what plane was where?" The other major question that morning, was "Is this real or is it the exercise(s)?"

They had every right to be confused, because the morning of September 11, the US military was conducting at least five major military exercises at the same exact time. One of the exercises was a "hijacked aircraft scenario that had a threat of planes hitting buildings." A rather strange coincidence, one would think. Of interest is that the Vice-President and PNAC founder, Dick Cheney, was running the exercises from a basement control room of the White House.

Serious questions also include the fact that no aircraft were successfully launched to intercept the "hijacked" planes, yet the FAA lost AA 11 at 8:17 AM, when the transponder was turned off and the plane went off its flight plan.

FAA regulations demand that such an incident be treated as a suspected hijacking, and that the plane be intercepted immediately. Yet Flight 11 continued unmolested, hitting Tower I some 26 minutes later.

NORAD/NORTHCOM had a very good track record on interceptions previously. From January 1, 2001, until September 11, 2001, they had successfully intercepted 67 aircraft within a matter of minutes. However, on 9/11, they could not intercept *any* of the aircraft. In the private sector, as well as the military, such failure would normally send heads rolling. But since 9/11, there have been no reports of anyone being so much as demoted or chastised. No one. New York and our nation's Capitol were absolutely undefended on the morning of 9/11. This alone should raise serious questions to all Americans.

One might ask, "OK, if these facts are true, why hasn't the American media looked into this?"

To discuss that further, one must reflect on the history of the press when covering governmental actions.

- In 1898, the United States declared War on Spain following the destruction of the *U.S.S Maine* in Havana Harbor. The attack was blamed on the Spanish, but was later discovered to have been an internal explosion due to coal dust in the hold of the ship.

- In 1933, the Reichstag Fire gave Hitler an opportunity to take greater power in Germany. It turned out that the Nazis actually started the fire, blaming others as an excuse to limit civil liberties and pass massive social control laws.

- In 1941, the Japanese attack on Pearl Harbor put the United States into WWII. Only much later was it discovered the US had cracked the Japanese code, and Roosevelt knew the attack was coming. History suggests that Roosevelt's failure to warn Pearl Harbor was an intentional act to get the US into War with Germany.—something the majority of the public did not want to do at the time.

- In 1965, a PT boat "attack" on two US Navy destroyers angered the public to the point where LBJ could ask Congress for the Gulf of Tonkin Resolution—an authorization for the massive build up in Viet-Nam. The attack never happened. It was manufactured to start the Viet-Nam War.

- In 1990–91, George H.W. Bush moved to act against Iraq, after a fifteen year old girl told of atrocities done by the Iraqis in Kuwait. Chief among the crimes? Throwing babies to the floor to die, so the Iraqis could steal incubators from hospitals. It turns out the girl was the daughter of the Kuwaiti Ambassador, and was coached on how to testify, tearfully, to Congress by a Washington public relations firm. It was a lie, created to garner support for the Gulf War.

As we can see, a well placed deception can start a war. And, note that all of this important information only came out well *after the fact.* The wars were successfully started, the "mission accomplished." Also note that, aside from a few scattered reports, the Media failed to bring the truth out in a timely manner about any of these events.

We have long been proud of that very basic First Amendment right —the freedom of the press. But the press is rarely rewarded when it breaks news that angers the powers that be. Carl Bernstein and Bob Woodward were very close to not only losing their jobs over Watergate, but to destroying *The Washington Post* completely. If there had been no "Deep Throat", their story would have died, untold. Nixon would have served out his second term. The war in Vietnam might not have ended. It is a great example of the power of the press, where it can bring forth the truth as the natural watchdog of government or other wrongdoing.

But things have changed since 1973.

News is now a corporate conglomerate. It's said that ninety percent of the news is controlled by just five corporations. These corporations don't have a Hippocratic Oath. They don't have an obligation to provide the truth. They have no obligation to be absolutely accurate or to dig deeper into suspicious activity. There's no incentive on moral or principled grounds; no obligation to serve the public with uncomfortable facts. There is but one important thing for these corporations —money.

At the top of these corporations are men who enjoy rubbing shoulders with the power elite of government and industry. They also enjoy entertainment stories about Pamela Anderson or Britney Spears. And, apparently they enjoy "missing blond" stories equally as much, judging by the evening Cable News.

Reporters, be it television, radio or print, are in danger of losing their jobs if they stray too far from the company line. This situation is only too obvious when the neocon spin gets heavy coverage, and government misdeeds are minimalized. There are some signs that this is changing, yet I can imagine no greater threat to our democracy than outright control over the mainstream press.

So, like the JFK assassination and other major national questions, the press does not do its important job of finding the truth. More and more we must hope that whistleblowers have the courage to step forward. And some have. Then they are ordered not to testify while they feel the heat of Presidential or other pressure. Ambassador Joseph Wilson and his wife Valerie Plame are examples, Sibel Edmonds is another.

Since it's evident that the press has been largely deficient, with rare exceptions, it is interesting that our newest medium, the internet, has arisen as a response to the vacuum. Strangely, the public has been slow to take the internet seriously, partly because anything that criticizes the powers that be, is immediately subject to a concerted attack by a White House that spent $1.6 billion on public relations and fake news stories in 2005.

But the internet is gaining respectability. It has broken stories that have proven accurate and it has been a public forum for dissenter and neocon alike. Perhaps the internet's greatest contribution will be the facts about 9/11 that the mainstream media refuses to acknowledge.

I tend to think that Truth cannot be totally ignored. Eventually, like hydraulics, if you step hard on it somewhere, it will squeeze out somewhere else.

So we the people have a problem. Do we believe the official story about 9/11, that nineteen Arabs carried off this major disaster, co-coordinated from a cave in Afghanistan? Or does the truth lie somewhere else? Were the hijackers themselves *allowed* to proceed? Even to the point where our own air defense was quiet on that morning? Since we cannot depend on mainstream news to ask the questions and find the answers, we have to look to people that have thoroughly studied the facts.

And the facts overwhelmingly point to some sort of government involvement with the specific purpose of starting a never-ending War on Terrorism. Never-ending is the operative word. When you have a common enemy for the foreseeable future, you have the situation in Orwell's *1984*. Oceania versus Eurasia, a war that is serving the purpose of the power elite and can be manipulated on every level, with staged attacks to keep the fear alive.

When one asks the question "Why?", the Administration's response is that "they hate our freedoms." But if one reflects upon that, it makes no sense. Simple jealousy? Isn't it far more logical that terrorism is a response by those that are oppressed themselves? And we have to ask – who, then is the oppressor? Is Iraq simply the latest example of oppression and occupation? The United States has spent millions creating fourteen permanent bases there. And a billion dollar "Embassy City". That doesn't sound like we are planning to pull out as soon as we can.

The Aftermath of 9/11

Clearly the first major question in any criminal case, is *cui bono*? Who benefits? 9/11 created "opportunities", according to this administration. The more obvious ones are:

- To beef up military and security spending in a massive way, to provide the wherewithal to successfully maintain and "win" many simultaneous foreign wars (the PNAC plan).
- To create a state of fear, a demand that the government "do something" to protect us from the "evil terrorists."
- To rally universal support for this administration to fight the War on Terror; as Bush said, "If you are not with us, you are against us."
- To quickly pass laws that give the government more power over all Americans. The unread "Patriot Act" was pre-written and just needed the right moment to sail, unquestioned, through Congress.
- The power to suppress dissent. This is extremely important. If you are against the war, you are automatically on the side of the terrorists. Perhaps the Democratic loyal opposition was basically "disappeared" with this mighty move. Recall that any protest against war was considered un-American. This served the Administration well.
- To create entirely new government departments (Homeland Security, Immigration and Customs Enforcement, etc.) These departments automatically create more intrusions on privacy and amass more information on ALL Americans.
- To secure America's oil supplies for the future, rather than move toward a more sensible energy policy.
- To eventually excuse any otherwise unconstitutional acts under the guise of the never-ending "War on Terror". Chief among these is the Presidential claim that he can wire-tap Americans on a massive level, with basically no accountability.

In short, every single effect of the events of 9/11, has been to deny civil rights and give unwarranted power to the government and corporations—most of that to the Executive Branch alone. Somehow, we faced down mass destruction by thousands of nuclear weapons for many years, without losing major portions of our Constitution or privacy—but now you can be wiretapped without a warrant in direct contradiction to the 4th Amendment of the Constitution.

So the attack on 9/11 has changed America in critical ways. It could be, strangely enough, considered a success. It has brought about major shifts in American policy and internal structural change. Again, who benefited? Was it the so-called "terrorists"?

I, and an increasing number of others, believe the facts of 9/11 tell their own story. It is beholden upon a society that believes in a democratic republic and the Constitution, that we be active in the running of our country; that we demand the truth. What are the facts surrounding 9/11?

Those facts are presented in the volume in your hands. They have been carefully researched and discussed by professionals in their respective fields. I, and the various authors herein, believe that the facts are overwhelming and self-evident to anyone who inquires with an open mind.

The future of our country demands that we pay attention: that we look at evidence, that we don't call things "impossible" simply because they seem at first glance to be unlikely. Clearly at stake is the future of our children, our very Constitution, and millions of lives here and abroad. That should be enough reason to seek the evidence.

To preserve this Republic, we need to know what the truth actually is. The real conspiracy is the one being perpetrated against the American people.

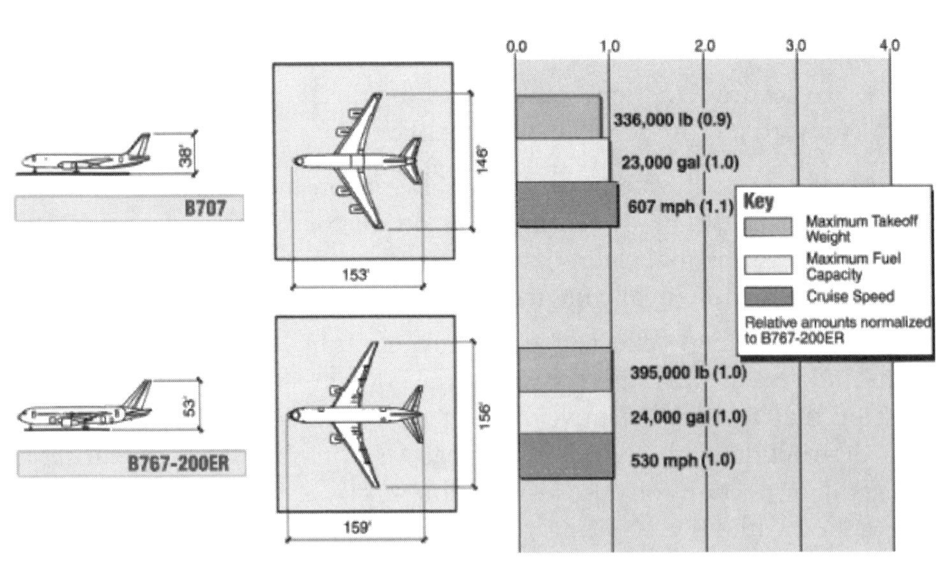

As Frank DiMartini observed, the towers were designed to withstand the impact of the then-largest commerical airliners, Boing 707s. The 767s that presumably hit the buildings were very comparable in their mass and dimensions.

PART I: THE BIG PICTURE

1

9/11: The Myth and the Reality

David Ray Griffin

Although I am a philosopher of religion and a theologian, I have spent most of my time during the past three years on 9/11—studying it, writing about it, and speaking about it. In this lecture, I will try to make clear why I believe this issue worthy of so much time and energy. I will do this in terms of the distinction between myth and reality.

I am here using the term "myth" in two senses. In one sense, a myth is an idea that, while widely believed, is false, failing to correspond with reality. In a deeper sense, which is employed by students of religion, a myth serves as an orienting and mobilizing story for a people, a story that reminds them who they are and why they do what they do.

When a story is called a myth in this sense—which we can call Myth with a capital "M"—the focus is not on the story's relation to reality but on its function. This orienting and mobilizing function is possible, moreover, only because Myths with a capital "M" have religious overtones. Such a Myth is a Sacred Story.

However, although to note that a story functions as a Myth in the religious sense is not necessarily to deny its truth, a story cannot function as a Sacred Myth within a community or nation unless it is believed to be true. In most cases, moreover, the truth of the Myth is taken on faith. It is not a matter of debate. If some people have the bad taste to question the truth of the Sacred Story, the keepers of the faith do not enter into debate with them. Rather, they ignore them or denounce them as blasphemers.

According to the official story about 9/11, America, because of its goodness, was attacked by fanatical Arab Muslims who hate our freedoms. This story has functioned as a Sacred Myth for the United States since that fateful day. And this function appears to have been carefully orchestrated. The very next day, President Bush announced his intention to lead "a monumental struggle of Good versus Evil."[1] Then on September 13, he declared that the following day would be a National Day of Prayer and Remembrance for the Victims of the Terrorist Attacks. And *on* that next day, the president himself, surrounded by Billy Graham, a cardinal, a rabbi, and an imam, delivered a sermon in the national cathedral, saying:

Our responsibility to history is already clear: to answer these attacks and rid the world of Evil. War has been waged against us by stealth and deceit and murder. This nation is peaceful, but fierce when stirred to anger. . . . In every generation, the world has produced enemies of human freedom. They have attacked America, because we are freedom's home and defender. And the commitment of our fathers is now the calling of our time. . . . [W]e ask almighty God to watch over our nation, and grant us patience and resolve in all that is to come...And may He always guide our country. God bless America.[2]

Through this unprecedented event, in which the president of the United States issued a declaration of war from a cathedral, French author Thierry Meyssan observed in 2002, "the American government consecrated . . . its version of events. From then on, any questioning of the official truth would be seen as sacrilege."[3]

That attitude has remained dominant in the public sphere until this day, as the official account has continued to serve as a Sacred Story. When people raise questions about this story, they are either ignored, ridiculed as conspiracy theorists, or—as Charlie Sheen has recently experienced—attacked personally.

When anyone asks what right the administration has to invade and occupy other countries, to imprison people indefinitely without due process, or even to ignore various laws, the answer is always the same: "9/11." Those who believe that US law and international law should be respected are dismissed as having "a pre-9/11 mind-set."

Given the role the official account of 9/11 has played and continues to play, the most important question before our country today is whether this account, besides being a Myth in the religious sense, is also a myth in the pejorative sense—that is, whether it is simply false.

As a philosopher of religion, I would emphasize that the fact that a story has served as a Myth in the religious sense does not necessarily mean that it fails to correspond with reality. Many religious accounts contain at least a kernel of truth that can be defended in terms of a rational examination of the relevant evidence.

In many cases, however, stories that have served as religious Myths cannot stand up to rational scrutiny. When such a story is stripped of its halo and treated simply as a theory, rather than an unquestionable dogma, it cannot be defended as the best theory to account for the relevant facts. The official account of 9/11 is such a theory. When challenges to it are not treated as blasphemy, it can easily be seen to be composed of a number of ideas that are myths in the sense of not corresponding with reality.

Using the word "myth" from now on only in this pejorative sense, I will discuss nine of the major myths contained in the official story about 9/11. I will thereby show that the official account of 9/11 cannot be defended, in light of the relevant evidence, against the main alternative account, according to which 9/11 was an inside job, orchestrated by people within our own government. I will begin with a few myths that prevent many people from even looking at the evidence for this alternative account.

Myth Number 1: Our political and military leaders simply would not do such a thing.

This idea is widely believed. But it is undermined by much evidence. The United States, like many other countries, has often used deceit to begin wars—for example, the Mexican-American war, with its false claim that Mexico had "shed American blood on the American soil,"[4] the Spanish-American war, with its "Remember the Maine" hoax,[5] the war in the Philippines, with its false claim that the Filipinos fired first,[6] and the Vietnam war, with its Tonkin Gulf hoax.[7]

The United States has also sometimes organized false flag terrorist attacks—killing innocent civilians, then blaming the attacks on an enemy country or group, often by planting evidence. We have even done this in allied countries. As Daniele Ganser has shown in his recent book *NATO's Secret Armies*, NATO, guided by the CIA and the Pentagon, arranged many such attacks in Western European countries during the Cold War. These attacks were successfully blamed on Communists and other leftists to discredit them in the eyes of the voting public.[8]

Finally, in case it be thought that US military leaders would not orchestrate such attacks against US citizens, one needs only to read the plan known as Operation Northwoods, which the Joint Chiefs of Staff worked up in 1962, shortly after Fidel Castro had overthrown the pro-American dictator Batista. This plan contained various "pretexts which would provide justification for US military intervention in Cuba." American citizens would have been killed in some of them, such as a "Remember the Maine!" incident, in which: "We could blow up a U.S. ship in Guantánamo Bay and blame Cuba."[9]

At this point, some people, having seen evidence that US leaders would be morally capable of orchestrating 9/11, might avoid looking at the evidence by appeal to

Myth Number 2: Our political and military leaders would have had no motive for orchestrating the 9/11 attacks.

This myth was reinforced by *The 9/11 Commission Report*. While explaining why al-Qaeda had ample motives for carrying out the attacks, this report mentions no motives that US leaders might have had. But the alleged motive of al-Qaeda—that it hated Americans and their freedoms—is dwarfed by a motive held by many members of the Bush-Cheney administration: the dream of establishing a global *Pax Americana*, the first all-inclusive empire in history.

This dream had been articulated by many neoconservatives, or neocons, throughout the 1990s, after the disintegration of the Soviet Union made it seem possible. It was first officially articulated in the Defense Planning Guidance of 1992, drafted by Paul Wolfowitz on behalf of then Secretary of Defense Dick Cheney—a document that has been called "a blueprint for permanent American global hegemony"[10] and Cheney's "Plan . . . to rule the world."[11]

Achieving this goal would require four things. The first of these was getting control of the world's oil, especially in Central Asia and the Middle East. When the Bush-Cheney administration came to power, it had already made plans to attack Afghanistan and Iraq. The second was a technological transformation of the military, in which fighting from space would become central. A third would be an enormous increase in military spending, to pay for these new wars and for weaponizing space. A fourth need was to modify the doctrine of preemptive attack to one of preventive attack, so that America would be able to attack other countries even if they posed no imminent threat.

These four elements would, moreover, require a fifth: an event that would make the American people ready to accept these imperialistic policies. As Zbigniew Brzezinski explained in his 1997 book, *The Grand Chessboard*, the American people, with their democratic instincts, are reluctant to authorize the money and human sacrifices necessary for "imperial mobilization," and this refusal "limits . . . America's . . . capacity for military intimidation."[12] But this impediment could be overcome if there were "a truly massive and widely perceived direct external threat"[13]—just as the

American people were willing to enter World War II only after "the shock effect of the Japanese attack on Pearl Harbor."[14]

This same idea was suggested in 2000 in a document entitled *Rebuilding America's Defenses*, which was put out by a neo-con think tank called the Project for the New American Century, many members of which—including Cheney, Rumsfeld, and Wolfowitz—became central members of the Bush administration. This document, referring to the goal of transforming the military, said that this "process of transformation . . . is likely to be a long one, absent some catastrophic and catalyzing event—like a new Pearl Harbor."15

When the attacks of 9/11 occurred, they were treated like a new Pearl Harbor. Several members of the Bush administration even spoke of 9/11 as providing opportunities. Secretary of Defense Rumsfeld said that 9/11 created "the kind of opportunities that World War II offered, to refashion the world."[16] It created, in particular, the opportunity to attack Afghanistan and Iraq; to increase the military budget enormously; to go forward with military transformation; and to turn the new idea of preemptive warfare into official doctrine. This doctrinal change was announced in the 2002 version of the *National Security Strategy*, which said that America will "act against . . . emerging threats before they are fully formed."[17]

So, not only did the Bush administration reap huge benefits from 9/11. These were benefits that it had desired in advance. The idea that it would have had no motives for orchestrating 9/11 is a myth. But there is one more myth that keeps many people from looking at the evidence. This is

Myth Number 3: Such a big operation, involving so many people, could not have been kept a secret, because someone involved in it would have talked by now.

This claim is based on a more general myth, which is that is impossible for secret government operations to be kept secret very long, because someone always talks. But how could we know this? If some big operations have remained secret until now, we by definition do not know about them. Moreover, we do know of some big operations that *were* kept secret as long as necessary, such as the Manhattan Project to create the atomic bomb, and the war in Indonesia in 1957, which the United States government provoked, participated in, and was able to keep secret from its own people until a book about it appeared in 1995.[18] Many more examples could be given.

We can understand, moreover, why those with inside knowledge of 9/11 would not talk. At least most of them would have been people with the proven ability to keep secrets. Those who were directly complicit would also be highly motivated to avoid public disgrace and the gas chamber. Those people who had inside knowledge without being complicit could be induced to keep quiet by means of more or less subtle threats—such as: "Joe, if you go forward with your plans to talk to the press about this, I don't know who is going to protect your wife and kids from some nutcase angered by your statement." Still another fact is that neither the government nor the mainstream press has, to say the least, shown any signs of wanting anyone to come forward.

I come now to

Myth Number 4: The 9/11 Commission, which has endorsed the official account, was an independent, impartial commission and hence can be believed.

One needs only to look at the reviews of *The 9/11 Commission Report* on Amazon.com to see that this assumption is widely accepted. Perhaps this is partly because in the Preface, the Commission's chairman and vice chairman tell us that the Commission sought "to be independent, impartial, thorough, and nonpartisan." But these terms do not describe the reality. The 9/11 Commission's lack of impartiality can be partly explained by the fact that Chairman Thomas Kean, most of the other commissioners, and at least half of the members of the staff had conflicts of interest.[19]

The most serious problem, however, is that the executive director, Philip Zelikow, was essentially a member of the Bush-Cheney administration. He had worked with Condoleezza Rice on the National Security Council in the administration of the first President Bush. When the Republicans were out of office during the Clinton administration, Zelikow and Rice wrote a book together. Rice then, as National Security Advisor for the second President Bush, had Zelikow help make the transition to the new National Security Council. After that, Zelikow was appointed to the President's Foreign Intelligence Advisory Board.

Zelikow was, therefore, the White House's man inside the 9/11 Commission. As executive director, he guided the staff, which did virtually all the work of the Commission.[20] Zelikow was in position, therefore, to decide which topics would be investigated and which ones not. One disgruntled member reportedly said at the time, "Zelikow is calling the shots. He's skewing the investigation and running it his own way."[21]

Accordingly, insofar as the Commission was supposed to be investigating the failure of the Bush administration to prevent the attacks, the Commission was no more independent and impartial than if Dick Cheney had been running it. (The only difference is that no one got shot.)

Zelikow's ideological and personal closeness to the Bush administration is shown by one more fact that has until now not been widely known, even within the 9/11 truth movement. I mentioned earlier the Bush administration's *National Security Strategy* statement of 2002, in which the new doctrine of preemptive warfare was articulated. The primary author of this document, reports James Mann in *Rise of the Vulcans*, was none other than Philip Zelikow.

According to Mann, after Rice saw a first draft, which had been written by Richard Haass in the State Department, she, wanting "something bolder," brought in Zelikow to completely rewrite it.[22] The result was a very bellicose document that used 9/11 to justify the administration's so-called war on terror. Max Boot described it as a "quintessentially neo-conservative document."[23]

We can understand, therefore, why the Commission, under Philip Zelikow's leadership, would have ignored all evidence that would point to the truth: that 9/11 was a false flag operation intended to authorize the doctrines and funds needed for a new level of imperial mobilization.

The suggestion that 9/11 was a false flag operation brings us to:

Myth Number 5: The Bush administration provided proof that the attacks were carried out by al-Qaeda terrorists under the direction of Osama bin Laden.

One of the main pieces of alleged proof involved the claim that the baggage of Mohamed Atta, called the ringleader of the hijackers, was discovered at the Boston airport, from which Flight 11 departed. This baggage, besides containing Atta's passport and driver's license, also contained various types of incriminating evidence, such as flight simulator manuals, videotapes about Boeing airliners, and a letter to other hijackers about preparing for the mission. But the bags also contained Atta's will. Why would Atta have intended to take his will on a plane that he planned to fly into the World Trade Center? There are also many other problems in this story.[24] We appear to have planted evidence.

Another element of the official story about the alleged hijackers is that they were very devout Muslims. *The 9/11 Commission Report* said that Atta had become very religious, even "fanatically so."[25] The public was thereby led to believe that these men would have had no problem going on this suicide mission, because they were ready to meet their maker. Investigative reporter Daniel Hopsicker, however, discovered that Atta loved cocaine, alcohol, gambling, pork, and lap dances.[26] Several of the other alleged hijackers, the *Wall Street Journal* reported, had similar tastes.[27] The Commission pretends, however, that none of this information was available. While admitting that Atta met other members of al-Qaeda in Las Vegas shortly before 9/11, it says that it saw "no credible evidence explaining why, on this occasion and others, the operatives flew to or met in Las Vegas."[28]

Another problem in the official account is that, although we are told that four or five of the alleged hijackers were on each of the four flights, no proof of this claim has been provided. The story, of course, is that they did not force their way onto the planes but were regular, ticketed passengers. If so, their names should be on the flight manifests. But the flight manifests that have been released contain neither the names of the alleged hijackers nor any other Arab names.[29] We have also been given no proof that the remains of any of these men were found at any of the crash sites.

One final little problem is that several of these 19 men, according to stories published by the BBC and British newspapers, are still alive. For example, The *9/11 Commission Report* named Waleed al-Shehri as one of the hijackers and reproduced the FBI's photograph of him. It even suggested that al-Shehri stabbed one of the flight attendants shortly before Flight 11 crashed into the north tower.[30] But as BBC News had reported 11 days after 9/11, al-Shehri, having seen his photograph in newspapers and TV programs, notified authorities and journalists in Morocco, where he works as a pilot, that he is still alive.[31]

But if there are various problems with the government's story about the hijackers, surely it presented proof that Osama bin Laden was behind the operation? Insofar as this belief is widely held, it also is a myth. Secretary of State Colin Powell promised to provide a white paper providing proof that the attacks had been planned by bin Laden, but this paper was never produced. British Prime Minister Tony Blair did provide such a paper, which was entitled "Responsibility for the Terrorist Atrocities in the United States." But it begins with the admission that it "does not purport to provide a prosecutable case against Usama Bin Laden in a court of law."[32] (So, evidence good enough to go to war is not good enough to go to court!) And even though the Taliban said it would hand bin Laden over if the United States were to present evidence of his involvement in 9/11, Bush refused.[33]

This failure to provide proof was later said to be unnecessary because bin Laden, in a video allegedly found in Afghanistan, admitted responsibility for the attacks. This "confession" is now widely cited as proof. However, the man in this video has darker skin, fuller cheeks, and a broader nose than the Osama bin Laden of all the other videos.[34] We again seem to have planted evidence.

There are, moreover, other problems in the official account of Osama bin Laden. For one thing, in June of 2001, when he was already America's "most wanted" criminal, he reportedly spent two weeks in the American Hospital in Dubai, at which he was treated by an American doctor and visited by the local CIA agent.[35]

Also, after 9/11, when America was reportedly trying to get bin Laden "dead or alive," the US military evidently allowed him to escape on at least four occasions, the last one being the "battle of Tora Bora," which the *London Telegraph* labeled "a grand charade."36 Shortly thereafter, Bush said: "I don't know where he [bin Laden] is. . . . I just don't spend that much time on him. . . . I truly am not that concerned about him."[37] (Sometimes the truth slips out.)

In any case, the idea that the Bush administration has provided proof for its claims about Osama bin Laden and the al-Qaeda hijackers is a myth. I turn now to:

Myth Number 6: The 9/11 attacks came as a surprise to the Bush administration.

Nothing is more essential to the official story than this idea. About 10 months after 9/11, for example, FBI Director Robert Mueller said: "To this day we have found no one in the United States except the actual hijackers who knew of the plot."[38] There is much evidence, however, that counts against this claim.

The Put Options: One type of evidence involves an extraordinarily high volume of "put options" purchased in the three days prior to 9/11. To buy put options for a particular company is to bet that its stock price will go down. These extraordinary purchases included two, and only two, airlines—United and American—the two airlines used in the attacks. They also included Morgan Stanley Dean Witter, which occupied 22 stories of the World Trade Center.

The price of these shares did, of course, plummet after 9/11, resulting in enormous profits for the purchasers. These unusual purchases, as the *San Francisco Chronicle* said, raise "suspicions that the investors . . . had advance knowledge of the strikes."[39] It would appear, in other words, that those who made the purchases knew that United and American airliners were going to be used in attacks on the World Trade Center.

The 9/11 Commission tried to show these suspicions to be unfounded. It claimed, for example, that the purchases for United Airlines do not show that anyone other than al-Qaeda had foreknowledge of the attacks, because 95 percent of these options were purchased by "[a] single U.S.-based institutional investor with no conceivable ties to al Qaeda."[40] But the Commission thereby simply begged the question at issue, which is whether some organization other than al-Qaeda was involved in the planning.

Also, the Commission ignored the other crucial point, which is that US intelligence agencies closely monitor the stock market, looking for any anomalies that might provide clues about untoward events in the works.[41] Therefore, regardless of who orchestrated the attacks, the US government would have had intelligence suggesting that United and American airliners were to be used for attacks on the World Trade Center.

Bush and the Secret Service: Further evidence of advance knowledge is shown by the behavior of President Bush and his secret service agents during the photo-op at the school in Florida that morning. According to the official story, when Bush was first told that a plane had struck one of the Twin Towers, he dismissed the incident as merely a "horrible accident," which meant that they could go ahead with the photo-op.[42] News of the second strike, however, would have indicated—assuming that the strikes were unexpected—that terrorists were using planes to attack high-value targets. And what could have been a higher-value target than the president of the United States?

His location at the school had been highly publicized. The Secret Service agents should have feared, therefore, that a hijacked airliner might have been bearing down on the school at that very minute, ready to crash into it. It is standard procedure for the Secret Service to rush the president to a safe location when there is any sign that he may be in danger. And yet these agents allowed the president to remain another half hour, even permitting him to deliver an address on television, thereby announcing to the world that he was still at the school.

Would not this behavior be explainable only if the head of the Secret Service detail knew that the planned attacks did not include an attack on the president? The 9/11 Commission, of course, did not ask this question. It was content to report that "[t]he Secret Service told us they . . . did not think it imperative for [the president] to run out the door."[43] Maintaining decorum, in other words, was more important than protecting the president's life. Can anyone seriously believe that highly trained Secret Service agents would act this way in a situation of genuine danger?

Mineta's Report about Cheney: The attack on the Pentagon, as well as the attack on the World Trade Center, was said to be a surprise, even though it occurred over a half hour after the second strike on the Twin Towers. A Pentagon spokesperson, in explaining why the Pentagon was not evacuated before it was struck, claimed that "[t]he Pentagon was simply not aware that this aircraft was coming our way."[44] The 9/11 Commission claimed that there was no warning about an unidentified aircraft heading towards Washington until 9:36 and hence only "one or two minutes" before the Pentagon was struck at 9:38.[45]

But this claim is contradicted by Secretary of Transportation Norman Mineta's testimony about an episode that occurred in the Presidential Emergency Operations Center under the White House. In open testimony to the 9/11 Commission, Mineta gave this account:

> *During the time that the airplane was coming in to the Pentagon, there was a young man who would come in and say to the Vice President, "The plane is 50 miles out." "The plane is 30 miles out." And when it got down to "the plane is 10 miles out," the young man also said to the Vice President, "Do the orders still stand?" And the Vice President . . . said, "Of course the orders still stand. Have you heard anything to the contrary?"*[46]

Mineta said that that this final exchange occurred at about 9:25 or 9:26.[47] According to Mineta's account, therefore, Cheney knew about an approaching aircraft more than 12 minutes before 9:38, when the Pentagon was struck. Assuming that Cheney would not have kept this information from his good friend Donald Rumsfeld, Mineta's testimony contradicts the claim of the Pentagon and the 9/11 Commission that there was no advance knowledge, at least not sufficient advance knowledge to have evacuated the Pentagon, which would have saved 125 lives.

This example affords one of the clearest examples of the fact that the Zelikow-led 9/11 Commission cannot be trusted. Having claimed that there was no knowledge that an aircraft was approaching the Pentagon until the last minute or so, it simply omitted Mineta's testimony to the contrary, which had been given in open testimony to the Commission itself, from its final report. Then, to rule out even the possibility that the episode reported by Mineta could have occurred, it claimed that Cheney did not even arrive in the Presidential Emergency Operations Center until almost 10:00 o'clock, hence about 20 minutes after the Pentagon was struck.[48] But this claim, besides contradicting Mineta's eyewitness testimony that

Cheney was already there when Mineta arrived at 9:20, also contradicts all other reports as to when Cheney had arrived there, including a report by Cheney himself.[49]

In light of this information about the put options, the Secret Service, and Mineta's testimony, we can reject as a myth the idea that the attacks were unexpected. However, even if the attacks had been unexpected, should they not have been intercepted? This brings us to:

Myth Number 7: US officials have explained why the hijacked airliners were not intercepted.

Actually, there is a sense in which this statement is true. US officials *have* explained why the US military did not prevent the attacks. The problem, however, is that they have given *three* explanations, each of which is contradicted by the others and none of which is a *satisfactory* explanation. Let me explain.

According to standard operating procedures, if an FAA flight controller notices anything that suggests a possible hijacking, the controller is to contact a superior. If the problem cannot be fixed quickly (within about a minute), the superior is to ask NORAD—the North American Aerospace Defense Command—to send up, or "scramble," jet fighters to find out what is going on. NORAD then issues a scramble order to the nearest air force base with fighters on alert.

The jet fighters at NORAD's disposal could respond very quickly: According to the US Air Force website, F-15s can go from "scramble order" to 29,000 feet in only 2.5 minutes, after which they can fly over 1800 miles per hour.[50] Therefore—according to General Ralph Eberhart, the head of NORAD—after the FAA senses that something is wrong, "it takes about one minute" for it to contact NORAD, after which, according to a spokesperson, NORAD can scramble fighter jets "within a matter of minutes to anywhere in the United States."[51]

These statements were, to be sure, made after 9/11, so we might suspect that they reflect a post-9/11 speed-up in procedures. But an Air Traffic Control document put out in 1998 warned pilots that any airplanes persisting in unusual behavior "will likely find two [jet fighters] on their tail within 10 or so minutes."[52] If these procedures had been carried out on the morning of 9/11, AA Flight 11 and UA Flight 175 would have been intercepted before they could have reached Manhattan, and AA Flight 77 would have been intercepted long before it could have reached the Pentagon.

Such interceptions are routine, being carried out about 100 times a year. A month after 9/11, the *Calgary Herald* reported that in the year 2000, NORAD had scrambled fighters 129 times. Do these scrambles regularly result in interceptions? Just a few days after 9/11, Major Mike Snyder, a NORAD spokesperson, told the *Boston Globe* that "[NORAD's] fighters routinely intercept aircraft."[53] Why did such interceptions not occur on 9/11?

During the first few days, the public was told that no fighter jets were sent up until after the strike on the Pentagon at 9:38. However, it was also reported that signs of Flight 11's hijacking had been observed at 8:15. That would mean that although interceptions usually occur within "10 or so" minutes after signs of trouble are observed, in this case 80 or so minutes had elapsed before fighters were even airborne. This story suggested that a "stand-down" order had been issued.

Within a few days, however, a second story was put out, according to which NORAD *had* sent up fighters but, because notification from the FAA had been very slow in coming, the fighters arrived too late. On September 18, NORAD made this second story official, embodying it in a timeline, which indicated when NORAD had been notified by the FAA about each airplane and when it had scrambled fighters in response.[54]

Critics showed, however, that even if the FAA notifications had come as late as NORAD's timeline indicated, NORAD's jets would have had time to make the interceptions.55 This second story did not, therefore, remove the suspicion that a stand-down order had been given.

Hoping to overcome this problem, *The 9/11 Commission Report* provided a third account, according to which, contrary to NORAD's timeline of September 18, 2001, the FAA did not notify NORAD about Flight 175 until after it had struck the south tower or about Flight 77 until after it had struck the Pentagon. But there are serious problems with this third story.

One problem is the very fact that it is the third story. Normally, when a suspect in a criminal investigation keeps changing his story, we get suspicious. Let's say that the police ask Charlie Jones where he was Saturday night. He says he was at the movie theater, but they say, "No, the movie theater has been closed all week." Then Charlie says, "Oh, that's right, I was with my girl friend." But, the police say, "No, we checked with her and she was home with her husband." If at that point Charlie says, "Oh, now I remember, I was home reading my Bible," you are probably not going to believe him. And yet that's what we have here. The military told one story right after 9/11, another story a week later, and a third story through *The 9/11 Commission Report* in 2004.

A second problem with this third story is that it contradicts several features of the second story, which had served as the official story for almost three years.

For example, NORAD's timeline of September 18, 2001, had indicated that the FAA had notified it about Flight 175 exactly 20 minutes before it hit its target and about Flight 77 some 14 minutes before the Pentagon was struck. The 9/11 Commission maintains that both of these statements were "incorrect"—that, really, there had been no notification about these flights until after they hit their targets. This, it claims, is why the military had failed to intercept them.[56] But if NORAD's timeline was false, as the Commission now claims, NORAD must have been either lying or confused. But it is hard to believe that it could have been confused one week after 9/11. So it must have been lying. But if the military's second story was a lie, why should we believe this third one?

Further scepticism about this third story arises from the fact that it is contradicted by considerable evidence. For example, the Commission's claim that the military did not know about Flight 175 until it crashed is contradicted by a report involving Captain Michael Jellinek, a Canadian who on 9/11 was overseeing NORAD's headquarters in Colorado. According to a story in the *Toronto Star*, Jellinek was on the phone with NORAD as he watched Flight 175 crash into the south tower. He then asked NORAD: "Was that the hijacked aircraft you were dealing with?"—to which NORAD said "yes."[57]

The 9/11 Commission's claims about Flights 175 and 77 are also contradicted by a memo sent to the Commission by Laura Brown of the FAA. Her memo stated that at about 8:50 the FAA had set up a teleconference, in which it started sharing information with the military about all flights. She specifically mentioned Flight 77, indicating that the FAA had been sharing information about it even before the formal notification time of 9:24. Her memo, which is available on the Web,58 was discussed by the 9/11 Commission and read into its record on May 23, 2003.59 But Zelikow's *9/11 Commission Report* fails to mention this memo.

Because of these and still more problems, which I have discussed in my book on the 9/11 Commission's report and also in a lecture called "Flights of Fancy",[60] this third story does not remove the grounds for suspicion that a stand-down order had been issued.

There is, moreover, ear-witness testimony for this suspicion. An upper management official at LAX [Los Angeles International Airport], who needs to remain anonymous, has told me that he overheard members of LAX Security—including officers from the FBI and LAPD—interacting on their walkie-talkies shortly after the attacks. In some cases, he could hear both sides of the conversation. At first, the LAX officials were told that the airplanes that attacked World Trade Center and the Pentagon had not been intercepted because the FAA had not notified NORAD about the hijackings. But later, he reports, they were told that NORAD *had* been notified but did not respond because it had been "ordered to stand down." When LAX security officials asked who had issued that order, they were told that it had come "from the highest level of the White House."[61]

Accordingly, the idea that the attacks could not have been prevented is a myth. I turn now to:

Myth Number 8: Official Reports have explained why the Twin Towers and Building 7 of the World Trade Center collapsed.

This claim suffers from the same problem as the previous one: We have had *three* explanations, each of which contradicts the others and none of which is anywhere close to adequate. The first explanation, widely disseminated through television specials, was that the buildings collapsed because their steel columns were melted by the jet-fuel-fed fires. But this explanation contained many problems, the most obvious of which is that steel does not begin to melt until about 2800 degrees F, while open fires based on hydrocarbons such as kerosene—which is what jet fuel is—cannot under the most ideal circumstances rise above 1700 degrees.

A second explanation, endorsed by *The 9/11 Commission Report*, is a "pancake" theory, according to which the fires, while not melting the steel, heated it up sufficiently to cause the floors weakened by the airplane strikes to break loose from the steel columns—both those in the core of the building and those around the outside. All the floors above the strike zone hence fell down on the floor below the strike zone, causing it to break free, and this started a chain reaction, so the floors pancaked all the way down. But this explanation also suffered from many problems, the most obvious of which was that it could not explain why the buildings collapsed into a pile of rubble only a few stories high. The core of each of the Twin Towers consisted of 47 massive steel columns. If the floors had broken loose from them, these columns would have still been sticking up a thousand feet in the air. *The 9/11 Commission Report* tried to cover up this problem by claiming that the core of each tower consisted of "a hollow steel shaft."[62] But those massive steel columns could not be wished away.

The definitive explanation was supposed to be the third one, issued by the National Institute of Standards and Technology, often simply called NIST. The NIST Report claimed that when the floors collapsed, they, rather than breaking free from the columns, pulled on them, causing the perimeter columns to become unstable. This instability then increased the gravity load on the core columns, which had been weakened by tremendously hot fires in the core, which, NIST claims, reached 1832°F, and this combination of factors resulted in "global collapse."[63]

But, as physicists Jim Hoffman and Steven Jones have shown, this account is riddled with problems. One of these is that NIST's claim about tremendously hot fires in the core is completely unsupported by evidence. NIST's own studies found no evidence that any of the core columns had reached temperatures of even 482°F (250°C).[64] A second problem is that, even if this sequence of events had occurred, NIST provided no explanation as to why it would have produced global—that is, total—collapse. The NIST Report asserts that "column failure" occurred in the core as well as the perimeter columns. But this remains a bare assertion. There is no plausible explanation of why the core columns would have broken, or even buckled, so as to produce global collapse.[65]

And this is only to begin to enumerate the problems in NIST's theory, all of which follow from the fact that it, like the previous two theories, is essentially a fire theory, according to which the buildings were brought down primarily by fire. In the case of the Twin Towers, of course, the impact of the airplanes is said to have played a role. But most experts who support the official theory attribute the collapses primarily to the fires. NIST, for example, says that the main contribution of the airplanes, aside from providing jet fuel, was to dislodge a lot of the fire-proofing from the steel, thereby making it vulnerable to the fires.[66] But these fire-theories face several formidable problems.

First, the fires in these three buildings were not very hot, very big, or very long-lasting, compared with fires in some steel-frame high-rises that did *not* collapse. A 1991 fire in Philadelphia burned 18 hours, and a 2004 fire in Caracas burned 17 hours, without causing even a partial collapse.[67] By contrast, the fires in the north and south towers burned only 102 and 56 minutes, respectively, before they collapsed, and neither fire, unlike the Philadelphia and Caracas fires, was hot enough to break windows.

Second, total collapses of steel-frame high-rise buildings have never—either before or after 9/11—been brought about by fire alone, or fire combined with externally produced structural damage. The collapse of Building 7 has been recognized as especially difficult to explain. It was not hit by a plane, so the explanation has to rely on fire alone; and yet, because there was no jet fuel to get a big fire started, this building had fires on only two or three floors, according to several witnesses[68] and all the photographic evidence.[69]

FEMA admitted that the best explanation it could come up with had "only a low probability of occurrence."[70] *The 9/11 Commission Report* implicitly admitted that it could not explain the collapse of Building 7 by not even mentioning it. The NIST Report, which could not claim that the fireproofing had gotten knocked off the steel of *this* building, has yet to offer an explanation as to why it collapsed.

And NIST, like the 9/11 Commission, evidently did not want citizens asking why Building 7 collapsed even though it was not hit by any plane. On its Website, it states that one of its objectives is to determine "why and how World Trade Center buildings 1, 2, and 7 collapsed after the initial impact of the aircraft"—thereby implying that building 7, like the Twin Towers, *was* hit by a plane.[71]

In any case, a third problem with the official account of the collapse of these three buildings is that all prior and subsequent total collapses of steel-frame high-rises have been caused by explosives in the procedure known as "controlled demolition." This problem is made even more severe by the fact that the collapses of these three buildings manifested many standard features of the most difficult type of controlled demolition, known as implosion. I will mention seven such features.

First, the collapses began suddenly. Steel, if weakened by fire, would gradually begin to sag. But as one can see from videos available on the Web,[72] all three buildings are completely motionless up to the moment they begin to collapse.

Second, if these huge buildings had toppled over, they would have caused enormous death and destruction. But they came straight down. This straight-down collapse is the whole point of the type of controlled demolition called implosion, which only a few companies in the world can perform.[73]

Third, these buildings collapsed at virtually free-fall speed, which means that the lower floors, with all their steel and concrete, were offering no resistance to the upper floors.

Fourth, as mentioned earlier, the collapses were *total* collapses, resulting in piles of rubble only a few stories high. This means that the enormous steel columns in the core of each building had to be broken into rather short segments—which is what explosives do.

Fifth, great quantities of molten steel were produced, which means that the steel had been heated up to several thousand degrees. Witnesses during the clean-up reported, moreover, that sometimes when a piece of steel was lifted out of the rubble, molten metal would be dripping from the end.[74]

Sixth, according to many fire fighters, medical workers, journalists, and World Trade Center employees, many explosions went off before and after the collapses. For example, Fire Captain Dennis Tardio, speaking of the south tower, said: "I hear an explosion and I look up. It is as if the building is being imploded, from the top floor down, one after another, *boom, boom, boom*."[75] Firefighter Richard Banaciski said: "It seemed like on television [when] they blow up these buildings. It seemed like it was going all the way around like a belt, all these explosions."[76]

Thanks to the release in August of 2005 of the oral histories recorded by the Fire Department of New York shortly after 9/11, dozens of testimonies of this type are now available. I have published an essay on them, which will be included—along with an essay on "The Destruction of the World Trade Center," which I am here summarizing—in a forthcoming book on 9/11 and Christian faith.[77]

A seventh feature of controlled implosions is the production of large quantities of dust. In the case of the Twin Towers, virtually everything except the steel—all the concrete, desks, computers—was pulverized into very tiny dust particles.[78]

The official theory cannot explain one, let alone all seven, of these features—at least, as Jim Hoffman and Steven Jones have pointed out, without violating several basic laws of physics.[79] But the theory of controlled demolition easily explains all of these features.

These facts are inconsistent with the notion that al-Qaeda terrorists were responsible. Foreign terrorists could not have obtained access to the buildings for the hours needed to plant the explosives. Terrorists working for the Bush-Cheney administration, by contrast, *could* have gotten such access, given the fact that Marvin Bush and Wirt Walker III—the president's brother and cousin, respectively—were principals of the company in charge of security for the World Trade Center.[80] It is most unlikely that al-Qaeda terrorists would have had the courtesy to ensure that these huge buildings came straight down, rather than falling over onto other buildings. They also would not have had the necessary expertise.

Another relevant fact is that evidence was destroyed. An examination of the buildings' steel beams and columns could have shown whether explosives had been used to slice them. But virtually all of the steel was removed before it could be properly examined,[81] then put on ships to Asia to be melted down.82 It is usually a federal offense to remove anything from a crime scene. But here the removal of over 100 tons of steel, the biggest destruction of evidence in history, was carried out under the supervision of federal officials.[83]

Evidence was also apparently planted. The passport of one of the hijackers on Flight 11 was allegedly found in the rubble, having survived the fire caused by the crash into the North Tower and also whatever caused everything else in this building except the steel to be pulverized.[84] As a story in the *Guardian* said, "the idea that [this] passport had escaped from that inferno unsinged would [test] the credulity of the staunchest supporter of the FBI's crackdown on terrorism."[85]

To sum up: The idea that US officials have given a satisfactory, or even close to satisfactory, explanation of the collapse of the World Trade Center buildings is a myth. And they have implicitly admitted this by refusing to engage in rational debate about it. For example, Michael Newman, a spokesman for NIST, reportedly said during a recent interview that "none of the NIST scientists would participate in any public debate" with scientists who reject their report. When Newman was asked why NIST would avoid public debate if it had confidence in its report, Newman replied: "Because there is no winning in such debates."[86] In that same interview, Newman had compared people who reject the government's account of the collapses with people who believe in Bigfoot and a flat earth. And yet he fears that his scientists would not be able to show up these fools in a public debate!

In any case, I come now to the final myth, which is:

Myth Number 9: There is no doubt that Flight 77, under the control of al-Qaeda hijacker Hani Hanjour, struck the Pentagon.

There are, in fact, many reasons to doubt this claim.

We have, in the first place, reasons to doubt that the aircraft that hit the Pentagon was under the control of Hani Hanjour. For one thing, the aircraft, before striking the Pentagon, reportedly executed a 270-degree downward spiral, and yet Hani Hanjour was known as a terrible pilot, who could not safely fly even a small plane.[87] Russ Wittenberg, who flew large commercial airliners for 35 years after serving in Vietnam as a fighter pilot, says that it would have been "totally impossible for an amateur who couldn't even fly a Cessna to maneuver the jetliner in such a highly professional manner."[88]

Moreover, as a result of that very difficult maneuver, the Pentagon's west wing was struck, but terrorists brilliant enough to get through the US military's defense system would have known that this was the worst place to strike, for several reasons: The west wing had been reinforced, so the damage was less severe than a strike anywhere else would have been. This wing was still being renovated, so relatively few people were there; a strike anywhere else would have killed thousands of people, rather than 125. And the secretary of defense and all the top brass, whom terrorists would presumably have wanted to kill, were in the *east* wing. Why would an al-Qaeda pilot have executed a very difficult maneuver to hit the west wing when he could have simply crashed into the roof of the east wing?

A second major problem with the official story: There are reasons to believe that the Pentagon was struck only because officials at the Pentagon wanted it to be struck. For one thing, Flight 77 allegedly, after making a U-turn in the mid-west, flew back to Washington undetected for 40 minutes. And yet the US military, which by then clearly knew that hijacked airliners were being used as weapons, has the best radar systems in the world, one of which, it even brags, "does not miss anything occurring in North American airspace."[89] The idea that a large airliner could have slipped through, especially during a time of acutely heightened alert, is absurd.

Also, the Pentagon is surely the best defended building on the planet.[90] It is not only within the P-56-A restricted air space that extends 17 miles in all directions from the Washington Monument, but also within P-56-B, the three-mile ultra-restricted zone above the White House, the Capitol, and the Pentagon. The Pentagon is only a few miles from Andrews Air Force Base, which has at least three squadrons with fighter jets on alert at all times. (The claim by *The 9/11 Commission Report* that no fighters were on alert the morning of 9/11 is wholly implausible, as I have explained in my critique of this report.[91])

The Pentagon, moreover, is reportedly protected by batteries of surface-to-air missiles, so if any aircraft without a US military transponder were to enter the Pentagon's airspace, it would be shot down.[92] Even if the aircraft that hit the Pentagon had been Flight 77, therefore, it could have succeeded only because officials in the Pentagon turned off its missiles as well as ordering the fighters from Andrews to stand down.

A third major problem with the official story is that there is considerable evidence that it could not have been Flight 77 because it was not a Boeing 757. For one thing, the strike on the Pentagon, unlike the strikes on the Twin Towers, reportedly did not create a detectable seismic signal.[93]

Also, according to several witnesses and many people who have studied the available photographs, both the damage and the debris were inconsistent with a strike by a large airliner. That issue, however, is too complex to discuss here, as is the issue of precisely what should be inferred from the conflicting eyewitness testimony.

I conclude by pointing out that the suspicion that the Pentagon was not struck by a 757, as the government claims, is supported by the fact that evidence was destroyed. Shortly after the strike, government agents picked up debris and carried it off.[94] Then the entire lawn was covered with dirt and gravel, so that any remaining forensic evidence was *literally* covered up.[95]

The videos from security cameras at the nearby Citgo gas station and at the Sheraton Hotel, which would surely show what really hit the Pentagon, were immediately confiscated by agents of the FBI, and the Department of Justice has to this day refused to release them.96 If these videos would prove that the Pentagon was really hit by a 757, most of us would assume, the government would release them.

Conclusion

It would seem, for many reasons, that the official story of 9/11, which has served as a religious Myth in the intervening years, is a myth in the pejorative sense of a story that does not correspond to reality. One sign of a story that is a myth in this sense, I have pointed out, is that it cannot be rationally defended, and the official story has never been publicly defended against informed criticism by any member of NIST, the 9/11 Commission, or the Bush administration.

An illustration: After Charlie Sheen had made public his skepticism about the official story, CNN's "Showbiz Tonight" wanted to have a debate, about the points he had raised, between a representative of the government and a representative of 9/11Truth.org. But the producers reportedly could find no member of the government willing to appear on the show. In this unwillingness of the government to appear on an entertainment show to answer questions raised by an actor, we would seem to have the clearest possible sign that the government's story is myth, not reality. If so, we must demand that the government immediately cease implementing the policies that have been justified by this myth.

When charges were brought against some members of Duke University's lacrosse team in March of 2006, the president of the university immediately cancelled all future games until the truth of the charges could be decided. But surely, as serious as the charges were in that case, the charges against the official story of 9/11 are far more serious, for this story, serving as a national religious Myth, has been used to justify two wars, which have caused many tens of thousands of deaths; to start a more general war on Islam, in which Muslims are considered guilty until proven innocent; to annul and violate civil rights; and to increase our military spending, which was already greater than that of the rest of the world combined, by hundreds of billions of dollars, partly so that weapons can be put into space.

Congress needs to put the implementation of these policies on hold until there is a truly independent investigation, carried out by qualified individuals who are not members of the very circles that, if 9/11 truly *was* a false flag operation, planned it, carried it out, and then covered it up.

Notes

1. "Remarks by the President in Photo Opportunity with the National Security Team" (www.whitehouse.gov/news/releases/2001/09/20010912-4.html), quoted in Thierry Meyssan, *9:11: The Big Lie* (London: Carnot, 2002), 77.
2. "President's Remarks at National Day of Prayer and Remembrance" (www.whitehouse.gov/news/releases/2001/09/20010914-2.html), quoted in Meyssan, *9/11: The Big Lie*, 76-77.
3. Meyssan, *9/11: The Big Lie*, 79.
4. Howard Zinn, *A People's History of the United States* (1980; New York: HarperPerennial, 1990), 150. Richard Van Alstyne, *The Rising American Empire* (1960; New York, Norton, 1974), 143.
5. Stuart Creighton Miller, *Benevolent Assimilation: The American Conquest of the Philippines, 1899-1903* (New Haven: Yale University Press, 1982), 11.
6. Ibid., 57-62.
7. George McT. Kahin, *Intervention: How America Became Involved in Vietnam* (Garden City: Anchor Press/Doubleday, 1987), 220; Marilyn B. Young, *The Vietnam Wars 1945-1990* (New York: HarperCollins, 1991), 119.
8. Daniele Ganser, *NATO's Secret Armies: Operation Gladio and Terrorism in Western Europe* (New York: Frank Cass, 2005).
9. This memorandum can be found at the National Security Archive, 30 April 2001 (http://www.gwu.edu/~nsarchiv/news/20010430). It was revealed to US readers by James Bamford in *Body of Secrets: Anatomy of the Ultra-secret National Security Agency* (2001: New York: Anchor Books, 2002), 82-91.

10. Andrew J. Bacevich, *American Empire: The Realities and Consequences of U.S. Diplomacy* (Cambridge: Harvard University Press, 2002), 44.
11. David Armstrong, "Dick Cheney's Song of America," *Harper's*, October, 2002.
12. Zbigniew Brzezinski, *The Grand Chessboard: American Primacy and Its Geostrategic Imperatives* (New York: Basic Books, 1997), 35-36.
13. Ibid., 212.
14. Ibid., 212, 24-25.
15. Project for the New American Century, *Rebuilding America's Defenses: Strategy, Forces and Resources for a New Century*, September 2000 (www.newamericancentury.org), 51.
16. "Secretary Rumsfeld Interview with the New York Times," *New York Times*, 12 October 2001. Similar sentiments were expressed by Condoleezza Rice and President Bush. On Rice, see Nicholas Lemann, "The Next World Order: The Bush Administration May Have a Brand-New Doctrine of Power," *New Yorker*, 1 April 2002 (http://www.newyorker.com/fact/content/articles/020401fa_FACT1), and Rice, "Remarks by National Security Adviser Condoleezza Rice on Terrorism and Foreign Policy," 29 April 2002 (www.whitehouse.gov); on Bush, see "Bush Vows to 'Whip Terrorism,'" Reuters, 14 September 2001, and Bob Woodward, *Bush at War* (New York: Simon & Schuster, 2002), 32.
17. *The National Security Strategy of the United States of America*, September 2002 (www.whitehouse.gov/nsc/nss.html), cover letter.
18. Audrey R. Kahin and George McT. Kahin, *Subversion as Foreign Policy: The Secret Eisenhower and Dulles Debacle in Indonesia* (Seattle: University of Washington Press, 1995).
19. *The 9/11 Commission Report: Final Report of the National Commission on Terrorist Attacks upon the United States*, Authorized Edition [New York: W. W. Norton, 2004], xv. David Ray Griffin, *The 9/11 Commission Report: Omissions and Distortions* (Northampton: Interlink Books, 2005), 285-95.
20. Chairman Thomas Kean and Vice Chairman Lee Hamilton, in their Preface, say: "The professional staff, headed by Philip Zelikow, . . . conducted the exacting investigative work upon which the Commission has built" (*The 9/11 Commission Report: Final Report of the National Commission on Terrorist Attacks upon the United States*, Authorized Edition [New York: W. W. Norton, 2004], xvi-xvii).
21. These statements are quoted in Peter Lance, *Cover Up: What the Government is Still Hiding about the War on Terror* (New York: Harper-Collins/ReganBooks, 2004), 139-40.
22. James Mann, *Rise of the Vulcans: The History of Bush's War Cabinet* (New York: Viking, 2004), 316, 331.
23. Max Boot, "Think Again: Neocons," *Foreign Policy*, January/February 2004, 18 (http://www.cfr.org/publication/7592/think_again.html).
24. See Rowland Morgan and Ian Henshall, *9/11 Revealed: The Unanswered Questions* (New York: Carroll & Graf, 2005), 180-83.
25. *The 9/11 Commission Report*, 116.
26. Daniel Hopsicker, *Welcome to Terrorland: Mohamed Atta and the 9/11 Cover-up in Florida* (Eugene: MacCowPress, 2004). These details from Hopsicker's book are summarized in his "Top Ten things You Never Knew about Mohamed Atta," Mad Cow Morning News, June 7, 2004 (www.madcowprod.com/index60.html), and in an interview in the Guerrilla News Forum, 17 June 2004 (www.guerrillanews.com/intelligence/doc4660.html), summarized in NPH, 2nd ed., 243n1.

27. "Terrorist Stag Parties," *Wall Street Journal*, 10 October 2001 (http://www.opinionjournal.com/best/?id=95001298).
28. *The 9/11 Commission Report*, 248.
29. The flight manifest for AA 11 that was published by CNN can be seen at www.cnn.com/SPECIALS/2001/trade.center/victims/AA11.victims.html. The manifests for the other flights can be located by simply changing that part of the URL. The manifest for UA 93, for example, is at www.cnn.com/SPECIALS/2001/trade.center/victims/ua93.victims.html.
30. *The 9/11 Commission Report*, 19-20.
31. David Bamford, "Hijack 'Suspect' Alive in Morocco," BBC News, 22 September 2001 (http://news.bbc.co.uk/1/hi/world/middle_east/1558669.stm). Several other alleged hijackers were reported to be alive in David Harrison, "Revealed: The Men with Stolen Identities," *Telegraph*, 23 September 2001 (www.portal.telegraph.co.uk/news/main.jhtml?xml=/news/2001/09/23/widen23.xml). At least one of these claims, that involving Ahmed al-Nami, was based on a confusion. The al-Nami contacted by Harrison was 33, whereas the man of that name who was supposedly on Flight 93, which supposedly crashed in Pennsylvania, was only 21. See Christine Lamb, "The Six Sons of Asir," *Telegraph*, 15 September 2002 (http://www.portal.telegraph.co.uk/news/main.jhtml?xml=/news/2002/09/15/wdoss215.xml). But no such explanation seems possible with Waleed al-Shehri, since the FBI photograph is clearly of a still-living man of that name.
32. Francis A. Boyle, "Bush, Jr., September 11th and the Rule of Law," which can be found in *The Criminality of Nuclear Deterrence: Could The US War On Terrorism Go Nuclear?* (Atlanta: Clarity Press, 2002) or at http://www.ratical.org/ratville/CAH/CrimNukDetSI.html.
33. "White House Warns Taliban: 'We Will Defeat You'" (CNN.com, 21 September 2001). Four weeks after the attacks began, a Taliban spokesman said: "We are not a province of the United States, to be issued orders to. We have asked for proof of Osama's involvement, but they have refused. Why?" (Kathy Gannon, AP, "Taliban Willing To Talk, But Wants U.S. Respect" [http://www.suburbanchicagonews.com/focus/terrorism/archives/1001/w01taliban.html]).
34. See "The Fake bin Laden Video" (http://www.whatreallyhappened.com/osamatape.html).
35. Richard Labeviere, "CIA Agent Allegedly Met Bin Laden in July," *Le Figaro*, 31 October 2001. This story was also reported in Anthony Sampson, "CIA Agent Alleged to Have Met Bin Laden in July," *Guardian*, 1 November 2001 and Adam Sage, "Ailing bin Laden 'Treated for Kidney Disease,'" *London Times*, 1 November 2001.
36. Telegraph, 23 February 2002; Griffin, *The 9/11 Commission Report: Omissions and Distortions*, 60.
37. President George W. Bush, Conference, 13 March 2002 (http://www.whitehouse.gov/news/releases/2002/03/20020313-8.html).
38. Philip Shenon, "FBI Gave Secret Files to Terrorist Suspect," *New York Times*, 28 September 2002, citing Mueller's testimony to Congress on 18 June 2002.
39. *San Francisco Chronicle*, 29 September 2001.
40. *The 9/11 Commission Report*, 499 n. 130.

41. Investigative journalist Michael Ruppert, a former detective for the Los Angeles Police Department, has written: "It is well documented that the CIA has long monitored such trades—in real time—as potential warnings of terrorist attacks and other economic moves contrary to U.S. interests" ("Suppressed Details of Criminal Insider Trading Lead Directly into the CIA's Highest Ranks," From the Wilderness Publications (www.fromthewilderness.com or www.copvcia.com), 9 October 2001. Nafeez Ahmed, besides quoting Ruppert's remark, points out that "UPI reported that the U.S.-sponsored ECHELON intelligence network closely monitors stock trading," citing United Press International, 13 February 2001. See Nafeez Ahmed, *The War on Freedom: How and Why America Was Attacked September 11, 2001* (Joshua Tree, Calif.: Tree of Life Publications, 2002), 120.
42. CNN, 4 December 2001, *The Daily Mail*, 8 September 2002, and ABC News, 11 September 2002.
43. *The 9/11 Commission Report*, 39.
44. "Air Attack on Pentagon Indicates Weaknesses," *Newsday*, 23 September 2001.
45. *The 9/11 Commission Report*, 34.
46. "Statement of Secretary of Transportation Norman Y. Mineta before the National Commission on Terrorist Attacks upon the United States, May 23, 2003" (available at www.cooperativeresearch.org/timeline/2003/commissiontestimony052303.htm).
47. Ibid.
48. *The 9/11 Commission Report*, 40.
49. See the summary of evidence in Griffin, *The 9/11 Commission Report: Omissions and Distortions*, 241-44, which includes discussion of the fact that the Commission cited no evidence for its revisionist timeline.
50. Cited in Griffin, *The 9/11 Commission Report: Omissions and Distortions*, 140.
51. Ibid.
52. Ibid., 141.
53. See the *Calgary Herald*, 13 October 2001, and Glen Johnson, "Otis Fighter Jets Scrambled Too Late to Halt the Attacks," *Boston Globe*, 15 September 2001 [http://nl.newsbank.com/nl-search/we/Archives?p_action=print]). At an average of 100 scrambles a year, fighters would have been scrambled about 1000 times in the decade prior to 9/11. One of the many falsehoods in a essay entitled "9/11: Debunking Myths," which was published by *Popular Mechanics* (March 2005), is its claim that in the decade before 9/11, there had been only *one* interception, that of golfer Payne Stewart's *Learjet*. This essay's "senior researcher," 25-year old Benjamin Chertoff, has (on a radio show) tried to reconcile this claim with the fact that fighters are scrambled about 100 times per year by saying that these statements speak only of scrambles, not interceptions. But Chertoff's position would require the claim that only one of the 1000 scrambles in that period resulted in interceptions—that the other 999 fighters were called back before they actually made the interception. Besides being highly improbable, this interpretation contradicts Major Snyder's statement that interceptions are carried out routinely.
54. Griffin, *The 9/11 Commission Report: Omissions and Distortions*, 141-43.
55. Ibid., 139-48.
56. Ibid., 192.
57. Ibid., 176.

58. Laura Brown, "FAA Communications with NORAD on September 11, 2001," available at http://www.911truth.org/article.php?story=20040812004217 97.
59. National Commission on Terrorist Attacks Upon the United States, May 23, 2003 (http://www.911commission.gov/archive/hearing2/9-11Commission_Hearing_2003-05-23.htm). Commissioner Richard Ben-Veniste, who read the memo into the record, reported that he had been told that it had been authored by two "high level individuals at FAA, Mr. Asmus and Ms. Schuessler." However, I was told by Laura Brown during a telephone conversation on 15 August 2004, that she had written the memo.
60. Griffin, *The 9/11 Commission Report: Omissions and Distortions*, 155-226; "Flights of Fancy: The 9/11 Commission's Incredible Tales of Flights 11, 175, 77, and 93," *Global Outlook*, 12 (Fall-Winter 2006), and in *Christian Faith and the Truth Behind 9/11* (Louisville: Westminster John Knox Press, 2006).
61. "My Observation of LAX Security Events on 9/11," by an Upper Management LAX Official. Although this official needs to remain anonymous, he has said that he would be willing to take a polygraph test if his anonymity could be protected.
62. *The 9/11 Commission Report*, 541 note 1.
63. *Final Report of the National Construction Safety Team on the Collapses of the World Trade Center Towers* (Draft), June, 2005, usually called the NIST Report, 28, 143.
64. And, as Jim Hoffman says, NIST's claim about these tremendously hot fires in the core is especially absurd given the fact that the core "had very little fuel; was far from any source of fresh air; had huge steel columns to wick away the heat; [and] does not show evidence of fires in any of the photographs or videos." All the evidence, in other words, suggests that none of the core columns would have reached the temperatures of some of the perimeter columns ("Building a Better Mirage: NIST's 3-Year $20,000,000 Cover-Up of the Crime of the Century," 911 Research, Dec. 8, 2005 (http://911research.wtc7.net/essays/nist/index.html).
65. See Hoffman, ibid., and Stephen E. Jones, "Why Indeed Did the WTC Buildings Collapse?" in David Ray Griffin and Peter Dale Scott, eds., *9/11 and the American Empire: Intellectuals Speak Out* (Northampton: Interlink, 2006); also available at www.scholarsfor911truth.org/WhyIndeedDidtheWorldTradeCenterBuildingsCompletelyCollapse.pdf.
66. The NIST Report (xliii and 171) says: "the towers withstood the impacts and would have remained standing were it not for the dislodged insulation (fireproofing) and the subsequent multifloor fires."
67. "High-Rise Office Building Fire One Meridian Plaza Philadelphia, Pennsylvania," FEMA (http://usfa.fema.gov/fire-service/techreports/tr049.shtm); "Fire Practically Destroys Venezuela's Tallest Building" (http://www.whatreallyhappened.com/venezuela_fire.html).
68. Chief Thomas McCarthy of the FDNY said that while the firefighters "were waiting for 7 World Trade to come down," there was "fire on three separate floors" (Oral History of Thomas McCarthy, 10-11). Emergency medical technician Decosta Wright said: "I think the fourth floor was on fire. . . . [W]e were like, are you guys going to put that fire out?" (Oral History of Decosta Wright, 11). These quotations are from the 9/11 oral histories recorded by the New York Fire Department at the end of 2001 but released to the public (after a court battle) only in August 2005, at

which time they were made available on a *New York Times* website (http://graphics8.nytimes.com/packages/html/nyregion/20050812_WTC_GRAPHIC/met_WTC_histories_full_01.html).

69. A photograph taken by Terry Schmidt can be seen on page 63 of Eric Hufschmid's *Painful Questions: An Analysis of the September 11th Attack* (Goleta, Calif.: Endpoint Software, 2002) or on Schmidt's website (http://www.nycwireless.net/Images/wtc2/). According to Schmidt, this photo was taken between 3:09 and 3:16 PM, hence only a little over two hours before Building 7 collapsed. It shows that on the north side of the building, fires were visible only on floors 7 and 12. Therefore, if there were more fires on the south side, which faced the Twin Towers, they were not big enough to be seen from the north side.
70. FEMA Report #403, World Trade Center Building Performance Study, May 2002 (www.fema.gov/library/wtcstudy.shtm), Ch. 5, Sect. 6.2, "Probable Collapse Sequence."
71. Reported in Ed Haas, "Government spokesman says, 'I Don't Understand the Public's Fascination with World Trade Center Building Seven,'" *Muckraker Report*, 21 March 2006 (http://www.teamliberty.net/id235.html), referring to NIST's "Investigation of the Sept. 11 World Trade Center Disaster" (http://wtc.nist.gov/pubs/factsheets/faqs.htm), as accessed on 20 March 2006.
72. See Jim Hoffman's website (http://911research.wtc7.net/index.html) and Jeff King's website (http://home.comcast.net/~jeffrey.king2/wsb/html/view.cgi-home.html-.html), especially "The World Trade Center Collapse: How Strong is the Evidence for a Controlled Demolition?"
73. Implosion World (http://www.implosionworld.com/dyk2.html).
74. Professor Allison Geyh of Johns Hopkins, who was part of a team of public health investigators who visited the site shortly after 9/11, wrote: "In some pockets now being uncovered they are finding molten steel," *Magazine of Johns Hopkins Public Health*, Late Fall, 2001. Dr. Keith Eaton, who somewhat later toured the site with an engineer, said that he was shown slides of "molten metal, which was still red hot weeks after the event" (The Structural Engineer, 3 September 2002: 6). On the dripping steel, see Trudy Walsh, "Handheld APP Eased Recovery Tasks," *Government Computer News*, 21/27a, 11 September 2002 (http://www.gcn.com/21_27a/news/19930-1.html) and Jennifer Lin, "Recovery Worker Reflects on Months Spent at Ground Zero," *Knight Ridder*, 29 May 2002 (http://www.messenger-inquirer.com/news/attacks/4522011.htm).
75. Quoted in Dennis Smith, *Report from Ground Zero: The Story of the Rescue Efforts at the World Trade Center* (New York: Penguin, 2002), 18.
76. Oral History of Richard Banaciski, 3-4. See next note.

    "Explosive Testimony: Revelations about the Twin Towers in the 9/11 Oral Histories," in Griffin, *Christian Faith and the Truth Behind 9/11*. It is also available at 911Truth.org (http://www.911truth.org/article.php?story=20060118104223192). The oral histories of 9/11 recorded by the Fire Department of New York are available at a NYT website (http://graphics8.nytimes.com/packages/html/nyregion/20050812_WTC_GRAPHIC/met_WTC_histories_full_01.html).
77. David Ray Griffin, *Christian Faith and the Truth Behind 9/11*.

78. Jim Hoffman, "The North Tower's Dust Cloud: Analysis of Energy Requirements for the Expansion of the Dust Cloud Following the Collapse of 1 World Trade Center," Version 3, 9-11 Research.wtc7.net, 16 October 2003 (http://911research.wtc7.net/papers/dustvolume/volume.html). The available evidence, Hoffman says, suggests that the dust particles were very small indeed—on the order of 10 microns. Also Colonel John O'Dowd of the U.S. Army Corps of Engineers said: "At the World Trade Center sites, it seemed like everything was pulverized" ("The World Trade Center: Rise and Fall of an American Icon," The History Channel, 8 September 2002).
79. Jones, "Why Indeed Did the WTC Buildings Collapse?" See also David Ray Griffin, "The Destruction of the World Trade Center: Why the Official Account Cannot Be True," in Paul Zarembka, ed., *The Hidden History of 9-11-2001* (Amsterdam: Elsevier, March, 2006), and in Griffin, *Christian Faith and the Truth behind 9/11*. This essay is also available at 911Review.com, 9 December 2005 [http://911review.com/articles/griffin/nyc1.html]). For Hoffman's analyses, see http://911research.wtc7.net/essays/nist/index.html. For videos of the WTC collapses, see in particular "9/11/01 WTC Videos" (http://911research.wtc7.net/wtc/evidence/videos/index.html).
80. See Griffin, *The 9/11 Commission Report: Omissions and Distortions*, 31-32.
81. The official investigators found that they had less authority than the clean-up crews, a fact that led the Science Committee of the House of Representatives to report that "the lack of authority of investigators to impound pieces of steel for examination before they were recycled led to the loss of important pieces of evidence" (see the report at http://www.house.gov/science/hot/wtc/charter.htm).
82. "Baosteel Will Recycle World Trade Center Debris," Eastday.com, 24 January 2002 (http://www.china.org.cn/english/2002/Jan/25776.htm).
83. This removal was, moreover, carried out with the utmost care. Each truck was equipped with a Vehicle Location Device, connected to GPS. "The software recorded every trip and location, sending out alerts if the vehicle traveled off course, arrived late at its destination, or deviated from expectations in any other way" (Jacqueline Emigh, "GPS on the Job in Massive World Trade Center Clean-Up," 1 July 2002 [http://securitysolutions.com/ar/security_gps_job_massive]).
84. Another problem with this story is that there were at least two versions of it. One said that the passport was found in the rubble the day after 9/11, the other that it was found minutes after the attack (see Morgan and Henshall, *9/11 Revealed*, 68).
85. Anne Karpf, "Uncle Sam's Lucky Finds," *Guardian*, 19 March 2002 (http://www.guardian.co.uk/september11/story/0,11209,669961,00.html).
86. Haas, "Government spokesman says, 'I Don't Understand the Public's Fascination with World Trade Center Building Seven.'"
87. *New York Times*, 4 May 2002, and CBS News, 10 May 2002, quoted under "Was Hani Hanjour Even on Flight 77 and Could He Have Really Flown It to Its Doom?" in Killtown's "Did Flight 77 Really Crash into the Pentagon?" (thewebfairy.com/killtown/flight77), 19 October 2003. Even *The 9/11 Commission Report* acknowledges that Hanjour was "a terrible pilot" in some passages (225-26, 242, 520n56).
88. Greg Szymanski, "Former Vietnam Combat and Commercial Pilot Firm Believer 9/11 Was Inside Government Job," *Lewis News*, Sunday, 8 January 2006 [http://www.lewisnews.com/article.asp?ID=106623]).

89. "PAVE PAWS, Watching North America's Skies, 24 Hours a Day" (www.pavepaws.org).
90. Besides the fact that this is what we would expect, this is evidently what Pentagon officials tell their employees. April Gallop, who was working in the Pentagon on 9/11, has reportedly said that during her classified tour when she was first assigned to the Pentagon, she was told that it was the best-defended building in the world (John Judge, "Pentagon and P-56 Preparations and Defenses and the Stand-Down on 9/11," Ratville Times, Jan. 11, 2006 [www.ratical.org/ratville/JFK/JohnJudge/P56A.html]).
91. See the evidence in Griffin, *The 9/11 Commission Report: Omissions and Distortions*, 159-64.
92. Thierry Meyssan, who has referred to these anti-missile batteries (*Pentagate* [London: Carnot, 2002], 112, 116), has said with regard to his source of information: "The presence of these anti-missile batteries was testified to me by French officers to whom they were shown during an official visit to the Pentagon. This was later confirmed to me by a Saudi officer."
    John Judge, co-founder of 9-11 Citizens Watch, has reported that he learned about the missiles from his father, John Joseph Judge, a WWII Army Air Corps veteran who worked at the Pentagon after the war until his death in 1965. Young John Judge, whose mother also worked at the Pentagon, spent much time there. In the late 1950s, he says, his father pointed out the location of an air-to-surface missile.
    Judge also reports that in 1998, he was given a tour of the Pentagon by Colonel Robinson, the long-time director of security. While they were outside talking about threats from terrorists, Robinson pointed to the roof and said, "we have cameras and radar up there to make sure they don't try to run a plane into the building." Since cameras and radars by themselves would not stop anything, Judge concluded, Robinson's statement implicitly referred to anti-aircraft missiles (John Judge, "Pentagon and P-56 Preparations and Defenses and the Stand-Down on 9/11," Ratville Times, 11 January 2006 [www.ratical.org/ratville/JFK/JohnJudge/P56A.html].
    The Pentagon, to be sure, has denied that it had any anti-aircraft batteries at that time, saying that they had thought them "too costly and too dangerous to surrounding residential areas" (Paul Sperry, "Why the Pentagon Was So Vulnerable," WorldNetDaily, 11 September 2001 [http://www.wnd.com/news/article.asp?ARTICLE_ID=24426]). But can anyone believe that Pentagon officials would have let such considerations prevent them from protecting themselves?
93. Won-Young Kim and Gerald R. Baum, "Seismic Observations during September 11, 2001, Terrorist Attack" (http://www.mgs.md.gov/esic/publications/download/911pentagon.pdf).
94. Karen Kwiatkowski, who was working at the Pentagon that morning, reports that "any physical remains of the aircraft that hit the Pentagon were quickly carted away to some unknown location, so we have no physical evidence that the aircraft really was Flight 77 or even a Boeing 757" ("Assessing the Official 9/11 Conspiracy Theory," in David Ray Griffin and Peter Dale Scott, eds., *9/11 and the American Empire: Intellectuals Speak Out* (Northampton: Interlink, 2006). Photographic evidence of this removal can be seen on Eric Hufschmid's video, "Painful Deceptions" (available at www.EricHufschmid.Net).

95. A photograph showing this literal cover-up can be seen in Ralph Omholt, "9-11 and thc Impossiblc:Thc Pcntagon. Part One of an Online Journal of 9-11" (http://www.physics911.net/omholt.htm).
96. On the confiscation of the film from the Citgo gas station and the Sheraton Hotel, respectively, see Bill McKelway "Three Months On, Tension Lingers Near the Pentagon," *Richmond Times-Dispatch*, 11 December 2001 (http://news.nationalgeographic.com/news/2001/12/1211_wirepentagon.html), and Bill Gertz and Rowan Scarborough, "Inside the Ring," *Washington Times*, 21 September 2001. Scott Bingham, who has tried to get videos of the Pentagon strike released under the Freedom of Information Act, has his lawsuit and the official response posted on his website (http://www.flight77.info). See also "Government Responds to Flight 77 FOAI Request," 911Truth.org, 24 August 2005 (http://www.911truth.org/article.php?story=20050824131004151).

NOTE: This lecture was delivered 30 March 2006, at Grand Lake Theater in Oakland for Progressive Democrats of the East Bay. Abbreviated versions of it were given in San Francisco for the Democratic World Federalists on April 2nd and the Commonwealth Club on April 3rd.

According to The 9/11 Commission Report (2004), page 305, the South Tower came down in 10 seconds. Estimates for the North Tower range from 10–14 seconds. A grand piano in free fall through air would have taken 12–13 seconds to hit the ground. This means that the towers "collapse" under gravitational attraction alone *would have been physically impossible. These times alone imply that the buildings were destroyed using powerful sources of energy beyond gravity.*

2

Thinking about "Conspiracy Theories": 9/11 and JFK

James H. Fetzer

The phrase "conspiracy theory" harbors an ambiguity, since conspiracies are widespread and theories about them need not be mere speculations. The application of scientific reasoning in the form of inference to the best explanation, applied to the relevant evidence, establishes that the official account of the events of 9/11 cannot be sustained. Objective measures of evidential support using liklihoods establish that the WTC was brought down through the use of controlled demolition and that the Pentagon was not hit by a Boeing 757. Since these hypotheses have high likelihoods and the only alternatives have likelihoods that range from zero to null (because they are not even physically possible), assuming that sufficient evidence has become available and "settled down" these conclusions not only provide better explanations for the data but are proven beyond a reasonable doubt.

"Conspiracy Theories"

We need to come to grips with conspiracies. Conspiracies are as American as apple pie. All they require is that two or more persons collaborate in actions to bring about illegal ends. When two guys knock off a 7/11 store, they are engaged in a conspiracy. Most conspiracies in our country are economic, such as Enron, WorldCom, and now Halliburton as it exploits the opportunities for amassing profits in Iraq. Insider trading is a simple example, since investors and brokers collaborate to benefit from privileged information.[1] Ordinarily, however, the media does not describe them as "conspiracies" The two most important conspiracies in our history are surely those involving JFK and 9/11.

One fascinating aspect of 9/11 is that the official story involves collaboration between some nineteen persons in order to bring about illegal ends and thus obviously qualifies as a "conspiracy theory" When critics of the government offer an alternative account that implicates key figures of the government in 9/11, that obviously qualifies as a "conspiracy theory" too. But what matters now is that *we are confronted by alternative accounts of what happened on 9/11, both of which qualify as "conspiracy theories" It is therefore not rational to dismiss one of them as a "conspiracy theory" in favor of the other. The question becomes, Which of these two "conspiracy theories" is more defensible?*

There is a certain ingenuity in combining "conspiracy" with "theory" because the word "theory" can be used in the weak sense of a speculation, conjecture, or guess to denigrate one account or another for political or ideological reasons without acknowledging that "theory" can also be used in the stronger sense of an empirically testable, explanatory hypothesis. Consider Newton's theory of gravitation or Einstein's theory of relativity as instances. The psychological ploy is to speak as though all "theories" were guesses, none of which ought to be taken seriously. Various different cases, however, can present very different problems. Evidence can be scarce, for example, or alternatives might be difficult to imagine.

Moreover, there are several reasons why different persons might arrive at very different conclusions in a given case. These include that they are not considering the same set of alternative explanations or that they are not employing the same rules of reasoning. The objectivity of science derives, not from transcending our human frailties, but from its inter-subjectivity. Different scientists confronting the same alternatives, the same evidence, and the same rules of reasoning should arrive at all and only the same conclusions about which hypotheses are acceptable, which are rejectable, and which should be held in suspense.[2] And, in the search for truth, scientific reasoning must be based upon all the available relevant evidence, a condition called *the requirement of total evidence*, and is otherwise fallacious.[3]

Scientific Reasoning

Scientific reasoning characterizes a systematic pattern of thought involving four stages or steps, namely: puzzlement, speculation, adaptation, and explanation.[4] Something occurs that does not fit comfortably into our background knowledge and expectations and thus becomes a source of puzzlement. Alternative theories that might possibly explain that occurrence are advanced for consideration. The available relevant evidence is brought to bear upon those hypotheses and their measures of evidential support are ascertained, as well as where additional evidence may be obtained on the basis of observation, measurement, and experiment. The weight of the evidence is assessed, where the hypothesis with the strongest support is the preferable hypothesis. When sufficient evidence becomes available, the preferable hypothesis also becomes acceptable in the tentative and fallible fashion of science.[5]

Among the most important distinctions that need to be drawn in reasoning about alternative scenarios for historical events of the kind that matter here are those between different kinds of necessity, possibility and impossibility.[6] Our language imposes some constraints upon the possible as functions of grammar and meaning. In ordinary English, for example, a freshman is a student, necessarily, because to be a freshman is to be a student in the first year of a four-year curriculum. By the same token, it is impossible to be a freshman and not be a student. The first is a logical necessity, the second a logical impossibility. Since a conspiracy requires at least two conspirators, if there were not at least two conspirators, it is not logically possible that a conspiracy was involved; if there were, then necessarily there was.

More interesting than logical necessities, possibilities and impossibilities, however, are physical necessities, possibilities and impossibilities.[7] These are determined in relation to the laws of nature, which, unlike laws of society, cannot be violated, cannot be changed, and require no enforcement. If pure water freezes at 32° F at sea level atmospheric pressure, for example, then it is physically necessary for a sample of pure water to freeze when its temperature falls below 32° F at that pressure. Analogously, under those same conditions, that a sample of pure water would not freeze when its temperature falls below 32° F is physically impossible. And when a sample of pure water is not frozen at that pressure, it is justifiable to infer that it is therefore not at a temperature below its freezing point of 32° F.[8]

Laws of nature are the core of science and provide the principles on the basis of which the occurrence of events can be systematically explained, predicted, and retrodicted.[9] They therefore have an important role to play in reasoning about specific cases in which those principles make a difference. In legal reasoning, for example, the phrase, "beyond a reasonable doubt" means a standard of proof that requires subjective conviction that is equal to "moral certainty"[10] In the context of scientific reasoning, the meaning of that same phrase is better captured by the objective standard that an explanation is "beyond a reasonable doubt" when no alternative is reasonable. Notice that the falsity of hypotheses that describe the occurrence of events that are physically impossible is beyond a reasonable doubt.[11]

Probabilities and Likelihoods

An appropriate measure of the weight of the evidence is provided by likelihoods, where the likelihood of an hypothesis *h*, given evidence *e*, is determined by the probability of evidence e, if that hypothesis were true.[12] Hypotheses should be tested in pairs, *h1* and *h2*, where the relationship between the hypotheses and the evidence may be regarded as that between possible causes and effects. Thus, suppose in a game of chance, you were confronted with a long series of outcomes that would have been highly improbable if the coin were symmetrical (if the dice were fair, or if the deck were normal). If such a run would be far more probable if the coin were bent (if the dice were loaded, if the deck were stacked), then the likelihood that the coin is bent (the dice are loaded, the deck is stacked) is much higher than the likelihood the coin is symmetrical (dice are fair, deck is normal).

A better grasp of probabilistic reasoning follows from distinguishing between two kinds of probabilities as properties of the world. The first is *relative frequencies*, which simply represent "how often" things of one kind occur in relation to things of another kind. This includes averages of many different varieties, such as the average grade on a philosophy exam in a course on critical thinking. The second is *causal propensities*, which reflect "how strong" the tendencies are for outcomes of a certain kind to be brought about under specific conditions.[13] Frequencies are brought about by propensities, which may differ from one case to another. When the class averages 85 on the first exam, that does not mean every student scored 85 on the exam. It might even be the case that no student actually had that score. But each students' own score was an effect of his propensity to score on that exam.

It can be easy to confuse "how often" with "how strong" but some examples help to bring their difference home. Canoeing on the Brule River in Wisconsin is not a hazardous pastime, but a 76-year old woman was killed on 15 July 1993 when a tree that had been gnawed by a beaver fell and landed on her. The tree fell and hit the woman on the head, as she and her daughter paddled past it.[14] The tree was about 18 inches in diameter and 30 to 40 feet tall and stood about 10 to 20 feet up the river bank. So while hundreds and hundreds of canoeists had paddled down the Brule River before and escaped completely unscathed, this woman had the misfortune to be killed during "a freak accident" It was improbable in terms of its relative frequency of occurrence yet, given those particular conditions, the causal propensity for death to result as an effect of that specific event was great.

When the same causally relevant conditions are subject to replication, then the relative frequencies that result tend to be reliable evidence of the strength of the causal propensity that produced them. But when those conditions can vary, how often an outcome occurs may not indicate the strength of that tendency on any specific trial. We commonly assume smoking diminishes life spans, which is usually true. But a 21-year old man was confronted by three thugs who, when he failed to respond quickly enough, shot him. He might have been killed, but a metal cigarette lighter deflected the .25-caliber bullet and he lived.[15] Once you appreciate the difference, three principles that relate probabilities of these kinds become apparent, namely: that propensities cause frequencies; that frequencies are evidence for propensities; and that propensities can explain frequencies. But it depends on the constancy of the relevant conditions from one trial to another.[16]

The Case of JFK

Conspiracy theories have to be assessed using principles of scientific reasoning. In the case of JFK, the difficulty has not been a dearth of evidence but sorting through the superabundance of conflicting and even contradictory physical, medical, witness, and photographic "evidence" to ascertain which is authentic and which is not. Something qualifies as evidence in relation to an hypothesis only when its presence or absence or its truth or falsity makes a difference to the truth or falsity of that hypothesis. But "evidence" can be planted, faked, or fabricated to provide a false foundation for reasoning.[17] That has proven to be true here. Once the task of sorting things out has been performed, it becomes relatively simple to draw appropriate inferences about the general character of the assassination on the basis of what we have learned about the cover-up.

Early studies by Harold Weisberg, Mark Lane, and Sylvia Meagher, for example, were instrumental in establishing that *The Warren Report* (1964) could not be sustained on the basis of evidence available even then (Weisberg 1965; Lane 1966; Meagher 1967). According to the official account, a lone assassin fired three shots from the sixth floor of the Texas School Book Depository Building, scoring two hits. One of those hits is supposed to have entered at the base of the President's neck, passed through without hitting any bony structures and exited just above his tie. It then entered the back of Governor John Connally, who was seated in front of him, shattered a rib, exited his chest and injured his right wrist before being deflected into his left thigh. The bullet alleged to have followed this trajectory was later "found" in virtually pristine condition.

This sequence of events appears so improbable that the missile that caused all of this damage has come to be known as the "magic bullet"[18] The jacket and the shirt JFK was wearing both have holes about 5½ inches below the collar. An autopsy diagram verified by the President's personal physician shows a wound at that same location. A second diagram prepared by an FBI observer shows the wound to the back below the wound to the throat. The death certificate executed by the President's personal physician also places that wound at the level of the third thoracic vertebra, about 5½ inches below the collar. Even photographs taken during re-enactments of the shooting show patches on stand-ins for the President at that location.[19]

Although *The Warren Report* tries to imply that the "magic bullet" theory is not indispensable to its conclusions, that is a gross misrepresentation. No less an authority than Michael Baden, M.D., who chaired the forensic panel that reviewed the medical evidence when the case was reinvestigated by the House Select Committee on Assassinations in 1977-78, has remarked that, if the "magic bullet" theory is false, then there had to have been at least six shots from three different directions.[20] An especially disturbing aspect of this situation is that all the evidence described here was not only available to the HSCA in 1977–78 but had been discussed quite extensively in those early books by Weisberg, Lane, and Meagher (Weisberg 1965; Lane 1966; Meagher 1967). The government has simply ignored their discoveries.[21]

Recent Scientific Studies

Since the release of Oliver Stone's film, *JFK*, in 1991, research on the assassination evidence (conducted by the best qualified persons who have ever studied the case)[22] has revealed that the autopsy X-rays have been altered in several ways, that another brain was substituted for that of JFK during its examination, and that the home movie ostensibly taken by a spectator named Abraham Zapruder has not only been extensively edited but actually recreated by reshooting each of its frames (Fetzer 1998; 2000; 2003).[23] The film was redone using techniques of optical printing and special effects, which allow combining any background with any foreground to create any impression that one desires, and included removing series of frames that would have given the plot away, such as that the driver pulled the limousine to the left and stopped after shots began to be fired.[24]

The alterations of the medical evidence include "patching" a massive defect in the back of the head caused by a shot from in front, in the case of the lateral cranial X-ray, and adding a 6.5 mm metallic slice to the anterior/posterior X-ray, in an evident attempt to implicate a 6.5 mm weapon in the assassination, which have been exposed by means of optical density studies.[25] Adapting a simple technique from physics, David W. Mantik, M.D., Ph.D., on the basis of objective measurements and repeatable experiments, has been able to prove that the JFK autopsy X-rays are not authentic. And, by even simpler comparisons between descriptions from experienced and professional physicians at Parkland Hospital describing extensive damage to the brain of JFK, Robert Livingston, M.D., a world authority on the human brain, has concluded that the diagrams and photographs of a brain that are stored in the National Archives must be of a brain other than that of John Fitzgerald Kennedy.[26]

The evidence establishing the recreation of the Zapruder film comes from diverse sources, including that frame 232 was published in *Life* with physically impossible features; that a mistake was made in introducing the Stemmons Freeway sign into the recreated version; that the "blob" and blood spray was added on to frame 313; that the driver's head turns occur too rapidly to even be humanly possible; that the Governor's left turn has been edited out of the film; that Erwin Swartz, an associate of Abraham Zapruder, reported having observed blood and brains blown out to the back and left when he viewed the original film; that several Secret Service agents observed brains and blood on the trunk of the limousine; that others have viewed another and more complete version of the film; and that Homer McMahon, an expert at the National Photographic Interpretation Center, studied a very different film on that very night.[27]

Other evidence that has long been available to serious students of the death of JFK includes multiple indications of Secret Service complicity in setting him up for the hit.[28] There was no welding of the manhole covers; no coverage of open windows; the motorcycles were placed in a non-protective formation; agents did not ride on the limousine; an improper route, including a turn of more than 90°, was utilized; the vehicles were in an improper sequence; the limousine slowed nearly to a halt at Houston and Elm; the limousine was actually brought to a stop after bullets began to be fired; the agents were non-responsive; brains and blood were washed from the limousine at Parkland before the President was even pronounced dead; the autopsy X-rays and photographs were taken from the morgue; and the limousine was sent to Ford Motor Company, stripped down and completely rebuilt, on 25th November 1963.[29]

Patterns of Reasoning

Records released by the Assassination Records Review Board (ARRB) have shown that Gerald Ford (R-MI), a member of the commission, had the description of the wound changed from "his uppermost back" which was already an exaggeration, to "the base of the back of his neck" to make the "magic bullet" theory more plausible (Fetzer 1998, p. 177). And Mantik has now proven that no bullet could have taken the trajectory ascribed to the "magic bullet" because cervical vertebrae intervene (Fetzer 2000, pp. 3–4). So the vastly influential accounts of the death of JFK that take it for granted as their foundation—*The Warren Report*, *The House Select Committee on Assassinations Report*, and Gerald Posner's *Case Closed*—are not only false but provably false and not even anatomically possible.

The wound to his throat and the wounds to Connally have to be explained on the basis of other shots and other shooters. We now know that JFK was hit four times—in the throat from in front; in the back from behind; and twice in the head: in the back of the head from behind and then in the right temple from in front.[30] We know Connally was hit at least once and another shot missed and injured a bystander. It thus turns out that Michael Baden, M.D., was correct when he observed that, if the "magic bullet" theory is false, then there had to have been at least six shots from at least three different directions. The theory is not even anatomically possible and, with at least one to Connally and one miss, there had to have been at least six shots.[31]

Anatomical impossibility, of course, is one kind of physical impossibility, insofar as humans are vertebrates with vertebrae, including those of the cervical variety. The wound observations of the attending physicians at Parkland and at Bethesda were cleverly concealed by Arlen Specter, now a United States Senator from Pennsylvania but then a junior counsel to the Warren Commission. Specter did not ask the doctors what they had observed or what they had inferred from what they had observed, but instead posed a hypothetical question: "If we assume that the bullet entered the base of the back of the neck, traversed the neck without impacting any bony structures, and came out just above the level of the tie" he asked, "would that be consistent with describing the neck wound as a wound of exit?" In response to this trivial question, they dutifully replied that it would be, but Malcolm Perry, M.D., who had performed a tracheostomy through the wound and had described it three times as a wound of entry during a press conference, added that he was not in the position to vouch for or to verify the assumptions he had been asked to make, which of course was true.[32]

The discoveries about the X-rays, the brain, and the Zapruder film are also powerful. What makes these discoveries so significant as evidence is that none of these things could possibly have been done by Lee Harvey Oswald, the alleged assassin, who was either incarcerated or already dead. Other theories, moreover, can be rejected on similar grounds. The Mafia, for example, could not have extended its reach into the Bethesda Naval Hospital to alter X-rays under the control of agents of the Secret Service, medical officers of the United States Navy, and the President's personal physician. Neither pro- nor anti-Castro Cubans could have substituted one brain for another. Nor could the KGB, which probably had the same ability as Hollywood and the CIA to fabricate movies, have been able to gain possession of the Zapruder film to subject it to alteration. Which raises the question, Who had the power to make these things happen? Given what we know now, the answer is no longer difficult to discern. It required involvement at the highest levels of the American government.

Insofar as the "magic bullet" theory describes the occurrence of events that are not only provably false but actually physically impossible, that it cannot possibly be true is beyond reasonable doubt. Moreover, the discovery that the autopsy X-rays have been altered, that another brain has been substituted, and that the Zapruder film has been recreated imply a very meticulous and carefully planned cover-up in which the alleged assassin could not have been involved. The identification of more than a dozen indications of Secret Service complicity means that the evidence has "settled down"[33] The probability of the evidence on the lone-assassin hypothesis does not even rise to zero, since it posits a physically impossible sequence, whose value is better set at null.[34] The probability of the evidence on a conspiracy scenario, by comparison, is extremely high, depending upon the competence and the power of those who carried it out. There is in fact no reasonable alternative to a fairly large-scale conspiracy in the death of our 35th President, which means that it has been established beyond a reasonable doubt.[35]

The Case of 9/11

It has taken nearly forty years for the deception to have been decisively settled on the basis of objective scientific evidence. In the case of 9/11, however, we are vastly more fortunate. As a consequence of inquiries by

Nafeez Ahmed (2002), Thierry Meyssan (2002), Paul Thompson (2004), Michael Ruppert (2004), and David Ray Griffin (2004, 2005), among others, we already know that the official account of 9/11 cannot possibly be correct. That account contends that nineteen Arabs, with feeble ability to pilot aircraft, hijacked four airliners and then executed demanding maneuvers in order to impact the World Trade Center and the Pentagon;[36] that the damage created by their impact combined with the heat from burning jet fuel brought down WTC1 and WTC2; that WTC7 was the first building in history to be brought down by fire alone; and that the Pentagon was struck by United Flight 77, which was a Boeing 757.[37] The basic problem with this "conspiracy theory" as in the case of JFK, is that its truth would violate laws of physics and engineering that cannot be transgressed.

The extremely high melting point of structural steel (about 2,800° F) is far above the maximum (less than 1,800° F) that could have been produced by jet fuel under optimal conditions. Underwriters Laboratories had certified the steel used in the World Trade Center to 2,000° F for at least 3–4 hours.[38] Even lower maximum temperatures result after factoring in insulation, such as asbestos, and the availability of oxygen.[39] Since steel is a good conductor, any heat applied to one part of the structure would have been dissipated to other parts. WTC1, the North Tower, was hit first at 8:46 am and collapsed at 10:29 am, whereas the South Tower, hit second at 9:03 am, collapsed at 9:59 am. They were exposed to fires for roughly an hour and a half and an hour, respectively. Insofar as most of the fuel was burned off in the gigantic fireballs that accompanied the initial impacts, that these towers were brought down by fuel fires that melted the steel is not just improbable but physically impossible.[40]

Most Americans may not realize that no steel-structure high-rise building has ever collapsed from fire in the history of civil engineering, either before or after 9/11. If we assume that those fires have occurred in a wide variety of buildings under a broad range of conditions, that evidence suggests that these buildings do not have a propensity to collapse as an effect of fire. That makes an alternative explanation, especially the use of powerful explosives in a controlled demolition, an hypothesis that must be taken seriously. Indeed, there appear to be at least ten features of the collapse of the Twin Towers that are expectable effects of controlled demolitions but not from fires following aircraft impacts.[41] They include that the buildings fell about the rate of free fall; that they both collapsed virtually straight down (and into their own "footprints"); that almost all the concrete was turned into very fine dust; that the collapses were complete, leaving virtually no steel support columns standing; that photographic records of their collapse show "demolition waves" occurring just ahead of the collapsing floors; that most of the beams and columns fell in sections of 30′ to 40′ in length; that firemen reported hearing sequences of explosions as they took place; that seismological events were recorded coincident with aircraft impacts and again when the buildings collapsed; and that pools of molten metal were observed in the subbasements for weeks after.[42]

The situation here is analogous to what we encountered with multiple indications of Secret Service complicity in setting up JFK for the hit. Suppose, as before, we adopt a value of 1 time in 10 for any one of these features to occur as a causal consequence of an aircraft impact and ensuing fire. We know that is a fantastically high number, since this has never occurred before or since. But, for the sake of argument, let us assume it. Then if we treat these features as having propensities that are independent and equal, for those ten features to have occurred on any single event of this kind would have a propensity equal to 1 over 1 followed by ten zeros, that is, 1/10,000,000,000, which is one chance in ten billion! Of course, since there were two such events—given TWC1 and TWC2—the probability that they would both display these same ten features on the very same occasion is equal to the product of one in ten billion times one in ten billion, which is 1 over 1 followed by twenty zeros, or 1/100,000,000,000,000,000,000. This is a very small number. And these calculations assume values that are far too high.[43]

9/11: The Pentagon

The Pentagon case should be the most accessible to study, since it only depends upon observations and measurements, which are the most basic elements available for any scientific investigation. Indeed, photos taken prior to the collapse of the Pentagon's upper floors supply evidence that, whatever hit the Pentagon, it cannot possibly have been a Boeing 757.[44] The plane was 155′ long, with a wing span of 125′ and stood 36′ high with its wheels retracted. The initial point of impact (prior to the collapse of the floors above) was only about 10′ high and 16–17′ wide, about the size of the double-doors on a mansion. A meticulous engineering study with careful measurements has been conducted that offers powerful evidence that the official story cannot possibly be correct. The damage done appears to have been inflicted by a smaller aircraft, such as an F-16, or by the impact of a cruise missile, as an alternative possibility.[45] The amount of damage is simply not consistent with what would have occurred had the building been hit by a plane with the mass and the dimensions of a Boeing 757.

Unofficial variations on the official account include that the Boeing 757 first hit the ground and then bounced into the building, that the plane's engines plowed across the lawn before it entered the building, or that its right wing-tip hit and caused it to "cartwheel" into the Pentagon.[46] None of these accounts is remotely consistent with the smooth, green, and unblemished lawn. It is all the more remarkable, therefore, that the Secretary of Defense had the lawn resurfaced as though it had been damaged during the attack. Photographs of the lawn were taken immediately after the attack that demonstrate it was not damaged at all.[47] Anyone who only viewed the lawn after its reconstruction, however, would be more likely to accept the official account. And it is of more than passing interest that far more damage could have been caused by less demanding maneuvers if the plane had been crashed through the roof of the building as opposed to hitting a newly reconstructed wing that was largely bereft of personnel and records—as though the "terrorists" wanted to inflict minimal damage.

Had a Boeing 757 hit the Pentagon, it would have left massive debris from the wings, the fuselage, the engines, the seats, the luggage, the bodies, and the tail. Look at photographs taken shortly after the impact before the upper floors fell, however, and you will observe none of the above: no wings, no engines, no seats, no luggage, no bodies, no tail. It does not require rocket science—or even the calculation of any probabilities—to recognize that something that large cannot possibly have fit through an opening that small and left no remnants in the form of wings sheered off, debris scattered about, and so on. One piece of fuselage alleged to have come from the plane appears to have been planted evidence, which was moved around and photographed in more than one location.[48] But if massive debris from the fuselage, wings, engines, seats, luggage, bodies, and tail were not present at the scene, the scene cannot have been of the crash of a 757. The argument involved is about as simple as they come.

The principle of logic involved is known as *modus tollens*, which states that, if p then q, but not q, then not p. If q must be true when p is true, but q is not true, then p is not true, either. This is an elementary rule of deductive reasoning, employment of which is fundamental to scientific investigations. If you want to test an hypothesis, deduce what must be true if that hypothesis is true and attempt to ascertain whether those consequences are true. If they are not true, then the hypothesis is false. Q.E.D. If a Boeing 757 had hit the Pentagon, as the government has alleged, it would have left debris of specific kinds and quantities. Photographs and measurements show no debris of those kinds and quantities. As long as these photographs are authentic and those measurements are correct—which concerns the quality of the evidence for not *q* and appears to be rather difficult to dispute—then no Boeing 757 hit the Pentagon.[49] Q.E.D.

What Really Happened?

The remnants of the single engine found inside offer clues as to what actually hit the Pentagon. Boeing 757s are powered by two Pratt and Whitney turbofan engines, with front-rotor elements about 42′ in diameter and high-pressure rear stages that are less than 21′ in diameter. The part found was less than 24′ in diameter and, it turns out, actually matches, not the turbofan engine, but the front-hub assembly of the front compressor for the JT8D turbojet engine used in the A-3 Sky Warrior jet fighter.[50] Since cruise missiles have a 20′ diameter, moreover, they appear to be too small to accommodate this component. It follows that the Pentagon was not hit by a Boeing 757 or by a cruise missile but, given this evidence, was probably struck by an A-3 Sky Warrior instead. The available relevant evidence is not consistent with the government's official account, which deserves to be rejected. Its likelihood given the evidence is actually null, while the alternative A-3 hypothesis makes the relevant evidence highly probable and has high likelihood as a clearly preferable explanation.

This conjecture, which the evidence suggests, receives additional support from other sources. Two civilian defense contract employees, for example, have reported that A-3 Sky Warriors were covertly retrofitted with remote control systems and missile-firing systems at the Ft. Collins-Loveland Municipal Airport, a small civilian airport in Colorado, during the months prior to 9/11. According to information they supplied, "separate military contractors—working independently at different times—retrofitted Douglas A-3 Sky Warriors with updated missiles, Raytheon's Global Hawk unmanned aerial vehicle (UAV) remote control systems, new engines and fire control systems, transponders, and radio-radar-navigation systems—a total makeover—seemingly for an operation more important than their use as a simple missile testing platform for defense contractor Hughes-Raytheon."[51] These reports substantiate the alternative.

If a small fighter jet rather than a Boeing 757 had hit the Pentagon, that would tend to explain the small impact point, the lack of massive external debris, and a hole in the inner ring of the building, which the fragile nose of a Boeing 757 could not have created. It would also suggest why parts of a plane were carried off by servicemen, since they might have made the identification of the aircraft by type apparent and falsified the official account.[52] A small fighter also accommodates the report from Danielle O'Brien, an air traffic controller, who said of the aircraft that hit, "Its speed, maneuverability, the way that it turned, we all thought in the radar room—all of us experienced air traffic controllers—that it was a military plane."[53] Nothing moves or maneuvers more like a military plane, such as a jet fighter, than a military plane or a jet fighter, which could also explain how it was able to penetrate some of the most strongly defended air space in the world—by emitting a friendly transponder signal.

Another line of argument suggests that the evidence has "settled down" Confirming that the engine found at the Pentagon was indeed a JT8D, Jon Carlson has proposed that the plane used in the attack must have been a Boeing 737, which also uses them.[54] That contradicts the use of a 757, of course, but it would also be vulnerable to a parallel argument about the absence of debris of the right kinds and quantities. Both are incompatible with the smooth and unblemished landscape, which should have been massively disrupted by the wake turbulence that would have been generated by any plane of those dimensions at that low height, a phenomenon even known to rip tiles off roofs at ordinary altitudes.[55] These and still other lines of argument establish that, whatever hit the Pentagon, it cannot have been a Boeing 757 (or a 737). It may be that controversy over this specific point has been so strenuous because it offers such a clear and obvious indication of the government's complicity.

Preferability Versus Acceptability

New York events require only slightly more sophisticated analysis. We know that the government's account posits a physically impossible sequence of events whose probability is null. So a probability of zero is merely a close approximation to null. If the buildings were brought down by controlled demolition, by contrast, then the steel would not have had to have melted or to be significantly weakened from heat, but would have been blown apart by the precise placement of explosives. And the propensity that the building would have collapsed at about the rate of free fall and that there would have been enough energy to pulverize concrete would have been very high. Since the buildings did fall at approximately the rate of free fall and there was enough energy to convert concrete into fine dust, the evidential support for this alternative is very high. It would have been quite easily confirmed by metallurgical study of what remained of the structural steel, but it was rapidly removed and sent to China by an extremely efficient company named "Controlled Demolition, Inc."

The measure of evidential support here can be captured more precisely by the use of likelihoods. The likelihood of an hypothesis (*h1*), the official account, on the basis of the available evidence *e*, is equal to the probability of *e*, if that hypothesis were true. The probability of the evidence as an effect of the official account of the cause, we have found, is approximately zero. The likelihood of the alternative, (*h2*), the demolition hypothesis, on the available evidence *e*, by contrast, is extremely high. One hypothesis is preferable to another when the likelihood of that hypothesis on the available evidence is higher than the likelihood of its alternative. Insofar as the likelihood of (*h1*) on e is very low, while the likelihood of (*h2*) on *e* is very high, the demolition hypothesis (*h2*) is obviously preferable to alternative (*h1*), based upon *e*.

A preferable hypothesis is not acceptable until sufficient evidence becomes available, which occurs when the evidence "settles down" or points in the same direction. Any concerns on this score are resolvable by adding that there were vast pools of molten metal in the sub-basements of WTC1 and WTC2 for weeks after their collapse.[56] This would be inexplicable on (*h1*) but highly probable on (*h2*). If any more proof were necessary, we know that Larry Silverstein, who leased the WTC, said that WTC7 was "pulled" which means it was brought down using explosives.[57] This occurred hours after the other buildings came down. No plane ever hit WTC7 and its collapse was perfectly symmetrical and again occurred at virtually free-fall speed. The building could not have been "pulled" without prior placement of explosives. The collapses of WTC1 and of WTC2 were very similar and equally suggestive of controlled demolition.

A new documentary, "Loose Change" includes a photographic record that offers very powerful substantiation of the controlled demolition of WTC1 and WTC2 by providing additional evidence that explosives were used to bring them down. The videotape includes eyewitness reports of firemen and other first responders, who heard what they reported to be the sounds of sequences of explosions in rapid sequence ("Boom! Boom! Boom!").[58] It displays the effects of massive explosions that occurred at the subbasement level just before the aircraft impacts, recorded at 0.9 and 0.7 on the Richter scale, and events of magnitudes of 2.1 and 2.3 of 10 and of 8 seconds duration, respectively, concurrent with their collapse.[59] And it also explores a remarkable, odd series of "security related" interruptions of security cameras and other safeguards, which involved vacating large portions of WTC1 and of WTC2 for intervals that would have allowed for the placement of explosives to have occurred. This remarkable documentary dramatically contradicts the government's account.

Beyond a Reasonable Doubt

A conclusion may be described as having been established "beyond a reasonable doubt" when no alternative conclusion is reasonable. In this case, hypothesis (*h2*), controlled demolition, can explain the available evidence with high probability and consequently possesses a corresponding high likelihood.[60] But hypothesis (h1), the government's account, can explain virtually none of the available evidence and has an extremely low likelihood. Indeed, strictly speaking, given that it even requires violations of laws of physics and engineering, the likelihood of (h1) is actually null. When seismic, molten metal, and eyewitness evidence—and especially the collapse of WTC7, which was never hit by any plane—are taken into account, the evidence also appears to have "settled down" *Thus, a scientific analysis of the alternatives on the basis of the available evidence demonstrates that the government's account of the collapse due to heat from fires cannot be sustained and that the alternative of a controlled demolition has been objectively established beyond a reasonable doubt.*

This conclusion receives support from other directions, moreover, since the project manager who was responsible for supervising the construction of these buildings has observed that they were constructed to withstand the impact from the largest commercial airplanes then available—namely, Boeing 707s—and that the structural design was so sophisticated airplane crashes would have been analogous to sticking pencils through mosquito netting.[61] It's not as though the possibility of events of this kind had never been given consideration in the construction of 110-story buildings! This observation reinforces the conclusion that the government's account is not just "less defensible" than the alternative. The likelihood of the demolition hypothesis is very high, while the likelihood of the government's account is actually null, which is a value that is less than zero. This means that the official story cannot possibly be true.

It follows that, when these "theories" are subject to the kinds of systematic appraisal appropriate to empirically testable alternative explanations, one of them turns out to be overwhelmingly preferable to the other. Since they are both "conspiracy theories" however, we have discovered that at least some "conspiracy theories" are subject to empirical test and that, based upon likelihood measures of evidential support, one of them is strongly confirmed while the other is decisively disproven. Indeed, strictly speaking, the inconsistency of the government's account with natural laws makes it physically impossible, a nice example of the falsification of a theory on the basis of its incompatibility with scientific knowledge. So some "conspiracy theories" are not only subject to empirical test but have actually been falsified by the available evidence.[62]

The fact that the government's "conspiracy theory" cannot be sustained needs to be widely disseminated to the American people. Not all "theories" are mere guesses and many of them are empirically testable. In this case, elementary considerations have proven that one "conspiracy theory" is false (indeed, as we have discovered, it cannot possibly be true), while the alternative appears to be true (on the basis of measures of probability and likelihood). Since the (*h1*) alternative to (*h2*) is unreasonable and no other alternative appears remotely plausible, the demolition hypothesis (h2) has actually been established beyond a reasonable doubt. That, I believe, is something the American people need to understand. With only slight exaggeration, this government makes a practice of lying to us all the time. It has lied about tax cuts, the threat of global warming, the reasons for going to war in Iraq, and dozens of other major issues. Some lies are bigger than others. This one—about the causes and the effects of 9/11—counts as a monstrosity!

Who Had the Power?

The observation that the government's official account cannot be sustained and that the alternative has been established beyond a reasonable doubt is not tantamount to an assertion of omniscience. Scientific reasoning in the form of inference to the best explanation applied to the available relevant evidence yields the result that, in the case of JFK, the official account of Lee Harvey Oswald as a lone assassin is not even physically possible, which means that it has null probability. It cannot possibly be true. And, in the case of 9/11, the same principles applied to the available relevant evidence yields the result that the official account of the events of that day are not even physically possible, which means that they have null probabilities, too. These conclusions are objective discoveries that anyone using the same rules of reasoning applied to the same evidence and considering the same alternatives would reach.[63]

Conclusions in science are always tentative and fallible, which means the discovery of new evidence or new alternatives may require reconsideration of the inferential situation. The suggestion could be made, for example, that the South Tower fell first because it was hit on a lower floor and to one side of the building, where the lack of symmetry caused it to fall. But that ignores the load-redistribution capabilities built into the towers, which would have precluded that outcome. The claim has also been advanced that the steel only had to weaken, not melt. But the heat generated by the fuel fires never reached temperatures that would weaken the steel and, if it had, the buildings would have sagged asymmetrically, not completely collapsed all at once, as in fact was the case. The buildings both fell abruptly, completely, and symmetrically into their own footprints, which is explicable on the controlled demolition hypothesis but not on the official account. Similar considerations apply to the Pentagon hit. Even if the wings had been shorn off, a Boeing 757—which weighed 100 tons!—cannot have entered the building through that tiny opening and not have left massive debris. Both the government's "explanations" violate laws of nature. They cannot possibly be true.

Which raises the question, Who had the power to make these things happen and to cover it up? Once the evidence has been sorted out and appropriately appraised, the answer is no longer very difficult to find. Like the assassination of JFK, the events of 9/11 required involvement at the highest levels of the American government. This conclusion, moreover, receives confirmation from the conduct of our highest elected officials, who took extraordinary steps to prevent any formal investigation of 9/11 and, when it was forced upon them by tremendous political pressure, especially from the survivors of victims of these crimes, they did whatever they could to subvert them. There are good reasons for viewing *The 9/11 Commission Report* (2004) as the historical successor to and functional equivalent of *The Warren Report* (1964).[64]

I therefore believe that those of us who care about the truth and the restoration of responsible government in the United States have an obligation to make use of every possible media venue from talk radio and the internet to newspapers and television whenever feasible. The American people can act wisely only when they know the truth. So, while the truth is said to "make us free," the truth only matters when the American people are able to discover what is true. Obstacles here that are posed by the government-dominated mass media, including the use of stooge "reporters" and of prepackaged "news releases," only make matters that much more difficult. As John Dean asks in *Worse than Watergate* (2004), if there has ever been an administration more prone to deceiving the American people in our history, which one could it be?

Ubiquitous Conspiracies

Moreover, we must overcome the inhibition to talk openly about conspiracies. That the United States is now engaged in a conspiracy to control the world's oil in relation to Afghanistan, Iraq, Iran, and Venezuela comes as no surprise.[65] Read John Perkins' *Confessions of an Economic Hitman* (2004) or Robert Barnett's *The Pentagon's New Map* (2004) for modern extensions of the predominant attitudes of the recent past elaborated by Peter Dale Scott in *Deep Politics and the Death of JFK* (1993). But not all conspiracies are global in character and many are more limited in scope, such as the effort to keep an Italian journalist from returning to Italy from her captivity in Iraq, which seems to have been deliberately contrived to contain information about war crimes committed by American forces in Falluja.[66]

If anyone doubts the ubiquitous presence of conspiracies, let them take a look at any newspaper of substance and evaluate the stories that are reported there. During an appearance on Black Op Radio, for example, I went through a single issue of *The New York Times* (Wednesday, 18 March 2005), which I chose as suitable for a case study. Multiple conspiracies are addressed throughout, including the WorldCom scandal, atrocities in Iraq and in Afghanistan (involving the murder of at least twenty-six inmates), the assassination of Refik Hariri in Lebanon, the use of counterfeit news by our own government, an SEC suit against Qwest for fraud, the 125 bank accounts of Augusto Pinochet, on and on.[67]

Efforts to promote the view that "conspiracy theories" must never be taken seriously continue unabated. A recent example of my acquaintance appears in the December 2004 issue of *Scientific American Mind* (December 2004), its "premiere issue" This issue features an article, "Secret Powers Everywhere" whose author is identified as Thomas Gruter of the University of Munster in Germany. [68] Its theme is that, while "most individuals who revel in tales of conspiracies are sane" they tend to "border on delusion" This is a very unscientific article for a publication that, like its sibling, *Scientific American*, focuses on science. We have discovered that conspiracies are ubiquitous and amenable to scientific investigation. This article thus appears to be only the latest in an ongoing series of propagandistic assaults upon our rationality.[69]

Although it ought to go without saying, no "conspiracy theory" should be accepted or rejected without research. Each case of a possible conspiracy has to be evaluated independently based on the principles of logic and the available relevant evidence. Conspiracies flourish and time is fleeting. We lack the resources to confront them all. But we need the intelligence and the courage to promote truth in matters of the highest importance to our country and to the world at large. We must do whatever we can to uncover and publish the truth and to expose the techniques so skillfully deployed to defeat us. History cannot be understood—even remotely!—without grasping the prevalence of conspiracies. And American history is no exception.

According to the official account, Flight #77 skimmed the ground at over 500 mph before hitting the Pentagon at the ground floor. This would have been aerodynamically impossible, because at that speed a pocket of compressed gas beneath the fuselage would have prevented the plane from coming closer than about 60 feet to the ground.

Notes

1. The recent indictment of former Speaker of the House Tom DeLay for money laundering and the investigation of Senate Majority Leader Bill Frist for insider trading are even being referred to as "conspiracies" See "Big Money, Big Influence, Big Trouble" *Duluth News Tribune* (4th December 2005).
2. Properties whose presence or absence depends upon and varies with different observers or thinkers are said to be "subjective" (Fetzer and Almeder 1993, p. 99). Beliefs are "rational" when they satisfy suitable standards of evidential support with regard to acceptance, rejection, and suspension (Fetzer and Almeder 1993, pp. 13–14).
3. Some relevant evidence may not be available and some available evidence may not be relevant (Fetzer and Almeder 1993, p. 133). The fallacy that results from picking and choosing your evidence (call it "selection and elimination") is known as "special pleading" a common practice by editorial writers, politicians, and used-car salesmen.
4. Some alternative models of science include Inductivism, Deductivism, Hypothetico-Deductivism, Bayesianism (which comes in many different variations), and Abductivism, whose alternative strengths and weaknesses are assessed in Fetzer 1981, 1993, and 2002. The most defensible appears to be Abductivism, which is adopted here. Abductivism envisions science as a process of four steps or stages, puzzlement, speculation, adaptation, and explanation, where the basic rule of reasoning is inference to the best explanation.
5. Acceptance within scientific contexts is "tentative and fallible" because new evidence or new hypotheses may require reconsideration of inferential situations. Conclusions that were once accepted as true may have to be rejected as false and conclusions once rejected as false may have to be accepted as true, as the history of science progresses.
6. In philosophical discourse, differences like these are known as "modal" distinctions.
7. And an event is historically possible (relative to time *t*) when its occurrence does not violate the history of the world (relative to *t*). Historical possibility implies both physical and logical, and physical implies logical, but not conversely. See Fetzer and Almeder 1993. For a detailed technical elaboration, see Fetzer 1981, pp. 54–55.
8. The example ignores the phenomena of supercooling. Some natural laws are causal and others are non-causal, while causal laws can be deterministic or indeterministic (or probabilistic). On the differences between kinds of laws, see Fetzer 1981, 1993, and 2002. Laws of society, such as speed limits on highways, of course, can be violated, can be changed, and require enforcement.
9. Scientific explanations of specific events explain why those events occur through their subsumption by means of covering laws. Predictions and retrodictions offer a basis for inferring that an event will occur or has occurred but, depending upon their specific form, may or may not explain why. See Fetzer 1981, 1993, and 2002.
10. The term "proof" sometimes simply refers to specific evidence or an illustration of a principle or theorem, as in the case of a laboratory experiment. For a discussion of the meaning of "proof" in legal contexts, abstract contexts, and scientific contexts, see James H. Fetzer, "Assassination Science and the Language of Proof," in Fetzer 1998

11. Thus, the stage of adaptation (of hypotheses to evidence) entails the exclusion of hypotheses that are inconsistent with the evidence. Like acceptance, rejection in science is also tentative and fallible, since the discovery of new alternatives or new evidence may require rejecting previously accepted alternatives, and conversely.
12. Formally, $L(h/e) = P(e/h)$, that is, the likelihood of h, given e, is equal to the probability of e, given h. For propensities as opposed to frequencies, the formula may be expressed as $NL(h/e) = NP(e/h)$, that is, the nomic likelihood of h, given e, equals the nomic probability of e, given h. See Fetzer 1981, 1993, and 2002.
13. Strictly speaking, relative frequencies are collective properties that do not belong to its individual members, while propensities are distributive properties that belong to each of its members, but may not be the same for every member in the collective. Under constant conditions, relative frequencies are evidence for causal propensities.
14. "Woman canoeing Brule River is killed in freak accident" *Duluth News Tribune* (16th July 1993), p. 1A. If those same unusual conditions were to be replicated over and over, of course, the relative frequency for death while canoeing would become extremely high. Enthusiasm for paddling the Brule River would no doubt diminish.
15. "Cigarette Lighter Saves Man from a Bullet" *National Enquirer* (6th July 1993), p. 21. In another case, a man who walked away unharmed after his truck hit a utility pole was killed as he left the crash scene, stepped on two downed power lines, and was electrocuted. His luck had run out. *Duluth News Tribune* (11th October 1993), p. 2D.
16. The sequences of cases that make up collectives are properly envisioned as sets of single cases, where the cause of each single case is the propensity that was present on that occasion. Laws of nature describe what would happen for any single case of the kind to which it applies up to the values of its propensities (Fetzer 1982, 1991, 2002).
17. The discovery that the autopsy X-rays have been altered, that someone else's brain was substituted for that of JFK, and that the Zapruder film has been recreated thus afford striking examples of the tentative and fallible status of scientific knowledge, where conclusions previously regarded as true must be rejected as false. See below.
18. Rather like the beaver on the Brule River, it seems to have been responsible for what would otherwise have appeared to have been a most improbable outcome. The difference, however, is that the Brule River incident actually occurred, while the "magic bullet" phenomenon cannot have occurred. It is not physically possible.
19. Warren Commission drawings of the alleged path of the "magic bullet" along with photographs of the holes in the jacket and shirt, the autopsy diagram, the death certificate, and some re-enactment photographs may be found in Galanor 1998, which presents available and relevant evidence contradicting *The Warren Report.*
20. Baden no doubt meant to imply that, since it would be absurd to suppose there had been as many as six shots from three directions, the "magic bullet" theory must be true. Recent scientific research has not only established that the "magic bullet" theory is physically impossible but that there had to have been at least six shots.
21. When the available relevant evidence proves that *The Warren Report*, which is the official government account of the assassination of JFK, is false, yet the government refuses to revise its phony "explanation" of the cause of his death, it is abusive to demean the serious investigators as "buffs"

22. These include Robert B. Livingston, M.D., a world authority on the human brain, who was also an expert on wound ballistics; David W. Mantik, M.D., Ph.D., a Ph.D. in physics who is also an M.D. and board-certified in radiation oncology; and John P. Costella, Ph.D., an expert in electromagnetism and the physics of moving objects.
23. The authenticity of the Zapruder film has dedicated proponents, such as Josiah Thompson, the author of an early study (Thompson 1967), and David Wrone, the author of a recent study (Wrone 2003). For a critique of the critics' arguments, go to "The Great Zapruder Film Hoax Debate," http://www.assassinationscience.com. Some of their arguments were already refuted by the "Preface" to Fetzer 2003.
24. The witnesses to the limousine stop range from Roy Truly, Oswald's supervisor in the Texas School Book Depository, to Richard DellaRosa, who has viewed another and more complete film that includes the limo stop. See, for example, David W. Mantik, "How the Film of the Century was Edited," in Fetzer 1998, pp. 274–275; Vince Palamara, "59 Witnesses: Delay on Elm Street," in Fetzer 2000, pp. 119–128; and Richard DellaRosa, "The DellaRosa Report," in Fetzer 2003, Appendix E. This was such an obvious indication of Secret Service complicity that it had to be taken out.
25. With respect to the medical evidence, see David W. Mantik, "The JFK Assassination: Cause for Doubt," with its "Postscript: The President John F. Kennedy Skull X-Rays," in Fetzer 1998, pp. 93–139; and Robert Livingston, "Statement 18 November 1993," in Fetzer 1998, pp. 161–166. See also Fetzer 2000, 2003. Blunders were committed along the way. For example, while the 6.5 mm metallic slice was intended to implicate an obscure 6.5 mm weapon, the weapon itself only has a muzzle velocity of 2,000 fps and is not a high-velocity weapon. So if JFK was killed by the impact of high-velocity bullets, as his death certificates, the Warren Commission and the HSCA supposed, then he was not killed by Lee Harvey Oswald. See Weisberg 1965, Model and Groden 1976, and Groden and Livingstone 1989.
26. Livingston's conclusion has now been reinforced by the recent discovery that two supplemental brain examinations were conducted, one with the real brain, the other with the substitute. See Douglas Horne, "Evidence of a Government Cover-Up: Two Different Brain Specimens in President Kennedy's Autopsy," Fetzer 2000, pp. 299–310.
27. A summary of evidence for alteration may be found in James H. Fetzer, "Fraud and Fabrication in the Death of JFK," in Fetzer 2003, pp. 1–28. See especially John P. Costella, Ph.D., "A Scientist's Verdict: The Film is a Fabrication," in Fetzer 2003, pp. 145–238. It had to be recreated by reshooting the frames for technical reasons related to sprocket hole images that have the effect of linking one frame to another. That the cinematic techniques for recreating the film were available in 1963 has been established by David Healy, "Technical Aspects of Film Alteration," in Fetzer 2003, pp. 113–144. The Disney film, "Mary Poppins," for example, with its elaborate special effects, was completed in 1963 and released in 1964. For easy access to the evidence, see John P. Costella, "The JFK Assassination Film Hoax: An Introduction," at *http://www.assassinationscience.com.*
28. See, for example, Vincent Palamara, "Secret Service Agents who believed there was a conspiracy," http://www.geocities.com/zzzmail/palarma.htm; Vincent Palamara, "The Secret Service: On the Job in Dallas," in Fetzer 2000; and Vincent Palamara,

"Survivor's Guilt: The Secret Service and the Failure to Protect the President" 1995; Lifton 1980; Marrs 1989; Livingstone 1992; and Fetzer 1998, 2003.

29. When the Assassination Records Review Board (ARRB), which was established by Congress to declassify documents and records held by the CIA, the FBI, the NSA, and other agencies in the wake of the surge of interest generated by Oliver Stone's *JFK*, was drafting requests for copies of its presidential protection reports for some of his trips during 1963, the Secret Service destroyed them. See Fetzer 2000, pp. 12–13.
30. Even the mortician observed that the deceased had a massive defect to the back of his head, a small entry wound to the right temple, several small puncture wounds to the face, and a wound to the back about five to six inches below the collar. (See, for example, Fetzer 2003, pp. 8–9.) This information should have been easily available. Even *The Warren Report* describes the holes in the shirt and jacket he was wearing as "53/8 inches below the top of the collar" in the jacket and as "5 3/4 inches below the top of the collar" in the shirt, contradicting its own declared conclusions (Warren 1964, p. 92). David W. Mantik, believes that the small puncture wounds were caused by shards of glass when the bullet that hit his throat passed through the windshield.
31. There appear to have been eight, nine, or ten shots from six locations. See, for example, Richard F. Sprague, "The Assassination of President John F. Kennedy," *Computers and Automation* (May 1970), pp. 29–60; James H. Fetzer, "Assassination Science and the Language of Proof," in Fetzer (1998), pp. 349–372; and David W. Mantik, "Paradoxes of the JFK Assassination: The Medical Evidence Decoded," in Fetzer 2000, pp. 219–297.
32. Lane already noticed this deceptive performance (Lane 1966, "The Hypothetical Medical Questions" Appendix II). Perry, who had performed the tracheostomy, was not in the position to vouch for or to verify the assumptions that he had been asked to make, because he knew they were false! The press conference transcript, where he described the wound three times as a wound of entry, was not provided to the Warren Commission, but has been published in Fetzer (1998) as Appendix C.
33. There were others, including that the crowd was allowed to spill into the street, the 112th Military Intelligence Group was ordered to "stand down" and a flatbed truck that would normally precede the limo for camermen to film was cancelled. Even on the unreasonable assumption that, say, one time in ten, the Secret Service "forgets" to weld the manhole covers, to cover the open windows, and such, then the probability that there would be a dozen independent events of this kind is equal to 1 over 1 followed by a dozen zeros, 1/1,000,000,000,000, or one in a trillion. Even if we arbitrarily discount half of them, the probability that there would be a half-dozen independent events of this kind is equal to 1 over 1 followed by a half-dozen zeros, 1/1,000,000, or one in a million. Since hypotheses in science are rejected when they have improbabilities of 1 in twenty or more, these alternatives must be rejected.
34. The difference is that between events that, while extremely rare, can in fact occur and those that are impossible because their occurrence would violate laws of nature. The accidental death of the woman canoeing on the Brule River had a probability of zero, but it was not physically impossible or it could never have occurred. The prime numbers occur with diminishing relative frequency among the natural numbers and have a limiting frequency of zero, but there are infinitely many of them,

nonetheless. It is therefore important, as a point of logic, to distinguish between "zero" and "null"

35. Those who make a last-ditch stand on behalf of the government's position often insist that, if there had a been a large-scale conspiracy, then some of those involved would have talked—and no one has talked! Proof that they don't know what they are talking about may be found in many places, including Noel Twyman's *Bloody Treason* (1997), where on a single page (285) he lists eight prominent figures who talked! None of this inhibits late night MSNBC-show hosts from fawning over Gerald Posner.
36. The identity of the alleged hijackers remains very much in doubt. Nila Sagadevan, "9/11—The Real Report" (forthcoming), has observed that none of the names of the Arabs who are supposed to have committed these crimes are included in the flight manifests for any of the planes. Others, such as Griffin (2004, 2005), have observed that not only were fifteen of the nineteen from Saudi Arabia and none from Iraq, but that at least six of those alleged to have been involved have turned up alive and well and living in Saudi Arabia. The FBI has not bothered to revise its list, but it should be apparent that the probability that they died in the crash, yet are still alive, is null.
37. A French human-rights activist and investigative journalist, Thierry Meyssan, was among the first to observe that the government's account of the attack upon the Pentagon did not comport with the evidence. He published two of the earliest books on 9/11, *Pentagate* (2002a) and *9/11: The Big Lie* (2002b). Meyssan has been the target of many attacks, including by James S. Robbins, "9/11 Denial" (2002), whose rebuttal consists of two assertions, "I was there. I saw it" Whatever he may have thought he saw does not affect the evidence Meyssan emphasizes. See, for example, the web site http://www.asile.org/citoyens/numero13/pentaone/erreurs_en.htm.
38. Notice that the magnitude of the differences that are involved here is very large (http://reopen911.org/Core.htm). The melting point of iron is 2795° F, but steel as a mixture has a melting point dependent upon its composition. Thus, typical structural steel has a melting point of about 2750° F. The maximum temperature of air-aspirated, hydrocarbon fires without pre-heating or pressurization is about 1,700° F. Even if the temperatures of those fires had reached as high as 1,700-2,000° F, as FEMA suggests, there was not enough time for sufficient heat to have been produced to have caused the steel to melt (Hufschmid 2002, pp. 32–40). Underwriters Laboratories had in fact certified that the steel used in construction could withstand temperatures of 2,000° F several hours before even any significant softening would have occurred. http://www.prisonplanet.com/articles/november2004/121104easilywithstood.htm
39. It certainly would not have melted at the lower temperatures of around 500° F to which, NIST estimated, they were exposed, given the conditions present in the towers (http://www.prisonplanet.com/articles/november2004/121104easilywithstood.htm). Nor would they have melted at temperatures as high as 1,200° or 1,300° F, as other estimates suggest (Griffin 2004, p. 13). The hottest temperature measured in the South Tower was about 1,375° F, far too low to cause the steel to melt, even if the exposure time had been much longer than 56 minutes. (See below.)

40. In the case of 9/11, as in the case of JFK, physical impossibilities lie at the core of the cover-up. What is impossible cannot happen, but many people are able to believe impossible things, especially when they are unaware of the laws that are involved and the specific conditions that were present. Gullibility tends to be a function of ignorance.
41. Griffin 2005, pp. 26–27. Griffin's recent study, "The Destruction of the World Trade Center" in Griffin 2006, adds even more. As Frank A. DeMartini, who was project manager for the construction of World Trade Center, during an interview recorded in January 2001, explained, "The building was designed to have a fully loaded 707 crash into it—that was the largest plane at the time. I believe that the building could probably sustain multiple impacts of jet liners because this structure is like mosquito netting on your screen door—this intense grid—and the plane is just a pencil puncturing that screen netting. It really does nothing to the screen netting" (http://www.prisonplanet.com/articles/november2004/121104designedtotake.htm). Three other engineers involved in the project—Lee Robertson, Aaron Swirski, and Hyman Brown—offered similar opinions (http://www.rense.com/ general17/eyewitnessreportspersist.htm). DeMartini died at the towers on 9/11.
42. See the discussion of seismic phenomena in Section 10. Peter Tully, President of Tully Construction, who was involved in the process of clearing the site, reported seeing pools of "molten steel" an observation that was confirmed by Mark Loizeaux, President of Controlled Demolition, who said they had been found at the subbasement level as low as seven levels down. Moreover, those pools remained "three, four, and five weeks later, when the rubble was being removed" (http://www.americanfreepress.net/09_03_02/NEW_SEISMIC_/new_seis-mic_.html). These extreme temperatures would not result from either burning fuel or collapse due to the "pancake effect," which would have propensities of zero or null, but would be expectable effects of the use of powerful explosives to bring them down.
43. Indeed, most of these features would have a null propensity on the official account. Suppose, for example, that the collapse was brought about by a "pancake" effect, with one floor falling and overwhelming the capacity of the lower floor to support it. Suppose, further, that the collapse of one floor onto another occurred at an average speed of ½ second per floor. (Try dropping a set of keys from various heights and measure the time!) Even if the initial collapse occurred more slowly and increased with the increase in falling mass, even though resistance was increasing, too, for all 110 floors to collapse—using averages, it would not matter which collapsed first or where the planes hit!—would have taken about 55 seconds. The buildings actually fell in about ten seconds, as even *The 9/11 Report* itself concedes (Zelikow 2004, p. 305). That, however, is about the speed of free fall through air for objects encountering no resistance at all. If these assumptions are even remotely correct, then that the buildings should have collapsed so much faster than 55 seconds would appear to be physically impossible on a "pancake" account. Eric Hufschmid, "Painful Deceptions" (2003), a video he produced, has shown that seismic data has confirmed that towers came down in about 10 seconds.
44. See, for example, http://www.assassinationscience.com/911links.html. This site includes many important studies of the Pentagon crash, such as a set of PowerPoint studies by Jack White. It also includes the links to many of the reports cited in

this chapter, including "Hunt the Boeing!" which presents Meyssan's analysis in a series of photographs. I have found that links to evidence that tends to contradict the government's account do not always work normally, however, and sometimes just simply disappear. Similar photographs are found in Meyssan (2002a), color photo section, pp. vi–vii. The same conclusion is drawn by Eric Hufschmid (Hufschmid 2002).

45. A photograph is archived at http://www.assassinationscience.com/911links.html. Another photograph suggests that the width may even be considerably less than 16–17 feet, perhaps much closer to ten feet, but it appears to be of two windows that were blown out of the second floor instead (http://www.serendipity.li/wot/crash_site.htm*). Notice several unbroken windows in the impact area and the lack of collateral da*mage. According to A. K. Dewdney and G. W. Longspaugh, the maximum diameter of the fuselage is about 12 feet, 4 inches, with a wingspan of 125 feet (http://www.physics911.net/missingwings.htm). They found, "*The initial (pre-collapse) hole made by the alleged impact on the ground floor of Wedge One of the building is too small to admit an entire Boeing 757*" and "*Wings that should have been sheered off by the impact are entirely absent. There is also substantial debris from a much smaller jet-powered aircraft inside the building*" They conclude with a "high degree" of certainty that no Boeing 757 struck the Pentagon and with a "substantial degree" of certainty that it was struck by a small jet, like an F-16.

46. Bloggers observed the proliferation of inconsistent stories about what happened at the Pentagon, where some were saying that the wing hit the grass and it "cartwheeled" into the Pentagon, others saying that it "nose dived" into the Pentagon, others saying that it flew "straight into" the Pentagon, others saying that it hit the helicopter pad and the wreckage flew into the Pentagon: "Why so many different stories? Are these people seeing different things?" (http://www.abovetopsecret.com/forum/thread71124/pg11). The Pentagon said the crew of a C-130 had watched the attack take place while circling Washington, D.C. (http://www.ratical.org/ratville/CAH/linkscopy/C130sawF772P.html).

47. Go to http://www.asile.org/citoyens/numero13/pentagone/erreurs_en.htm for a photograph of the construction. Compare it with other photographs of the lawn, which can be found at http://www.assassinationscience.com/911links.html, including in the PowerPoint studies of Jack White. The lawn seems to be as smooth as a putting green.

48. Slide 20 of Jack White's PowerPoint studies displays two photographs of the same piece of "aircraft debris" with two different backgrounds (*http://www.assassination-science.com/911links.html*). Another study supporting the impossibility of a Boeing 757 having passed through that entry point includes photos not only of the same piece of alleged debris but others showing two men in suits carrying what appears to be the same or similar pieces and an enormous box being carried from the site by six or eight servicemen, who have covered it up completely by using blue and white plastic tarps (http://www.geocities.com/s911surprise3b/american_airlines_flight_77/).

49. Hufschmid (Hufschmid 2002, Chapter 9), concludes that the building may have been hit by a Predator drone, which could have been painted to resemble an American Airlines aircraft. Most arguments for the official government account tend to emphasize eyewitnesses who said that they saw a Boeing 757 hit the Pentagon. (See note 37 above.) But the physical evidence overwhelmingly outweighs the contrary

eyewitness evidence, since it is not physically possible that an aircraft of those dimensions hit the building at that location and left no trace. Think of driving a car through your front door for a comparison.

50. See http://www.simmeringfrogs.com/articles/jt8d.html, which includes photos of a JT8D turbojet engine and the remnant found at the crash site. A similar conclusion is drawn by http://www.physics911.net/missingwings.htm., which concludes that this part cannot have come from a Boeing 757 but was probably from a small fighter jet, such as an F-16. The F-16 and the A-3 Sky Warrior are both attack jets. With a lenghth of 76 feet and a height of 22 feet, the Skywarrior is about half the size of a 757. Both pages are also accessible from http://www.assassinationscience.com/911links.html.
51. The workers' reports about these activities may be read at "Secret Global Hawk Refit for Sky Warrior!" (http://portland.indymedia.org/en/2005/05/318250.shtml).
52. See http://www.geocities.com/s911surprise3b/american_airlines_flight_77/.
53. She is quoted by Meyssan (2002a) on p. I and on pp. 96-97. The original source is http://www.abcnews.go.com/sections/2020/2020/2020_011014_atc.feature.htm.
54. The JT8D, however, was superceded in 737s by CFM56 engines in the early 1980s. A new study by Russell Pickering, however, raises serious questions about the JT8D evidence, leaving me more certain that there was no 757 than confident that it was an A-3. See "The JT8D and A3 Skywarrior Pentagon Theory: What Is It and Where Did It Come From?", http://www.rense.com/general70/jt.htm. Jon Carlson, "FBI Hides 85 Pentagon Videos and 9/11 Truth" http://www.rense.com/general69/91185.htm, relates that, "the Power Hour has found that Pentagon 9/11 'witnesses' were given prepared written statements to say that a commercial airliner hit the Pentagon" As a former Marine Corps officer, I can confirm that it would have been effortless to acquire the testimony of any number of enlisted that they personally observed Bruce Wayne drive the Batmobile into the Pentagon that morning. I wonder how many of us could tell the difference between a 767, a 757, or a 737, for example, especially when whatever hit was only observable for a brief span of time? AA Flight 77 left the radar screen in the vicinity of the Kentucky-Ohio border. One possible explanation for what became of it is that it went down and the bodies were transported back to a makeshift morgue in Washington, D.C., an hypothesis that may merit more investigation.
55. Wake turbulence occurs as an unavoidable effect of aircraft operation and "is generated when the difference in air pressure above and below the wings of an aircraft causes the air to spiral at the aircraft's wing tips" It dissipates rapidly in windy conditions, but in still conditions, "the spirals sink toward the ground and degrade slowly" (http://www.aeru.com/au/pages/page189.asp). Pilots are offered instructions for avoiding the problem (see "FAA Advisory Circular, AC-90-23E: CAUTION WAKE TURBULANCE" http://www.fcitraining.com/article14_fci_training_jul04.htm. The effects can be substantial, which gives rise to the following dilemma: if a 757 was flying low enough to impact the hit point on the ground floor with the official trajectory, then it should have massively disrupted the lawn; but the lawn was not massively disrupted. And if it was not flying low enough to massively disrupt the lawn, then it was not flying low enough on that trajectory to hit that point on the ground floor. Indeed, at heights low enough to impact the ground floor, the engines

or even fuselage would have been expected to plow the ground, which clearly did not occur.

56. See note 42 above and the discussion of this important point that may be found at http://www.americanfreepress.net/09_03_02/NEW_SEISMIC_/new_seis-mic_.html.
57. During a PBS documentary, "America Rebuilds" broadcast 10th September 2002, Larry Silverstein remarks, "I remember getting a call from the, er, fire department commander, telling me that they were not sure they were gonna be able to contain the fire, and I said, 'We've had such terrible loss of life, maybe the smartest thing to do is pull it.' They made that decision to pull and we watched the building collapse" (http://911research.wtc7.net/wtc/evidence/pullit.html). That, however, could not have occurred unless the building contained prepositioned explosives. If WTC7 had prepositioned explosives, that strongly suggests WTC1 and WTC2 had them as well.
58. In this respect, "Loose Change" corroborates earlier reports from eyewitnesses to explosions, such as http://www.chiefengineer.org/article.cfm?seqnum1=1029 and http://www.resne.com/general17/eyewitnessreortspersist.htm. See also David Ray Griffin, "Explosive Testimony: Revelations about the Twin Towers in the 9/11 Oral Histories" in Griffin 2006 and at 911Truth.org (http://911truth.org/article.php?story=20060118104223192).
59. WTC1, hit first but falling second, had events of 0.9 and of 2.3 on the Richter scale, while WTC2, hit second but falling first, had events of 0.7 and 2.1 on the Richter scale. These differences may be important. See, for example, http://www.americanfreepress.net/09_03_02/NEW_SEISMIC_/new_seismic_.html and http://www.democraticunderground.com/duforum/DCForumID43/5189.html, which includes the seismic record from Columbia University's Lamont-Doherty Earth Observatory.
60. For additional discussion, including many more links, see, for example, http://www.propagandamatrix.com/articles/july2005/060705controlleddemolition.htm.
61. See note 41. The properties of Boeing 707s and Boeing 767s are very similar.
62. United Flight 93, which went down in Pennsylvania, may be an easy case. Persons living in the area at the time have contacted me and told me they heard an explosion before the plane crashed, but the FBI would not even write it down. Others told me that they had been taken to an area far larger than the official crash scene to search for debris and body parts, but the Sheriff who accompanied them told them that, if they were to repeat this, he would deny it. A former Inspector General who used to supervise air crashes for the Air Force told me that, if the plane had crashed as it was officially described, it should have occupied an area about the size of a city block; but the debris is actually scattered over an area of some eight square miles. There is also a report the plane was shot down by a "Happy Hooligans" Air National Guard officer, one Major Rick Gibney, at http://www.letsroll911.org/articles/flight93shotdown.html.
63. On the objectivity of scientific reasoning, see Fetzer 1981, 1993, and 2002.
64. For more discussion and evidence, see Ahmed 2002, Meyssan 2002, Griffin 2004, Thompson 2004, Ruppert 2004, and Griffin 2005 and forthcoming.

65. See "Mission Accomplished: Big Oil's Occupation of Iraq," BUZZFLASH.COM (2 December 2005), http;//www.buzzflash.com/contributors/05/12/con05464.html.
66. See "Hostage's shooting 'no accident'" (http://news.bbc.co.uk/go/fr/-/2/hi/ europe/4323361.stm) and "Dead Messengers: How the U.S. Military Threatens Journalists" (http://www.truthout.org/docs_2005/030605.shtml). The *New York Times* has recently lost one of its own, "Reporter Working for Times Abducted and Slain in Iraq," *The New York Times* (20th September 2005), although *The Times* has not suggested that he was deliberately targeted by the American military. See, for example, "The Twilight World of the Iraqi News Stringer," *The New York Times* (25th September 2005). For another troubling report, see "US forces 'out of control', says Reuters chief," http://www.guardian.co.uk/Iraq/Story/0,2763,1580244,00.html.
67. The discussion is archived at *http://www.blackopradio.com/*. Go to "archived shows 2005" and scroll down to Part 2, Archived Show #213. Other examples of probable conspiracies making their way into the national media include financing propaganda in Iraqi ("U.S. Is Said to Pay to Plant Articles in Iraq Papers" *The New York Times*, 1 December 2005) and the DeLay-inspired G.O.P. redistricting of Texas ("Lawyer's Voting Rights Memo Overruled," *The New York Times*, 3rd December 2005).
68. I have received an email from "Dr. med. Thomas Gruter" (25th January 2005) in which he advises me that he has not been a member of the faculty at Munster for nearly twenty years and never was a professor. He is a medical doctor and journalist writing on scientific subjects. He asked *Scientific American Mind* to correct this, but it never did. He faulted the magazine's translation of his German, which, he wrote, should have said, "Most conspiracy believers are certainly sane, even if the dividing line to a delusional disorder of thinking may be ill-defined (or fluid)" So the problem could have arisen from an editor's decision to publish an English translation without verification from the author.
69. A distinction must be drawn between rationality of belief and rationality of action. Rationality of belief involves accepting, rejecting, and holding beliefs in suspense on the basis of the available relevant evidence and appropriate principles of reasoning. Rationality of action involves adopting means that are efficient, effective, or reliable to attain your aims, objective, or goals. Lying about tax cuts (global warming, Iraq) can be a rational act if it is an efficient, effective, or reliable means to attaining goals, which may be political, economic, or personal. And they can attain their aims even if they are ultimately discovered. Assessments of comparative rationality with respect to belief must take into account that persons are rational in their beliefs when they incorporate the principles that define it. Since the "community of scientists" can be littered with phonys, charlatans, and frauds, "scientists" are those who adhere to the principles of science. Analogously, "rational persons" are those who adhere to the principles of rationality. They tend to converge. See Fetzer 1981, 1993, 2000.

Book References

Ahmed, N. M. 2002: *The War on Freedom: How and Why America was Attacked, September 11th, 2001* (Joshua Tree: Tree of Life Publications, 2002).

Barnett, T. P. M. 2004: *The Pentagon's New Map: War and Peace in the Twenty-first Century* (New York: Putnam, 2004).

Dean, J. 2004: *Worse than Watergate: The Secret Presidency of George W. Bush* (New York: Little, Brown, 2004).

Fetzer, J. H. 1981: *Scientific Knowledge: Causation, Explanation, and Corroboration* (Dordrecht: Reidel, 1981).

Fetzer, J. H. 1993: *Philosophy of Science* (New York, Paragon House, 1990).

Fetzer, J. H. 2002: "Propensities and Frequencies: Inference to the Best Explanation" *Synthese* 132/1–2 (July August 2002), pp. 27–61.

Fetzer, J. H., ed. 1998: *Assassination Science: Experts Speak Out on the Death of JFK* (Chicago, Catfeet Press/Open Court, 1998).

Fetzer, J. H., ed. 2000: *Murder in Dealey Plaza: What We Know Now that We Didn't Know Then* (Chicago: Catfeet Press/Open Court, 2000).

Fetzer, J. H., ed. 2003: *The Great Zapruder Film Hoax: Deceit and Deception in the Death of JFK* (Chicago, Catfeet Press/Open Court, 2003).

Fetzer, J. H. and R. F. Almeder 1993: *Glossary of Epistemology/Philosophy of Science* (New York: Paragon House, 1993).

Galanor, S. 1998: *Cover-Up* (New York: Kestrel, 1998).

Griffin, D. R. 2004: *The New Pearl Harbor* (Northampton, Olive Branch Press, 2004).

Griffin, D. R. 2005: *The 9/11 Commission Report: Omissions and Distortions* (Northampton: Olive Branch Press, 2005).

Griffin, D. R. 2006: *Christian Faith and the Truth Behind 9/11* (Lexington, Westminster John Knox, 2006:

Groden, R. and H. Livingstone 1989: *High Treason: The Assassination of President Kennedy and the New Evidence of Conspiracy* (Boothywyn: The Conservatory Press, 1989).

Hacking, I. 1965: *Logic of Statistical Inference* (Cambridge: Cambridge University Press, 1965).

Hufschmid, E. 2002: *Painful Questions: An Analysis of the September 11th Attack* (Goleta: End-point Software, 2002).

Lane, M. (1966), *Rush to Judgment* (New York: Holt, Rinehart, Winston, 1966).

Lifton, D. 1980: *Best Evidence: Disguise and Deception in the Assassination of John F. Kennedy* (New York, Macmillan, 1980).

Livingstone, H. 1992: *High Treason 2: The Great Cover-Up* (New York, Carroll Graf, 1992).

Marrs, J. 1989: *Crossfire: The Plot that Killed Kennedy* (New York, Carroll Graf, 1989).

Meagher, S. 1967: *Accessories after the Fact* (Indianapolis: Bobbs-Merrill, 1967).

Meyssan, T. 2002a: *Pentagate* (London: Carnot, 2002).

Meyssan, T. 2002b: *9/11: The Big Lie* (London, Carnot, 2002).

Model, P. and R. Groden 1976: *JFK: The Case for Conspiracy* (New York: Manor, 1976).

Palamara, V. 1995: *Survivor's Guilt: The Secret Service and the Failure to Protect the President* (Self-Published: Xerox, 1995).

Perkins, J. 2004: *Confessions of an Economic Hitman* (San Francisco: Berrett-Koehler, 2004).

Posner, G. 1993: *Case Closed: Lee Harvey Oswald and the Assassination of JFK* (New York: Random House, 1993).

Robbins, J. S. 2002: "9/11 Denial" *The National Review On-Line* (9th April 2002), http://nationalreview.com/robbins/robbins040902.asp.

Ruppert, M. 2004: *Crossing the Rubicon: The Decline of the American Empire at the End of the Age of Oil* (Garbiola Island: New Society, 2004).

Scott, P. D. 1993: *Deep Politics and the Death of JFK* (Berkeley: University of California Press, 1993).

Thompson, J. 1967: *Six Seconds in Dallas* (New York, Bernard Geis, 1967).

Thompson, P. 2004: *The Terror Timeline: Year by Year, Day by Day, Minute by Minute* (New York, Regan, 2004).

Twyman, N. 1998: *Bloody Treason: On Solving History's Greatest Murder Mystery: The Assassination of John F. Kennedy* (Rancho Santa Fe: Laurel Publishing, 1997).

Warren, E. et al. 1964: *Report of the President's Commission on the Assassination of President John F. Kennedy* (New York: St. Martin's Press, 1964).

Weisberg, H. 1965: *Whitewash: The Report on the Warren Report* (New York: Dell, 1965).

Wrone, D. 2003: *The Zapruder Film: Reframing JFK's Assassination* (Lawrence: University Press of Kansas, 2003).

Zelikow, P., et al. 2004: *The 9/11 Commission Report: Final Report of the National Commission on Terrorist Attacks Upon the United States* (New York, Norton, 2004).

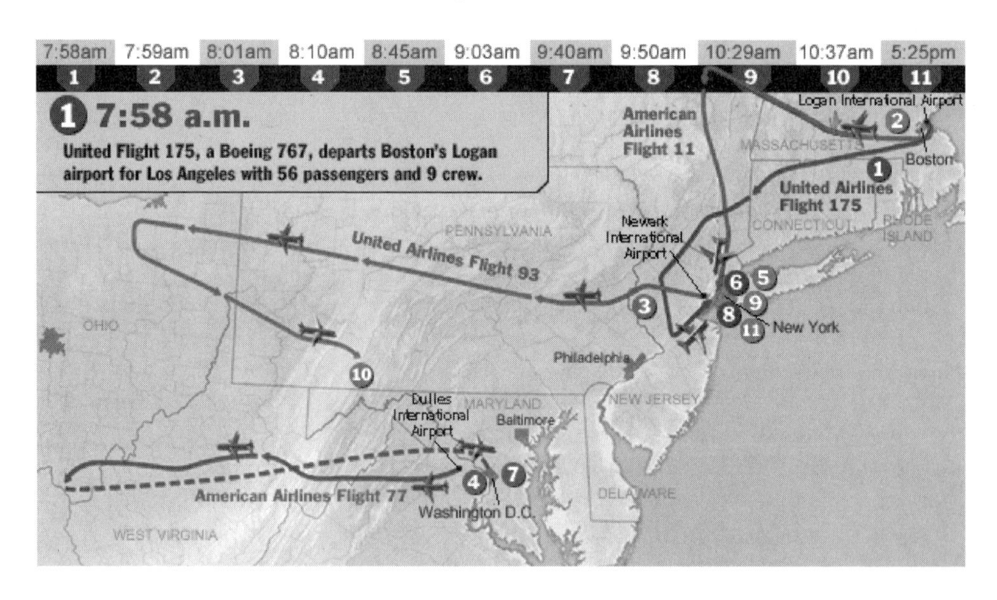

Flight 77 was not on the radar screen between the Kentucky-Ohio border back to Washington, indicating the plane was not in the air during that interval. Norman Mineta's testimony to the 9/11 commision provides powerful evidence that Dick Cheney issued a "stand-down order" to insure an incoming plane would not be shot down. A smaller plane appears to have been substituted for the original Boeing 757.

3

9/11
A Photographic Portfolio of Death and Devastation

Jack White

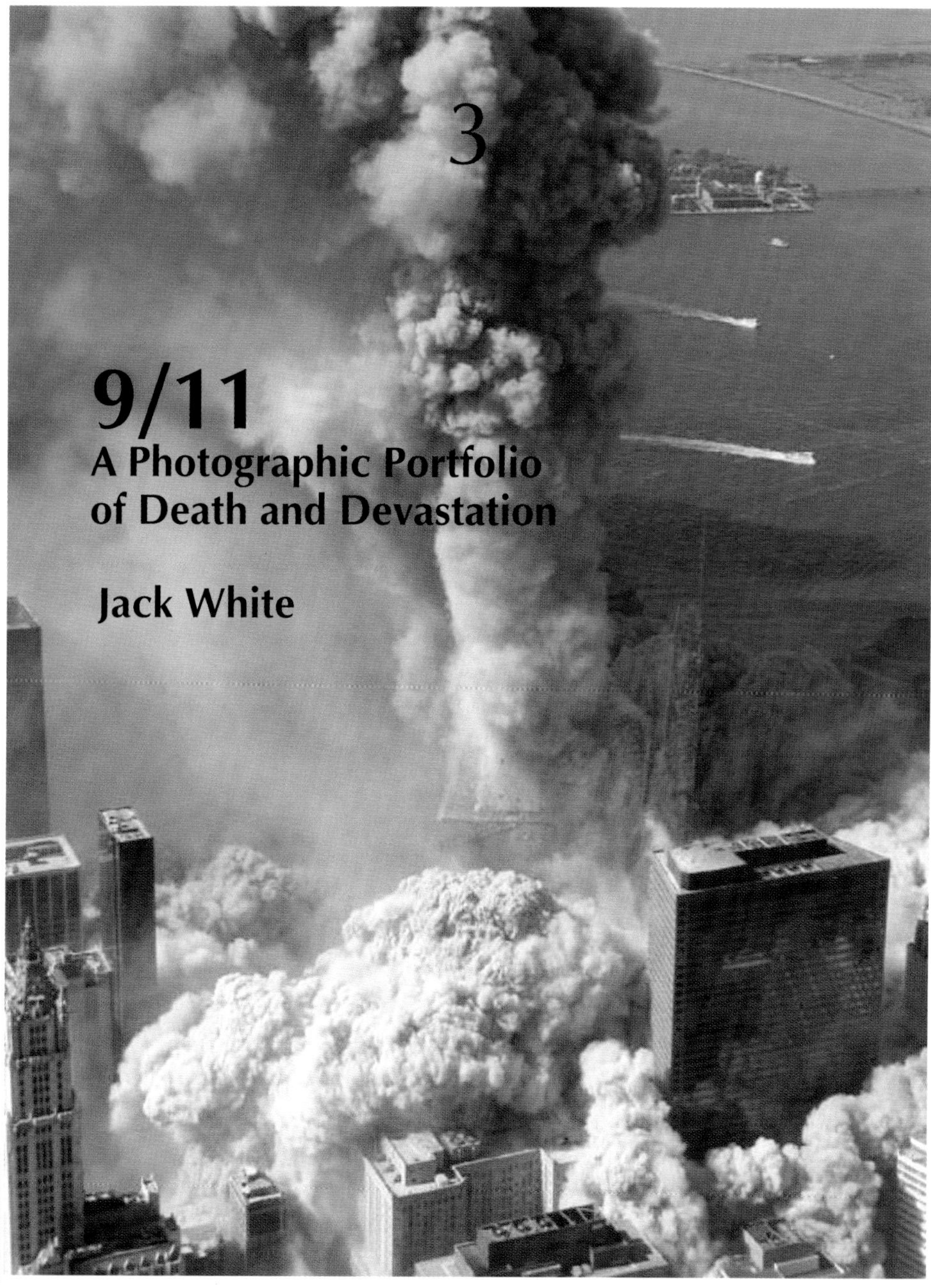

The most surreal scene in history was witnessed by millions of people worldwide on television as it happened. Yet the plumes of smoke and the incredible dust clouds from the the pulverization of two of the world's tallest buildings within minutes of each other could not adequately portray the horror of thousands of people dying and the total destruction of many buildings. This photo shows Building 7 amid the dust clouds, serenely waiting its turn to fall about seven hours later for no apparent reason. Two five-hundred-thousand ton buildings were converted to dust in approxiately ten seconds each. According to *The 9/11 Commission Report* (2004), the buildings were destroyed by the combination of jet-plane impacts and jet-fuel based fires which caused the steel to weaken and bring about a "pancake collapse." The photographic record makes that very difficult to believe.

Left to right, top to bottom: Demolition starts badly; the top 300 feet of WTC-2 tilted as much as 23 degrees before being "blown to Kingdom come." No one had ever attempted to demolish a building the size of a twin tower, and the dust cloud from WTC-1 helped to distract and cover up problems in destroying WTC-2. As the buildings disintegrated, huge steel columns many feet long were scattered like matchsticks for hundreds of feet. The tower peeled downward as dark explosions shot up, while white ones exploded outward. Above the white explosions, the tower is turning to dust as the lower part awaits its fate. At lower right, as explosions destroy WTC-2, huge sections of disintegrating steel "wheatchex" showered down on WTC-3, the Marriott Hotel. According to the "official account," fires that caused a collapse due to gravity brought down these buildings.

Bill Biggart

James R. Tourtellotte

Along Vesey Street were WTC buildings 5, 6, and 7. Lower photo shows two huge cavities in eight-story WTC-6 at center and a smaller but striking gash on the side of Building 5 just above. Neither building was struck by significant debris from either of the Twin Towers, right. Across Vesey Street, at left, is a neat pile that was the 47-story Building 7, which imploded and fell at the speed of gravity into its own footprint. Top photo shows a gash on the side of Building 3, with walls of WTC-1 reeling oddly nearby. Other photos of the hole in Building 6 show little debris of any kind within, which is very difficult, even impossible, for the government to explain. How could a collapse of the towers possibly account for this?

WTC-7, above right, during the attack on the Twin Towers, appears undamaged except for a modest fire at street level. Below right, WTC-7 (on the right) still appears in no distress long after both towers had fallen. Frames (above) from video of the collapse of WTC Building 7 shows a perfectly controlled demolition of WTC-7, which was two blocks away from WTC-1 and 2 and only superficially hit by debris from 1 and 2. At 5:20 PM, over six hours after WTC-1 and WTC-2 fell, WTC-7 came down in free fall into its own footprint, a sure sign of controlled demolition, which causes a "kink" in the center of the building. The official story claims that diesel fuel reservoirs in the building exploded, resulting in fires that brought the building down, even though there is no recorded case of the fire-induced collapse of a large steel-protected building; and only very small fires were burning when WTC-7 "collapsed." Diesel fuel does not explode, and it burns at low temperatures

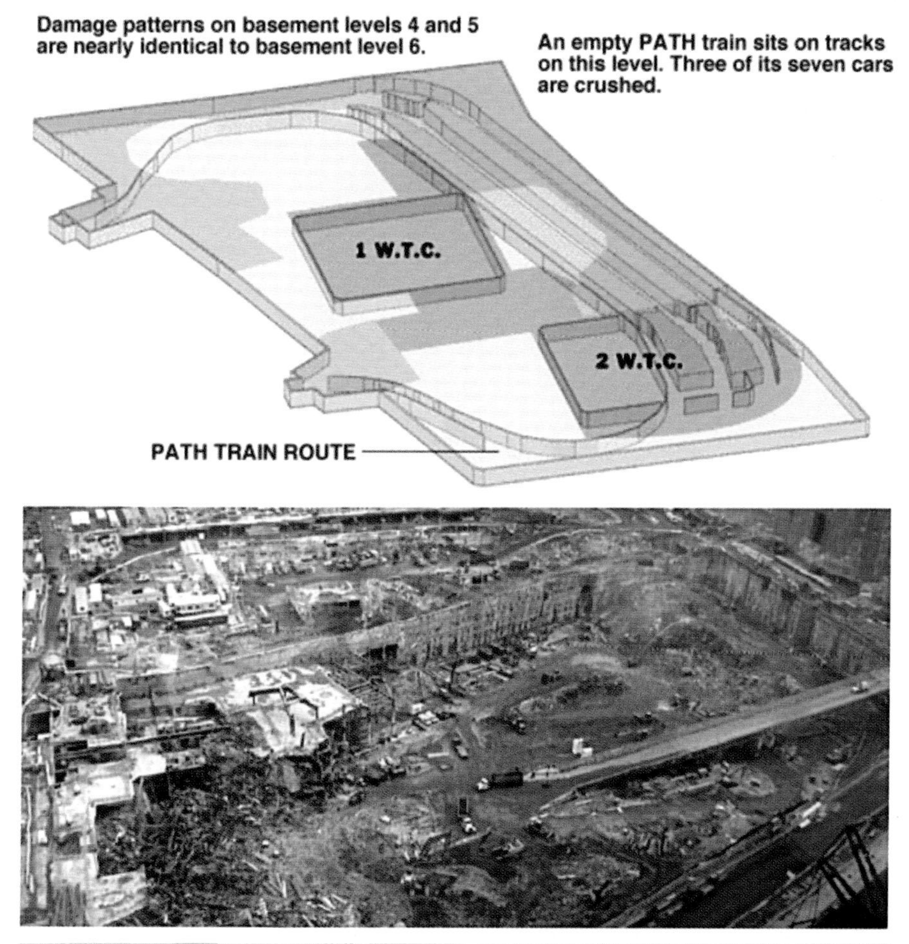

The World Trade Center was built on bedrock, protected by an underground "bathtub" or foundation ring (top, left, and diagram) down seven stories below the surface of lower Manhattan to prevent flooding by the Hudson River, only a block away. On September 11 the bathtub mysteriously remained without significant damage despite two huge towers collapsing on it. It was not built to withstand such colossal impact. No foundation structure could remain unscathed after a mountain of quarter-mile high material was dropped on it twice. The intact bathtub appears to contradict the official theory of gravity-driven collapse in which virtually the entire weight of the Twin Towers would crash into the bathtub. Even subway cars within the bathtub were not crushed, lower right.

At bottom, a mysterious explosion shot by an "unknown" photographer before any fire trucks arrived purports to show the explosion of Flight 77 within the building. Researchers wonder how a photographer happened to be directly under the incoming flight with a camera and capture such a remarkable image; some suspect the image was faked and others that it was a later occurrence. At top are official "before and after" photos of the alleged impact point; upper right shows where the wall collapsed directly over the "impact point" but upper left shows the same area before the wall collapsed, and unbroken windows and undamaged wall are seen at the "impact point" of the "plane," which was 125 feet wide and 44 feet tall. Hard to believe.

At top, fire trucks from National Airport arrived at the Pentagon within ten minutes and had all fires out within seven minutes. They saw no aircraft wreckage or damage to the lawn. They did not know there had been a "plane crash" because the main fire they found was a burning trailer. The stream of water at left had been a "plane crash" because the main fire they found was a burning trailer. The stream of water at left is being sprayed at the alleged impact point, yet the wall is not visibly breeched. At bottom, a Pentagon security camera captures an image said to be an "incoming plane" (red rectangle), yet it is much too small to be a Boeing 757 (inset) like American Airlines Flight 77, plus it is emitting a trail of smoke like a missile.

United Airlines Flight 93, a huge Boeing 767, allegedly crashed at high speed into a field near Shanksville, Pennsylvania, leaving virtually no crash debris and little damage to grass or trees. Witnesses described and photos confirm only a small trench in the grassy field. The official story says the soft ground "swallowed" the entire plane and its occupants. A lady named Val McClatchy allegedly took the photo at top of a small puff of smoke claimed to be the plane exploding near her home, yet pieces of the plane were found up to eight miles away. A coroner called to the scene saw not a single body, but the official story said DNA identified all victims.

PART II: WHAT WE KNOW NOW

4

A Refutation of the Official Collapse Theory

Judy Wood

Abstract

The World Trade Center towers were over one quarter mile tall. We were told the Twin Towers "collapsed" in about ten seconds. We evaluate if this is physically possible. An example using billiard balls is presented as a mental exercise to help visualize a minimum collapse time one would expect.

Introduction

Very shortly after the events of September 11, 2001, the U.S. government proclaimed its certitude concerning who the attackers were—nineteen Arab suicide bombers under the guidance of one Osama bin Laden. What followed in quick succession were 'authoritative' pronouncements, through NOVA and a few academicians, about what brought the WTC towers down. This early public consensus of 'the authorities' was that the buildings could not withstand the horrific onslaught of the plane crashes and subsequent fires.

Since that time questions have arisen about the veracity of the Official Government Theory of the events of 9/11. One area of particular interest has been the issue of the WTC tower "collapses." Could they have indeed been brought down as a consequence of the apparent air strikes against them?

This article looks at that question from a single, simple perspective—that of the timing of those "collapses." Absent other forces, gravity alone must have generated them. We will examine whether that was possible, from the perspective of the law of gravity and the visual record.

The Value of Simplicity

What can you prove with simple models of an enormously complex situation?

Let's say I tell you that I ran, by foot,
to a store (10 miles away), then
to the bank (5 more miles), then
to the dog track (7 more miles), then
to my friend's house (21 more miles),
then home . . . all in 2 minutes.

To disprove my story, you could present a simple case. You could present that the world's record for running just one mile is 3:43.13, or just under four minutes. So, it does not seem possible that I could have run over 40 miles in 2 minutes. That is, it does not seem possible for me to have run 43 miles in half the time it would take the holder of the world's record to run just one mile. Even if you gave me the benefit of having run all 43 miles at world-record pace, it would not have been possible for me to have covered that distance in two minutes. Remember, the proof need not be complicated. You don't need to prove exactly how long it should have taken me to run that distance. Nor do you need to prove how much longer it would have taken if I stopped to place a bet at the dog track. To disprove my story, you only need to show that the story I gave you is not physically possible. Now, let us consider if any of those collapse times provided to us seem possible with the story we were given.

How Long Did It Take the WTC Towers to Collapse?

Three distinct sources have provided data and/or opinions about how long it took for the WTC towers to collapse. (1) The Official Government Story, as expressed in *The 9/11 Commission Report* (2) Columbia University's Seismology Group record of the earth-shaking associated with the collapse, and (3) independent 9/11 researchers who have attempted to discern the collapse time through various methods involving video analysis.

Page 305 of *The 9/11 Commission Report*[1] states, "At 9:58:59, the South Tower collapsed in ten seconds, The building collapsed into itself, causing a ferocious windstorm and creating a massive debris cloud." (Chapter 9.[2] The August Fact Sheet "Answers to Frequently Asked Questions" by NIST states, "NIST estimated the elapsed times for the first exterior panels to strike the ground after the collapse initiated in each of the towers to be approximately 11 seconds for WTC 1 and approximately 9 seconds for WTC 2." (Question #6.)[3]

The height of the South Tower (WTC-2) is 1362 feet, and the height of the North Tower (WTC-1) is 1368 feet, which are nearly the same.[4] We will therefore assign the value of 10 seconds to the Official Government story.

Columbia University's Seismology Group recorded seismic events of 10 seconds and 8 seconds in duration, which correspond to the collapses of WTC2 and WTC1, respectively.

Information Based on Seismic Waves recorded at Palisades New York			
Seismology Group,[5] Lamont-Doherty Earth Observatory, Columbia University			
Event	**Origin time (EDT)** (hours:minutes:seconds)	**Magnitude** (equivalent seismic)	**Duration**
"Impact 1" at WTC1	08:46:26±1	0.9	12 seconds
"Impact 2" at WTC2	09:02:54±2	0.7	6 seconds
"Collapse 1," WTC2	09:59:04±1	2.1	10 seconds
"Collapse 2," WTC1	10:28:31±1	2.3	8 seconds

Table 1: Information Based on Seismic Waves recorded at Palisades New York

Because the exact nature of what caused the towers to be destroyed has not been determined, it is difficult to assign a clear meaning to the geological evidence. However, for our purposes we interpret the evidence here as suggesting a fall-time in the vicinity of free-fall.

The third source of data/opinion about fall times comes from independent researchers and is based on their examination of video footage. Here we have a range of suggested fall times, from approximately 9 seconds to perhaps as long as 15 or even 18 seconds (though the longer times seem to involve questionable reasoning.)[6]

One problem with attempting a video analysis is that the later part of the collapse is hidden in the immense pyroclastic-like dust clouds the event produced. Additionally, there is the issue of whether or not the videos reflect the absolute time involved or are affected by subtle time distortions.

From the evidence available, we will assume that the fall time must have been within the range of 9 to 15 seconds.

However, our purpose in the exercise below is to identify whether the Official Government Story is worthy of our belief. For that reason, we will assume the government's published value of 10 seconds for our fall time. Before we begin our analysis, we might ask ourselves, "Do any of these values seem reasonable as collapse times, from gravity alone, for buildings approximately one quarter mile in height?" Let's calculate a few values we can use as a reference.[4]

For the following, we will use the height of WTC-1 as 1368 feet and considered each floor to be a height of 12.44 feet. (1368/110 =12.44 ft/floor). We will assume bodies accelerate in accord with the law of gravity = 32.2 ft/sec² or 9.81 m/sec².

Case 1: Free-Fall Time of a Billiard Ball from the Roof of WTC-1

Let's consider the minimum time it would take a blue billiard ball to hit the pavement, more than ¼ mile below (see below). Start the timer when the ball is dropped from the roof of WTC-1. We'll assume this is in a vacuum, with no air resistance. (Note, large chunks of the building will have a very low surface area-to-mass ratio, so air resistance can be neglected.) From the rooftop of WTC-1, drop one (dark-blue) billiard ball over the edge. As it falls, it accelerates. If it were in a vacuum, it would hit the pavement, 1368 feet below, in 9.22 seconds, shown by the blue curve in the figure, below. It will take longer if air resistance is considered, but for simplicity, we will neglect air resistance. This means that the calculated collapse times are more generous to the official story than they need to be.

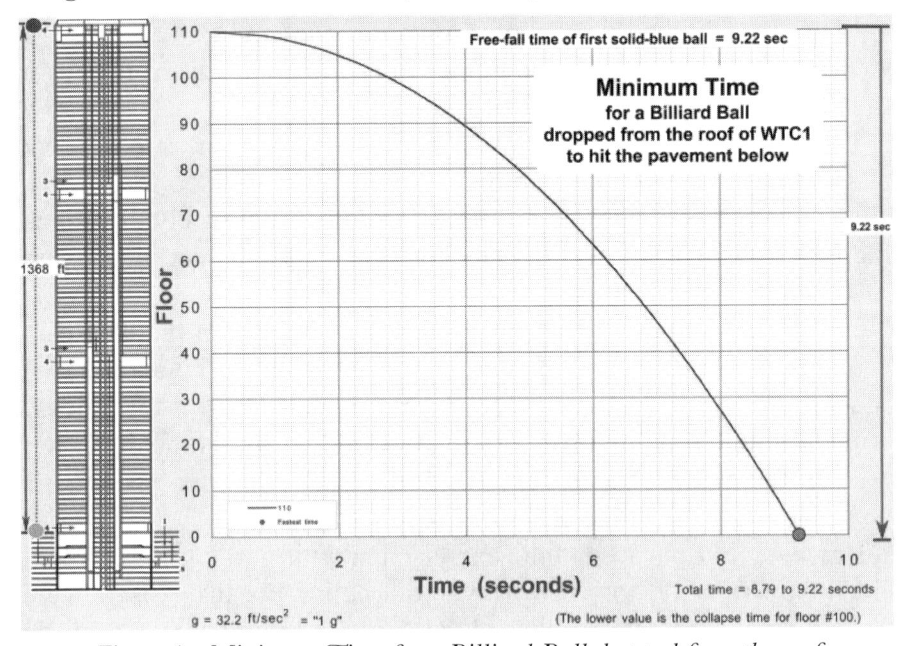

Figure 1. Minimum Time for a Billiard Ball dropped from the roof of WTC-1 to hit the pavement below, assuming no air resistance.

Notice that the billiard ball begins to drop very slowly then accelerates with the pull of gravity. If in a vacuum, the blue ball will hit the pavement, 1368 ft. below, 9.22 seconds after it is dropped. That is, unless it is propelled by explosives, it will take at least 9.22 seconds to reach the ground (assuming no air resistance).

Let's consider the "Pancake Theory"

The reason we need to consider the 'pancake theory' is that it is an integral part of the Official Government Story. According to the U.S. government (FEMA and vocal supporters of the official story such as Thomas Eagar[7]), the WTC towers fell by 'pancaking', propelled from gravity alone, in 10 seconds. Our purpose here is to examine the government claim to determine its likely veracity.

According to the pancake theory, one floor fails and falls onto the floor below, causing it to fail and fall on the floor below that one, and so forth. The "pancake theory" implies that this continues all the way to the ground floor. Even if the initial "collapse" should begin at the 80th floor, for a total collapse to occur, the 30 floors above the 80th floor would still need to 'pancake' to get the entire structure to the ground. Since there is no evidence of 30 floors remaining intact, we must assume this is what happened, although we do not know what mechanism may have caused such a total collapse.

What does the visual evidence suggest?

In the case of both WTC towers, not only did we fail to see a block of floors remaining intact at the completion of the event; we did not see any accumulation of floors at all. Rather, the video and photographic record clearly shows a pulverization of the floors throughout the event (see pictures below).

Thus, we cannot assume the floors stacked up like pancakes. Looking at the data, we therefore take the conservative approach. For the purposes of our analysis, we will assume that a falling floor initiates the fall of the one below, while itself becoming pulverized. In other words, when one floor impacts another, the small amount of kinetic energy from the falling floor is consumed by (a) pulverizing that floor forst and (b) breaking free the next floor. In reality, there is not enough kinetic energy to do either Trumpman[8], Hoffman[9], Grimmer.[10] But for the sake of calculating a "collapse" timing, we will assume there was. After all, millions of people believe they saw the buildings "collapse." Below are two schematics. Model A represents a true 'pancaking' of floors—that is, the floors remain intact and pile up like a stack of pancakes. Model B represents a disintegration of floors during the "collapse"—that is, the floors blow up like an erupting volcano from the top down.

Which of the two models, above, best matches the images below?

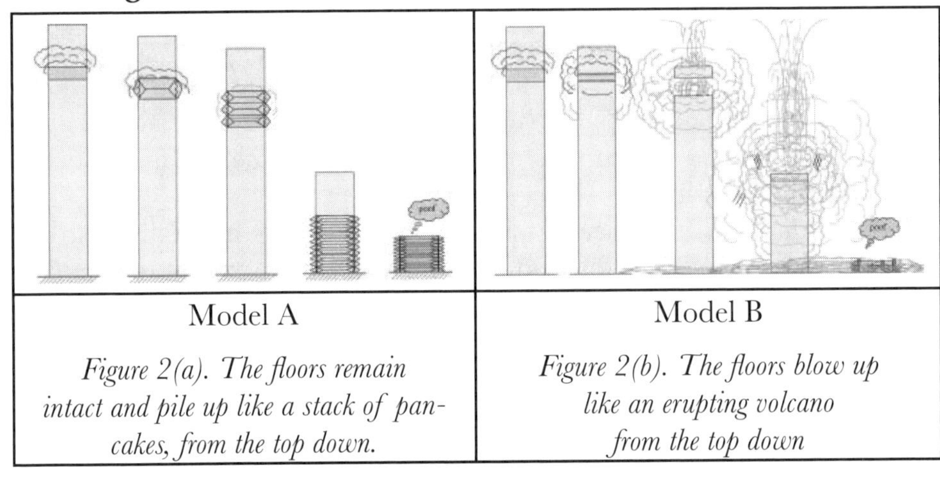

Model A	Model B
Figure 2(a). The floors remain intact and pile up like a stack of pancakes, from the top down.	*Figure 2(b). The floors blow up like an erupting volcano from the top down*

Figure 2(c). Note that the top "block" begins to disintegrate before the damaged zone starts to move downward. http://i18.photobucket.com/albums/b108/janedoe444/present/WTC-1_redLines.gif

Video clip courtesy of 911review.org[11]

Figure 3(a). WTC-2, demonstrating there is little to no free-fall debris ahead of the "collapse wave."

Figure 3(b). A layer of uniform dust left by the "collapse."

Figure 3(c). The rubble was not deep enough to reach the undercarriage of the black Cushman scooter in the foreground and the flagpoles in the background look full height.

Images from the "collapse." 3(a) WTC-2, demonstrating there is little to no free-fall debris ahead of the "collapse wave," 3(b) layer of uniform dust left by the "collapse,"and 3(c) WTC-7 on the afternoon of 9-11-01. WTC-7 is the tall skyscraper in the background, right, seen from WTC. plaza area, which shows evidence of pulverization, but none of pancaking. All reports from 'The Pile' confirm that, apart from the steel, nothing but fine powder remained.[12]

Kinetic energy cannot be spent in diametrically opposite tasks.

Figure 4. An earthquake-induced collapse in Pakistan suggests how much rubble and how little dust should have been at Ground Zero if the government's gravitational collapse story were true. Source of photo: Rolling Stone[13]

So, if there was enough kinetic energy for pulverization, there will be pancaking or pulverization, but not both. Energy can only be spent once; there will be pancaking or pulverization, but not both. If the potential energy is used to pulverize a floor upward and outward, it cannot also be used to accelerate the building downward. In order to have pancaking, a force is required to trigger the failure of the next floor. If the building above that floor has been pulverized, there can be no force pushing down. As observed in the pictures below, much of the material has been ejected upward and outward. Any pulverized material remaining over the footprint of the building will be suspended in the air and cannot contribute to a downward force slamming onto the next floor. With pulverization, the small particles have a much larger surface-area-to-mass ratio, and air resistance becomes significant. As we can recall, the dust took many days to settle out of the air—not hours or minutes. So, even though the mechanism to trigger the "pancaking" of each floor seems to elude us, let's consider the time we would expect for such a collapse

5(a). 5(b). 5(c). 5(d).

Figure 5. Images illustrating what really happened that day.

To illustrate the timing for this domino effect, we will use a sequence of falling billiard balls, where each billiard ball triggers the release of the next billiard ball in the sequence. This is analogous to assuming pulverization is instantaneous and does not slow down the process. In reality, this pulverization would slow down the "pancake" progression, so longer times would be expected. Thus, if anything, this means the calculated collapse times are more generous to the official story than they need to be.

Case 2: 'Progressive Collapse' in Ten-Floor Intervals

To account for the damaged zone, let's simulate the floor beams collapsing every 10th floor, as if something has destroyed 9 out of every 10 floors for the entire height of the building. This assumes there is no resistance within each 10-floor interval. That is, we use the conservative approach that there is no resistance between floor impacts. In reality there is, which would slow the collapse time further. Also, there was only damage in one 10-floor interval, not the entire height of the building. Thus, if anything, this means the calculated collapse times are more generous to the official story than they need to be. Refer to the figure below.

The clock starts when the blue ball is dropped from the roof (110th floor). Just as the blue ball passes the 100th floor, the red ball drops from the 100th floor. When the red ball passes the 90th floor, the orange ball drops from the 90th floor, . . . etc. Notice that the red ball (at floor 100) cannot begin moving until the blue ball reaches that level, which is 2.8 seconds after the blue ball begins to drop.

This approximates the "pancaking" theory, assuming that each floor within the "pancaking" (collapsing) interval provides no resistance at all. With this theory, no floor below the "pancake" can begin to move until the progressive collapse has reached that level. For example, there is no reason for the 20th floor to suddenly collapse before it is damaged.

With this model, a minimum of 30.6 seconds is required for the roof to hit the ground. Of course it would take longer if accounting for air resistance. It would take longer if accounting for the structure's resistance that allows pulverization. The columns at each level would be expected to absorb a great deal of the energy of the falling floors. Thus, if anything, this means the calculated collapse times are more generous to the official story than they need to be.

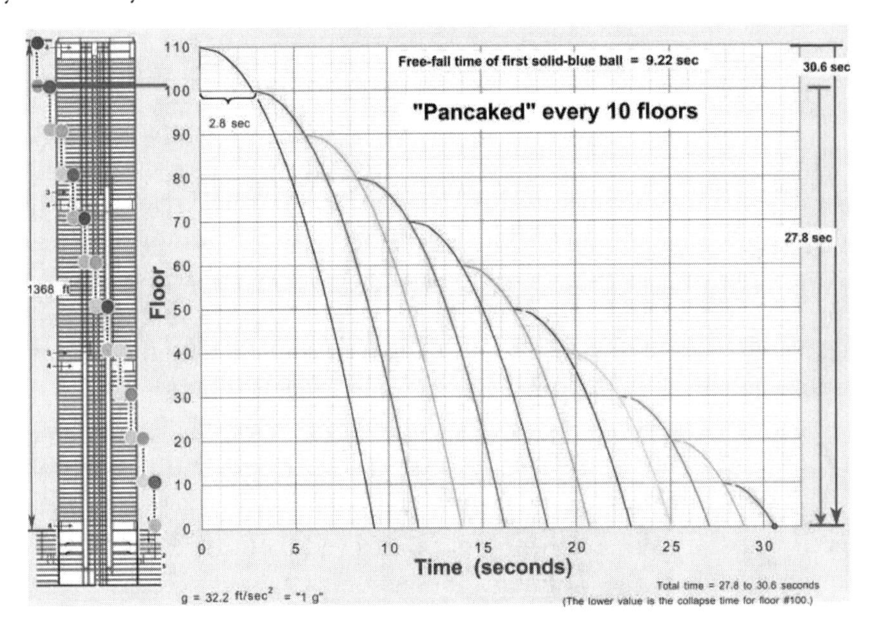

Figure 6. Minimum time for the collapse, if nine of every ten floors have been demolished prior to the "collapse."

Case 3: 'Progressive Collapse' in One-Floor Intervals

Similar to Case 2, above, let's consider a floor-by-floor progressive collapse. Refer to the figure below:

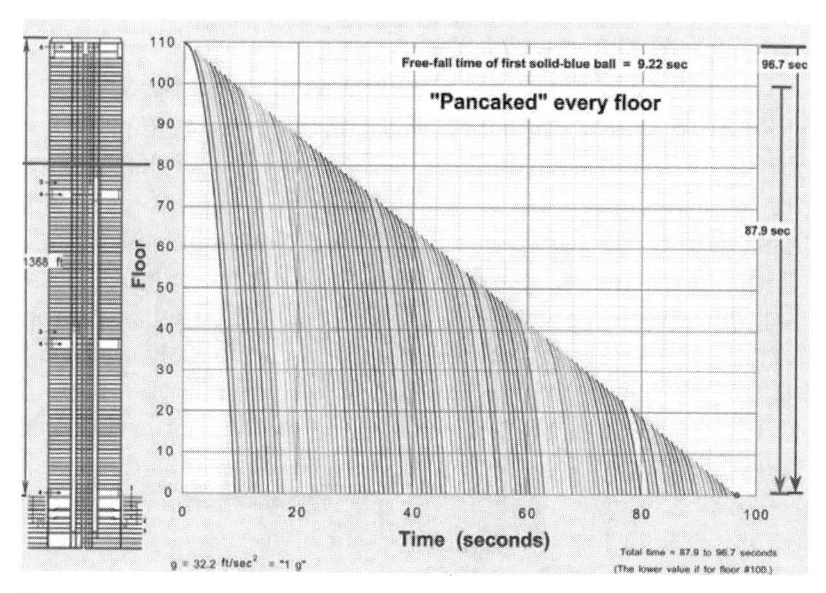

Figure 7. Minimum time for the collapse, if every floor collapsed like dominos.

Case 4: A 'Progressive Collapse' at <u>Near</u> Free-Fall Speed

Now, consider the chart below.

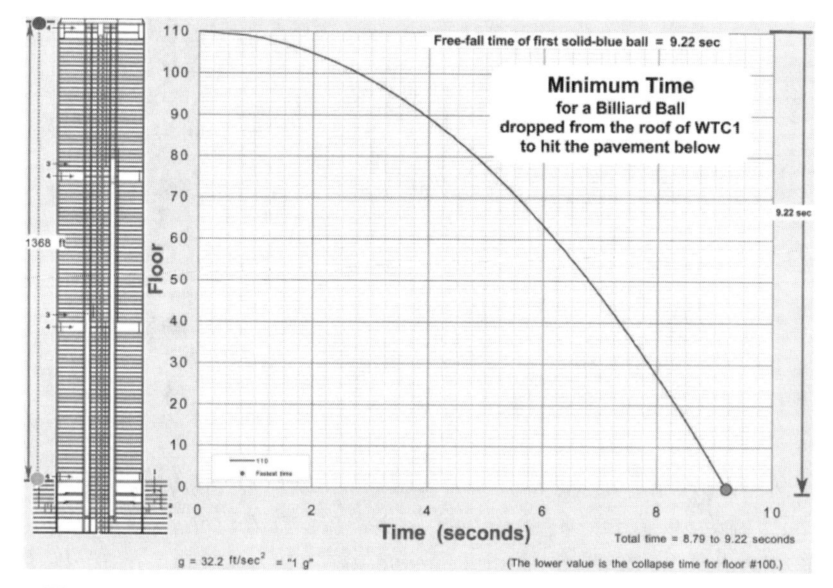

Figure 8. Minimum Time for a Billiard Ball dropped from the roof of WTC-1 to hit the pavement below, assuming no air resistance.

Let's say that we want to bring down the entire building in the time it takes for free-fall of the top floor of WTC-1. (Use 9.22 seconds as the time it would take the blue ball to drop from the roof to the street below, in a vacuum.) So, If the entire building is to be on the ground in 9.22 seconds, the floors below the "pancaking" must start moving before the "progressive collapse" reaches that floor, below. To illustrate this, use the concept of the billiard balls. If the red ball (dropped from the 100th floor) is to reach the ground at the same time as the blue ball (dropped from the 110th floor), the red ball must be dropped 0.429 seconds after the blue ball is dropped. But, the blue ball will take 2.8 seconds after it is dropped, just to reach the 100th floor in free fall. So, the red ball needs to begin moving 2.4 seconds before the blue ball arrives to "trigger" the red ball's motion. I.e., each of these floors will need a 2.4 second head start. But this creates yet another problem. How can the upper floor be destroyed by slamming into a lower floor if the lower floor has already moved out of the way?

Case 2, above, shows the red ball being dropped just as the blue ball passes that point. Remember, I'm assuming the building was turning to dust as the collapse progressed, which is essentially what happened. So, for the building to be collapsed in about 10 seconds, the lower floors would have to start moving before the upper floors could reach them by gravity alone.

Figure 9. Horizontal plumes below the "collapse wave" in the North Tower during top-down collapse. Realizing that, for example, the 40th floor needs to start moving before any of the upper floors have "free-fallen" to that point, why would it start moving? There was no fire there. And, if anything, there is less load on that floor as the upper floors turn to dust. In the picture (at right), notice that WTC-2 is less than half of its original height, yet has no debris that has fallen ahead of the demolition wave.

Did we see this? I believe it's pretty clear in some of the videos. The "wave" of collapse, progressing down the building, is moving faster than free-fall speed. This would require something like a detonation sequence.

Figure 10. WTC-2, demonstrating there is little to no free-fall debris ahead of the "collapse wave."

Why Does the Ground Rumble for only 8 Seconds While WTC-1 "Disappeared?"

Figure 11. Dust from "collapse." I don't think this part of the building made a thud when it hit the ground.

This part of the building surely took a lot longer to hit the ground as dust than it would have if it came down as larger pieces of material. We know that sheets of paper have a very high surface-area-to-mass ratio and will stay aloft for long periods of time, which is why paper is an excellent material for making toy airplanes. The alert observer will notice that much of the paper is covered with dust, indicating that this dust reached the ground after the paper did. In the above picture, there are a few tire tracks through the dust, but not many, so it was probably taken shortly after one (or both) of the towers were down.

Figure 12. Note, if some part must stop and then restart its descent every floor, the total collapse time must be more than 10 seconds.

Given that the building disintegrated from the top down, it is difficult to believe there could be much momentum to transfer, anyway. Also, consider the energy required to pulverize the floor between each "pancake." After being pulverized, the surface-area/mass is greatly increased and the air resistance becomes significant. I don't believe this pulverized material can contribute any momentum as it "hangs" in the air and floats down at a much-much slower rate than the "collapsing" floors.

The people in Figure 3(b) look like they've just come out of hiding, curious to see what just happened and to take pictures. If there had been a strong wind blowing the dust around, it would blow the paper away before it would have blown the dust onto the paper. So, the fact that much of the randomly-landed paper is covered with dust indicates the relative aerodynamic properties of this dust. Also, notice the dark sky as well as the haze in the distance. This was a clear day with no clouds in the sky... except for the dust clouds. This overcast appearance as well as the distant haze can only be explained by dust from the "collapse" that is still suspended in the air.

In a conventional controlled-demolition, a building's supports are knocked out and the building is broken up as it slams to the ground. In a conventional controlled-demolition, gravity is used to break up the building. Here, it seems that the only use of gravity was to get the dust out of the air.

Now, let's consider reality.

Questions:

1. How likely is it that all supporting structures on a given floor will fail at exactly the same time?
2. If all supporting structures on a given floor did not fail at the same time, would that portion of the building tip over or fall straight down into its own footprint?
3. What is the likelihood that supporting structures on every floor would fail at exactly the same time, and that these failures would progress through every floor with perfect symmetry?

Conclusion

So, if motion must be restarted at every floor, the total collapse time must be more than 10 seconds. Given that the building disintegrated from the top down, it is difficult to believe there could be much momentum to transfer, if any. Also, consider the energy required to pulverize the floor between each "pancake." After being pulverized, the surface-area/mass is greatly increased and the air resistance becomes significant. I don't believe this pulverized material can contribute any momentum as it "hangs" in the air and floats down at a much-much slower rate than the "collapsing" floors.

In conclusion, the explanations of the collapse that have been given by *The 9/11 Commission Report* and NIST are not physically possible. A new investigation is needed to determine the true cause of what happened to these buildings on September 11, 2001. The "collapse" of all three WTC buildings may be considered the greatest engineering disaster in the history of the world and deserve a thorough investigation.

Acknowledgments

I gratefully acknowledge comments and contributions by James Fetzer, Morgan Reynolds, Jeff Strahl, and especially Alex Dent, for providing the initial motivation and encouragement.

REFERENCES

1. 9/11 Commission Report http://www.9-11commission.gov/report/index.htm 2. Page 305, 9/11 Commission Report, Chapter 9., html, pdf http://www.9-11commission.gov/report/index.htm
   http://www.9-11commission.gov/report/911Report_Ch9.htm
   http://www.9-11commission.gov/report/911Report_Ch9.pdf
3. Fact Sheet (Answers to Frequently Asked Questions) by NIST http://wtc.nist.gov/pubs/factsheets/faqs_8_2006.htm
4. The height of the South Tower (WTC2) is 1362 feet, and the height of the North Tower (WTC1) is 1368 feet. http://www.infoplease.com/spot/wtc1.html
5. Seismology Group, Lamont-Doherty Earth Observatory, Columbia University http://www.ldeo.columbia.edu/LCSN/Eq/20010911_WTC/fact_sheet.htm
6. Other values http://911research.wtc7.net/essays/demolition/seismic.html
   http://911research.wtc7.net/wtc/analysis/collapses/freefall.html#timeline
7. The Collapse: An Engineer's Perspective http://www.pbs.org/wgbh/nova/wtc/collapse.html
8. Wayne Trumpman (September 2005) http://911research.wtc7.net/papers/trumpman/CoreAnalysisFinal.htm
9. Jim Hoffman http://911research.wtc7.net/papers/dustvolume/index.html
10. D.P. Grimmer, June 20, 2004 http://www.physics911.net/thermite.htm
11. WTC1 http://i18.photobucket.com/albums/b108/janedoe444/present/WTC1_redLines.gif (Video clip courtesy of 911review.org)
12. http://reddit.com/info/iq0i/comments/ciqdw
13. Rolling Stone, Issue 988, December 1, 2005 Page 80

APPENDIX A

Governing Equations:

$x_2 = x_1 + v_1 t + (1/2) at^2$ (1)

$t = SQRT(2H/a)$ (1a)

$v_2 = v_1 + at$ (2)

where, x1 is the initial position

x2 is the final position

v1 is the initial speed

v2 is the final speed

t is the time for this interval

a is the acceleration, the coefficient of gravity.

APPENDIX B

For those concerned about Conservation of Momentum and Conservation of Energy

Conservation of Momentum

The amount of momentum (p) that an object has depends on two physical quantities: the mass and the velocity of the moving object.

$\mathbf{p}_1 = m_1 * \mathbf{v}_1$

where p is the momentum, m is the mass, and v the velocity.

If momentum is conserved it can be used to calculate unknown velocities following a collision.

$(\mathbf{m}_1 * \mathbf{v}_1)i + (\mathbf{m}_2 * v2)i = (\mathbf{m}_1 * \mathbf{v}_1)f + (\mathbf{m}_2 * \mathbf{v}_2)_f$

where the subscript i signifies initial, before the collision, and f signifies final, after the collision.

If $(\mathbf{m}_1)_i = 0$, and $(\mathbf{v}_2)i = 0$, then $(\mathbf{v}_2)f$ must $=0$.

So, for conservation of momentum, there cannot be pulverization.

If we assume the second mass is initially at rest [(v2)i = 0], the equation reduces to

$(\mathbf{m}_1 * \mathbf{v}_1)_i = (\mathbf{m}_1 * \mathbf{v}_1)f + (\mathbf{m}_2 * \mathbf{v}_2)_f$

As you can see, if mass m1 = m2 and they "stick" together after impact, the equation reduces to ,

$(\mathbf{m}1 * \mathbf{v}_1)_i = (\mathbf{2m}_1 * \mathbf{v}_{new})_f$

or $v_{new} = (1/2) * v1$

If two identical masses colliding and sticking together, they will travel at half the speed as the original single mass.

Conservation of Energy

In elastic collisions, the sum of kinetic energy before a collision must equal the sum of kinetic energy after the collision. Conservation of kinetic energy is given by the following formula:

$(1/2)(m_1 * \mathbf{v}^2_1)i + (1/2)(m_2 * \mathbf{v}^2_2)_i = (1/2)(m_1 * \mathbf{v}^2_1)_f + (1/2)(m_2 * \mathbf{v}^2_2)_f +$ (**Pulverize**) + (**Fail Floor Supports**)

where (Pulverize) is the energy required to pulverize a floor and (Fail Floor Supports) is the energy required to fail the next floor.

If $(1/2)(m_1 * \mathbf{v}^2_1)_i + (1/2)(m_2 * \mathbf{v}^2_2)_i =$ (Pulverize) + (Fail Floor Supports), there well be no momentum transfer.

In reality, $(1/2)(\mathbf{m}1 * \mathbf{v}21)i + (1/2)(\mathbf{m}2 * \mathbf{v}22)i <$ (Pulverize) + (Fail Floor Supports),

So, for conservation of energy, we must assume there is some additional energy such that,

$(1/2)(\mathbf{m}_1 * \mathbf{v}^2_1)_i + (1/2)(\mathbf{m}_2 * \mathbf{v}^2_2)_i +$ (Additional Energy) = (Pulverize) + (Fail Floor Supports),

where (Additional Energy) is the additional amount of energy needed to have the outcome we observed on 9/11/01.

APPENDIX C:

Assuming elastic collisions:

Assume that the top floor stays intact as a solid block weight, Block-A. Start the collapse timer when the 109th floor fails. At that instant, assume floor 108 miraculously turns to dust and disappears. So, Block-A can drop at free-fall speed until it reaches the 108th floor. After Block-A travels one floor, it now has momentum. If all of the momentum is transferred from Block-A to Block-B, the next floor, Block-A will stop moving momentarily, even if there is no resistance for the next block to start moving.

$$(\mathbf{m}_1 * \mathbf{v}_1)_i = (\mathbf{m}_2 * \mathbf{v}_2)_f$$

If Block-A stops moving, after triggering the next sequence, the mass of Block-A will not arrive in time to transfer momentum to the next "pancaking" between Block-B and Block-C. In other words, the momentum will not be increased as the "collapse" progresses.

However, as we can observe, the building disintegrated from the top down and there was no block of material. Recall the physics demonstration shown below. (I believe everyone who has finished high school has seen one of these momentum demonstrations at some point in his/her life.)

a. conservation of momentum if ***no*** *pulverization,* ***no*** *structural resistanc*

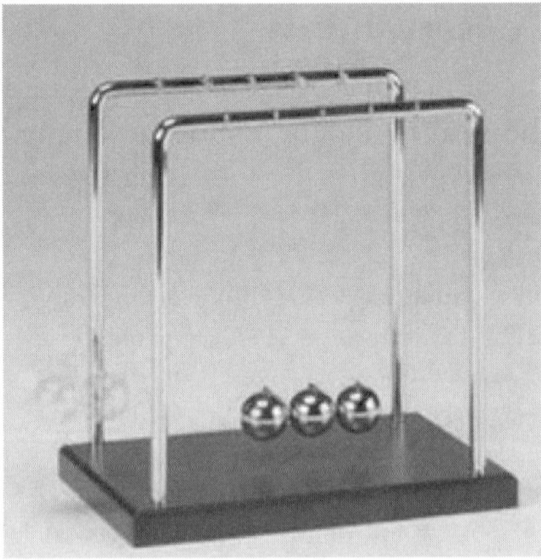

b. w/pulverization there's no mass left to impact, so there's no momentum to transfer

5

Intersecting Facts and Theories about 9/11

Joseph P. Firmage

The attacks of September 11th 2001 have resulted in significant changes both in the geopolitical order of nations and in the lives of billions of citizens across the planet. From two wars and growing instability across the Middle East, to the powers that states are exercising upon each other and their citizens, to your removal of tennis shoes at the airport security gate, the forces unleashed on that dark day are still reverberating throughout the world.

In the immediate weeks and months following 9/11, we felt a near-universal sense of horror and intense desire for effective response against the perpetrators of the attacks. We also felt a sense of urgency, as another wave of terror seemed possible at any time. The anthrax scare reinforced the imperative that all other restraining considerations should be swept aside in the interests of protecting lives, and regular terror alerts kept apprehension palpable among policy-makers and the public. The psychology of most citizens across the world's most powerful nation became focused: Islamic terrorism was the new evil, and it demanded an unprecedented response. Aggressive wars were launched, billions in new defense contracts signed, sweeping legislation empowering the executive approved, global and domestic surveillance operations unleashed, and a War President was born.

In this climate there was neither political space nor institutional leadership for a proper forensic examination of what actually happened on September 11th. It would take extended lobbying by increasingly exasperated family members of victims before any official investigation would be undertaken. Nonetheless, prior to, during, and after the tenure of the 9/11 Commission a growing network of researchers developed an increasingly comprehensive map of the situation preceding, during, and following 9/11.

While the researchers involved in this truly *independent* investigation are of varying discipline and credentials, the best of them have done a highly competent job of: (1) employing only credible sources to assemble as complete a picture of 9/11-related facts as is possible without access to classified material, and (2) conservatively synthesizing the implications of these facts in comparison to the conclusions of the 9/11 Commission investigation. The best of these researchers have reached a disturbing conclusion: the events of 9/11 were the result of either passive complicity among certain elements within the Bush administration and the terrorists, or, more likely, a self-inflicted wound on the nation orchestrated by such elements to create a new reality in geopolitical affairs.

One of the challenges in comprehending the circumstances of 9/11 is the sheer volume of material spanning two decades that must be studied for one to become comfortable reaching any conclusions. Intelligent people new to this controversy feel a sense of drowning when they begin to study what happened on 9/11. Having explored this subject deeply, I thought it might be useful to create a summary accessible to larger numbers of people. That is the purpose of what follows.

In the chart below, forty-two facts of significance are listed, intersecting three possible theories about the nature of 9/11. The three alternative theories considered are:

1. the official conspiracy theory in which nineteen Islamic radicals caught the US off guard;

2. the theory that elements within the Bush administration knew of the impending attacks and allowed them to happen; and

3. the theory that such officials architected the attacks and caused them to happen.

4. Based upon the details behind the facts, I have assigned each fact a degree of compatibility—**sensible**, **plausible**, or **suspicious**—to each theory. Below the table are summaries of the reasoning employed to assign compatibility, along with references for interested readers I conclude with responses to four objections that might be raised to this analysis.

	Sensible / Plausible / Suspicious	19 highjackers caught us off guard	Let it happen	Create new reality
1	Origin of Al-Qaeda from CIA-backed Mujahedeen			
2	Angry Islamists want to kill Americans			
3	Previous terror attacks attributed to al-Qaeda			
4	Historical relationship of Bush officials and clandestine operations			
5	Similarity between PNAC agenda and 9/11 aftermath			
6	Bill Clinton's failure to neutralize bin Laden			
7	George W. Bush's negligence in dealing with bin Laden			
8	Some alleged hijackers may have flight trained at U.S. military bases			
9	Lack of response to warnings from 11 countries about attacks			
10	Lack of response to warnings from U.S. agents about attacks			
11	Cheney's early 2001 assignment over counter-terrorism and war games			
12	Rumsfeld's mid 2001 assignment over NORAD response to hijackings			
13	WTC security anomalies			
14	Plan for invasion of Afghanistan in place on 9/10			
15	Allegedly devout Muslim hijackers out partying prior to 9/11			
16	Options trading in days preceding 9/11			
17	Jeb Bush's preparation for Florida State of Emergency			
18	Funder of Atta meeting with top U.S. officials during week of 9/11			
19	Wargames underway simulating hijacked airlines			
20	Slow Bush and Secret Service response to attacks			
21	Third large airplane in restricted airspace over Manhattan during attacks			
22	Lack of Pentagon response to incoming aerial threat			
23	Failure of air defense to intercept hijackings			
24	Demolition-like collapse of WTC 1, 2 and 7			
25	Anomalies surrounding Pentagon attack			
26	Molten metal at WTC site for weeks			
27	Immediate destruction of evidence at WTC sites			
28	Initiation of broad domestic surveillance programs			
29	Disappearance of Cheney for weeks			
30	Hijacker names missing from flight manifests			
31	Several alleged hijackers discovered alive and well			
32	Destruction of air traffic control tape from 9/11			
33	Sole confession of bin Laden in questionable video			
34	Shutdown of Congress by domestic military strain of anthrax			
35	Silencing of whistleblowers			
36	Resistance to 9/11 investigations			
37	Resistance to testimony under oath			
38	Promotion of key counterterrorism officials post 9/11			
39	Failure to catch bin Laden			
40	Promotion of threat psychology			
41	Lack of attention to Homeland Security hotspots			
42	Numerous obvious, key omissions from 9/11 Commission report			

Discussion of Facts and Theories

Let us briefly describe each of these facts—along a rough chronology—and the basis for assigning compatibility with the three theories proposed to explain them.

1. The Origin of al-Qaeda from the CIA-backed Mujahedeen

Working in tight collaboration with its Pakistani counterpart (ISI), the CIA launched during the 1980s a comprehensive program to cultivate thousands of radical Muslims throughout Afghanistan, as a means to draw the USSR into a quagmire and suffer a strategic Cold War defeat in this vital Central Asian territory. One of the key assets for the CIA in this campaign was Osama bin Laden. The program went so far as to involve the creation and teaching of a violence- and terror-infused curriculum to young children (who were taught to do math with graphs showing units in tanks or guns, for example). Millions of these textbooks were still in use throughout the 1990s. A large segment of the Mujahedeen eventually were reorganized by bin Laden into al-Qaeda, whose mission allegedly became the liberation of the Islamic world from Western domination.

These facts are compatible with the official conspiracy theory, though the long history between CIA, ISI, bin Laden and the Mujahedeen suggests that clandestine intelligence elements in the US—official or private—may have had closer and more enduring ties to al-Qaeda than generally believed.[1]

2. Angry Islamists Want to Kill Americans

Numerous professional texts have surveyed the long history of tension between Islamic populations and Western policies. There is more than ample evidence to support a radical Islamic motive to perpetrate 9/11-level—or greater—violence.

Yet since "false flag" operations work best when general public fear of whoever is to be falsely blamed pre-exists, the existence of real and serious threats from radical Islamic elements remains compatible with theories of US complicity or causation on 9/11.[2]

3. Previous Terror Attacks Attributed to al-Qaeda

Numerous terror attacks throughout the 1990s were attributed to al-Qaeda. The conservative assessment here is to take the official explanations at face value and agree that al-Qaeda demonstrated the intention and capability to attack US interests, though it is useful to review the history of these events with an open mind.[3]

4. Historical Relationship of Bush Officials and Clandestine Operations

A common refrain heard from the left—less often from the right—in response to suspicions about the official 9/11 story goes something like this: "The Bush administration has demonstrated such incompetence on so many fronts that it strains the imagination to think they could of have pulled off something so elaborate, and kept it a secret."

This argument ignores three key facts.

First, while George W. Bush may be intellectually challenged across the board, and while neoconservatives may have a gravely naive, overreaching geopolitical agenda, Bush officials in key national security positions have superlative experience in managing clandestine operations, and have repeatedly demonstrated ruthless, systematic, detail-oriented control over sensitive programs and information. The historical preoccupation of key officials across the Bush administration with clandestine operations—both legal and illegal—is well known to historians of the field.

Second, vastly larger programs have remained secret for decades. A few examples: the National Security Agency has a larger budget and more employees than the CIA. It was organized in 1949. This entire agency of the federal government remained completely hidden from the public until more than three decades later. One of the programs run by NSA, believed to have started in the 1940s, was Project Shamrock, through which all major transatlantic telegraph cables were tapped with the co-operation of AT&T and other communications carriers. This vast program—involving people building, installing and running equipment all over the world, and numerous others watching and translating conversations—was kept entirely secret until the 1990s. Most American citizens have never heard of this program to this day. Serious students of the US national security apparatus know how effective its systems can be in controlling information and people, and compartmentalizing information and tasks into a startlingly small number of hands.

Third, the official 9/11 story asks us to believe that only a couple of dozen poorly trained Islamic radicals deftly maneuvered through the world's most powerful intelligence gathering and military machine. How much easier might it have been for a similar number of people to do so, employing many unknowing others for secondary, compartmented tasks, if those handful with full knowledge of the plan also knew every aspect of the US intelligence and military machine, and were in key positions governing its activities and responses?

The historical association between Bush officials, government and private intelligence networks, and clandestine operations argues against the notion that incompetence allowed 9/11 to occur, and therefore this fact must raise suspicion.[4]

5. Similarity between the PNAC Agenda and the 9/11 Aftermath

The degree of forethought that may have gone into the events of 9/11 is suggested by the similarity of its aftermath to the geopolitical agenda set forth by the neoconservative think tank, Project for a New American Century, in its 2000 manifesto: "Rebuilding America's Defenses: Strategies, Forces and Resources for a New Century."

This document was written for George W. Bush's team before the 2000 Presidential election. It was commissioned by future Vice President Cheney, future Defense Secretary Rumsfeld, future Deputy Defense Secretary Paul Wolfowitz, Florida Governor Jeb Bush (Bush's brother), and future Vice President Cheney's Chief of Staff Lewis Libby.

The explicit statements concerning the utility of a "new Pearl Harbor" and the central roles played by Afghanistan and Iraq in configuring a new world order in which American supremacy is unchallengeable, are strikingly prescient of what was fortuitously made feasible by 9/11.

Few would argue that we would be in Afghanistan and Iraq today had the attacks of 9/11 never occurred. It is therefore reasonable to be suspicious of the spectacularly convenient conformance between the PNAC manifesto, the rise to power of those who wrote the document and 9/11's absolutely essential role in facilitating its implementation.[5]

6. Bill Clinton's Failure to Neutralize bin Laden

Some commentators have assigned much of the blame for 9/11 on the Clinton administration, for failing to deal with the bin Laden threat more effectively. It is empirically true that Clinton's team did not neutralize bin Laden. As references demonstrate, the reasons for that failure remain unclear, thus this failure can reasonably be assessed as compatible with any of the three theories proposed.[6]

7. George W. Bush's Negligence in Dealing with bin Laden

The performance of George W. Bush's administration in dealing with bin Laden is more troubling. The record clearly indicates that the administration took few concrete steps to strengthen counter-terrorism despite what CIA Director George Tenet called an intelligence community "with its hair on fire" from the frequency and credibility of warnings.

Several steps were taken that can be interpreted as obstructing pre-existing counter-terrorism plans and capabilities. For example, prior to 9/11, the Bush administration instructed intelligence officials to back off Saudi Arabia, discontinued plans made under Clinton for employing submarines and Predator drones to hunt for al-Qaeda leaders, suspended US co-operation in a pre-existing effort to track international terrorist financing networks, refused to seek a FISA warrant to hack into a suspect's computer, translated key communications late and mistranslated others, and ignored repeated, urgent warnings about impending attacks.

Indeed, the White House's Counterterrorism and Security Group chaired by Cheney, which met two or three times a week under Clinton, rarely convened under Bush prior to 9/11.[7]

8. Some Alleged Hijackers May Have Flight Trained at US Military Bases

According to *Newsweek* and *The Washington Post* in stories published days after 9/11, between three and five of the alleged hijackers may have received training at US military installations in the years leading up to 2001. In fact, three of the registrants with names matching alleged hijackers used the same address at the Pensacola Naval Air Station (known as the "cradle of US Naval aviation") eliminating the possibility of mere similarity of names as an explanation for this troubling coincidence.

Other alleged terrorists trained at a Florida flight school that many in the region believe had been utilized by the CIA. It has been alleged that Jeb Bush ordered records removed from its offices within twenty-four hours of the attacks . . . a rather speedy police action since the government allegedly had not connected the dots prior to 9/11. It has also been alleged that the owner of the flight school—Rudi Dekkers, constantly in trouble with the law—was deported by the INS prior to his possible testimony to the 9/11 Commission.[8]

9. Lack of Response to Warnings from Eleven Countries about Attacks

Among the most damning of pre-9/11 evidence raising suspicion of the official theory is the multitude of high-level, at times urgent, warnings supplied to the US by the intelligence services of other nations. These warnings often included specific targets or methods of attack, and in one case included names of four of the alleged hijackers. Among the countries communicating relevant threat intelligence to the U.S prior to 9/11: Great Britain, Russia, Germany, Afghanistan, Egypt, Jordan and Israel. For example, astonishingly, Russian President Vladimir Putin publicly stated on Fox News in 2002 that he ordered his intelligence agencies to alert the US in the summer of 2001 that suicide pilots were training for attacks on US targets. It is interesting that two countries in the best position to know about the impending attacks—Pakistan and Saudi Arabia—apparently forwarded no warnings at all.

In any case, the repeated claims by Bush administration officials to the effect that "no one ever imagined this kind of thing could happen" are entirely incompatible with the seniority, volume, and specificity of international warnings received in months prior to 9/11.[9]

10. Lack of Response to Warnings from US Agents about Attacks

The record of domestic warnings from field agents of the FBI and CIA (and other civilians) is lengthy and troubling, particularly when juxtaposed with contemporaneous intelligence received from abroad. As but two examples, an agent at the Phoenix office of the FBI wrote an extensive memo outlining the "inordinate" number of suspicious individuals taking flight training courses in Arizona, who he suspected were linked to al-Qaeda. Agents in the Minneapolis office of the FBI were so frustrated that they became suspicious of a mole at headquarters because of the obstacles put in their path. They were attempting—unsuccessfully—to gain approval from higher ups to obtain a FISA search warrant for Moussaoui's computer.

Other agents have tried in recent years to go public as whistleblowers—describing strangely negligent behavior of certain officials prior to 9/11—and have been gagged by court order under the State Secrets privilege.[10]

11. Cheney's Early 2001 Assignment over Counter-terrorism and War Games

On May 8th 2001, President Bush appointed Dick Cheney to head the new Office of National Preparedness, with responsibility to co-ordinate all federal programs to respond to an attack on the homeland. Cheney was given power over "all federal programs dealing with weapons of mass destruction consequence management within the Departments of Defense, Health and Human Services, Justice, and Energy, the Environmental Protection Agency, and other federal agencies . . ." This covered "training and planning" which had to be "seamlessly integrated, harmonious and comprehensive" in order to "maximize effectiveness." This position would afford Cheney the total legal authority to manage a 9/11-type situation as it unfolded. As it turned out, he would need such power and appeared very comfortable exercising it. As former terrorism czar Richard Clarke wrote in *Against All Enemies*, "I was amazed at the speed of the decisions coming from Cheney and, through him, from Bush." According to most reports, this Office was just beginning to hire staff members a few days prior to 9/11.

Again, in the context of the warnings from home and abroad, the long alleged history of a bin Laden threat and the longer history of key Bush officials' preoccupation with global threat management, the administration's pre-9/11 behavior suggests neglect and obstruction of obvious, urgent, loudly-called-for defensive measures and yet refined, thorough advance calculation and planning for offensive measures in the war on terrorism to come.[11]

12. Rumsfeld's Mid-2001 Assignment over NORAD Response to Hijackings

Less than one month later, another link of the chain of command was set in place relevant to later events on 9/11. Except for "immediate responses" that do not require "potentially lethal support" all requests for military assistance during hijackings were to be approved only by the Secretary of Defense, a change to a protocol which for years had allowed lower-level military commanders the authority to respond to requests from FAA for military assistance. Effectively, the entire chain of command under Rumsfeld was stripped of the ability to approval potentially lethal assistance in the specific event of a hijacking or derelict airborne object.

On its own this alteration of protocol would not justify suspicion. In the context of the rest of the pattern of behavior among key officials before and after 9/11, this fact must be deemed troubling.[12]

13. WTC Security Anomalies

A number of strange facts fall under the heading of WTC security anomalies. Among them:

- George W. Bush's brother was a Director and his cousin was the CEO of the security firm responsible for the design of the electronic security network of the World Trade Center prior to and during 9/11;
- Numerous phone threats of bombs placed WTC on high alert in weeks prior to 9/11;
- Employees of WTC reported rare "power-down" alerts in days leading up to 9/11 in which power was shut down to various floors for maintenance work, rendering security controls and video cameras inoperative; many workers were seen entering and leaving the buildings;
- At least one security guard at WTC reported the abrupt removal of explosive-sniffing dogs five days prior to 9/11;
- John O'Neill quit his job as FBI counterterrorism expert in part because of obstruction of his investigations of al-Qaeda and became head of WTC security, starting in late August 2001; he was killed three weeks later in the attacks.[13]

14. Plan for Invasion of Afghanistan in Place on 9/10

A plan for the invasion of Afghanistan had been in preparation for months and reached the White House for President Bush's signature during the week before 9/11. This conforms to the activities of US officials in the region, who in meetings during the summer of 2001 made it known to the Taliban government that it must choose whether to receive a "carpet of bombs" or a "carpet of gold" during negotiations over the construction of a pipeline through the country. Former Pakistani Foreign Secretary Niaz Naik later said he was told by American officials—again, prior to 9/11—that military action to overthrow the Taliban was planned to "take place before the snows started falling in Afghanistan, by the middle of October at the latest."

That pre-9/11 prediction was exactly correct.[14]

15. Allegedly Devout Muslim Hijackers out Partying Prior to 9/11

Ringleader Mohamed Atta and other alleged hijackers were frequently seen in the US and the Philippines partying—drinking heavily, using drugs, cavorting with women and spending considerable money. This portrait is incompatible with the official narrative in which the hijackers are portrayed as devout Muslims preparing to meet their maker, but is compatible with the notion that some or all of the alleged hijackers were not devout Muslims but were directly or indirectly serving as assets or patsies for elements within the Bush administration.[15]

16. Options Trading in Days Preceding 9/11

During the first ten days of September and beginning possibly earlier, unusually high levels of "put options" were placed on the stocks of American and United airlines and corporate tenants of the World Trade Center. The 9/11 Commission later concludes "The SEC and the FBI, aided by other agencies and the securities industry, devoted enormous resources to investigating this issue, including securing the co-operation of many foreign governments. These investigators have found that the apparently suspicious trading consistently proved innocuous." Though known to government investigators, the identities of the parties placing these put options have never been revealed. There should be no reason why such identities must remain concealed if the official story is true.

According to Dylan Ratigan of *Bloomberg Business News*, "This would be one of the most extraordinary coincidences in the history of mankind if it was a coincidence."[16]

17. Jeb Bush's Preparation for Florida State of Emergency

On September 7th 2001, George W. Bush's brother and Florida Governor Jeb Bush signed Florida Executive Order No. 01-261 which states, in part:

I hereby delegate to The Adjutant General of the State of Florida all necessary authority, within approved budgetary appropriations or grants, to order members of the Florida National Guard into active service . . . for the purpose of training to support law-enforcement personnel and emergency-management personnel in the event of civil disturbances . . .

This order effectively placed the Florida National Guard, a unit of the federal US Army, in service of Florida law enforcement and the Florida Emergency Management department four days prior to 9/11.

On the morning of September 11th, Jeb Bush signed Florida Executive Order No. 01-262 immediately after the second WTC tower fell, making Florida the first state in the US to declare a "State of Emergency"—even before New York and Washington D.C.:

> I hereby declare that a state of emergency exists in the State of Florida . . . The authority to suspend the effect of any statute or rule governing the conduct of state business, and the further authority to suspend the effect of any order or rule of any governmental entity . . . The authority to seize and utilize any and all real or personal property as needed to meet this emergency . . . The authority to order the evacuation of any or all persons from any location in the State of Florida, and the authority to regulate the movement of any or all persons to or from any location in the State; The authority to regulate the return of the evacuees to their home communities . . . I hereby order the Adjutant General to activate the Florida National Guard for the duration of this emergency.

This latter move may be plausible given the presence of the President of the United States in the state during surprise attacks by terrorists. In the context of complicity theories, however, it is quite sensible that these two orders—*numerically back-to-back, four days apart, one before and one on 9/11*—were put in place in case the plan went awry and it became necessary to take extraordinary measures to protect one or both Bushes from their own government or citizenry.

Under complicity theories, the additional sightings of suspicious Middle Eastern men stalking President Bush in Sarasota Florida earlier that morning—driving a large van and requesting entrance to the resort where he was staying—might have provided later evidence for and a means to trigger a state of emergency, if it became necessary.[17]

18. Funder of Atta Meeting with Top US Officials during Week of 9/11

At the moment of the attacks, Pakistan's ISI Director Lt. Gen. Mahmoud Ahmad was at a breakfast meeting at the Capitol with the chairmen of the House and Senate Intelligence Committees, Senator Bob Graham (D) and Representative Porter Goss (R) (Goss is a ten-year veteran of the CIA's clandestine operations wing). The meeting is said to have lasted at least until the second plane hit the WTC. Graham and Goss later co-head the joint House-Senate investigation into the 9/11 attacks, which made headlines for saying there was no "smoking gun" of Bush's knowledge before 9/11. Senator Graham should have been aware of a report made to his staff the previous month that one of Mahmoud's subordinates had told a US undercover agent that the WTC would be destroyed. Evidence suggests that attendee Mahmoud had previously ordered that $100,000 be sent to hijacker Mohamed Atta. Also present at the meeting were Senator Jon Kyl (R) and the Pakistani ambassador to the US, Maleeha Lodhi. All or most of the people in this meeting had previously met in Pakistan just a few weeks earlier. Senator Graham said of the meeting: "We were talking about terrorism, specifically terrorism generated from Afghanistan." The *New York Times* reported that bin Laden was specifically discussed.

In an interview with ABC News the FBI confirmed that the alleged 9/11 ringleader, Mohammed Atta, had been financed from unnamed sources in Pakistan:

> As to September 11th, federal authorities have told ABC News they have now tracked more than $100,000 from banks in Pakistan, to two banks in Florida, to accounts held by suspected hijack ring leader, Mohammed Atta. As well . . . *Time Magazine* is reporting that some of that money came in the days just before the attack and can be traced directly to people connected to Osama bin Laden. It's all part of what has been a successful FBI effort so far to close in on the hijackers' high commander, the money men, the planners, and the mastermind.

Less than two weeks later, *Agence France Presse* and *The Times of India*, quoting an official Indian intelligence report, confirmed the money used to finance the 9/11 attacks had been "wired to WTC hijacker Mohammed Atta from Pakistan, by Ahmad Umar Sheikh, at the instance of [ISI Chief] General Mahmoud [Ahmad]." Officials in Pakistan and the US later claimed that the Indian intelligence report was propaganda intended to create tension between the US and Pakistan. But according to the AFP (quoting the Indian intelligence source): "The evidence we have supplied to the US is of a much wider range and depth than just one piece of paper linking a rogue general to some misplaced act of terrorism."

The ISI chief who was meeting with top US intelligence figures in the days leading to and on the morning of 9/11, who is alleged to have previously ordered the transfer of $100,000 to Mohamed Atta, was fired less than thirty days later.[18]

19. Wargames Conducted on 9/11 Simulating Hijackings

In the days leading up to and including 9/11, the US military was conducting between four and six war game exercises and operations involving aircraft from or in the northeastern US. At least one of those exercises involved the simulation of hijacked aircraft, and others sent northeast fighters to Canada for scenarios involving invasion by Russian aircraft. In some such exercises, fake aircraft signals were "inserted" into the air traffic control systems of NORAD and the FAA in order to test the response protocols of the air traffic and air defense network.

In other such exercises, real aircraft were piloted by war gamers as if they were hijacked and flown to test all aspects of the civil-military response process, including scrambled jets.

Some researchers have suggested that Cheney was the lead authority involved in these exercises on 9/11. That's an important question, but is less relevant a factor than the degree to which such exercises degraded the response capacity of FAA and NORAD on 9/11. Numerous officials across the FAA and military are recorded on transcripts from 9/11 asking if "this is real world or exercise." One key figure in the air defense command involved in the exercise is quoted on NORAD tapes as saying "the hijack's not supposed to be for another hour." Another stated: "I've never seen so much real-world stuff happen during an exercise."

In the context of this analysis, these are shocking revelations. It appears certain that fake or real hijacking signals were injected into the air defense network on 9/11, and thus the failure to get fighters off the ground and to the right places in time to make a difference becomes sensible.

On their own, such exercises would not raise suspicion. Juxtaposed with the other facts, they do.[19]

20. Slow Bush and Secret Service Response to Attacks

As the US military was conducting operations and exercises involving aircraft from or in the northeast, and while real planes were striking the World Trade Center, President Bush was reading a story about a pet goat to schoolchildren in Florida. He was informed of the second plane strike at 9:07 a.m. The Commander in Chief of the US armed forces then proceeded to do nothing for seven minutes.

It is interesting to actually sit oneself down and wait out seven minutes with the notion in mind that you have just been informed that the country you are responsible to protect has just been attacked. Bush was informed of the first strike before even entering the classroom; he later stated or misstated that he watched the first strike on television outside the classroom—something that would have been impossible unless secret cameras were rolling, since the first public video of the first plane strike did not emerge until September 12th. Either way, we must keep in mind that, under the official theory, there was no advance knowledge of the scale of the day's events; there may have been scores of hijacked airlines, biological or nuclear weapons, or any other number of possible immediate threats facing the nation.

As unusual as it seems for the Commander in Chief to have waited at least seven minutes before even getting up, the behavior of the Secret Service around him is at least as unfathomable. The man they were sworn to protect with their lives was in a pre-announced public place on television during an attack in which airplanes were being used to strike symbols of US power. For all anyone allegedly knew, the President himself was a target. They did not yank him out of the chair and pull him into the limousine and rush him to Air Force One.

This strange lack of response is more sensible under the complicity theories in which at least Bush and possibly some others in his entourage were aware of what was going to happen that day, knew that the classroom was in no danger from the attacks and that Vice President Cheney had things under control back in the White House.[20]

21. Third Large Airplane in Restricted Airspace over Manhattan During Attacks

Commercial jets are prohibited from flying at low altitudes around the borough of Manhattan. Of course, two planes violated that rule on 9/11 to tragic effect. However video, photographic and eyewitness testimony has clearly placed a third commercial-size jet aircraft circling at low altitude while the first tower is burning and continuing as the second tower is struck. No such plane is mentioned in the 9/11 Commission report or in any official investigation. If it was a commercial jet, it was flying illegally, its pilot was taking risks flying close to billowing clouds of smoke and was presenting an obvious target for the fighters that would arrive too late. It is not plausible that this third plane was a commercial passenger flight.

The complicity theories resolve the mystery of the third aircraft: it was most likely involved in the operation, perhaps providing observational data or offering a flying platform nearby to manage part of the attack—a platform that could get in and get out quickly and relatively discretely. It would also explain Bush's statement that he saw the first plane strike the WTC before the rest of the world could have.

Note that the author of the article revealing the third plane claims that he has received threats against himself and his family for having written the article (referenced below). The author reported that the source of these threats suggested that he drop out of the 9/11 research project and that his article should "go away."[21]

22. Failure of Air Defense to Intercept Hijackers

An excellent summary of the failure of the US air defense network is available at the reference cited below, excerpted here:

> It is standard operating procedure to scramble jet fighters whenever a jetliner goes off course or radio contact with it is lost. Between September 2000 and June 2001, interceptors were scrambled 67 times. In the year 2000 jets were scrambled 129 times.
>
> There are several elements involved in domestic air defense. FAA's air traffic control system continuously monitors air traffic and notifies NORAD of deviations of any aircraft from their flight-paths or loss of radio contact. NORAD monitors air and space traffic continuously and is prepared to react immediately to threats and emergencies. It has the authority to order units from the Air National Guard, the Air Force, or other armed services to scramble fighters in pursuit of jetliners in trouble.
>
> The air defense network had, on September 11th, predictable and effective procedures for dealing with just such an attack. Yet it failed to respond in a timely manner until after the attack was over, more than an hour and a half after it had started. The official timeline describes a series of events and mode of response in which the delays are spread out into a number of areas. There are failures upon failures, in what might be described as a strategy of layered failures, or failure in depth. The failures can be divided into four types.
>
> **Failures to report**: Based on the official timeline, the FAA response times for reporting the deviating aircraft were many times longer than the prescribed times. [The "official" timeline has shifted several times, thus shifting blame back and forth between FAA and NORAD; the overall lack of response is what's relevant]

> **Failures to scramble**: NORAD, once notified of the off-course aircraft, failed to scramble jets from the nearest bases.
>
> **Failures to intercept**: Once airborne, interceptors failed to reach their targets because they flew at small fractions of their top speeds.
>
> **Failures to redeploy**: Fighters that were airborne and within interception range of the deviating aircraft were not redeployed to pursue them.
>
> Had there not been multiple failures of each type, one or more parts of the attack could have been thwarted. NORAD had time to protect the World Trade Center even given the unbelievably late time, 8:40, when it claims to have first been notified. It had time to protect the South Tower and Washington even given its bizarre choice of bases to scramble. And it still had ample opportunity to protect both New York City and Washington even if it insisted that all interceptors fly subsonic, simply by redeploying airborne fighters.

The details behind each of these failures—including the precise timelines, actions, and locations of air defense network activity—are a matter of public record and can be explored at the referenced source. Particularly suspicious is the fact that the first four fighters scrambled on 9/11 were initially sent and held over the Atlantic before being told where to fly. They were given shoot-down orders only after all four planes had crashed.

The co-chairmen of the 9/11 Commission have recently released a new book, *Without Precedent*, which states in this regard: "Fog of war could explain why some people were confused on the day of 9/11, but it could not explain why all of the after-action reports, accident investigations and public testimony by FAA and NORAD officials advanced an account of 9/11 that was untrue."[22]

23. Lack of Pentagon Response to Incoming Aerial Threat

After two planes had struck the World Trade Center, one would think that there would be near-instant response to a third threat. The Pentagon became aware that Flight 77 had been hijacked no later than when it learned that its transponder was turned off at 8:56 a.m. According to the official narrative, it crashed into the Pentagon at 9:37 a.m., leaving it approaching the nation's nerve center for forty minutes with no fighter response able to intervene. The Pentagon was well prepared for aerial attacks, with batteries of anti-aircraft guns surrounding the headquarters of the world's most powerful military. They did not fire a shot that day.

Norman Mineta, Secretary of Transportation at the time, revealed the extent of knowledge of the threat to the Pentagon, and in so doing may have revealed Cheney's role in the events of that day, during testimony to the 9/11 Commission regarding events in the White House Situation Room that morning:

> During the time that the airplane was coming [towards] the Pentagon, there was a young man who would come in and say to the Vice President . . . the plane is 50 miles out . . . the plane is 30 miles out. . . . and when it got down to the plane is 10 miles out, the young man also said to the Vice President, "Do the orders still stand?" And the Vice President turned and whipped his neck around and said "Of course the orders still stand, have you heard anything to the contrary!??"

Regardless of what those orders were (to shoot it down? to leave it alone?) this statement is startling because it reveals the degree of situational awareness in the Situation Room. Given the state of affairs at that time on 9/11, it is extremely difficult for the official story to account for the fact that the Pentagon was struck by anything, and that no fighter or anti-aircraft device could intercept a hijacked airliner forty minutes after it became a known threat, almost an hour after the first plane struck the World Trade Center.[23]

24. Demolition-like Collapse of WTC 1, 2, and 7

Of all the facts discussed in this survey, the nature of the collapse of three World Trade Center buildings ranks among the most significant. There are several mysteries about these collapses:

- Never in the history of modern civilization has a steel-framed skyscraper collapsed due to fire;
- The fires in the buildings were much shorted-lived than other fires that have damaged skyscrapers in the past;
- The World Trade Center buildings were built to very high standards; they were highly redundant structures intentionally designed to withstand the direct impact of a commercial jetliner and much larger fires;

- Scores of firefighters, police, workers, outside witnesses and journalists reported hearing explosive detonations throughout the buildings just before and during their collapse;
- There is clear visible evidence of 'squibs' (demolition explosions) on the sides of the towers during their collapse;
- Towers 1 and 2 fell to the ground within one and three seconds of free-fall velocity, something that is physically impossible if the floors of the buildings are meeting—let alone overcoming—the resistance of intact steel and concrete structure throughout their fall;
- The concrete of the towers is pulverized to a fine dust, something that would not occur if the floors of the towers simply "pancaked" upon each other;
- The towers fell almost perfectly into their own footprints;
- The buildings had been transferred from public to private ownership only a few weeks earlier, and their new owner took out insurance that specifically included acts of terrorism.

The case of World Trade Center 7 is most revealing:

- It was never struck by an airplane;
- The fires inside (allegedly due to falling debris from the collapse of the other towers) were relatively small;
- It fell at exactly free-fall velocity; without controlled demolition this is impossible according to the laws of physics;
- It fell symmetrically into its footprint;
- Its owner is on videotape saying he suggested to fire officials that the building be "pulled"—jargon for controlled demolition; shortly after that suggestion, it collapsed in precisely the manner of a controlled demolition;
- It housed offices of the CIA and New York's emergency management center, among others;
- Evidence of explosive compounds has been found in at least one of the few remaining pieces of once-molten iron that were not illegally destroyed;

- The collapse of WTC 7 was never addressed by the 9/11 Commission.

These facts all bluntly conflict with the official theory of 9/11. These facts are completely consistent with controlled demolition of WTC 1, 2 and 7.[24]

25. Anomalies Surrounding Pentagon Attack

Researchers have accumulated a number of unanswered questions concerning the attack on the Pentagon, suggesting that an airplane may not have struck, or may not have been the only thing to strike, the headquarters of the US military:

- There are conflicting eyewitness reports about what was seen striking the building; some calling it a large jet aircraft, others describing a smaller plane-like vehicle (a description that fits certain types of missiles used by the US military);
- The debris on the ground did not include identifiable large pieces of a commercial jet that would be expected in the debris, such as two giant engines; the official story suggests they were vaporized, which is physically impossible at impact temperatures;
- The pattern of damage on the outside of the building does not match the shape and size of a 757;
- The damage into the core of the Pentagon reaches too far, in the form it takes, to be explained by the relatively lightweight, hollow body of a 757; the damage pattern to the reinforced concrete wall of the inner "C-Ring" is a perfectly round, small hole that is consistent with the kinds of shaped charges used in missiles;
- Several surveillance videos recording the impact area of the Pentagon were confiscated by the FBI immediately after the event and have never been released;
- The piloting of Flight 77 during its descent to the Pentagon has been universally described by trained pilots as "extremely challenging for an expert" and seemingly outside the capabilities of a hijacker described by his flight trainer as unfit to fly a Cessna;
- The flight plan appears designed to limit damage to the Pentagon, rather than maximize it: the angle of the attack is low, the side of

the building hit was recently rebuilt, hardened, partially occupied and 180° from Donald Rumsfeld's office;

- A military cargo plane was seen following Flight 77; the same plane wound up seventeen miles from the crash site of Flight 93.

Some researchers place great weight on these anomalies, suggesting that the physical evidence—or lack thereof—at the Pentagon site is the "smoking gun" of 9/11. I do not share that opinion, as other evidence addressed in this study is far less ambiguous. Cumulatively, however, these observations raise suspicion of the official account, particularly in light of surrounding facts.[25]

26. Molten Metal at WTC Site for Weeks

From a scientific point of view, one of the most troubling mysteries about the destruction of the World Trade Center towers was the molten metal seen throughout the wreckage not only immediately after their collapse, but for weeks and weeks afterward. Collapsing concrete and steel does not create circumstances—even with fires burning—in which molten iron drips through the wreckage at many levels forming pools below, as the photographic, video and witness testimony clearly confirms existed. On the other hand, controlled demolition involves cutting hundreds of steel beams with specially designed high-temperature explosives, creating pools of molten iron that can persist and even spread (if sheltered in an "oven" of debris) for weeks.[26]

27. Immediate Destruction of Evidence at WTC Sites

Conveniently, a bio-terror exercise had been scheduled for 9/12 in lower Manhattan, which meant that officials from various agencies had arrived earlier. They were then put to work at WTC on 9/11. As Mayor Rudolph Giuliani later testifies, "hundreds of people . . . from FEMA, from the federal government, from the state, from the State Emergency Management Office" had come to New York to take part in the exercise. Giuliani stated that the equipment for the exercise was in place on 9/11, so when his emergency operations center (in WTC-7) collapsed, he moved his emergency operations center to the site of the planned bio-terror exercise.

Immediately after the collapse of the towers, federal agents and police secured the WTC area. Contrary to federal and state laws concerning crime scenes, the debris from WTC was never subjected to a forensic investigation. Over subsequent weeks and months, thousands of tons of steel beams were evacuated from the site to the port in secured conveys—with GPS devices tracking every vehicle—and then shipped to Asia to be melted and reused for other construction. Thus, the most crucial physical evidence to reveal the causes of the collapse of the towers was intentionally and illegally destroyed without public examination. At least one of the few pieces of once-molten metal that somehow got around this process has been examined. Residue was discovered consistent with the use of the kind of explosive used in controlled demolition.

The journal *Fire Engineering* boldly editorialized:

> Respected members of the fire protection engineering community are beginning to raise red flags, and a resonating theory has emerged: The structural damage from the planes and the explosive ignition of jet fuel in themselves were not enough to bring down the towers. . . .
>
> *Fire Engineering* has good reason to believe that the "official investigation" blessed by FEMA and run by the American Society of Civil Engineers is a half-baked farce that may already have been commandeered by political forces whose primary interests, to put it mildly, lie far afield of full disclosure. Except for the marginal benefit obtained from a three-day, visual walk-through of evidence sites conducted by ASCE investigation committee members—described by one close source as a "tourist trip'—no one's checking the evidence for anything.
>
> Some citizens are taking to the streets to protest the investigation sellout. Sally Regenhard, for one, wants to know why and how the building fell as it did upon her unfortunate son Christian, an FDNY probationary firefighter. And so do we.
>
> Clearly, there are burning questions that need answers. Based on the incident's magnitude alone, a full-throttle, fully resourced, forensic investigation is imperative. More important, from a moral standpoint, [are considerations] for the safety of present and future generations.

That's a strong statement from real experts that has been ignored by the 9/11 Commission, the Bush administration and the mainstream media.[27]

28. Initiation of Broad Domestic Surveillance Programs

As we all now know, several secret domestic surveillance programs were initiated shortly after 9/11. It is quite sensible that such programs would be initiated under any of the three theories. If the official narrative is true, then it is not unreasonable for the executive branch to desire the ability to map networks of potential terrorists inside the US, including suspect US citizens, and listen in on their communications.

However, it is not sensible that such programs would be vigorously concealed from legally-mandated, secret judicial and congressional oversight. The totality and vigor of their concealment become more sensible under the complicity theories, whereby an ultra-secret program must exist to spy not only on terrorists, but on those involved in or on course to reveal official complicity in 9/11. Serious students of national security are very well aware that those involved in highly sensitive operations routinely "sign away" their right to privacy and expect all of their communications to be tapped. Others who might represent a threat of disclosure of officials involved in 9/11—like journalists and investigators—have not signed away such rights, though most of us would not be surprised to find our names on the watch list of one or more of these surveillance programs.

Further recent developments reinforce suspicion on this point. Recently-drafted "compromise" legislation would permit the FISA court to review the *constitutionality* of these surveillance programs, rather than requiring review of *each individual target* as is the case today. If that legislation passes, it will permit the administration to *avoid any external oversight of the identities of individuals targeted for invasive spying.* That is exactly what would be required by a program designed to "protect the national security" of a criminal administration.[28]

29. Disappearance of Cheney for Weeks

After the 9/11 attacks and continuing for several weeks, Vice President Cheney was rarely seen and was reported to be shifting among undisclosed locations as a contingency in case further attacks took out President Bush or otherwise demanded initiation of "continuity of government" plans for an alternate chain of command.

This is plausible under all three theories, but becomes imperative under complicity theories. In an operation as illegal as the one contemplated under those theories, the risk of exposure or even coup from within the government would be high and palpable.

If we accept, solely for the sake of discussion, that one of the complicity theories is true, then Cheney was almost certainly the key leader of the operation. It would be several weeks before he would have felt sufficiently informed of the aftershocks and information tributaries from 9/11 to come back into administrative routine.

30. Hijacker Names Missing from Flight Manifests

The official passenger manifests from American and United airlines for the four 9/11 flights contained no names identified as hijackers. This fact has never been explained.[29]

31. Several Alleged Hijackers Discovered Alive and Well

Several alleged hijackers were found to be alive overseas. They and their families saw their pictures on television and in newspapers in days following the attacks, and began talking to the press, which extensively covered this anomaly. Several reported that their passports were stolen. On September 20th, the London *Times* reported, "Five of the hijackers were using stolen identities, and investigators are studying the possibility that the entire suicide squad consisted of impostors."

After all of this, on September 27th, FBI Director Mueller stated merely, "We are fairly certain of a number of them," according to the next day's *South Florida Sun-Sentinel.*

This matter becomes suspicious because of the combination of two factors: the absence of hijacker names on flight manifests, and the failure of the FBI to supply any alternative names to those provided just after 9/11. If not them, who? Surely, if the official story is true, a forensic examination of the history of how the intelligence community acquired the names in the first place would lead to one or more new, real identities.[30]

32. Destruction of Air Traffic Control Tape from 9/11

Shortly before noon on 9/11, about sixteen people at the New York Air Route Traffic Control Center recorded their version of the response to the 9/11 attack. At least six were air traffic controllers who dealt with two of the hijacked airliners. But officials at the center never told higher-ups about the tape. Around this time, a quality-assurance manager, whose name has not been released, crushes the cassette recording in his hand, shreds the tape, and drops the pieces into different trashcans. This manager later asserted that keeping the tape would have been a violation of union rules and accident procedures. When he destroyed the tape, he had already received an email from the FAA instructing officials to safeguard all records that specifically stated, "If a question arises whether or not you should retain data, **Retain It**." Most, but not all, of the air traffic controllers involved made written statements about three weeks after 9/11, but it isn't clear how these might differ from what was on the tape. The unidentified manager wass later said to have been disciplined for this incident, though it isn't clear how.

Let us give the official theory the benefit of the doubt and characterize this event as plausible. It is certainly sensible with the two alternative theories.[31]

33. Shutdown of Congress by Domestic Military Strain of Anthrax

In early October 2001 four letters containing anthrax were mailed to NBC, the *New York Post*, and Democratic senators Tom Daschle and Patrick Leahy. Twenty-three people were infected and five people died. Panic swept the nation. On October 16th the Senate office buildings were shut down, followed by the House of Representatives, after twenty-eight congressional staffers tested positive for exposure to anthrax. A number of hoax letters containing harmless powder also turned up.

Initially it was suspected that either al-Qaeda or Iraq were behind the anthrax letters. However, further investigation led the US government to conclude that, "everything seems to lean toward a domestic source . . . Nothing seems to fit with an overseas terrorist type operation." In August 2002, the FBI named Steven Hatfill, a bio-weapons researcher who worked for the US government, as a "person of interest" in the case. Though he underwent intense scrutiny by the FBI, he was never charged with any crime. As of early 2007, no one else has been charged in relation to the anthrax letter attacks.

Later research determined that the biological strain of the anthrax used in 2001 was developed by the US military, and that it had been cultured no more than two years earlier.

The anthrax scare had the effect of shutting down the legislative branch of government in the highly sensitive weeks following 9/11. It sent a chill down the spine of Washington D.C. and the nation as a whole. Under complicity theories, these consequences would be helpful to inhibit strategic conversation about what happened on 9/11, accelerate passage of the Patriot Act and possibly even warn other factions in the government about how far the administration might go to achieve its objectives.[32]

34. Sole Confession of bin Laden Found in Questionable Video

On October 20th 2001, a video was allegedly shot of Osama bin Laden saying that al-Qaeda "instigated" the 9/11 attacks, and that 9/11 "was revenge for our people killed in Palestine and Iraq." The existence of this video was first revealed by the *Daily Telegraph* on November 11th, in an article which said the video was not made for public release via the al-Jazeera television network, as previous bin Laden tapes had been, but had been circulating for fourteen days among bin Laden's supporters. The *Daily Telegraph* claimed it had obtained access to the footage in the Middle East. On November 14th, Tony Blair referred to the video in a speech before the House of Commons and claimed, "The intelligence material now leaves no doubt whatever of the guilt of bin Laden and his associates." Yet the British government said it did not have a copy of the video, only information about it from intelligence sources. The *Daily Telegraph* noted that in four previous post-9/11 videos, bin Laden always denied responsibility for the attacks. As of this writing, the October 20th video has not been made public.

This video is allegedly different from a tape released publicly in December 2001 by the US, in which bin Laden again seemed to confirm his role in 9/11. However, a number of strange facts about this video soon emerged. For example, all previous videos had been made with the consent of bin Laden, and usually released to the Arabic television channel al-Jazeera. This video was supposedly recorded without his knowledge, found in a house in Afghanistan, and then passed to the CIA by an unknown person or group. Experts pointed out that it would be possible to fake such a video. So many people doubted the video's authenticity that Bush soon made a statement, saying it was "preposterous for anybody to think this tape was doctored. Those who contend it's a farce or a fake are hoping for the best about an evil man." The German television show *Monitor* conducted an independent translation that questioned the translation given by the US military. According to Professor Gernot Rotter, scholar of Islamic and Arabic Studies at the University of Hamburg:

> This tape is of such poor quality that many passages are unintelligible. And those that are intelligible have often been taken out of context, so that you can't use that as evidence. The American translators who listened to the tape and transcribed it obviously added things that they wanted to hear in many places.

The bin Laden seen in this video looks significantly heavier, has a differently-shaped nose and beard, as can be clearly seen in a comparison of stills from earlier and later footage, including an authenticated video released just a few weeks later on al-Jazeera showing a very gaunt bin Laden.

There are reports that bin Laden had from four to ten look-alike doubles at the time.

The video was played across Western television networks as if it was an open and shut conviction of bin Laden. This lucky find arrived as the first serious questions about what happened on 9/11 began to pop up across the Internet, at a time when the administration needed unwavering public support for its bold, aggressive foreign policy and domestic legislative agenda.[33]

35. Silencing of Whistleblowers

Whistleblowers on various aspects of the government's handling of 9/11 have been silenced through disciplinary action, court proceedings and, in some cases, invocation of the rarely-used State Secrets privilege. The curious case of FBI translator Sibel Edmonds is not unrepresentative.

Edmonds claims to have discovered that a co-worker was a foreign intelligence asset and was intentionally mistranslating intercepted communications among suspected terrorists. After her boss and others in the FBI failed to respond to her complaints, she wrote to the Justice Department's inspector general's office in March, 2002: "Investigations are being compromised. Incorrect or misleading translations are being sent to agents in the field. Translations are being blocked and circumvented." Edmonds was then fired and she sued the FBI. A second FBI whistleblower, John Cole, also claimed to know of security lapses in the screening and hiring of FBI translators. The supervisor who told Edmonds not to make those accusations and also encouraged her to go slow in her translations was later promoted.

Half a dozen or so cases like this, once again, suggest intention and not incompetence in the failure of the US military and intelligence community to stop 9/11 before it happened.[34]

36. Resistance to 9/11 Investigations

In prior national crises, such as the attack on Pearl Harbor and the assassination of John F. Kennedy, investigations were empanelled within a matter of days. In the case of 9/11 the nation would have to wait a half-year for House-Senate hearings, more than a year for a formal investigation to commence, and nearly three years for a final report. The Commission closed on August 21st 2004.

President Bush and Vice President Cheney fought these hearings and investigations at every possible turn. As but one of many examples, former

Senate majority leader Tom Daschle reported on a personal phone call from Cheney in January 2002: "The vice president expressed the concern that a review of what happened on September 11th would take resources and personnel away from the effort in the war on terrorism."

It was only after a rising uproar from families that a government-appointed "independent" commission would be established. And then, its rules were such that very few of its own members would have access to the most sensitive matters. One member, Senator Max Cleland, resigned from the commission with the words, "Bush is scamming America."

Cleland attacked his own commission after the other members cut a deal to accept highly limited access to CIA reports to the White House that may indicate advance knowledge of the attacks on the part of the Bush administration. "This is a scam," Cleland said. "It's disgusting. America is being cheated."

"As each day goes by," Cleland said, "we learn that this government knew a whole lot more about these terrorists before September 11th than it has ever admitted. . . . Let's chase this rabbit into the ground. They had a plan to go to war and when 9/11 happened that's what they did; they went to war."[35]

37. Resistance to Testimony Under Oath

Under extreme pressure and threats of subpoena, the administration finally gave in to demands that top officials testify before the 9/11 Commission. Bush and Cheney decided to permit Condoleezza Rice to testify under oath in public, but refused to do so themselves. They agreed only to have a private conversation with members of the Commission. . . and not separately, only together.

If the official story is true, how can one explain the totality of resistance to normal investigative proceedings, particularly the resistance to testimony under oath?[36]

38. Promotion of Key Counterterrorism Officials After 9/11

One of the more telling facts that has received unfortunately little attention from the mainstream press is that there have been no significant disciplinary actions against any US official as a result of the 9/11 investigations. One would think that an investigation into the worst attack on US soil in the history of the nation would identify not just broad categories of failure, but specifically identify people who failed their nation.

Those names are, in fact, known, just not widely published. The striking thing to realize is that a handful of officials in key points of "failure" leading up to 9/11 have since been promoted or awarded other commendations. The most prominent, of course, is CIA Director George Tenet, who was awarded the nation's highest honor, the Medal of Freedom. If the official narrative is true, these men and women should have been fired or worse. Had 9/11 occurred on someone's watch in a European or Asian nation, they would have resigned in disgrace.

Under the complicity theories the actions of the administration are sensible. These people would not need to be consciously complicit to receive such treatment; it is only necessary that they know some uncomfortable facts that if made public might further stress the already fact-challenged official narrative of 9/11.[37]

39. Failure to Catch bin Laden

A half-decade after 9/11, the alleged mastermind remains at large. There now exists a large body of evidence—spanning more than a decade—of repeated negligent failures to capture or kill the world's best known terrorist. Consider three of many examples, drawn from Paul Thompson, The *Terror Timeline*:

> Bin Laden gave a speech in front of about 1,000 supporters on November 10th, 2001, in the town of Jalalabad, Afghanistan. [*Christian Science Monitor*, 3/4/2002] On the night of November 13th, a convoy of 1,000 or more al-Qaeda and Taliban fighters escapes from Jalalabad and reaches the fortress of Tora Bora after hours of driving and then walking. Bin Laden is believed to be with them, riding in one of "several hundred cars" in the convoy. The US bombs the nearby Jalalabad airport, but apparently does not attack the convoy. [Knight Ridder, 10/20/2002; *Christian Science Monitor*, 3/4/2002] The Northern Alliance captures Jalalabad the next day. [*Sydney Morning Herald*, 11/14/2001]

> Ismail Khan's troops and other Northern Alliance fighters are reportedly ready to take back Pashtun areas from Taliban control at this time. Khan, governor of Herat province and one of Afghanistan's most successful militia leaders, later maintains that "we could have captured all the Taliban and the al-Qaeda groups. We could have arrested Osama bin Laden with all of his supporters." [*USA Today*, 1/2/2002] However, according to Khan, his forces

hold back at the request of the US, who allegedly do not want the non-Pashtun Northern Alliance to conquer Pashtun areas. British newspapers at the time report bin Laden is surrounded in a 30-mile area, but the conquest of Kandahar takes weeks without the Northern Alliance and bin Laden slips away (other accounts put him at Tora Bora). [CNN, 11/18/2001]

According to *Newsweek*, approximately 600 al-Qaeda and Taliban fighters, including many senior leaders, escape Afghanistan on this day. This is the first day of heavy bombing of the Tora Bora region (see November 16th, 2001). There are two main routes out of the Tora Bora cave complex to Pakistan. The US bombs only one route, so the 600 are able to escape without being attacked using the other route. Hundreds will continue to use the escape route for weeks, generally unbothered by US bombing or Pakistani border guards. US officials later privately admit they lost an excellent opportunity to close a trap. [*Newsweek*, 8/11/2002] On the same day, the media reports that the US is studying routes bin Laden might use to escape Tora Bora [*Los Angeles Times*, 11/16/2001], but the one escape route is not closed, and by some accounts bin Laden and others escape into Pakistan and will use this same route several weeks later (see November 28th–30th, 2001). High-ranking British officers will later privately complain, "American commanders had vetoed a proposal to guard the high-altitude trails, arguing that the risks of a firefight, in deep snow, gusting winds, and low-slung clouds, were too high." [*New York Times*, 9/30/2002]

Other examples abound. This repeated failure is hard to square with the official story, unless the administration has chosen to eliminate bin Laden at some future date, perhaps timed to achieve a political objective. Under the complicity theories, the same conundrum persists, but an additional possibility becomes sensible: that bin Laden has some form of continuing relationship with certain official or private US intelligence elements, and has maintained it ever since he was explicitly serving US interests in the 1980s.[38]

40. Promotion of Threat Psychology

Unquestionably, in the past five years the citizens of the United States have experienced the most intense wave of fear about homeland security since the Cuban missile crisis. This state of fear has been sustained by the constant stream of threat coverage coming from mainstream media. It is also sensible—that is, understandable—in any of the three theories proposed. Regardless of whether the attacks occurred as officially described, the administration has an interest in ensuring the right balance of concern and comfort in the psychology of the public.

Under either complicity theory, however, this unending stream of fear-inducing media can be seen as creating a "terror psychosis" in the US body-politic, making Americans unwittingly complicit in the global agenda of neoconservative criminals—a necessary condition for them to remain in power to carry out a complex, long-term agenda. One future indicator that 9/11 was caused to happen by US officials would be another terrorist attack, or the capture of bin Laden, timed conveniently for the 2006 or 2008 election cycles—both of which are crucial for neoconservatives to retain control of a highly unstable situation. A major attack in Europe would fit the bill, restoring 9/11-level fear here at home, pulling European populations toward neoconservative instincts, yet affording no one the ability to blame the Bush administration for lack of homeland security.

41. Lack of Attention to Homeland Security Hotspots

One of the strange things about post-9/11 homeland security is how little work has been done to secure truly sensitive areas and infrastructure from attack. Our nuclear plants, chemical factories, electricity grid, water and rail systems and shipping ports remain vulnerable to devastating attack, and proposals to fix security holes have frequently been blocked or ignored by the Bush administration. One example, cited from the reference below:

> Following 9/11, there was an urgent push to curtail some of these risks. Democratic senator Jon Corzine of New Jersey, whose state was home to nine of the 111 most vulnerable factories in the country, introduced legislation to police chemical producers; the bill passed unanimously in Senate committees and quickly garnered White House support. Named the Chemical Security Act, it sought to codify parameters for site security, ensure the safer transport of toxic materials (a single railcar filled with 33,000 gallons of chlorine could kill up to 100,000 people), and establish a timetable to shift away from the use of the most noxious chemicals. Some major chemical users have already been doing that voluntarily. In Washington, for instance, the city water treatment plant switched in 2001 from chlorine to a slightly more expensive, but less dangerous, bacteria remover. The change cost the average

> D.C. water consumer fifty cents per year, but reduced the risk of terrorist hijackings by eliminating hundreds of chlorine tankers rumbling through the capital region.
>
> The Chemical Security Act seemed set to sail through Congress. But as the memory of 9/11 grew dimmer, the petrochemical industry launched a well-co-ordinated and well-financed campaign to scuttle the bill. Led by the powerful American Petroleum Institute, lobby groups bombarded senators, members of Congress, and the White House with thousands of letters, position papers, and reports on the adverse economic impact of the Chemical Security Act. Chlorine and its derivatives went into products that accounted for forty-five percent of the nation's gross domestic product, they argued. Without chlorine components, they lamented, even the backyard gas grill would disappear. The American pastoral would be forever changed.
>
> The White House quickly cooled toward the idea of regulating chemical security. The seven Republican senators who had endorsed the bill in committee withdrew their support. And $5.7 million in petrochemical campaign contributions helped to ensure that Republicans took the Senate in the 2002 midterm elections and that the Chemical Security Act died without a vote. In its place, Senator James Inhofe (R-Okla.) proposed that chemical factories be allowed to police themselves and that the government have no oversight or enforcement powers over safety rules.

There are dozens of other examples of the Bush administration failing to take homeland security programs seriously. If indeed we are at serious risk of domestic terrorist attacks, then this behavior borders on criminal negligence. Concern was so severe that 9/11 Commission members came together again and issued a damning report, hoping to raise attention of policymakers. House Homeland Security Committee member Edward Markey had this to say about the report in December, 2005:

> The commission report is really a blistering, scalding indictment of the Bush administration. Without question, Congress deserves some blame as well, some significant blame. Again it's a Republican House and Senate so I think they are working in coordination with the Bush White House.

> But the criticism of the lack of securing of nuclear materials overseas, the lack of funding for first responders, having a coordinated communications system for a terrorist list that can be checked at any airport in the United States, the list goes on and on. The criticisms go on and on. This is four years after 9/11. The Bush administration has given a blank check to fight a war in Iraq but it's nickel and diming homeland security. That's what the 9/11 Commission has just reported.
>
> And I think that principally the blame lies at the top at the White House.

This policy—spending hundreds of billions on wars abroad while shortchanging homeland security—becomes sensible if foreign terrorists did not, in fact, take the Bush administration by surprise on 9/11. In that case, domestic security was not penetrated by foreign terrorists, but rather by domestic ones.

Regardless, we can all rest easier knowing that grandma's shoes were checked when she went through airport security. She is duly afraid, and is doing her duty.[39]

42. Numerous Obvious, Key Omissions from the 9/11 Commission Report

The final fact discussed in this survey is the indisputable failure of the 9/11 Commission to address at least one hundred matters highly relevant to accomplishing its charter: "to prepare a full and complete account of the circumstances surrounding the September 11th 2001 terrorist attacks, including preparedness for and the immediate response to the attacks."

Most of the inconvenient facts described above were either artfully dodged or not discussed at all by the Commission. A few of the 115 key omissions catalogued by Professor David Ray Griffin:

- The omission of the fact that Zbigniew Brzezinski in his 1997 book had said that for the United States to maintain global primacy, it needed to gain control of Central Asia, with its vast petroleum reserves, and that a new Pearl Harbor would be helpful in getting the US public to support this imperial effort;
- The omission of the fact that Unocal had declared that the Taliban could not provide adequate security for it to go ahead with its oil-and-gas pipeline from the Caspian region through Afghanistan and Pakistan;

- The omission of the report that at a meeting in July 2001, US representatives said that because the Taliban refused to agree to a US proposal that would allow the pipeline project to go forward, a war against them would begin by October;
- The omission of evidence that some key members of the Bush administration, including Donald Rumsfeld and his deputy Paul Wolfowitz, had been agitating for a war with Iraq for many years;
- The omission of notes of Rumsfeld's conversations on 9/11 showing that he was determined to use the attacks as a pretext for a war with Iraq;
- The omission of the statement by the Project for the New American Century that "the need for a substantial American force presence in the Gulf transcends the issue of the regime of Saddam Hussein";
- The omission of the fact that the Project for the New American Century, many members of which became key figures in the Bush administration, published a document in 2000 saying that "a new Pearl Harbor" would aid its goal of obtaining funding for a rapid technological transformation of the US military;
- The omission of the fact that Donald Rumsfeld, who as head of the commission on the US Space Command had recommended increased funding for it, used the attacks of 9/11 on that very evening to secure such funding;
- The failure to mention the fact that three of the men who presided over the failure to prevent the 9/11 attacks—Secretary Rumsfeld, General Richard Myers, and General Ralph Eberhart—were also three of the strongest advocates for the US Space Command;
- The omission of any mention of the FBI agents who reportedly claimed to have known the targets and dates of the attacks well in advance;
- The omission of David Schippers's claim that he had, on the basis of information provided by FBI agents about upcoming attacks in lower Manhattan, tried unsuccessfully to convey this information to Attorney General Ashcroft during the six weeks prior to 9/11 [Schippers was lead investigative counsel for the House Judiciary Committee handling the impeachment of Bill Clinton];

- The omission of the report that Attorney General Ashcroft was warned to stop using commercial airlines prior to 9/11;
- The omission of reports that both Mayor Willie Brown and some Pentagon officials received warnings about flying on 9/11;
- The omission of Gerald Posner's account of Abu Zubaydah's testimony, according to which three members of the Saudi royal family—all of whom later died mysteriously within an eight-day period—were funding al-Qaeda and had advance knowledge of the 9/11 attacks;
- The Commission's denial that it found any evidence of Saudi funding of al-Qaeda;
- The omission of Coleen Rowley's claim that some officials at FBI headquarters did see the memo from Phoenix agent Kenneth Williams;
- The omission of Chicago FBI agent Robert Wright's charge that FBI headquarters closed his case on a terrorist cell, then used intimidation to prevent him from publishing a book reporting his experiences;
- The omission of evidence that FBI headquarters sabotaged the attempt by Coleen Rowley and other Minneapolis agents to obtain a warrant to search Zacarias Moussaoui's computer;
- The omission of the 3.5 hours of testimony to the Commission by former FBI translator Sibel Edmonds—testimony that, according to her later public letter to Chairman Kean, revealed serious 9/11-related cover-ups by officials at FBI headquarters;
- The omission of the fact that General Mahmoud Ahmad, the head of Pakistan's intelligence agency (the ISI), was in Washington the week prior to 9/11, meeting with CIA chief George Tenet and other US officials;
- The omission of evidence that ISI chief Ahmad had ordered $100,000 to be sent to Mohamed Atta prior to 9/11;
- The Commission's claim that it found no evidence that any foreign government, including Pakistan, had provided funding for the al-Qaeda operatives;

- The omission of the fact that President Bush and other members of his administration repeatedly spoke of the 9/11 attacks as "opportunities".

It is this researcher's appraisal that negligence and incompetence can explain many things about the past six years, but they can explain neither these omissions nor the failure of the Bush administration to prevent the attacks of September 11th 2001.

A future commission will have the tragic job of explaining them in great detail.[40]

Possible Objections to this Analysis

Apart from inevitable, irrelevant *ad hominem* attacks—for which this researcher is a uniquely easy target by virtue of controversial, vocal stands on certain major debates in science—a number of genuinely relevant objections will be raised this analysis. Let me respond to four of them in advance.

Objection: *Your list of facts suffers from selection bias; you've excluded a whole laundry list of other facts that support the official theory.*

This is true. Including certain other facts would have the effect of "diluting the red with a sea of green" in the official theory column in the table above. However that would in no way mitigate the implications of this analysis. For example, the huge list of facts that establish the scope and depth of radical Islamic terror networks—explored in books cited under Fact 2 above—are compatible with the nineteen hijackers theory. But again, because false flag operations work best when there pre-exists a real or perceived threat from those to be falsely blamed, those facts remain plausible or sensible in the other two theories.

The official conspiracy theory cannot be saved by flooding away unsupportive facts with supportive ones. It can only be saved by a scientifically and journalistically credible rationalization of not one, not two, but fifteen or more central facts which systematically contradict it, and which systematically support one or both complicity theories.

Objection: *Lots of your sources come from the Internet. They can't be trusted.*

This is a common refrain from folks who do not understand how to recognize quality reporting and research online. The sources cited above are, in almost every case, highly credible. They are uniformly well documented, themselves citing only official documents and authorities, respected journals and news sources, recorded first-person testimony and other equally credible information.

This analysis cannot be refuted on grounds of non-credible sources.

Objection: *Your analysis does not have benefit of access to classified material.*

This objection sounds helpful for the official theory. However, it is not. Surely if there existed evidence more strongly incriminating those charged with the official conspiracy, its substance would have been loudly shared by the administration by now; sources and methods would not need to be compromised to reveal any such substance.

The startling paucity of evidence available to convict the alleged bin Laden-hijacker cabal is itself a suspicious fact. Hysteria and "group think" about Islamic terrorism cannot constitute incriminating evidence in a particular case.

Objection: *Too many people would have to be involved for complicity to remain secret this long after 9/11.*

This objection is the hardest one for 9/11 researchers to deal with, for the scale and audacity of the operation under either complicity theory is breathtaking. However, they are the only theories compatible with the surveyed facts.

This objection is best answered by an estimate of the minimum degree of complicity required to carry out a false flag operation in the form of 9/11. Such an operation would plausibly require, at a minimum:

- A core group of insiders, numbering a dozen or so, with full knowledge of the plan. That group would have to include at least one or two officials at each of the following institutions: the White House, NSC, FBI, CIA, Pentagon and NORAD. They would each have a very specific set of responsibilities to cause certain things to happen, and prevent other things from happening.

- A second orbit of people, numbering a hundred or so, responsible for carrying out particular aspects of the operation or providing logistical support for core insiders. Wherever possible, they would be carrying out such tasks as part of other classified or confidential programs with other objectives, genuine or artificially-created. For example, this group would include support staff running secure air defense and communications systems for the White House and Pentagon leaders. As another example, consider the people who would have placed explosives in the WTC buildings and fired them on 9/11. Demolition charges could have been placed after the 1993 bombing, or in days prior to 9/11, as part of a reasonable contingency plan that would enable city officials, or their new owner, to "pull" the towers down cleanly, in their own footprints, in the event that they were at risk of falling into other buildings as result of a future bombing. This second group would have to be closely monitored following 9/11, as they represent the most likely risks for exposure of the operation.
- A third orbit of people, numbering in the thousands, serving useful roles but would have no knowledge that anything improper is afoot. They would only discover their unwitting involvement through consideration of this kind of retrospective analysis; they would be aware only of how one facet of the official story is incompatible with their experience. This group would include people involved in war games, FAA flight control, FEMA and FBI officials on site in New York City for a bio-terror exercise, security officers keeping the WTC clear, and contractors simply following orders to transport steel beams away from a disaster zone.

Given the massive scale of intelligence agencies and clandestine operations that have been kept from the public for decades, a false flag project of 9/11 scale would be tiny by comparison. It would, however, be extremely explosive and risky, and thus every contingency conceivable in advance would be covered.

Unfortunately, this conforms to what we see from the outside looking in five years later: a coherent, interlocking set of activities and programs specifically designed to cause 9/11 to happen, make it look like we simply failed to connect the dots in time and obstruct the release of any information that suggests otherwise.

Conclusion

It is clear from this survey that a large number of vital facts about 9/11 do not conform to the official conspiracy theory, and do conform to complicity or causation theories. If that represents the truth of the matter, then an enormous range of consequences, considerations, and possible futures emerge. They will be the subject of writings by this and many other researchers.

If this intersection of facts and theories stands up, then the core of the neoconservative movement is behind one of the greatest crimes in history. In that case, I have no doubt whatsoever that those involved had the good of the world in mind in formulating and carrying out the operation. After all, the logic would have gone, a few thousand people lost is a painful but small price to pay for strategically transforming the entire geopolitical order. I have equally little doubt that they honestly believed that, by 2006, Central Asia and the Middle East would be starting down the path to an astonishing liberation of Western-style democracy and freedom, and 9/11 would have been remembered in a different way as US forces were greeted with welcome arms by repressed populations of the region. Tragically naive, but I believe they believed it.

They certainly would not have predicted the state of world affairs their actions—and inaction—have yielded. Others did predict the conflict and chaos that could be unleashed if imperial ends and means were at the core of a New American Century.

If 9/11 was a false flag operation, whether and how we restore integrity to our nation is likely to be the greatest test our democracy has ever faced. Some have suggested that confronting the truth of 9/11 will bring down not just an administration, but the republic. On the contrary, I believe that the republic will be radically strengthened: its citizens will be smarter, its laws will be respected, its transparency will be reestablished, its policies will be restructured, its relations will be restored and its honor will be reclaimed.

The process itself can be an example to the world of the true potential of democracy to overcome the most pernicious kind of evil—the evil within.

NOTES

1. http://cooperativeresearch.org/timeline.jsp?timeline=complete_911_timeline&before_9/11=sovietAfghanWar; Nafeez Ahmed, "Terrorism and Statecraft: Al-Qaeda and Western Covert Operations After the Cold War," in Paul Zarembka, ed., *The Hidden History of 9-11-2001* (Amsterdam: Elsevier, 2006), Research in Political Economy, Volume 23, pp. 149–188.
2. See Bassam Tibi, *The Challenge of Fundamentalism: Political Islam and the New World Disorder* (Berkeley: University of California Press, 2002 [1998]); John L. Esposito, *Unholy War: Terror in the Name of Islam* (Oxford: Oxford University Press, 2002).
3. http://cooperativeresearch.org/timeline.jsp?timeline=complete_911_timeline&before_9/11=warnings; Ahmed, "Terrorism and Statecraft."
4. See: Joseph Trento, *Prelude to Terror: The Rogue CIA and the Legacy of America's Private Intelligence Network* (New York: Carroll and Graf, 2005); James Risen, *State of War: The Secret History of the CIA And the Bush Administration* (New York: Free Press, 2006).
5. http://cooperativeresearch.org/searchResults.jsp?searchtext=PNAC&events=on&entities=on&articles=on&topics=on&timelines= on&projects=on&titles=on&descriptions=on&dosearch=on&search=Go Diana Ralph, "Islamaphobia and the 'War on Terror'," in Zarembka, *Hidden History of 9-11-2001*, pp. 261–300.
6. http://cooperativeresearch.org/entity.jsp?entity=clinton_administration.
7. http://cooperativeresearch.org/searchResults.jsp?searchtext=Bush+bin+laden&events=on&entities=on&articles=on&topics=on&t imelines=on&projects=on&titles=on&descriptions=on&dosearch=on&search=Go
8. *Newsweek* (September 15th 2001); *Washington Post* (September 16th, 2001); Jay Kolar, "What We Know About the Alleged Hijackers," in Zarembka, *Hidden History of 9-11-2001*, pp. 3–48; http://www.scoop.co.nz/stories/HL0212/S00058.htm.
9. http://cooperativeresearch.org/essay.jsp?article=essaytheytriedtowarnus.
10. http://cooperativeresearch.org/searchResults.jsp?searchtext=cia+fbi+warning&events=on&entities=on&articles=on&topics=on& timelines=on&projects=on&titles=on&descriptions=on&dosearch=on&search=Go
11. Don Jacobs, "The Military Drills on 9-11: 'Bizarre Coincidence' or Something Else?" in Zarembka, *Hidden History of 9-11-2001*, pp. 123–148; http://cooperativeresearch.org/context.jsp?item=a050801cheneytaskforce http://www.fromthewilderness.com/free/ww3/011805_simplify_case.shtml#bullmeans
12. http://cooperativeresearch.org/timeline.jsp?timeline=complete_911_timeline&startpos=700#a060101newpolicy
13. http://cooperativeresearch.org/timeline.jsp?timeline=complete_911_timeline&startpos=200#a1096stratesec http://la.indymedia.org/news/2004/04/108539.php Newsday (September 12th, 2001); http://cooperativeresearch.org/timeline.jsp?timeline=complete_911_timeline&startpos=800#a082301newjob.
14. http://cooperativeresearch.org/timeline.jsp?timeline=complete_911_timeline&startpos=700#a072101berlin http://ist-socrates.berkeley.edu/~pdscott/qf911.html.
15. http://cooperativeresearch.org/searchResults.jsp?searchtext=party+hijacker&events=on&entities=on&articles=on&topics=on&ti melines=on&projects=on&titles=on&descriptions=on&dosearch=on&search=Go#articles

16. http://cooperativeresearch.org/searchResults.jsp?searchtext=options+trading&events=on&entities=on&articles=on&topics=on&ti melines=on&projects=on&titles=on&descriptions=on&dosearch=on&search=Go; Paul Zarembka's "Initiation of the 9-11 Operation, with Evidence of Insider Trading Beforehand," in Zarembka, *Hidden History of 9-11-2001*, pp. 49–78; http://sun6.dms.state.fl.us/eog_new/eog/orders/2001/september/eo2001-261-09-07-01.html.
17. http://sun6.dms.state.fl.us/eog_new/eog/orders/2001/september/eo2001-262-09-11-01.html http://cooperativeresearch.org/essay.jsp?article=essayaninterestingday.
18. http://cooperativeresearch.org/timeline.jsp?timeline=complete_911_timeline&startpos=1000#a091101mahmoodmeeting; http://www.globalresearch.ca/articles/CHO206A.html.
19. Don Jacobs, "The Military Drills on 9-11: 'Bizarre Coincidence' or Something Else?" http://cooperativeresearch.org/timeline.jsp?timeline=complete_911_timeline&startpos=1000#a630vigilantguardian http://www.fromthewilderness.com/free/ww3/011805_simplify_case.shtml http://www.vanityfair.com/features/general/060801fege01.
20. http://cooperativeresearch.org/essay.jsp?article=essayaninterestingday.
21. http://worldtradecentertruth.com/Journal_4_Jet.pdf; Scholars for 9/11 Truth, "The Flying Elephant: Evidence for Involvement of a Third Jet in the WTC Attacks," *Journal of 9/11 Studies* 1. Pp. 26–39; Available here: http://www.journalof911studies.com.
22. http://911research.wtc7.net/planes/analysis/norad/ http://cooperativeresearch.org/timeline.jsp?timeline=complete_911_timeline&startpos=1100#a852otisscramble.
23. http://www.911truth.org/article.php?story=20050724164122860. Diana Ralph, "Islamaphobia and the 'War on Terror'," in Zarembka, *Hidden History of 9-11-2001*, pp. 246–48.
24. http://www.physics.byu.edu/research/energy/htm7.html; Steven E. Jones, "Why Indeed Did the WTC Buildings Collapse?, *Global Outlook* 11 (Spring 2006), pp. 47–70; David Ray Griffin, "The Destruction of the World Trade Center: Why the Official Account Cannot Be True," in Zarembka, *Hidden History of 9-11-2001*, pp. 223–260; Kevin Ryan, "What Is 9/11 Truth?—The First Steps," *Journal of 9/11 Studies* 2, pp. 1–6. Available here: http://www.journalof911studies.com.
25. http://www.pentagonresearch.com/ http://www.scholarsfor911truth.org/ArticleMeyer_10June2006.html.
26. http://www.physics.byu.edu/research/energy/htm7.html; Jones, "Why Indeed did the WTC Buildings Collapse?"
27. "Selling Out the Investigation," editorial in *Fire Engineering* (January 2002) http://www.physics.byu.edu/research/energy/htm7.html; Jones, "Why Indeed Did the WTC Buildings Collapse?"
28. http://www.hillnews.com/thehill/export/TheHill/News/Frontpage/051606/news1.html.
29. http://edition.cnn.com/SPECIALS/2001/trade.center/victims/AA11.victims.html and related pages; Kolar, "What We Know About the Alleged Hijackers."

30. http://cooperativeresearch.org/timeline.jsp?timeline=complete_911_timeline&startpos=1400#a091601stillalive; Kolar, "What We Know About the Alleged Hijackers."
31. http://cooperativeresearch.org/searchResults.jsp?searchtext=air+traffic+control+tape&events=on&entities=on&articles=on&topi cs=on&timelines=on&projects=on&titles=on&descriptions=on&dosearch=on&search=Go
32. http://cooperativeresearch.org/timeline.jsp?timeline=complete_911_timeline&startpos=1500#a1001anthraxattacks http://en.wikipedia.org/wiki/2001_anthrax_attacks.
33. http://cooperativeresearch.org/timeline.jsp?timeline=complete_911_timeline&startpos=1500#a102001instigated http://www.whatreallyhappened.com/osamatape.html; Kolar, "What We Know About the Alleged Hijackers."
34. http://cooperativeresearch.org/searchResults.jsp?searchtext=whistleblower&events=on&entities=on&articles=on&topics=on&ti melines=on&projects=on&titles=on&descriptions=on&dosearch=on&search=Go.
35. http://archives.cnn.com/2002/ALLPOLITICS/01/29/inv.terror.probe/ http://www.cnsnews.com/ViewPolitics.asp?Page=\Politics\archive\200206\POL20020611b.html http://www.911truth.org/article.php?story=2004052510414 5424. Bryan Sacks, "Making History: The Compromised 9-11 Commission," in Zarembka, *Hidden History of 9-11-2001*, pp. 223–260.
36. David Sanger, "Bush Gives in to 9/11 Panel," *New York Times* (31st March 2004).
37. http://cooperativeresearch.org/timeline.jsp?timeline=complete_911_timeline&startpos=1900#a120402promotions.
38. http://cooperativeresearch.org/searchResults.jsp?searchtext=tora+bora&events=on&entities=on&articles=on&topics=on&timelin es=on&projects=on&titles=on&descriptions=on&dosearch=on&search=Go
39. http://www.motherjones.com/news/feature/2004/09/08_400.html http://www.pbs.org/newshour/bb/terrorism/july-dec05/commission_12-5.html.
40. David Ray Griffin, "The 9/11 Commission Report: A 571-Page Lie," linked at http://www.serendipity.li/wot/571-page-lie.htm; Sacks, "Making History."

6

Some Holes in the Plane Stories

Morgan Reynolds and Rick Rajter

September 11th 2001 was a well-planned psy-op, deceptive at every level, intended to manipulate public opinion, and wildly successful in the short run. Given this background, virtually everything the government and its controlled media say must be construed as deception until independently proven otherwise.

A primary question is: Why investigate the alleged airliner crashes of 9/11? Because the key to the war on terror and world domination project is the blood libel (Webster Tarpley's term) that young Arabs hijacked specific flights and crashed them into US landmarks. Proof that the plane stories are false has tremendous value; that explains why there is such intense opposition to studying the evidence about crashes. To offer a personal note, in the battle over 9/11 truth, if someone tells us not to go someplace because it would be "divisive," we go there. If told to stay away, it must be important. Analysis and discussion are the only means to find the truth. Truth-seekers want the truth, right? So let's get on with it. Challenging the official story about each so-called crash matters for at least three reasons:

- If the perpetrators get away with airplane hoaxes, it only encourages more audacious, blood-soaked scams;
- Exposure of lies about airliners expands the proof that the government committed the 9/11 atrocities;
- Key to the government's war on terror and global domination project is the false belief that Arabs attacked the homeland; once people become aware that this legend is false, support for the war on Muslims will collapse.

The most obvious defect of the official story is the *absence or near-absence of conventional airplane wreckage* at each crash site. Government and controlled media claim that four large airliners crashed in the highly populated northeast during a terrorist attack. Okay, *show me debris*! The US Government could have ended airplane controversy long ago by allowing independent aircraft accident investigators to examine the unique serial numbers on time-change parts at each crash site and compare them to each plane's maintenance logbook. But there has been no NTSB, FBI, nor independent investigation of the so-called air crashes.

Four large commercial jets, allegedly hijacked, vanished within eighty minutes that morning, unprecedented events in the northeastern United States. We repeat, they vanished with nary a trace, without any reliable evidence of debris. This is so incredible that it rivals the collapses of three steel-framed skyscrapers on the same day at the same location, the only collapses allegedly caused by fires in history.

Our purpose is not to show what really happened but *what did not happen* with airplanes that morning. To repeat, the purpose is to expose more of the government's 9/11 lies. The mind-control theory about two 767s and two 757s crashing turns out to be a gigantic hoax. Physical facts at every turn refute the official tale about what gashed the Pentagon, Pennsylvania, and WTC towers that bloody morning. At the WTC specifically, a commuter plane, specially prepared aircraft, military planes, missiles or drones as some eyewitnesses reported or nothing at all may have hit the towers from outside. We do not yet have enough evidence to say. But whatever alternative theory might be advocated, it must cope with the lack of big plane debris.

Phantom Flights?

Before examining physical evidence—our principal task—many facts about the alleged flights discredit the official account. The Colgan Air flight 5930 Portland-Logan is riddled with questions[1] and AA Flights 11 and 77 were not scheduled that day.[2] Official BTS data are meticulously kept because of liability issues. The two American Airlines Boeing 767s in question—tail numbers N334AA and N644AA—were deregistered January 14th, 2002, months late but with no proof they were involved in the alleged flights.[3] Mohammed Atta supposedly left a rental car at Portland International and absurdly left a second car full of incriminating evidence at Logan, in other words, evidence was over-planted. And was Gate 26 or 32 used for the unscheduled Flight 11? The two United Airlines aircraft that allegedly crashed that day—tail number N612UA for Flight 175 and N591UA for

Flight 93—were in the BTS database but only deregistered four years later on 28th September 2005, despite a requirement that destroyed aircraft be deregistered within twenty-four hours.[4]

Further fueling suspicion, all four cross-country flights had improbably light loads with only twenty-seven percent occupancy while the airlines, government, and media never produced credible passenger manifests, a routine matter, and all inexplicably lacked Arab names.[5] This was incredibly sloppy work by the perpetrators. The controlled media have reported at least nine alleged hijackers alive while ongoing searches of birth, death, and marriage records suggest many passenger names were fake.[6] Families of air crash victims remain oddly silent, highly suspicious behavior as government lies and evades, while dissatisfied families of ground zero victims are outspoken.[7] Searches fail to show hull insurance paid on the four jetliners despite the small number of insurers in the industry. Then we have missing airport surveillance video tapes, an incredible string of nineteen airport security or screening failures, flights disappearing from conventional radar, missing flight data (fdr) and cockpit voice recorders (cvr), gagged flight controllers-firefighters-police-airline-employees, physically impossible cell phone calls[8] with fake dialogue[9] ("I see water and buildings. Oh my God! Oh my God!" "Hello, mom. This is your son Mark Bingham"), not to mention the technical impossibility of the purported Arabs to pilot the planes as advertised. Virtually nothing checks out in the official account about the alleged flights. The controlled media steer a wide berth from these problems in favor of canonizing the official conspiracy theory.

A Boeing 757 Vanishes into the Pentagon

Of the four 9/11 crashes, extensive research and facts most clearly refute the government's "a-757-went-into-the-Pentagon" whopper. Only a handful of 9/11 researchers defend the government story. The question is, did AA Flight 77 crash into the west side of the Pentagon at 9:37:46 on 11th September 2001 (aka Boeing 757 tail #N644AA, FAA-listed as destroyed and deregistered on 14th January 2002, four months late)? The answer is now beyond a reasonable doubt. We know for sure that something else blew holes in the Pentagon that morning, not a Boeing 757. Compelling evidence includes the following:

- After two major terrorist attacks on the WTC, a hijacked, unscheduled FL 77 supposedly wandered about the countryside for some forty minutes undisturbed as FAA bureaucrats and NORAD warriors went "hmmmm."

- After the second WTC hit at 9:03 a.m., NORAD and the NMCC failed to put up a Combat Air Patrol (CAP) over the nation's Capitol as part of the government's general military inactivity.
- The government released flight control transcripts on 16th October 2001, but terminated Flight 77's path twenty minutes before it allegedly crashed into the Pentagon and excluded Flight 93 entirely (Thompson, *The Terror Timeline*, p. 505), indicating that official lies were still being worked out at that late date.
- The Pentagon aircraft supposedly put on a stunt show, suggesting supreme skill in the cockpit, yet the terrorist-pilot decided to fly into the low-occupancy west side, bypassing the high-occupancy east where people like Rumsfeld and Paul Wolfowitz might have been killed. Supposedly passing over a supine White House which failed to launch its SAMs, the Pentagon too took no action as the aircraft performed an acrobatic 270-degree (or 330-degree, according to *The 9/11 Commission Report*) dive from seven thousand feet (an altitude known to the FAA despite the transponder off), and smashed into outer ring E of the Pentagon dead center at the first and second floors traveling at an alleged 530+ m.p.h. without an engine scraping the front lawn or disturbing construction material, after downing a few lamp posts on the highway with their associated debris seeming pointed the wrong way and felling no lamp posts on the service road nearer the Pentagon. Curiously, no uniformed Air Force member was killed but the toll on Naval Intelligence and Army was high. A suggested reason for the high toll for ONI, the oldest and once most important intelligence service, was payback, perhaps for its conviction of Israeli spy Jonathan Pollard.
- Confusion has even reigned over the exact time of the Pentagon event. There was an event at 9:31 a.m. or 9:32 a.m. but various official accounts set the attack between 9:37 and 9:50 a.m., the 9/11 Commission settling on 9:37:46 a.m.[10] No seismic signal confirms the time because monitors did not pick up the alleged crash of a 757 into the Pentagon though they are sensitive enough to detect a sonic boom.
- Hani Hanjour, the alleged pilot, "may not have had a ticket" (Thompson, *The Terror Timeline*, p. 493), was not listed on the passenger manifest and "couldn't fly" (pp. 193–94). Professional pilots

observe that it must have been "a crack pilot in the left seat" or remote control doing the flying (p. 493). Crack pilot John Lear doubts that he could have done such flying.

- The premiere smoking gun is that the Pentagon gash is too small both vertically and horizontally. A Boeing 757's tail is forty feet tall with landing gear up while the maximum height of the hole in the Pentagon could not have been thirty feet tall (two stories). The width of the hole was less than twenty feet before the façade collapsed, and windows above the impact hole were intact. The largest width claimed for the hole is ninety feet—more like fifty-two feet according to photographic expert Jack White—and that seems to be after the façade collapsed, not upon impact. The 757 wingspan is 125 feet, much larger than the width of the post-façade-collapse hole. The puny Pentagon Hole falsifies the government's "a-Boeing-757-hit-the-Pentagon" story. It is not a close call.
- A second smoking gun is that a 757 flying a nearly flat flight profile (no dive) at 500+ m.p.h. as alleged could not hit the Pentagon's ground floor because of an extremely powerful *ground effect* cushion beneath it. At high speeds, the highly energized wing-tip vortices and huge downwash sheet of a two-hundred-thousand-pound airliner make it physically impossible to get closer to the ground than one-half wingspan or about sixty feet in this case. The physical forces of the compressible gas called air, in other words, stirred by a high-speed 757 traveling flat near the ground make it impossible to land it at high speed. An aeronautical engineer proves this proposition in an article at www.physics911.net, and invites other engineers and pilots to prove him wrong.[11] Very few pilots have experienced the aerodynamic effects in this rare flight domain because they normally only get this close to the ground during landing at low speeds. Highly wing-loaded aircraft like the Global Hawk or B1-B can land at high speed but not lightly wing-loaded aircraft like the 757. In addition, a ground-hugging 757 spewing a one-hundred-thousand-pound thrust jetblast behind it would have blown trailer trucks and people away, phenomena absent in the flight path (see the first "Loose Change" DVD for an example). There would have been tremendous noise, virtually unmentioned in so-called eyewitness testimony. Laws of aerodynamics falsify the official account.

- The five frames (incorrectly dated September 12th!) and additional video released by the Pentagon in May 2006 to "prove" a 757 crashed into the Pentagon are fake. One absurdity is a jet engine vapor trail because jetliners do not leave vapor trails at ground level, only in frigid cold at high altitude! That fact alone shows the Pentagon's crude attempt to prove a 757 crashed into the Pentagon has failed. The video frames show no 757 although a partial missile-like-tip or A-3-like image appears. The pictures are so compromised that it does not matter what is pictured in these fakes. The explosion in the parking lot video looks like it was caused by a warhead or some kind of military ordnance but is the fireball real or photoshopped?
- The linear path through rings E, D, and C implies vehicle impact at an approximate 45-degree angle without any deflection. Geometry dictates that the hole would have to be as much as 1.5 times a 757's wingspan, or 187 feet. Therefore, the hole necessary to accommodate a 757 on a "non-magical" basis is about twice the width of the post-façade-collapse hole.
- 767s supposedly crashed through steel and concrete and then "shredded" in the WTC towers, while a smaller 757 allegedly penetrated a three-foot thick, reinforced concrete exterior at the Pentagon and continued on through two more Pentagon rings, a distance of at least 185 feet, poking a nine-foot diameter hole into C's inside ring and apparently blowing two additional holes inside ring C. That would imply little or no shredding and an amazingly strong fuselage with its fifteen-foot diameter. *The theorized crash behaviors at the WTC and Pentagon are obviously contradictory.* According to photographic expert Jack White, photos do show penetration into the second ring.
- Some apologists claim that a huge 757 vaporized on impact and left virtually no wreckage while penetrating three rings, an unprecedented event in air crash history. Vaporization would require heat intense enough to melt all the metal, including aluminum, tempered steel, carbon, and titanium, and heat the resulting liquids into gases. That is impossible with jet fuel. Losing over sixty tons of material? Ridiculous. Engineer Rick Rajter has proven the vaporization and liquification theories impossible.[12] For example, it would take more than Mach 15+ (twenty times the top speed of a 757) to generate

enough kinetic energy to vaporize aluminum, the primary material in jetliners.

- Government would have us believe that such "vaporizing" heat was selective enough to preserve sufficient fingerprints and DNA to identify victims. These miraculous results were courtesy the Armed Forces Institute of Pathology, the government's "trustworthy" producer of autopsies from Waco, TWA flight 800, and so forth. The chain of custody for the reported human remains is unspecified.
- We don't know exactly what hit the Pentagon (F-16, Global Hawk, A-3, cruise missile), if anything flying at all, but "certain missiles are specially conceived to have a piercing effect. . . . An airplane crashes and smashes. A missile of this type pierces" (Griffin, *The New Pearl Harbor*, p. 31). The tomahawk cruise missile is "the weapon of choice to strike reinforced, hardened targets."[13]
- In a "sheer coincidence," emergency vehicles were pre-positioned at the Pentagon (Thompson, *The Terror Timeline*, p. 421) and the FBI quickly confiscated tapes of the crash from the Pentagon service station and Sheraton hotel after the crash (probably Virginia DOT too).
- The hapless fire chief Ed Plaugher of Arlington, Virginia, said there were no recognizable airplane parts, at a press conference the next day.
- Many eyewitnesses at the Pentagon incident favor the military plane, missile or drone theory (Griffin, *The New Pearl Harbor*, p. 26, Holmgren)[14]. Secretary of Defense Donald Rumsfeld endorsed the missile theory in a famous (intentional?) slip of the tongue, referring to ". . . the missile [used] to damage this building." Others believe that there was no flying object at all, just interior explosions.[15]
- Eyewitnesses saw a C-130 later confirmed to be piloted by Lt. Col. Steve O'Brien flying low over the aircraft or missile that may have hit the Pentagon. Contrary to eyewitness accounts, O'Brien claimed that he was not close to the crash and explosion: "With all of the East Coast haze, I had a hard time picking him out." Reynolds was in Washington, D.C., that morning and there was never a clearer morning in the history of East Coast aviation. The man is a liar. O'Brien's C-130 showed up minutes later at the Pennsylva-

nia crash, raising the suspicion that O'Brien was at both events for black ops purposes. Some nineteen C-130s reportedly are equipped for electronic warfare/jamming/remote control capabilities (*The Terror Timeline*, pp. 513–14).

- CNN's Jamie MacIntyre and others reported that close inspection showed "no evidence of a plane having crashed anywhere near the Pentagon."
- The FBI seized all the tapes from the Citgo station, Sheraton Hotel, Virginia DOT, and the Pentagon. There may be as many as eighty-four tapes. Responding to a recent FOIA request, the government contends that the two tape segments released are the *only* ones showing "plane" footage.[16] This must be a lie or the Citgo, Sheraton, and DOT tapes would be released.

Conclusion? Irrefutable and abundant FACTS rule out the theory that AA Flight 77 flew into the Pentagon on 11th September 2001.

Real plane crashes leave body parts strewn about as well as plane parts.[17] "Numerous points based on the physical evidence of the crash site seem to make an overwhelming cumulative case against a 757 having crashed there," Hoffman concedes, "provided one ignores the eyewitness evidence. However, most of these points involve some error in evaluating the evidence."[18–19] There is no error.[20] Dismissing physical evidence in favor of eyewitness testimony inverts the ranking in science and law. Flight 77 advocates have extremely flimsy arguments.[21]

A Boeing 757 Vanishes into Pennsylvania Turf

After taking it on the chin in three reported crashes (with no verified plane wreckage) and sustaining horrific loss of life and property, the government's heartwarming albeit murderous script says America picked itself up off the canvas and roared back, setting up its eagerly-sought war on terror with the Beamer-Bush war cry, "Let's roll!" Objective evidence on behalf of this propaganda tale, however, is scarce indeed.

With no substantiated airplane wreckage again, powerful evidence refutes the Flight 93 fraud:

- Flight 93 was a scheduled flight beginning 5th September but the Arab hijackers allegedly bought tickets online on 24th–29th August before the flight existed. Of course there are no Arab names on the FL 93 passenger manifests. One researcher contends that FL 93's maiden Tuesday flight was on 9/11.[22] Maybe the evidence exists but we haven't seen a gate number at Newark nor heard credible eyewitnesses testify regarding boarding and wheels-up. There is no video of Arab hijackers boarding.

- The FAA registered Boeing 757 tail number N591UA as valid—the alleged Flight 93 aircraft—until September 2005. There are many fishy things about this tail number. United Airlines reportedly identified its Flight 93 as landing at Cleveland Hopkins International Airport on 9/11 and it was initially reported as a Boeing 767.[23–24]

- An "aerial view of the impact crater of Flight 93 suggests that the plane plunged into the soft ground on a nearly vertical trajectory," yet a debris field was reported as far away as eight miles. Since it was a virtually windless morning, the physics make no sense: a hole with vertical wing marks (but no wings!) about twenty feet long, a fraction of the 125 feet wingspan of an intact 757, suggests a nearly vertical trajectory into soft ground but debris over a reportedly wide area suggests an explosion within the plane or "holed" by an air-to-air missile, as Defense Secretary Rumsfeld said. A shoot-down might explain an eight-mile debris field but that would make the Road Runner "airplane-outline" hole "for the folks to see" impossible because the plane presumably would have broken up in mid-air.

- Eyewitnesses reported an airliner flying low from the west with no suicide spiral, yet a "vertical impact hole" is impossibly at the eastern edge of the woods. Instead of an expected horizontal crash field with plenty of aircraft wreckage, a debris-free smoking hole 20' x 10' completely contradicts the flight path seen by witnesses. No eyewitness actually saw impact.

- "There was no plane," according to Ernie Stull,[25] mayor of Shanksville.[26] "Everyone was puzzled, because the call had been a plane had crashed. But there was no plane." Reporter: "They had been sent here because of a crash, but there was no plane?" Reply: "No. Nothing. Only this hole." Like counterterrorism expert Van Romero on the WTC demolitions, Ernie later changed his mind. Money talks?

- "We haven't seen anything bigger than a phone book, certainly nothing that would resemble a part of a plane," said Capt. Frank

Monaco of the Pennsylvania State Police.[27] "[T]here was no tail section, no jet engines, no large sections of fuselage in view anywhere near the impact crater" (*9/11 Synthetic Terror*, p. 268).

- Nena Lensbouer was the first to go up to the smoking crater and she described a hole five to six feet deep and smaller than the twenty-four-foot trailer in her front yard.[28] She described hearing "an explosion, like an atomic bomb—not a crash."
- Coroner Wallace Miller was stunned at how small the smoking crater looked: "[L]ike someone took a scrap truck, dug a ten-foot ditch and dumped all this trash into it . . . there were no bodies there."[29] He marveled because there was not a drop of blood: "It's as if the plane had stopped and let the passengers off before it crashed."[30-31]
- Government has allowed no public access to the flight data and cockpit voice recorders it allegedly recovered. The FBI refused to allow a detailed investigation of the crash site, and it filled in the crater with dirt followed by topsoil and had scorched trees cut down and shredded into mulch (Tarpley, pp. 270–71), most likely hiding explosive residue from a missile or other source.
- One alternative theory claims the military shot down an airliner over Indian Lake and then cordoned off New Baltimore, eight miles from the diversionary smoking hole near Shanksville.[32]

Conclusion? No Boeing 757 crashed in the designated hole in Shanksville, Pennsylvania. It is physically impossible.

Fools like us are supposed to believe that two Boeings hit the steel WTC towers and were strong enough to cut out cartoon plane shapes but not even close to the same shape in soft ground in Pennsylvania. Flight 93 supposedly fell into a little bitty hole 20' x 10' x 5' insufficient to hold half the millions of parts of a 757. "United Airlines Flight 93 is the plane that crashed in Pennsylvania on September 11th, 2001," Jim Hoffman[33] asserts but nobody offers proof.

Extra! Extra! Two Boeing 767s Vanish into Skyscrapers

Most 9/11 researchers reject the government's 757 theory in the Pentagon and Pennsylvania incidents for lack of supporting evidence and compelling counterevidence. Skepticism about 767s disappearing into the twin towers is far less common. It's virtually a taboo topic but if we look at the gashes in the towers, a telling question arises: *How could two wide-body aluminum jetliners glide into massive steel and concrete towers without a single flap, panel, or part knocked to the ground below the impact walls, no Boeing debris in gashes, no visible deceleration and disappearance into the towers?*

The NIST report (pdf, p. 38), for instance, states about the south tower, "the aircraft completely disappeared into the building in a fifth of a second."[34] Completely disappeared, incredibly neat, no recycling needed! Diligent NIST scientists have no problem whatever with a fragile aluminum plane smashing into a heavy steel tower, the strongest building in the world, without suffering displacement of a single aluminum panel dropped to the ground below impact. We truly live in remarkable times.

Tower walls were composed of high-strength steel beams approximately 14 inches square on one-meter centers (39.37") surrounding windows with each column beam secured to others by steel spandrel plates about 52 inches x 10 feet forming a belt around each floor (see NIST pdf, p. 8). Steel beam thicknesses varied from 4" at the base and tapered from 5/8" to 1/4" in the WTC-1 impact zone and 13/16" to 1/4" in the WTC-2 impact zone. WTC floors were grids of steel topped by four inches of steel-reinforced lightweight concrete in corrugated steel pans weighing seven tons each. Walls effectively were dense webs of nearly forty-percent steel covered by aluminum and backed by steel and concrete floor grids mated to an incredibly strong and dense core of forty-seven cross-braced steel columns, concrete stairwells and elevator shafts.

In a violent encounter between an aluminum plane weighing nearly 140 tons loaded and a steel tower weighing 500,000 tons,[35] the plane, of course, would crumple, parts would be sheared off and the plane crushed. Aluminum has lower yield and failure strengths than steel and the Boeing 767 mass was a minuscule three hundredths of one percent of each tower's mass. "The impact did nothing," as UC Berkeley structural engineer A. Astaneh-Asl said, "the airplane did not do much damage."[36] Like a needle piercing into skin or a person falling through the ice on a lake, a 140-ton airplane flying at over 400 m.p.h. (NIST and FEMA claim an astounding 590 m.p.h. for WTC-2) might inflict some minor local damage without damaging the structure globally. In particular, the engines themselves, thrusting along full throttle at approximately 450–550 m.p.h., obviously could penetrate a steel tower, even possibly fly through it. But whatever blew those gashes in each tower, only thirteen percent or less of the upper perimeter columns on a few floors were broken and the upper structures remained intact. A fuselage, with only minor hyperbole, could be termed a hollow aluminum tube. Among large jetliner components, only engines and landing gear would retain serious structural integrity in a collision, in addition to small parts like actuators. Higher speeds increase kinetic energy by the square of speed and a frontal area of under twenty-five square meters could create minor local damage. Yet planes running into mountains,[37] construction equipment,[38] concrete barriers, and steel/concrete buildings[39] fare very poorly, just as speeding automobiles hitting a guardrail, telephone pole or tree do.[40] A plane flying into a WTC tower should crumple, break up, shatter and scatter pieces everywhere. The only issue is the exact pattern of destruction the building would wreak on its intruder.

But belief in the butter entry is so strong that a patient treatment is a must. A central question regarding each jetliner's disappearance is: *Would aluminum wing tips and tail break off against a steel wall or disappear entirely inside each building?*

Ordinarily the answer would be that wing tips and tail would shear off on impact and bounce to the ground below. Wing tips have enormous forward momentum at impact but begin to decelerate (assuming they are still attached to the plane) as the fragile nose and fuselage collide with a steel wall, five floors of steel-truss-steel-reinforced-concrete, and a steel inner core. This would wreak complete havoc on a plane, although the plane in the south tower videos with FL 175 entry resembles a hot knife piercing a tower with the resistance of soft butter.

The videos are absurd, perhaps explaining why their origins and cameramen remain mysterious. Since each tower gash was undersized for the entry of a 767, localized force applied by wing tips must have been insufficient to penetrate steel columns or spandrel plates. Video footage of a real jetliner should have shown repelled wreckage bounce to the ground. There was none in the videos and no reports of such wreckage we can find. A decelerating tail section would slow down, crumple and break off too, yet we saw not a trace of it. "The impact of the inner half of an empty wing significantly damaged exterior columns but did not result in their complete failure," NIST concedes (pdf, p. 105). In plainer terms, the hollow sections of the wings may damage steel columns but not fragment or break through them. Instead, the dense steel exterior of each tower would "reject" or "bounce back" so-called empty aluminum wings, especially the wing tips and outer sections.

Airplane crashes into buildings, especially steel skyscrapers, are rare events but there is some experience beyond airport terminal mishaps. The

Empire State building[41] and Tampa crashes[42] suggest that wings and tails break off, and even a fuselage does not penetrate far, at least at low speeds. Higher speeds increase kinetic energy and raise penetration power, but resistance by the Herculean towers would instantly dissipate this energy. A vertical dive by an El Al 747 cargo plane that must have weighed 300+ tons, twice the weight of an alleged 767 at a WTC tower, got the better of an approximately 12-story apartment building (with an abundance of debris and lack of wing outlines on the building's facade).[43]

Most of us would agree that planes are flimsy things, built to be lightweight, not resilient in a high-speed collision. As Marcus Icke points out: "Computer simulation and mathematical analysis of the impact by MIT, University of Purdue, and others indicate that upon impact the wings of the 767 would have shattered and the fuel ignited outside the tower's facade, the aircraft would have lost about twenty-five percent of its kinetic energy on impact and that the tail fin would have sheared off due to torsional forces. In layman's terms this means that the airplane would have decelerated sharply [emphasis added], crumpled up, and exploded against the tower's wall with only heavy objects like the engines and undercarriage puncturing the tower's facade. The entire airframe would not have glided through the outer wall and would not have left a large hole roughly the same shape and size of a Boeing 767–200." Ickes's accompanying photos support his analysis by showing an MD80 landing hard, with its airframe bending and tail breaking off.[44]

Jim Hoffman says, "In fact, jetliners are very light and fragile compared to buildings: they consist mostly of aluminum and have skin less than 2mm thick,"[45] but he tries to save the official theory with the following theory: "[T]he wing tips were shredded by the grating of meter-spaced columns."[46] This is the same story the NIST relies on to answer the implicit question: where is the wreckage? Why no debris? Wing tips, flaps, panels and tail allegedly shredded instead of fracturing and shearing off. Supposedly the assumed confetti then was deposited, absorbed or sucked inside the towers. This is an absurd proposition. Most steel beams and belt sections around the floors did not fail. Consequently, the wall must have rejected or repelled wing tips and tails because the gashes are seriously undersized. Hoffman offers no evidence for his "shred/wrap around" theory nor does he cite precedent from previous air crashes. A proposition about how wing tips might have breakable joints precisely placed to coincide with columns and belts, break and then wrap around and vanish is equally impossible. To put it as bluntly as possible: *All steel beam and belt sections that were "hit" and did not fragment must have rejected plane pieces and bounced them outside each tower, period.*

Suppose we explicitly enumerate the possibilities of a plane impact into a building by strength and speed. For simplicity, assume two possible values for airplane strength upon exterior impact (invincible or flimsy), two values for aircraft strength during penetration inside a WTC tower (invincible or flimsy) and two possible speed changes during the crash process (deceleration or no deceleration). The following eight combinations exhaust the possibilities:

1. Invincible/Invincible/No deceleration
2. Invincible/Invincible/Deceleration
3. Invincible/Flimsy/No deceleration
4. Invincible/Flimsy/Deceleration
5. Flimsy/Flimsy/No deceleration
6. Flimsy/Flimsy/Deceleration
7. Flimsy/Invincible/No deceleration
8. Flimsy/Invincible/Deceleration

Looking this pattern over, physics declares all the odd theories (1, 3, 5, 7) truly "odd" because they are impossible: a plane must decelerate at impact due to the laws of conservation of momentum and conservation of energy. Anyone who has ever dived into water realizes that his or her body slows down as it penetrates through the surface and begins to transfer momentum to the water.

Furthermore, physics rejects any theory that posits an invincible airplane (a plane remaining intact after a high speed collision with a steel skyscraper) that also disintegrates (flimsy) or shreds itself in the next instant in the same general physical environment (temperature, etc.) eliminating theories 3 and 4. Nor is theory 8 possible because a solid airplane cannot transform itself from flimsy to invincible, thereby eliminating theories 4 and 8. That leaves theories 2 and 6. Yet theory 2 is contrary to established facts including the fact that 767 aircraft are fragile rather than invincible and the holes in the towers were too small to allow passage of an intact 767 even if it were built to "invincible" standards. Theory 6 is physically possible but it implies crumpling upon impact and that is contrary to the WTC facts. *Conclusion: No Boeing 767 hit either WTC tower. QED*

In detail, we have:

Theory 1 is impossible because the 767 would fly through a tower and continue at the same speed, speeding out the other side like a .357 magnum bullet fired through 1 mm thick balsa wood. Further, a Boeing 767 cutting completely through a tower would seriously destabilize the tower by cutting substantial core sections and major sections of at least two walls. Theory 1 does not apply and is contrary to observation.

Theory 2 cannot apply for multiple reasons: i) the holes were too small to allow an intact 767 to pass through, ii) all parties agree 767s are not invincible and it is impossible to build them to such a standard; even the government felt obligated to produce photos of aircraft pieces, and iii) because of its large size relative to a tower, an intact 767 would almost certainly have been visible in a tower, on the ground below the impact hole or crashed at another site. All three observations contradict theory 2: undersized holes, agreed-upon impossibility of building an invincible plane, and no intact or crashed plane with its 3.1 million parts ever found in or around the Twin Towers.

Theory 3 is physically impossible because a solid like an airplane does not transform itself from invincible to flimsy within a fraction of a second in the same environment (temperature, etc.). Further, we would expect a sharp deceleration as the plane crumpled to fit into the 50 feet of space from the outer wall to the core.

As we peer into the hole, this wreckage cannot be seen.

Theory 4 is physically impossible because a solid like an airplane cannot transform itself from invincible to flimsy within an instant in the same general environment (temperature, etc.). Theory 4 posits deceleration, contrary to the videos. The government reports (FEMA/NIST) appear to support this impossible theory.

Theory 5 is physically impossible because a flimsy, high-speed object must decelerate sharply upon impacting an invincible object unless it acquires more energy from somewhere yet video evidence shows no deceleration.

Theory 6 is a logical, physically plausible combination that characterizes air disasters except for the four crashes within eighty minutes on the morning of 9/11. A 767 would be flimsy in a high-speed collision against a steel and concrete tower except for engines and undercarriage. Yet each tower had "clean" gashes free of airplane debris as if punctured by an invincible air vehicle. Flimsiness implies plenty of parts visible in gashes, elsewhere in each tower and on the ground below each impact site. These consequences of theory 6 are contrary to fact.

Theory 7 is physically impossible because a solid cannot transform itself from flimsy to invincible during a collision, given an essentially static environment. Further, a flimsy airplane must decelerate and fail to seriously penetrate a steel tower. Airplane pieces would be highly visible, contrary to observation.

Theory 8 is physically impossible because a solid cannot transform itself from flimsy to strong during a collision in a static environment. A flimsy airplane would decelerate but it would also leave visible debris, contrary to observation.

A skeptic might argue that Option 4 is possible because the plane would easily pierce the outer walls and then slow as it encountered more resistance further into the building. The problem with this is that it requires the plane to be slowing and/or disintegrating at the front while maintaining velocity in the rear.

But we're in luck! The government claims it has the rejoinder. NIST simulation videos purport to show how Theory 4 (Invincible/Flimsy/Deceleration), might have happened! Swaddled in twenty-million-dollar scientific trappings, this NIST flight of fantasy has some serious problems. First, NIST chooses Theory 4, a physical impossibility. Second, if that is not sufficient, NIST completely avoided modeling the official "progressive pancake collapse" theory for the obvious reason that such a model would conflict with all the data, especially near-free-fall-speed in all three skyscraper collapses. This omission signifies "the collapse of the pancake theory," as A.K. Dewdney says. Third, despite impressive computer power and a high level of detail, the magnitudes of the parameters were amped up by as much as twenty percent to get the desired results. Fourth, a simulation is only as good as the model (Garbage In/Garbage Out) so any engineer-modeler can play with the parameters and approximations until the desired result arrives. In the present case, they played plenty. By contrast, imagine NIST coming out with a model that found the invincible-penetration-then-obliteration theory contrary to physical law! Fifth, a model can only represent reality under given approximations and finite data. NIST denies curious scientists access to the model's proprietary codes and parameters so they cannot examine the model's behavior, especially against other data. Sixth, the time is barely readable on the two NIST videos and they cannot be downloaded for a frame-by-frame analysis with a regular PC. In short, a federal agency spends twenty million dollars and says, "Trust us."

Turning back to reality again, another physical problem for the official WTC theory is that the maximum spread across the north tower hole is 126 feet and the south tower spread is only 103 feet, openings insufficient to accommodate a 767 wingspan of 156 feet. And wings with momentum do not "fold back onto themselves" in order to slip through an undersized hole along with the fuselage. Momentum breaks wings off in a forward motion and they torque inward (pdf) during deceleration but there is no evidence that this happened.[47] Commenting on the Pentagon crash, Hoffman erroneously writes, "It would seem reasonable to assume that the wings and tail could have folded back and thereby avoided impacting those areas."[48] If I walk forward with my arms extended and bump into you, my arms would continue to move forward as my torso is stopped. Substitute fuselage for torso and the analogy is exact. Additionally, the forward thrust of the plane comes from the engines mounted on the wings. Engines thrusting near maximum power would continue pulling the wings *forward* as the fuselage collides, making a fold back doubly impossible. Also, the videos show no wing or tail fold-back, just intact entry.

The wings of a Boeing 767 are swept back approximately thirty-five degrees. This means wings would not strike a steel wall "flush" during the milliseconds of the crash process. Engines and wing roots impact first, almost simultaneously, and the wing tips, which are forty feet back, hit a fraction of a second later. The official theory must be that wing roots and engines break off steel columns and spandrel plates following penetration of the "powerful" nose and fuselage, while wings stay intact to burst subsequent columns, floors and spandrel plates further away from the fuselage. The only way for tips to reach into the building and enter the "Hoffman shredding stage" is for the wings to stay intact and plow or "saw" through the steel columns and floors like an angled carpenters cut during the progressive steel fragmentation process (thanks to Gerard Holmgren for this point). What's next? Aluminum instead of carbide blends to cut steel?

Science is nothing but refined common sense and this "sawing" theory is contrary to common sense. While a 767 would carry enormous "momentum" or kinetic energy at initial impact, resistance by steel columns, spandrel plates, floors and core would quickly consume its fixed energy supply because of tremendous resistance. A far more plausible sequence (virtually certain) would be that the violence of the collision and consequent deceleration would shatter and break airplane wing tips off based on empirical regularity alone in airplane crashes.

That leaves 767 proponents one hundred percent dependent on the shredding/wrap-around theory that all debris (a 767 has 3.1 million parts[49]) slipped neatly between columns and around the spandrel belt at each floor, as if vacuumed into the deep interior. That hypothesis lacks plausibility, positive evidence and precedent, among other defects. Wing spars[50] have considerable structural integrity in the vertical plane ("The wing tips were pulled up 15.5 feet from normal position over the top of the fuselage at a pressure of 1,200,000 pounds. The wing did not break . . ."[51]) and 767 wing disappearance on the impact walls is impossible without bigger gashes or perfect shredding and wrap around.

For the sake of argument, suppose that a plane's aluminum skin and frame were strong enough unaided to demolish braced steel walls and leave a tidy outline for "the folks to see." In addition to steel walls and multiple steel/concrete floors, within a tenth of a second the airliner would encounter resistance from a dense core occupying twenty-seven percent of each tower's floor space with forty-seven high-strength, cross-braced steel columns, three stair wells, multiple elevator shafts, and mechanical equipment within sixty feet of the WTC-1 impact wall and thirty-seven feet of the WTC-2 wall. Even a sturdy "knife slicer" aircraft would not travel far against such dense resistance. The energy to demolish the local steel and concrete of a tower is transferred from speed and the plane itself must slow because it has no new source of energy.

At 159 feet long a Boeing 767 is almost seventy-seven percent as long as any side of a tower, and planes do not crumple like accordions. Real terrorists would have flown much larger 747s into lower floors later in the day to maximize destruction and loss of life, but the 747 at 211.5' wide and 232' long would have been impossible to "sell" as vanishing. With smaller 767s anyone who thought about it for a minute nodded and said, "Oh I see, they disappeared inside. That figures."

Defenders of the 767 theory want to have their cake and eat it too: supposedly powerful aluminum 767s, wings and all, instantly bored through steel walls and floors yet crumbled in the next instant and vanished despite fuselage length and wingspan nearly the length of a tower wall. Both 767s were never seen again from any side of either tower, a dazzling combination of powerful entry and disintegration within a tenth of a second.

The two end points—easy tower penetration at high speed without visible deceleration and flight termination within 200 feet—are nonsense.

Faith in the Big Boeing Theory rests on two huge planes disintegrating completely into small pieces inside each tower, concealing all plane parts. The immense difficulty with this idea, also favored by the NIST, is how to reconcile an aluminum aircraft punching through steel in its path followed immediately by complete failure within 0.1 seconds, shredding completely and vanishing. The plane image at the south tower should have decelerated in the videos and plane parts like wing tips should have bounced off the wall and many of the 3.1 million parts should have been visible in the gashes. We did not see that. The government theory is impossible to accept unless the plane was rigged to explode or disintegrate upon contact with the wall, somehow facilitating its thorough destruction within. That might restore some plausibility to the 767 story but it is certainly not the government story. Such explosives would add immense complexity for the perpetrators in an already-complex crime package, violating the KISS rule. The basic problem remains that a large commercial jetliner could not punch a clean, debris-free hole into a steel tower wall to begin with. The plane would need plenty of help, explosive help of its own and/or explosives from inside the building. Even the explosions that occurred in the towers blew no aircraft parts out the tower gashes to settle below the impact walls. The planted parts on the ground near the WTC were on the opposite side of the impacts.

With respect to the south tower, it was astounding that the 9/11 maestros reproduced such wide-body aluminum magic within sixteen minutes in the same city block. If anything, more of the vaunted 767 should have been visible in the south tower because it was only thirty-seven feet to the core, barely more than a "1st and 10." UA 175 supposedly hit the south tower at 543 m.p.h. or higher, although air resistance makes this is a suspect speed for a 767 at sea level in the absence of a dive. The NIST report (pdf, p. 92) asserts a nearly flat approach with a descent angle of only six degrees below horizontal. UA 175 allegedly sliced through a hole two-thirds the wingspan of a 767, dumped abundant fuel in a spectacular fireball out the east side, keeping wings and tail section intact, and disappeared within the tower. After its silent entry into the south tower, UA 175's remaining kinetic energy dissipated within a quarter second and proved insufficient to penetrate the east or north wall. Apparently we are supposed to believe that a plane can penetrate a wall displaying no resistance, yet not penetrate an identical wall on the way out. Maybe the WTC architects created one-way plane-proof walls. Somebody call the patent office before others file first. We're going to be rich!

A minor eyebrow-raiser was the thirty-eight-degree banking angle implied by the angle of the south tower hole. Such a banking angle ordinarily would imply a left-hand turn north in the last few seconds but it would take a skilled pilot at the controls of a cumbersome jetliner, to say the least, to hit the 207' span at the alleged 543 m.p.h.

In summary:

There is no convincing physics for how two wide-body aluminum jetliners flying at high speed could glide through steel walls, concrete/steel floors and concrete/steel core via undersized gashes and no deceleration in videos, and then stop within a fifth of a second, disappearing without a trace.

What about the plane parts the government found? Engines and landing gear could have flown out of either tower, although we seem to lack solid eyewitness testimony and video evidence of large parts flying out. Perhaps the FBI will soon open its warehouse of evidence and verify the serial numbers from the time-change parts. Spencer suspects that a canister was propelled from the north-east corner of the South Tower with "debris" to support the passenger plane hoax.[52] Some photos and videos show unidentified objects shooting out, for example, p. 39 in Hufschmid's *Painful Questions*. The FBI and FEMA—a black ops agency with virtually no investigative expertise then headed by George W. Bush campaign manager and family loyalist Joe Allbaugh—displayed a few parts during their felonious mission to destroy crime-scene evidence. None of the parts are consistent with 767 crashes (substantial sections of unburned fuselage,[53] a 737 engine part, a piece of unburned landing gear) nor have they been independently verified and matched by serial number against the maintenance logs of the specified aircraft. One piece is a 737 engine part (CFM 56),[54] according to aircraft experts, rather than from a 767.[55] By contrast, the authorities found an alleged hijacker's paper passport that survived a fiery crash, subsequent fire and tower demolition. Its purpose obviously was to tell a bloodthirsty America whom to hate.

The 9/11 planners understood the physics of crashing aluminum jetliners into the steel towers. Logically enough, they did not rely on commercial 767s like backward "Arab terrorists" might. No, the deceivers used more reliable technology to get the desired special effects to foment war and its insider benefits.

Sorting out theories of "what really happened" awaits another day but note that nothing we have written here constitutes an endorsement of any particular alternative theory to the official 757/767 Big Boeing Theory lies. To reassure a few people out there, we want to state skepticism about the most controversial, "holograms," based on the implausibility of successfully projecting 3-D holograms of large commercial aircraft flying at high speed on a sunlit morning.[56] We seem to lack solid evidence that such break-through stealth technology existed or was used. We are not experts but understand that the big impediment would be a 360-degree display surface to project the deception to witnesses and cameras.

Video Fakery

All WTC videos showing butter-smooth entry into the south tower are fake because they show impossible physics in a collision between a plane and a steel tower. Skeptics need only watch the "non-collision" between FL 175 and WTC-2 frame by frame and see the absurdity of the plane acting like a hot knife entering a massive steel tower with the resistance of sponge cake. We can be easily fooled by special effects.[57] The videos show no deceleration, have well-timed zoom-outs by "amateurs," grainy planes with artificial-appearing lighting, a United airliner that looks pitch black in profile and on its underside on a brilliant sunny morning (or silver on its underside!), frame to frame deformation in tails-wings-engines-body, disappearing wings and stabilizers in single frames (which may be only interlacing effects), discolored sky in some frames, soundless impacts, planes morphing into liquid-like buildings without metal-to-metal smashing, premature and off-center flashes or explosions, and explosions and squibs near and far from the impact (we believe the last!). The footage was faked either by blue screen or computer graphic inserts.

Eyewitness testimony about a high-speed Boeing 767 flying the length of Manhattan at an altitude of about one thousand feet and crashing into the North Tower may be scarce, but we have a "lucky" video: "Two French documentary filmmakers are filming a documentary on New York City firefighters about ten blocks from the WTC. One of them hears a roar, looks up, and captures a distant image of the first WTC crash."[58] These fortunate Frenchmen were perfectly situated only ten blocks north of the tower and filmed the plane at low altitude, although it seems a distant image.[59] Despite top-notch equipment used by the pros, it's impossible to make out what the flying image or inject on the screen is frame-by-frame. Not surprisingly, it's been tagged a whazzit, blurry blob and flying pig. Any amateur would have gotten a clearer image.[60] Whatever the flying object is, it does not look like a commercial airliner to us. Was there an actual aircraft or projectile of some kind? We don't know, but if there was, someone tampered with the pixels so that no one can identify it in the video. Just like the five Pentagon parking lot frames dated September 12, the north tower video conceals more than it reveals.

Scientific Cover Up

Why would scientists at FEMA, NIST, Purdue University and MIT lie? The answers are simple:

- They are government employees, consultants or federally-funded scientists paid to arrive at a predetermined conclusion for their client, the government.
- Unlike impartial scientists who weigh one theory versus another for logic and evidence, theories supported by evidence that points to explosives, demolition and non-Big-Boeing causation are neither discussed nor discredited. They are simply ignored. While every theory does not require careful analysis, ignoring promising alternative theories is scientifically dishonest.

Responding to Critics

The government's story about 767s crashing into the twin towers is a sacred cow, even among 9/11 skeptics, so we expected lots of criticism when the first version of this paper appeared on March 5th 2006. Yet we have received little. Silence has been the main response but five issues seem to be the main areas of concern:

1. We're not video experts, so what do we know? TV fakery is impossible and besides, it would be impossible to fake over thirty videos.

   A) True, we're not video experts but it's easy for anyone to prove that any version of FL 175 entering WTC-2 is fake: just go frame-by-frame and watch the plane image meld into the building. Da, da, dat . . . dat's all folks! It's a cartoon. No wings breaking up, no tail breaking off, no flap or panel bouncing off, no nothing, just a smooth, silent entry into a massive steel tower built to withstand category-5 hurricanes. It's rubbish.

   B) TV inserts are common. Look at the "first-and-ten" yard marker on NFL broadcasts and inserted billboard ads. Real time inserts of pre-planned images are quite "real" (feasible).[61] While the controlled media still cover some news, they fabricate the rest.

   C) On the contrary, all the videos show a physically impossible aircraft entry into a steel skyscraper, therefore they must be fake.

2. There was a slowdown in the videos.

A) The videos are fakes, see 1 above, so it hardly matters whether they show deceleration or not.

B) So much the worse for the videos—among other blunders—they do not show significant deceleration, a serious defect. For example, a frame-by-frame analysis of the Fairbanks video and the Myers photographs show that the speed of the plane in the videos or pictures decelerates somewhere between zero and four percent when being as generous as possible to deceleration potential. A less generous pixel-by-pixel analysis shows the speed actually increasing between zero and two percent.[62]

3. It's the kinetic energy, stupid!

   Sorry, there was too much building to absorb 767-level kinetic energy and besides, the high-energy theory destroys itself because a truly "energetic" 767 could not destroy itself within WTC-2 after such slick penetration. A 767 traveling at 530+ m.p.h. would have approximately four billion joules. This number is impressive, but produces a contradiction in the official story: the South Tower image exhibited, at most, a four percent deceleration in velocity. Let's say the numbers are off by a factor of two and it's actually eight percent, yielding a bigger slowdown. Using the kinetic energy equation, an eight percent slowdown would still have eighty-five percent of its kinetic energy available once the plane was completely in the building. Are we to assume that the remaining eighty-five percent is insufficient to escape out the other side? If we move to a more reasonable two percent observed slowdown, there would be 96 percent of the original kinetic energy available. Amazingly, four billion joules of energy will get a plane into the building but not eject it out the other side.

4. The Garage Door Theory posits that explosives or thermite on board the plane and/or in the tower blew an opening sufficient to allow an intact Boeing jetliner 767 to enter, whereupon the fragile plane disintegrated within.

   A) There is no evidence for the theory, for example, no explosions pave the way for Boeing entry in the videos (despite a "flash") and no exploded plane debris was observed on the ground below the impact walls nor in the gash in either tower. Timing would be virtually impossible. The planners would have avoided such a risky psy-op scheme if only because the controlled media were available to spin any airplane story desired.

B) The gashes in both towers were too small to allow a 767 to enter, no matter how created. Even the wingspan of a 737 (112' 7") exceeded the 103' opening in the south tower. Thus, the same problems exist regarding lack of plane debris.

5. Some eyewitnesses say they saw an airliner crash into the south tower.

A) Purported eyewitness testimony that contradicts the laws of physics and the physical facts is worse than worthless.

B) Many eyewitnesses saw no planes, heard no jetliners and some claim that the initial explosion at each tower came from within.

C) Psy-op planners not only plant evidence but also hire actors and pay people to lie.

D) Memories are remarkably malleable and "one of the cleverest and most powerful techniques for planting highly implausible false memories involves the use of fake photographs."[63]

E) Drones, missiles, and other aircraft can be disguised to look like airliners.

F) Given all the conflicting reports, eyewitness testimony presently is inconclusive.

Conclusion

On 9/11 we had four astonishing, unverified and uninvestigated crashes. The airlines refuse to look at evidence that their planes did not crash as advertised.[64] Wreckage at the four sites was virtually nonexistent and no parts were verified by serial number despite this routine ID method in aircraft accident investigations. Government claims two Boeing 767s disappeared into the twin towers within a 16.5-minute interval, a Boeing 757 disappeared in the Pentagon, and another 757 crashed in rural Pennsylvania. All supposedly vanished through undersized holes. How stupid is that? Gullible Americans believed George W. Bush and marched off to war. "What fools these mortals be," Shakespeare wrote.

At the WTC two Boeing 767s reportedly smashed through dense steel walls, steel-concrete floors and a dense steel core without a sound or deceleration and shredded themselves into nothing with virtually all "crumbs" retained within the skyscrapers. We have no reliable reports about all the 767 debris that should have been seen by occupants within each tower (82 tons of airplane, dry weight, with 3.1 million parts). Despite 767s three-fourths as long and wide as each tower side, both WTC "airliners" disappeared without breaking off a tail section, fuselage or wing tips upon impact.[65]

These are physically impossible crashes. Airplanes do not exhibit completely different physical behaviors within one-twentieth of a second at a given place. They cannot be insuperable and shatter without slowing down in the next instant.

If the government wanted to prove that specific hijacked airliners crashed as advertised, it could show the time-change parts that uniquely identify each aircraft. Government could show the NSA and/or commercial satellite photos of the airliners going about their deadly business that morning. It could show dozens of Pentagon videos it is hiding, flight data recorders, cockpit voice recorders, and so much more. There is no chance, of course, of the perpetrators voluntarily doing anything of the sort. Fabricating more evidence at this point is risky for them too. The release of the Pentagon "video" was a fiasco. There are too many sharp analysts on the internet waiting to pounce.

The WTC demolitions are a proven fact and the official 9/11 airliner tales are hogwash, as proven here. Once again, the emperor's raiment is not in evidence. What really happened? We cannot say with real conviction. What is clear is that the government is lying about the four reported Big Boeing crashes.

We might never figure out exactly what happened with the four crashes/explosion events although every month we advance our knowledge and perhaps one day the controlled media, Congress or a public prosecutor, seized by a sense of responsibility, will tap this growing body of research, thereby igniting probes that lead to justice. Failing that, 9/11 researchers have already convicted the perpetrators before the bar of history. Disgraced, the murderers will not get away with the crime of the century. The Bush-Cheney-Rumsfeld cabal lives in infamy.

Notes

1. http://www.democraticunderground.com/discuss/duboard.php?az=show_mesg&forum=125&topic_id=12490&mesg_id=13789&page, http://team8plus.org/e107_plugins/content/content.php?content.16, http://www.911dossier.co.uk/attabag.html, http://www.whatreallyhappened.com/atta_9-11.html.
2. http://oldsydimc.cat.org.au/front.php3?article_id=36354.
3. http://www.faa.gov/about/office_org/headquarters_offices/avs/offices/afs/afs700/.
4. Ibid.
5. http://www.911closeup.com/index.shtml?ID=65.
6. http://www.wingtv.net/thornarticles/911passengerlist.html.
7. http://www.arcticbeacon.citymaker.com/articles/article.cfm/1518131/37580.
8. http://www.physics911.net/projectachilles.htm.
9. http://news.bbc.co.uk/1/hi/world/americas/1556096.stm.
10. http://www.pentagonresearch.com/098.html.
11. Also see pilot Ralph Omholt, ibid., for confirmation.
12. http://nomoregames.net/index.php?page=911&subpage1=vaporized_plane_theories.
13. http://www.fas.org/man/dod-101/sys/smart/bgm-109.htm.
14. http://members.iinet.net.au/~holmgren/witness.html.
15. http://www.maebrussell.com/9-11/Dear%20World%20Watcher.html.
16. Jim Marrs, Inside Job: Unmasking the 9/11 Conspiracies (San Rafael: Origin, 2006), second edition, Appendix A.
17. http://www.cnn.com/2005/WORLD/africa/10/23/nigeria.plane/.
18. http://911review.com/errors/pentagon/index.html.
19. http://www.signs-of-the-times.org/signs/hoffman_rebuttal.htm.
20. http://members.iinet.net.au/~holmgren/witness.html.
21. http://69.28.73.17/hoffman.html.
22. http://www.thoughtcrimenews.com/flight93notscheduled.htm.
23. http://thewebfairy.com/killtown/flight93.html#WCPO.
24. http://www.rense.com/general56/flfight.htm.
25. http://thewebfairy.com/911/93/noplane.htm.
26. http://thewebfairy.com/911/93/mayor1.htm.
27. http://911review.org/Wiki/Flight93Somerset.shtml.
28. http://thewebfairy.com/killtown/flight93.html#WCPO.
29. http://911review.org/Wiki/Flight93Somerset.shtml.
30. http://www.theage.com.au/articles/2002/09/09/1031115990570.html?oneclick=true.
31. http://www.post-gazette.com/headlines/20011015newsmaker1015p2.asp.
32. http://www.wingtv.net/flight93.html.
33. http://911review.com/attack/flights/f93.html.
34. http://wtc.nist.gov/pubs/NISTNCSTAR1Draft.pdf.
35. http://www.infoplease.com/spot/wtc1.html.
36. http://www.engr.psu.edu/ae/WTC/APAstanehReport.htm.
37. http://www.airdisaster.com/photos/tans222/photo.shtml.

38. http://www.airdisaster.com/photos/sq006/photo.shtml.
39. http://www.airdisaster.com/photos/n571pe/2.shtml.
40. http://www.car-accidents.com/pages/accident_story/11-11-04.html, http://www.car-accidents.com/pages/accident_story/11-1-04.html.
41. http://history1900s.about.com/od/1940s/a/empirecrash.htm, http://www.damninteresting.com/?p=179.
42. http://archives.cnn.com/2002/US/01/06/tampa.crash/.
43. http://www.airdisaster.com/photos/elal1862/photo.shtml.
44. http://dialspace.dial.pipex.com/prod/dialspace/town/pipexdsl/q/aqrf00/ggua175/.
45. http://911research.wtc7.net/pentagon/analysis/conclusions/damage.html.
46. http://911research.wtc7.net/wtc/evidence/aircraft.html.
47. http://www.engineering-eye.com/AUTODYN/customer/paper/pdf/ESHP_1.pdf.
48. http://911research.wtc7.net/pentagon/analysis/conclusions/damage.html.
49. http://www.photovault.com/Link/Technology/Aviation/FlightCommercial/Aircraft/Boeing767.html.
50. http://www.physics911.net/missingwings.htm
51. http://www.photovault.com/Link/Technology/Aviation/FlightCommercial/Aircraft/Boeing767.html.
52. http://www.serendipity.li/wot/spencer06.htm#further_evidence.
53. http://911hoax.com/gFuselageDebris.asp?intPage=29&PageNum=29.
54. http://www.rense.com/general65/911b.htm.
55. http://www.airdisaster.com/photos/ca129/5.shtml.
56. http://www.gallerize.com/What_Is_The_Hologram_Theory.htm.
57. http://www.media-criticism.com/911_video_fakes_01_2004.html.
58. http://www.cooperativeresearch.org/timeline.jsp?timeline=complete_911_timeline&day_of_9/11=aa11.
59. http://www.serendipity.li/wot/naudet/raphael.htm.
60. http://members.iinet.net.au/~holmgren/planevideos.html.
61. http://www.nodeception.com/articles/pixel.jsp.
62. Deceleration analysis from Rick Rajter is forthcoming at http://nomoregames.net. In the meantime, see http://nomoregames.net/index.php?page=911&subpage1=deceleration_WTC2_myers.
63. http://faculty.washington.edu/eloftus/Articles/2003Nature.pdf
64. http://www.prisonplanet.tv/articles/september2004/300904refusestoview.htm.
65. http://www.911closeup.com/index.shtml?ID=79.

References

Griffin, David Ray. *The New Pearl Harbor*. Northampton, Massachusetts: Olive Branch, 2004.

Marrs, Jim. *Inside Job: Unmasking the 9/11 Conspiracies*. San Rafael: Origin, 2004.

Tarpley, Webster G. *9/11 Synthetic Terror: Made in USA*. Joshua Tree: Progressive, 2005.

The 9/11 Commission Report: Final Report of the National Commission on Terrorist Attacks Upon the United States. Washington, D.C.: U.S. Government Printing Office, 2004.

Thompson, Paul. *The Terror Timeline*. New York: Regan, 2004.

The Pentagon unofficially "released" five frames from a video of the alleged hit. They have the wrong date and time, but conveniently identify the first frame as "plane" and the other as a series of "impacts." As Jack White has observed on page 81, if the tail had been the tail of a Boing 757, the plane, which is more than twice as long as the building is tall, would have been conspicuous. In his books, 9/11: The Big Lie *(2002) and* Pentagate *(2002), Thierry Meyssan emphasizes the difference in the kind of explosion that occurred here and that occurred at the Twin Towers. The Pentagon explosion appears to be a detonation with high energetic power.*

PART III: WHAT DOES IT MEAN?

7

The "War on Terrorism": A Double Fraud on Humanity

Elias Davidsson

Shortly after the mass murder[1] of 11th September 2001, the United States administration announced a global "war on terrorism" that knows no borders or time limits. Numerous states have since broadened police powers of secret surveillance, house and body searches, detention without trial and have defined new types of offences as "terrorist acts." Yet the factual premises to justify such radical assault on constitutional and human rights have not been produced. The "war on terrorism" is legally dubious and factually unjustified.

Among the effects of the major scourges affecting the international community, the harmful effects of "retail terrorism"[2] seem almost trivial compared to the "wholesale terrorism" committed by states, child mortality, civil wars, extreme poverty, illiteracy, environmental degradation, third-world debt, lack of clean water, hunger, AIDS, drug abuse, child prostitution and common murder. Any person is more likely to die from a lightning strike than from terrorism.[3] Drunken drivers cause a thousand times more deaths than terrorists, yet no one has claimed that these drivers threaten international peace and security.[4] Terrorism only appears as a global threat because governments say so and because mass media amplify this phenomenon beyond reasonable proportions.

In this essay it will be argued that the "war on terrorism" is not only a deceptive concept—in fact an oxymoron—represents but itself a form of terror. By designating terrorism as a global conspiracy threatening to attack anywhere and at any time, whole populations are terrorized to fear the unknown and consent to increased surveillance, security measures, and restrictions of liberties. The events of 9/11, as presented by the mass media, provided the necessary shock to prepare the American and West European public for supporting wars against other nations and accept increased police surveillance.[5] By exposing the "war on terrorism" as a fraud and the

9/11 crime as its fraudulent justification, it will be easier to mobilize public resistance against further wars and the creeping emergence of a totalitarian world order.[6]

The Genesis of the "War on Terrorism"

The etymology of the word terrorism can be traced to Robespierre and his "règne de la terreur," namely government intimidation of the People.[7] Today, the term is mainly used by states to create public fear against an elusive international conspiracy.[8] Yet the original meaning of the word terrorism, reflecting a state policy, is still employed by concerned scholars, such as Noam Chomsky, Ed Herman, and others. The vague concept of terrorism ("one person's terrorist is another person's freedom fighter") has prevented the adoption of an internationally recognized definition.[9] A less publicized point of contention is whether government policies intended to coerce or terrorize civilian populations by military attacks or economic sanctions (or the threat thereof) should be designated as terrorism.[10] The Statute of the International Criminal Court does not include terrorism on its list of international crimes.[11]

Through National Security Directive No. 179 of 20th July 1985, a high level US "Task Force on Combatting Terrorism" was established[12]. The rationale for this measure at the time was that "[i]nternational terrorism poses an increasing threat to US citizens and our interests. Terrorists are waging a war against, not only the United States, but all civilized society in which innocent civilians are intentional victims and our servicemen are specific targets." Yet, according to Joanna Bourke, "just seventeen people were killed by terrorists in America between 1980 and 1985."[13]

Even before the events of 9/11, the annual federal budget of the United States for combating terrorism had reached sums exceeding six billion dollars.[14] The budget of the FBI Counterterrorism program alone grew from $78.5 million in 1993 to $301.2 million in 1999,[15] a year in which six (6) Americans died worldwide of terrorist acts.[16]

Merely hours after the aircraft crashed in the United States on September 11th, 2001 (hereafter 9/11) before any evidence could be examined, "federal authorities" designated the main suspect: Osama bin Laden, the alleged head of al-Qa'ida.[17] Within three days the FBI claimed to have identified the nineteen "hijackers" and the links established between them and al-Qa'ida.[18]

The new existential enemy of "Western civilization" was now created, profitably replacing the former Soviet threat. This threat, as will be shown below, was a myth crafted carefully by intelligence services,[19] nurtured since then by mass media[20] and accepted uncritically by numerous authors and scholars. As a result of the events of 9/11, as presented by the media, "al-Qa'ida" became almost overnight the subject of innumerable books, studies, articles and comments, vying to analyze and demonstrate the workings of this elusive conspiracy.[21] Yet there is no credible evidence for the claim that "al-Qa'ida" was responsible for the crime of 9/11, nor is it certain that there exists, at all, an organization by the name of al-Qa'ida,[22] or whether the trademark al-Qa'ida merely refers to a CIA project of covert operations using Arab or Muslim patsies.[23]

The mass murder of 9/11 permitted the US administration to justify a new military doctrine of the pre-emptive use of force anywhere in the world in the name of an unlimited war against terrorism.[24] Secretary of Defense Donald H. Rumsfeld expounded this new strategy before it became official US policy. It was, for example, described in *The New York Times* of 27th September 2001 under the heading "A New Kind of War"[25] and in his speech to the North Atlantic Council on 18th December 2001.[26]

Later, Rumsfeld hinted the "war on terrorism" would never stop:

> I think we will eventually sufficiently damage the so-called al-Qa'ida terrorist network that it will not be able to function. But there are many other terrorist networks and people will form new groups. Just as we go to school on them, they go to school on us. As they see us do certain things they change their techniques and change how they're attacking and keep looking for themes or vulnerabilities or asymmetrical ways to damage us.[27]

Asked by a member of the audience "when you look two or three years down the road, do you have a picture in your mind as to how the war on terrorism comes to an end and what the end looks like?" Rumsfeld answered:

> On the assumption that human nature is not going to change dramatically in that period of time, one has to assume that there will be people who will be teaching the kind of thing that's being taught in too many Madrasas and too many locations around the world, that there will still be people who will be looking for ways to damage the West, the United States, and free people.
>
> Clearly a terrorist can attack at any time, any place, using any technique, and it's physically not possible to defend it every time in every place against every technique. . . . It is that co-operation

> across the globe that is putting pressure on terrorists. It does not mean that there will not be additional terrorist attacks that are successful. There will be. And there will be in country after country. There will be a lot fewer than there otherwise would have been.[28]

He also hinted at the value of the 9/11 mass murder for US global leadership:

> Citizens of more than eighty nations died that day,[29] And citizens of every nation saw, in an instant, that the threat of terrorism is no longer confined by borders, in either its origin or the targets of its deadly acts. In the global war against terrorism, President Bush has assembled the largest coalition in the history of mankind. The scope of this alliance is truly breathtaking in its breadth and its depth. Some ninety nations—nearly half of the countries on the face of the earth—are participating in the global war on terrorism.[30]

To sum up, the US Secretary of Defense forecast that there will be additional, successful, terrorist attacks "in country after country" and that "people will form new [terrorist] groups," whose primary motive will be "to damage the West, the United States, and free people." In his testimony, delivered before the House and Senate Armed Services Committees regarding Iraq on 18th September 2002, he emphasized this forecast: "Let there be no doubt: an attack will be attempted. The only question is when and by what technique. It could be months, a year, or several years. But it will happen. It is in our future."[31] To ensure that attacks would happen, he proposed the creation of a new organization, the Proactive, Pre-emptive Operations Group (P2OG), which would carry out secret missions to "stimulate reactions" among terrorist groups, to provoke them to commit acts that could be used to justify massive attacks by the US forces.[32]

The Crime of 9/11 Catalyzes Public Opinion

US media, as exemplified by an editorial in *Time* magazine, compared 9/11 to the attack on Pearl Harbor and urged a similar response: "A day cannot live in infamy without the nourishment of rage. Let's have rage. What's needed is a unified, unifying Pearl Harbor sort of purple American fury."[33] The report "Rebuilding America's Defenses" issued by the Project for a New American Century (PNAC), a right-wing institution established by Donald Rumsfeld, Richard Cheney, Paul Wolfowitz, Elliot Abrams, Jeb Bush and other neo-fascists,[34] suggested a year before 9/11 that "some catastrophic and catalyzing event—like a new Pearl Harbor" could speed up the "revolutionary" process of transforming the US military into "tomorrow's dominant force."[35]

The "new Pearl Harbor," needed to speed up the "revolutionary" transformation of the US defence establishment, materialized, as if by miracle, on 11th September 2001. Almost three thousand people died in this carefully planned, perfectly executed and dramatically publicized act of mass murder.[36] The 9/11 events caused a threefold surge in public support for increased defense spending and "a thirty percentage point increase in the number of *mothers* who felt that missile defense was a good idea post-9/11."[37] Support swelled for a "strong" Bush presidency as well as confidence in the government and the media. "Four out of five Americans are ready to give up some of their freedoms in return for more security; nearly half worry about becoming victims of a terrorist attack. [Attorney General John] Ashcroft has done his work well."[38]

Creating public fear permitted legislators to extend law-enforcement powers to a new category of individuals ("suspected terrorists") who could now be lawfully monitored, searched and detained without warrant.[39] The model legislation for such new police powers was the so-called USA Patriot Act, adopted in the United States shortly after 9/11.[40] Although the Act was criticized by human rights organisations, further restrictions to human rights (in the name of fighting against terrorism) were envisaged. Preventive law-enforcement, a policy that requires permanent surveillance of entire social, political, or ethnic groups,[41] is now increasingly applied by numerous governments under various pretexts, such as the need to fight terrorism, money laundering, child prostitution, or drug smuggling.[42]

Colin Powell, former US Secretary of State, admitted in 2004 that due to the disappearance of the Soviet bloc, the US was "running out of enemies," thus reducing the readiness of the public to maintain a high level of expenditures on defense-related services and products.[43] A new policy of fear-mongering was urgently needed to keep the military and the corporations happy. The events of 9/11 just happened to fulfil that role.[44]

In terms of foreign policy goals pursued by the neo-fascists in the US administration, the events of 9/11 provided invaluable, long-sought, opportunities, such as to create US client regimes in Afghanistan[45] and Iraq. Richard Clarke, former US Counterterrorism Co-ordinator, reported how eager US leaders were to use the events of 9/11 as justification for a war on Iraq, without even bothering to inquire who committed the atrocities.

He reported that when he returned to a conference in the White House at 2:00 A.M. on 12th September 2001:

> I walked into a series of discussions about Iraq. At first I was incredulous that we were talking about something other than getting Al Qaeda. Then I realized with almost a sharp physical pain that Rumsfeld and Wolfowitz were going to try to take advantage of this national tragedy to promote their agenda about Iraq . . . On [that] morning . . . [the] focus was already beginning to shift from Al Qaeda . . . Later in the day, Secretary Rumsfeld complained that there were no decent targets for bombing in Afghanistan and that we should consider bombing Iraq, which, he said, had better targets. At first I thought Rumsfeld was joking. But he was serious and the President did not reject out of hand the idea of attacking Iraq.[46]

Was the Crime of 9/11 a Case of International Terrorism?

On 12th September 2001, the UN Security Council adopted a resolution condemning the mass murder of 9/11 as an act of *international* terrorism.[47] The Council was not presented with any evidence proving that the crime was instigated from outside the United States. On 2nd October 2001, the US Ambassador at Large and Co-ordinator for Counter-terrorism, Frank Taylor, gave an *oral* presentation to the North Atlantic Council, NATO's top decision-making body.[48] On the basis of this presentation the Council "determined that the individuals who carried out the attacks belonged to the world-wide terrorist network of Al-Qaida, headed by Osama bin Laden and protected by the Taleban regime in Afghanistan."[49] Whatever evidence was presented then remains to this day secret.[50] Recalling the lies told by US administration officials and by British Premier Tony Blair regarding alleged Iraqi weapons of mass destruction,[51] one is entitled to remain sceptical about the quality of the evidence presented to NATO, let alone to the world at large, about the responsibility of any person or group in Afghanistan for the attacks of 9/11.

The US administration has failed to produce any evidence proving that al-Qaeda members, or even any Muslims, actually boarded the four aircraft that were allegedly flown onto the known landmarks on 9/11. Items of evidence the US administration could and should have produced to prove its case, but failed to produce, include, *inter alia*,

- the original passenger lists of the four allegedly hijacked aircraft (on which the names of the alleged hijackers would appear);[52]
- coupons of boarding cards (with the names of the alleged hijackers on them);
- payment records for purchased flight tickets (with names and credit card numbers of the alleged hijackers);
- testimonies of individuals who saw the passengers and alleged hijackers board the aircraft;
- hijackers' bodily remains.

Until the year 2006, the US authorities refused to release video evidence in their possession proving that flight AA77 crashed into the Pentagon. The reasoning offered for refusing to release this evidence was that it "would reasonably be expected to interfere with enforcement proceedings."[53] On 16th May 2006, the Pentagon released what American media described as "the first video images of American Airlines Flight 77 crashing into" the Pentagon. It is, however, impossible to distinguish an aircraft from this video, let alone to identify it. The Pentagon still refuses to release eighty-four other videos it apparently possesses from that day.[54]

Shortly after 9/11, British and Arab media reported that at least five of the nineteen individuals listed by the FBI as the "hijackers" (Abdulaziz Alomari, Wail al-Shehri, Salem al-Hazmi, Saeed al-Ghamdi and Ahmed al-Nami) were still living.[55] FBI Director Robert S. Mueller admitted twice on CNN (20th and 27th September 2001) that there is "no legal proof to prove the identities of the suicidal hijackers."[56] Yet, the FBI maintains on its website the names and photographs of the "living suicide hijackers" as if its own doubts about the "hijackers'" identities were of no consequence.[57] What proof is there that the alleged hijackers, if any, were Muslims at all and had any relation to al-Qa'ida, if their identities are even in doubt? The 9/11 Commission established by President George W. Bush, which purported to provide "the fullest possible account of the events surrounding 9/11,"[58] glossed entirely over this question.

Dismissing the need to prove US allegations on the responsibility of al-Qa'ida and Osama bin Laden for the mass murder of 9/11, Donald Rumsfeld contends that "in the age of weapons of mass destruction," standards of evidence sufficient to prove guilt "beyond a reasonable doubt"[59] are not appropriate:

> We still do not know with certainty who was behind the 1996 bombing of the Khobar Towers in Saudi Arabia—an attack that killed nineteen American service members. We still do not know who is responsible for last year's anthrax attacks. The nature of terrorist attacks is that it is often very difficult to identify who is ultimately responsible. Indeed, our consistent failure over the past two decades to trace terrorist attacks to their ultimate source gives terrorist states the lesson that using terrorist networks as proxies is an effective way of attacking the US with impunity."[60]

One of the characteristics of terrorism is, however, the intent of the perpetrators to attain a political gain through the threat or use of violence against civilians.[61] The primary aim of a terrorist is not to cause harm for its own sake, but to make a forceful, violent, political statement. In order for the message to be driven home, the terrorists must claim authorship. Violent acts, such as bombings and aircraft hijackings, which are claimed by no one (or are claimed by dubious, anonymous, groups), must be presumed to be "false flag" operations by intelligence services. Such covert operations are committed in order to destabilize enemy governments, strain relations between states, justify foreign military intervention or cast blame on an "enemy."[62]

The US government has not only failed to prove Osama bin Laden and al-Qa'ida's responsibility for 9/11 but actually did not relish having the events of 9/11 investigated. Merely twenty-four hours after the deadliest crime on US soil, Attorney General John D. Ashcroft made it clear that the priority was to "stop another attack," not to investigate the crime committed on the previous day. Bob Woodward and Dan Balz of the *Washington Post* reported that at a meeting of the National Security Council, convened by President George W. Bush in the White House's Cabinet Room in the morning of 12th September 2001,

> FBI Director Robert S. Mueller III began to describe the investigation underway to identify those responsible for hijacking the four airplanes the day before . . . But Attorney General John D. Ashcroft interrupted him. Let's stop the discussion right here, he said. The chief mission of US law enforcement, he added, is to stop another attack and apprehend any accomplices or terrorists before they hit us again. If we can't bring them to trial, so be it.[63]

Yet in the same morning, Ari Fleischer, the White House's spokesman, announced in a press conference—citing undisclosed intelligence sources—that "the perpetrators have executed their plan and, therefore, the risks are significantly reduced."[64] How could the White House know twenty-four hours after the events that the risks were "significantly reduced" unless it had foreknowledge of the terrorists' plan? It appears that Ari Fleischer's statement was too embarrassing for the White House: The transcript of this particular press conference cannot be found on the website of White House Press Briefings.[65] This statement, still found on various websites,[66] elicited neither questions nor further comments by the media nor a retraction from the White House, as one could have expected under the circumstances.

Four weeks after 9/11, Attorney General John Ashcroft and FBI Director Robert Mueller "ordered agents to drop their investigation of the attacks or any other assignment any time they learn of a threat or lead that might suggest a future attack."[67] One year after the events there was still no official investigation into 9/11.[68] While "investigations into past disasters and attacks such as Pearl Harbor, the Titanic, the assassination of President Kennedy and the Shuttle Challenger explosion were established in less than ten days,"[69] President Bush resisted for 411 days before grudgingly agreeing to form a National Commission to investigate the events of 9/11.[70] He did so only after having been allowed to nominate the Chairman and the Executive Director of the Commission and restrict the Commission's mandate, subpoena powers and funding. The Commission based its conclusions, published in its Final Report, on assumptions it did not check and did not apparently seek to check, such as the true identities of the "hijackers" and summaries compiled from reports by unnamed officials who allegedly interrogated al-Qa'ida leaders at undisclosed locations, at undisclosed dates, and under unknown conditions. The Final Report of the Commission of Inquiry may accurately be designated as an Omission Report, because its main characteristic is the omission of countless facts and items of evidence which counter the official account on 9/11.[71]

Fearing that evidence could emerge which would undermine the official account, some forensic evidence was destroyed. Steel from the collapsed World Trade Center towers was sold speedily as scrap metal to China and Korea before experts could examine it to determine the cause of the collapse.[72] Evidence that could have helped explain delays in dispatching fighters to intercept the "hijacked" aircraft was also intentionally destroyed.[73]

Many individuals who have been reported in mass media as sources for facts regarding the events of 9/11 (witnesses to the crashing of the aircraft and the collapses of the World Trade towers, employees of the airlines who saw passengers board the aircraft, family members and friends of crew and passengers who received phone calls from the aircraft, individuals who were acquainted with the alleged hijackers, and so on), either cannot be located or have been gagged by the FBI. Some of those who can be located even appear afraid to say what they know.[74] It is thus almost impossible to independently verify testimonies these people may have given to the FBI or to the media shortly after the events.[75] When the US authorities yielded to repeated demands by relatives of 9/11 victims to listen to the recording of the UA93 flight recorder (which was said to contain details on the passenger's struggle for control over the aircraft), they were warned not to reveal the contents of what they heard. They had to sign a non-disclosure agreement and were not allowed to take notes.[76] Similarly, a confidentiality agreement was demanded from fire officials and relatives in New York before they were allowed to listen to a tape of emergency radio transmissions between the fire fighters in the World Trade towers and ground personnel.[77]

The Congress, by enacting the Air Transportation Safety and System Stabilization Act, established the September 11th Victim Compensation Fund of 2001. Under the terms of this Act, a claimant for compensation "waives the right to file a civil action (or to be a party to an action) in any Federal or State court for damages sustained as a result of the terrorist-related aircraft crashes of September 11th, 2001."[78] The US Government paid 9/11 victims (and their next-of-kin) lavish compensations—thirty times the size of the largest previous disaster payout[79]—but thereby secured itself immunity against possible legal action by the victims, which would have compelled it to expose in court its own lies regarding the events of 9/11. Some relatives declined to accept this "shut-up money" and are struggling against heavy odds to have the truth on 9/11 revealed through court discovery procedures.[80]

According to the CIA, its "officers worked with foreign intelligence services to detain more than 2,900 al-Qa'ida operatives and associates in over ninety countries" in the aftermath of 9/11.[81] Yet as of May 2005 not a single "al-Qa'ida operative," nor anyone else, for that matter, has yet been convicted, anywhere, for participating in the 9/11 plot.[82] Two alleged top leaders of al-Qa'ida allegedly in US custody, Khalid Mohammed Sheikh and Ramzi Binalshibh, who according to the 9/11 Commission, admitted to US investigators to having planned and co-ordinated the 9/11 attacks,[83] have neither been charged for any crime nor brought before any court.[84] They are kept at undisclosed locations, if they are still living.[85] The alleged leader of al-Qa'ida, Osama bin Laden, designated by US Secretary of State Colin Powell as the person who "committed these [9/11] acts of murder,"[86] has not even been charged by the US authorities for his alleged part in this crime.[87] President George W. Bush declared on 15th September 2001, regarding Osama bin Laden: "If he thinks he can hide from the United States and our allies he will be sorely mistaken."[88] On 28th December 2001, the tone has already changed. Bush then said, "Our objective is more than bin Laden."[89] In Bush's State of the Union speech on January 2002, he did not even mention Osama bin Laden.[90] In March 2002 President Bush, asked in a press conference why nothing has been heard about Osama bin Laden, answered that he's "not that concerned about him . . . He's just a person who's now been marginalized."[91] The US administration finally admitted officially that it was not interested in arresting Osama bin Laden: On 6th April 2002, the Joint Chiefs of Staff Chairman Richard Myers stated: "The goal has never been to get bin Laden."[92] It appears that the US administration had never been really interested in catching him.[93]

Beyond the above facts, it is possible to prove mathematically that the official account on 9/11 cannot be true.[94]

Is Terrorism a Threat to International Peace and Security?

On October 19th 1999, Ambassador Richard C. Holbrooke, United States Representative to the United Nations, said at a meeting of the UN Security Council: "International terrorism is one of the most egregious threats to international peace and security."[95] In that year exactly six US nationals died worldwide from terrorist acts.[96] Mr. Holbrooke evidently did not have state terrorism in mind when he made his statement to the Council. The events of 9/11 permitted the United States to secure the adoption of Security Council resolutions designating acts of international terrorism as threats to international peace and security, a formulation designed to open the way for UN-authorized use of force under Chapter VII of the UN Charter.

By resolution 1373 (2001) the Security Council determined that "any act of international terrorism, constitute[s] a threat to international peace and security." By the provisions of this resolution, made with reference to Chapter VII of the UN Charter, the Council required all states to adopt national measures to combat terrorism. The Council also established a Counter-Terrorism Committee empowered to monitor the implementation of these measures and help states to increase their capability to combat terrorism.[97]

By Security Council resolution 1456 (2003), the Council designated terrorism as "*one of the most serious threats* to peace and security"[98] (emphasis added).

By designating terrorism as a "threat to international peace and security," and especially as "one of the most serious" threats, the Security Council implicitly gave member states a green light to enact measures that are normally only adopted in "states of emergency," including derogations from human rights. Ed Herman and David Peterson captured well the benefit of these Security Council resolutions for numerous governments:

> The "war against terrorism" has given a freer hand to terrorist governments that are "with us," like Russia's but also that of Israel. . . . China has also joined the fight against terrorism, and is expected to "use the international war against terror for a new crackdown on the Turkic-speaking Uighurs," . . . since September 11th (UPI, October 11th 2001). The new "war" has encouraged governments across the globe to ask for military support from the United States to fight their own "terrorists," and the Bush administration has already come through with aid to the Philippines and Indonesia in these local struggles.[99]

The events of 9/11 have provided oppressive governments with a justification to reconsider the use of torture. The US Department of Justice has endorsed the use of torture when interrogating "suspected terrorists" who are not US citizens.[100] Shipping "terror suspects" to countries known to use torture in interrogations (designated by the euphemism "extraordinary rendition") has been revealed as a covert practice practiced by the CIA with the tacit or active help of numerous governments.[101] The presumption of innocence, a cornerstone of civilized law since Magna Carta, is being turned on its head.[102] US officials who long before 9/11 had advocated "the expansion of presidential powers,"[103] obtained cause. Imperial rule was duly expanded in the United States in the form of Presidential Executive Orders.[104] By one such Executive Order, the President gave himself power to determine who is to be treated as a "terrorist,"[105] by another Executive Order, the President empowered himself to "confiscate"[106] Iraqi public assets.[107] Secret dockets in the US judicial system have been revealed.[108] European law-enforcement authorities are beginning to apply anti-terror legislation to peaceful protestors.[109] All these developments, which threaten fundamental liberties and democratic rights, have been justified by a contrived terrorist threat, itself resting on the 9/11 fable.

Is Terrorism an Existential Threat to Humanity?

The events of 9/11—as officially presented—led some politicians to equate terrorism with an existential threat to humankind. US Senator Richard G. Lugar, for example, asserted that Americans were now aware that "the United States is exposed to an existential threat from terrorism."[110] Canada's Justice Minister Irwin Cotler referred to terrorism as "an existential threat to the whole of the human family" in order to justify broadened police powers.[111] Tony Blair, Britain's Prime Minister, argued that the threat of terrorism "defined not by Iraq but by September 11th" is of a "different nature from *anything the world has faced before*"[112] (emphasis added).

The elusive nature of terrorism allows creative minds to fantasize about its threat. The scenario of Muslim terrorists getting hold of a nuclear device is widely used as a scare to justify radical law-enforcement measures against individuals and states.[113] While there is no evidence that any "terrorist organization" has acquired weapons of mass destruction, or is able to handle such weapons, it is theoretically possible that a secret terrorist group could purchase nuclear devices on the black market. Delivering such a device against a population is, however, hardly within the capabilities of clandestine, non-state groups. Such capabilities are only possessed by a handful of governments. Experts are divided regarding the ability of ordinary criminals, such as terrorists, to endanger without State support a large number of people, let alone a whole population.

The main threat for international peacc and security remains, as ever, measures pursued by powerful States, such as bombing campaigns, ethnic cleansing, economic sanctions, military occupation, the deployment of nuclear weapons and the militarization of space.

The Threat of Terrorism: Myth and Reality

When governments and international organizations designate terrorism as a "threat to international peace and security" or as an "existential threat to civilization," one would expect them to substantiate such claims with hard evidence, such as statistics on the number of victims from terrorism. However, an examination of the major declarations and resolutions by the United Nations, NATO, the European Union and other international organisations, reveals that none mentions any such statistics.[114] We could only identify one explanation for this absence: The number of terrorism casualties is so small, compared to that of other causes of death, that the release of such figures would expose the "war on terrorism" as a bad joke.

According to the report *Patterns of International Terrorism 2003*, issued by the US Department of State in April 2004,[115] exactly thirty-five (35) American citizens died from international terrorism worldwide in 2003. They were killed in the following countries: Kuwait (1); Colombia (1); Philippines (1); Israel (10); Palestinian occupied territories (6); Saudi Arabia (9); Iraq (5); Afghanistan (2), No US citizen died in 2003 as a result of international terrorism in Europe, Africa, Australia, and North America. In that same year, 16,503 persons were murdered in the US alone,[116] apparently too few to cause international concern.

The number of US casualties of international terrorism in previous years was: 1998 (12); 1999 (6); 2000 (23); 2001 (2689—a figure based on the disputed assumption that the events of 9/11 were acts of international terrorism); 2002 (27). European casualties of international terrorism are typically a few dozens a year.[117]

The above figures show that, in terms of fatal casualties, neither the US nor European governments can honestly claim that non-state terrorism represents a grave threat for their own citizens. Such a claim is preposterous. The fact that the yearly US federal budget for the fight against terrorism exceeded already eight billion dollars before the events of 9/11—when the number of American victims of terrorism could be counted on one's fingers[118]—demonstrates that the "war on terror" was not impelled by a real threat.

According to the statistical database of the US Department of State (referred to above), the number of worldwide fatal casualties of terrorism, all nationalities combined, was the following:

Year	Number of fatal casualties
2000	2,494
2001	4,379
2002	2,723
2003	2,385

To put casualty figures from terrorism into a global perspective, one should mention that about ten and a half million children die *yearly* of preventable causes[119] (or the equivalent of ten 9/11 tragedies *every single day*). This staggering number of child deaths is merely a symptom of an acute social and political pathology that nourishes threats to international peace and security. Yet this yearly Holocaust does not appear to sufficiently shock the conscience of UN Security Council members into undertaking enforcement measures and end this scourge. The Security Council has never designated extreme poverty, the lack of drinking water and massive child mortality as threats to international peace and security.

It should be emphasized that the above statistics only cover "retail terrorism," namely the commission of terrorist acts by disparate, non-state groups and individuals with limited resources. Victims of "wholesale terrorism" (state terrorism) that is, organized attacks by government forces, aimed to demoralize or coerce a population, are not counted as terrorism but as ordinary state policies,[120] even if their harmful consequences exceed by far all acts of retail terrorism.[121]

Conclusions and Recommendations

We have demonstrated that the "war on terrorism" is a convenient and fraudulent cover for wars of aggression and internal repression. This fraudulent "war on terrorism" is in turn based on a second fraud, namely that the events of 9/11 were an act of "international terrorism," rather than an act of mass murder whose perpetrators have not yet been identified and prosecuted.

A major challenge facing the world's peoples is how to deal with a situation in which the majority of governments appear to collude in deceiving public opinion on a non-existing threat, using this contrived threat as a means to stifle opposition and covering up one of the most egregious contemporary crimes.

Attempts to uncover the truth on the events of 9/11 through judicial means have not been successful. American courts regularly defer to government claims that it cannot disclose evidence because of security considerations. Most families of 9/11 victims have been induced by financial rewards to forfeit their right to the truth. Many others have been gagged or threatened with sanctions if they reveal what they know about the events.

No international forum has jurisdiction over the crime of 9/11 because the United States, on the soil of which this crime against humanity was committed, is not a party to the Rome Statute of the International Criminal Court and will certainly not co-operate with the Court in investigating the crime.

In order to strengthen international solidarity against the emergence of a new totalitarian order under US leadership, the following recommendations are suggested:

1. An international, independent, inquiry commission should be established, under the auspices of the UN General Assembly, whose task would be to provide a full, truthful and final account of the events of 9/11.

2. An international ad-hoc criminal tribunal should be established to try and punish those who instigated, planned, facilitated and committed the crime against humanity committed on 9/11, as well as those who knowingly covered up the crime and protected its perpetrators.

3. The dissemination and maintenance of terrorism scares by governments should be designated as a criminal offence under international law.

NOTES

1. The author considers that "mass murder" is the most appropriate *prima facie* designation for the events of 9/11.
2. The author is indebted to Ed Herman and David Peterson for the terms "retail" and "wholesale" terrorism. The former term refers to terrorist acts by non-state, mostly clandestine, groups. The latter refers to measures committed at the behest of and with the resources of states. See "The Threat of Global State Terrorism," at http://zmag.org/Zmag/Articles/jan02herman.htm.
3. On an average year about eighty-two persons die in the US from lightning strikes. See: http://wonder.cdc.gov/wonder/prevguid/m0052833/m0052833.asp.
4. John W. Dean, "Liberties Disappearing Before Our Eyes," *Los Angeles Times* (21st September 2003), at http://www.globalpolicy.org/wtc/liberties/2003/0921disappearing.htm.
5. See, Richard Norton-Taylor, "Warning on Spread of State Surveillance," *Guardian* (21st April 2005), at http://www.guardian.co.uk/international/story/0,3604,1464412,00.html.
6. See, particularly, Jean-Claude Paye, "La fin de l'Etat de droit: La lutte antiterroriste de l'etat d'exception à la dictature, *La Dispute/SNÉDIT*, Paris (2004)
7. http://www.etymonline.com/index.php?term=terrorism.
8. The "criminal offense of terrorism was a new offense created in Senate Bill 184 and was defined in terms of the commission of an existing specified offense, coupled with the intent to either 1) intimidate or coerce a civilian population, 2) influence the policy of any government by intimidation or coercion, or 3) affect the conduct of any government by the act that constitutes the offense of terrorism." Individuals who committed the criminal offense "would be facing a penalty that is one degree higher than the most serious underlying specified offense that he or she is alleged to have committed." At http://www.ccao.org/newsletter/cab200204.htm.
9. See, for example, Brian Whitaker, "The Definition of Terrorism," *Guardian* (7th May 2002), at http://www.guardian.co.uk/elsewhere/journalist/story/0,7792,487098,00.html.
10. Based on the US statutory definition of international terrorism [US legal code (Title 18 § 2331)], comprehensive economic sanctions would include all the constitutive elements of this statutory crime. Such measures have been shown to (a) be "dangerous to human life"; (b) "appear to be intended to coerce a civilian population"; (c) "appear to be intended to influence the policy of a government by . . . coercion"; (d) "transcend national boundaries in terms of the means by which they are accomplished".
11. The Rome Statute of the International Criminal Court, at http://www.un.org/law/icc/statute/romefra.htm.
12. At http://www.gwu.edu/~nsarchiv/NSAEBB/NSAEBB55/nsdd179.pdf.
13. Cited by Linda Maher in the Sunday Business Post Online (13th March 2005), in her review of the book *Fear: A Cultural History* by Joanna Burke http://archives.tcm.ie/businesspost/2005/03/13/story3026.asp.
14. John Parachini, Center for Non-proliferation Studies, Testimony before the House Subcommittee on National Security, Veterans Affairs and International Relations, 26th July 2000, Figure 1, p. 1, [http://cns.miis.edu]). For FY 1998 the figure was

$6.5 billion, for FY 2000 $8.4 billion (source: Monterey Institute of International Studies, http://cns.miis.edu/research/cbw/terfund.htm).

15. Louis Freeh, Director FBI, Statement before the US Senate Committee on Appropriations Subcommittee for the Departments of Commerce, Justice, and State, the Judiciary, and Related Agencies, 4th February 1999, page 1, (http://www.fas.org/irp/congress/1999_hr/990204-freehct2.htm).
16. See statistics on international terrorism on the Department of State website, at http://www.state.gov/s/ct/rls/pgtrpt/2003/33771.htm.
17. Associated Press, 11th September 2001: "Today, Our Nation Saw Evil."
18. Associated Press, 14th September 2001, "19 People Identified by the FBI as Hijackers aboard the Four Planes that Crashed Tuesday."
19. See, for example, Michel Chossudovsky, "Fabricating an Enemy," at http://www.nadir.org/nadir/initiativ/agp/free/chossudovsky/fabricatingenemy.htm.
20. As an example, the French newspaper of record, *Le Monde*, published five hundred articles in 2003, which referred to "terrorism." Not a single person in France died during that year from terrorism. Maureen Dowd, a regular contributor to the *New York Times*, wrote on 20th August 2003: "The Bush team has now created the very monster that it conjured up to alarm Americans into backing a war on Iraq."
21. A search of the string "al Qaeda" on the website of what is presented as the World's Largest Online Library (Questia), yielded 141 books, practically all written after 9/11. The same search yielded 4,728 newspaper articles, 451 journal articles, and 2,637 magazine articles. At http://www.questia.com/SM.qst?act=search&keywordsSearchType=1000&keywords=%22Al%20Qaeda%22.
22. Referring to his meeting with an unnamed al Qa'ida expert at the Rand Corporation Leonid Shebarshin, ex-chief of the Soviet Foreign Intelligence Service, said: "We have agreed that [al-Qaeda] is not a group but a notion . . . The fight against that all-mighty ubiquitous myth deliberately linked to Islam is of great advantage for the Americans as it targets the oil-rich Muslim regions." Source: *Moscow News* (23rd March 2005), at http://mosnews.com/news/2005/03/21/shebarsh.shtml; see also Brendan O'Neill, "Does al-Qaeda exist?" 28th November 2003, at http://www.spiked-online.com/Articles/00000006DFED.htm. A good overview of the al-Qa'ida myth is provided by Standard Schaeffer in his interview with historian R.T. Naylor, "Al Qaeda Itself Does Not Exist" (21st June 2003), CounterPunch, at http://www.twf.org/News/Y2003/0622-Qaeda.html.
23. See, for example, Michel Chossudovsky, "Who Is Osama Bin Laden?" at http://www.globalresearch.ca/articles/CHO109C.html.
24. The National Security Strategy of the United States of America, signed by President George W. Bush on 17th September 2002, at http://www.informationclearinghouse.info/article2320.htm.
25. Mirrored at http://www.aldeilis.net/aldeilis/index.php?option=content&task=view&id=459&Itemid=107.
26. At http://www.defenselink.mil/speeches/2001/s20011218-secdef1.html.
27. At a *Fortune* Global Forum meeting, 11th November 2002, at http://www.defenselink.mil/speeches/2002/s20021111-secdef.html.
28. Ibid.
29. According to an accurate list, merely thirty-six (not eighty) nationalities were represented among the victims of 9/11. See Victims by Country and Citizenship, at

http://www.september11victims.com/september11victims/COUNTRY_CITIZENSHIP.htm.
30. Ibid.
31. "Rumsfeld Says Issue in Iraq is Disarmament, Not Weapons Inspections," United States Mission to the European Union, at http://www.useu.be/Categories/GlobalAffairs/Sept1802RumsfeldIraqDisarmament.html.
32. See Chris Floyd, "The Pentagon Plan to Provoke Terrorist Attacks," CounterPunch, 1st November 2002, at http://www.counterpunch.org/floyd1101.html.
33. Lance Morrow, "The Case for Rage and Retribution," Time (September 11th, 2001; cited in David Ray Griffin, *The New Pearl Harbor: Disturbing Questions about the Bush Administration and 9/11* (Northampton, Massachusetts: Olive Branch, 2004), p. xi. The thesis that Pearl Harbor took America by surprise is now discredited. In his 1982 book *Infamy: Pearl Harbor and Its Aftermath*, Pulitzer-prize winner John Toland reveals that almost everything the Japanese were planning to do "was known to the United States" on the morning of the attack, via intercepted messages never communicated to commanders at Pearl Harbor. (Cited by Heather Wokusch in "Infamy: Pearl Harbor, 911 and the Coming Outrage," CommonDreams.org, September 10th, 2004, at http://www.commondreams.org/views04/0910-06.htm; Robert B. Stinnett's *Day of Deceit*, published in 2000, goes further: "After 16 painstaking years of uncovering documents through the Freedom of Information Act, respected journalist and historian, Bob Stinnett, now charges that US government leaders at the highest level not only knew that a Japanese attack was imminent, but that they had deliberately engaged in policies intended to provoke the attack . . . and the purpose of this plan was to draw a reluctant, peace-loving American public into the war for good or ill" ("Pearl Harbor: Official Lies in an American War Tragedy?" Introductory remarks by David Theroux at the Independent Institute, 24th May 2000 http://www.independent.org/events/transcript.asp?eventID=28).
34. The author thinks that the term "neo-fascist" captures better the ideology of the ruling elite in the United States than the commonly used term "neo-con" ("neo-conservatives"). The "neo-fascist" ideology is predicated on the construction of a powerful "national security state," a disregard for human rights, an increase of covert and mass surveillance, deliberate manipulation of the citizenry and use of the State to promote corporate interests.
35. Project for the New American Century, "Rebuilding America's Defenses," September 2000, p. 51, at http://www.newamericancentury.org/RebuildingAmericasDefenses.pdf.
36. Exactly 2,948 persons were confirmed dead according to http://www.september11victims.com/september11victims/STATISTIC.asp. The manner of the attack was designed and the targets selected with the dramatic impact on ordinary people in mind.
37. "The Impact of September 11 on Public Opinion: Increased Patriotism, Unity, Support for Bush; More Interest in News," A Brookings/Harvard Forum, 27th March 2002, at: http://www.brookings.edu/comm/transcripts/20020327.htm, mirrored on www.juscogens.org.
38. Dennis Jett, "The Politics of Fear," *Christian Science Monitor* (17th June 2002). Dennis Jett is dean of the International Center at the University of Florida.
39. A Google search on 19th May 2005 yielded 152,000 web pages on the string "suspected terrorist."

40. The official title of the USA Patriot Act is: "Uniting and Strengthening America by Providing Appropriate Tools Required to Intercept and Obstruct Terrorism Act of 2001," H.R. 3162
41. The policies are initially directed at specific "risk" groups (Muslims, aliens). After being accepted by the general public, the group targeted for surveillance may be widened to what officialdom designates as "disruptive" groups (trade unions, anti-globalization, and environmental movements). For a literature review on "preventive law-enforcement," see Dean at note 5 above.
42. A representative argument for increased levels of surveillance can be found in the speech given by Germany's Federal Minister of the Interior, Otto Schily, at Witten/Herdecke University on 21st February 2005, see: http://www.bmi.bund.de/cln_012/nn_332136/Internet/Content/Nachrichten/Reden/2005/02/Schily__International__Cooperation__on__Fighting__Crime__en.html.
43. See, for example, Robert Higgs, "World War II and the Military-Industrial-Congressional Complex," *Freedom Daily* (1st May 1995), The Independent Institute, at http://www.independent.org/newsroom/article.asp?id=141. At a Press Conference of 26th May 2004, held at the Department of State, Colin Powell said: "[W]ell, you know, the Soviet Union is gone, the Warsaw Pact is gone, you know, *I'm running out of enemies*." See Transcript at http://hongkong.usconsulate.gov/uscn/state/2004/052601.htm, mirrored at: http://www.aldeilis.net/aldeilis/content/view/1603/130.
44. See Ruth Rosen, "Politics of Fear," *San Francisco Chronicle* (30th December 2002), at http://www.commondreams.org/views02/1230-02.htm; William Schroder, "American Imperialism and the Politics of Fear: Before Iraq, There Was the Philippines," CommonDreams.org, 15th February 2005, at http://www.commondreams.org/views05/0215-22.htm; Institute of Race Relations, "The Politics of Fear: Civil Society and the Security State," June 2004, at http://www.irr.org.uk/2004/june/ak000011.html; Bill Van Auken, "Two 'Sting' operations raise disturbing questions about US terror alert." World Socialist Web Site, August 2004, at http://www.wsws.org/articles/2004/aug2004/stng-a11.shtml.
45. Apparently, the US had planned before 9/11 to invade Afghanistan. See, inter alia, "US 'planned attack on Taliban'," BBC, 18th September 2001, citing Niaz Naik, a former Pakistani Foreign Secretary, at http://news.bbc.co.uk/1/hi/world/south_asia/1550366.stm.
46. Richard Clarke, *Against All Enemies* (New York: Free Press, 2004), Chapter 1.
47. SC Resolution 1368 (2001), OP 1, at http://www.un.org/News/Press/docs/2001/SC7143.doc.htm.
48. Suzanne Delay, "A Nation Challenged: The Evidence: NATO says US Has Proof Against bin Laden Group," *New York Times* (3rd October 2001), mirrored at http://www.aldeilis.net/aldeilis/content/view/1493.
49. NATO Update, 3rd October 2001, at http://www.nato.int/docu/update/2001/1001/e1002a.htm.
50. The secret nature of this dossier was confirmed to the author in a letter from Iceland's Ministry of Foreign Affairs of 18th February 2005 (Iceland is member of NATO and of the North Atlantic Council).
51. See, for example, the Downing Street Secret Memo of 23rd July 2002 (signed by Matthew Rycroft). It documents how the UK Government fixed facts to justify the invasion of Iraq. Posted on 1st May 2005 at the *Sunday Times* (London) website: http://www.timesonline.co.uk/article/0,,2087-1593607,00.html.

52. The passenger lists from the four flights of 9/11 (AA11, AA77, UA93 and UA175) published by various media, do not contain Arab names.
53. This was the answer from the Department of Justice to a private FOIA request for such information. Both the letter of request and the answer are reproduced as facsimile posted on http://www.flight77.info/.
54. See, for example, NBC Online, "Video of 9/11 Plane Hitting Pentagon Is Released" (16th May 2006), http://www.msnbc.msn.com/id/12818225/; see, however, Steve Watson, "FBI Withholding 84 More Tapes of Pentagon on 9/11," 17th May 2006 at http://www.infowars.net/articles/may2006/170506Pentagon_videos.htm.
55. A collection of articles regarding the "living hijackers" is found on: http://www.aldeilis.net/aldeilis/index.php?option=content&task=category§ionid=10&id=97&Itemid=107.
56. Cited by Timothy W. Maier, "FBI Denies Mix-Up Of 9/11 Terrorists," on Insight on the News, 11th June 2003, at http://www.realnews247.com/fbi_denies_mix-up_of_911_terrorists.htm.
57. Names of alleged hijackers': http://www.fbi.gov/pressrel/pressrel01/091401hj.htm.Photographs of alleged hijackers: http://www.fbi.gov/pressrel/penttbom/penttbomb.htm.
58. *The 9/11 Commission Report*, Preface, p. xvi.
59. A legal discussion of the expression "beyond reasonable doubt" can be found on http://www.jud.state.ct.us/CriminalJury/2-8.html.
60. Testimony of US Secretary of Defense Donald H. Rumsfeld before the House and Senate Armed Services Committees regarding Iraq, 18th–19th September 2002, at http://www.defenselink.mil/speeches/2002/s20020918-secdef.html.
61. Proposed definition by Boaz Ganor, "Defining Terrorism: Is One Man's Terrorist Another Man's Freedom Fighter?" at http://www.ict.org.il/articles/define.htm.
62. The most notorious cases of "false flag" operations in the twentieth century are the burning of the Reichstag (Berlin, 1933); the Lavon Affair (Israel/Egypt 1954), http://www.aljazeera.com/cgi-bin/conspiracy_theory/fullstory.asp?id=193]; and Operation Northwood (USA/Cuba, 1962), which was planned but not executed [see http://www.fromthewilderness.com/free/ww3/11_20_01_op_nwoods.html]. For a more comprehensive list of "false flag" operations (or synthetic terror), see: "False Flag Terrorism," at http://www.aldeilis.net/aldeilis/content/category/24/257/141.
63. Bob Woodward and Dan Balz, "We Will Rally the World" [A review of the events of 12th September 2001] *Washington Post* (28th January 2002), at http://www.washingtonpost.com/ac2/wp-dyn?pagename=article&node=&contentId=A46879-2002Jan27¬Found=true, mirrored at: http://www.aldeilis.net/aldeilis/content/view/1604/107.
64. White House Morning Briefing by Ari Fleischer, 12th September 2001, at 9:57 a.m. See http://usinfo.org/usia/usinfo.state.gov/topical/pol/terror/01091210.htm, mirrored on http://www.aldeilis.net/aldeilis/index.php?option=content&task=view&id=464&Itemid=107.
65. White House. Press Briefings by Date, at http://www.whitehouse.gov/news/briefings.
66. Jim Drinkard, "Air Force One, White House Were Targeted," *USA Today* (13th September 2001), at http://usatoday.com/news/nation/2001/09/11/worldtradecenter.htm; US Embassy in Canberra (http://canberra.usembassy.gov/hyper/2001/0912/epf305.htm); GovExec.com (http://www.govexec.com/dailyfed/0901/091201cd3.

htm); and CNN (http://transcripts.cnn.com/TRANSCRIPTS/0305/20/bn.05.html).

67. Philip Shenon and David Johnston, "F.B.I. Shifts Focus to Try to Avert Any More Attacks," *New York Times* (9th October 2001), at http://www.nytimes.com/2001/10/09/national/09INQU.html, mirrored at http://www.aldeilis.net/aldeilis/index.php?option=content&task=view&id=346&Itemid=107.
68. See Patrick Martin, "One Year After the Terror Attacks," 12th September 2002, Centre for Research on Globalisation, http://globalresearch.ca/articles/MAR209A.html.
69. Citizens critique of flawed 9/11 Commission process, 23rd July 2004, at http://www.911citizenswatch.org/modules.php?op=modload&name=News&file=article&sid=353.
70. On November 15th 2002, the US Congress approved legislation creating an independent commission—the National Commission on Terrorist Attacks Upon the United States—to "examine and report on the facts and causes relating to the September 11th terrorist attacks" and "make a full and complete accounting of the circumstances surrounding the attacks." President Bush signed it into law on November 27th, 2002.
71. For a thorough, critical discussion of the 9/11 Commission, see particularly David Ray Griffin's book *The 9/11 Commission Report: Omissions and Distortions* (Northampton, Massachusetts: Olive Branch, 2005).
72. See, for example, Christopher Bollyn, "The British Knights Who "Cleaned Up 911'," on http://www.aldeilis.net/aldeilis/index.php?option=content&task=view&id=468&Itemid=107.
73. Matthew Wald, "Destruction of FAA Tapes," *New York Times* (6th May 2004); Sara Kehaulani Goo, "FAA Managers Destroyed 9/11 Tapes," *Washington Post* (6th May 2004, mirrored on: http://portland.indymedia.org/en/2004/05/287757.shtml.
74. Daniel Hopsicker, "FBI 'Harassing and Intimidating' 911 Witnesses," Rense.com, 12-11.03, at http://www.rense.com/general45/witnesses.htm; also private communications by the author with two firefighters.
75. We say "may have given to the FBI," because in many cases media did not cite their sources or cited anonymous law-enforcement sources. It is impossible to know the exact nature of the testimonies.
76. Gail Sheehy, "9/11 Tapes Reveal Ground Personnel Muffled Attacks," *New York Observer* (20th June 2004);"Let's Roll," *Daily Mail* (27th July 2002); Stevenson Swanson, "Flight 93 Tape Ends Doubts for Families," *Chicago Tribune* (19th April 2002); "Our Loved Ones Died Heroes," CBS News, 18th April 2002.
77. "Firefighers Reached Crash Zone," BBC 4, August 2002, at http://news.bbc.co.uk/2/hi/world/americas/2171606.stm, also "Feds Withhold Crucial WTC Evidence" at http://www.911dossier.co.uk/hj03.html.
78. See: www.treasury.gov/offices/domestic-finance/atsb/hr2926.pdf.
79. Maggie Farley, "More than $38 Billion Paid to 9/11 Victims," *Los Angeles Times* (8th November 2004), at: http://www.latimes.com/news/nationworld/nation/la-110804compensation_lat,0,44112.story?coll=la-home-headlines.
80. See Walter Gilberti, "Bush Administration Moves to Stifle Discovery in 9/11 Lawsuits," World Socialist Web Site, 2nd August 2002, at http://www.wsws.org/articles/2002/aug2002/bush-a02.shtml; also: "9/11 Widow Beverly Eckert Declares, 'My Silence Cannot Be Bought'," 27th December 2003; "9/11 Families Reject

'Bribe,' Sue U.S.," 27th December 2003; "Ellen Mariani Would 'Eat Dirt' Before Accepting Bush's 9/11 Hush Money," 12th December 2003. September 11th Lawsuits. http://archive.democrats.com/preview.cfm?term=September%2011%20Lawsuits.

81. George J. Tenet, Director of CIA, Testimony Before the Senate Select Committee on Intelligence, 6th February 2002: Support to the War on Terrorism and Homeland Security http://www.cia.gov/cia/reports/Ann_Rpt_2002/swtandhs.html.
82. Only one person, Zacarias Moussaoui, has been sentenced to life imprisonment, *inter alia*, for his alleged foreknowledge of the 9/11 plot (not for participating in the plot). The sentence was based on his confession, which he retracted afterwards. Many observers doubt his sanity. A list of court documents regarding his case is found on the website of FindLaw, at http://news.findlaw.com/legalnews/us/terrorism/cases/index.html.
83. Staff Statement no. 16, 9/11 Commission, at www.9-11commission.gov/staff_statements/staff_statement_16.pdf.
84. "DOJ Attorney Warns of Immediate and Irreparable Harm to National Security in Arguments Before Appeals Court," CACI—Proud Partner in Homeland Security, at http://www.caci.com/homeland_security/moussaoui_14.shtml.
85. "Top al-Qaeda Suspect in US Custody," BBC News, 16th September 2002, at http://news.bbc.co.uk/2/hi/south_asia/2261136.stm; but see also Paul Thompson, "Is There More to the Capture of Khalid Shaikh Mohammed than Meets the Eye?" Center for Co-operative Research, 4th March 2003, at http://www.cooperativeresearch.net/timeline/main/essayksmcapture.html.
86. Interview with Colin Powell on NBC's "Meet the Press" on 23rd September 2001, posted on http://www.aldeilis.net/aldeilis/index.php?option=content&task=view&id=371&Itemid=107.
87. The Surgeon (pseudonym), "Osama bin Laden Has Not Been Indicted for the Attacks of 9/11?" ttp://www.aldeilis.net/aldeilis/index.php?option=content&task=view&id=312&Itemid=107.
88. Christopher Newton, "Bush Says bin Laden Cannot Hide, Tells Troops to Prepare," Associated Press, 15th September 2001.
89. "Terrorist Attacks Timeline," Associated Press, 19th August 2002, at http://billstclair.com/911timeline/2002/ap081902b.html.
90. President Bush State of the Union address, CNN, 29th January 2002, at http://archives.cnn.com/2002/ALLPOLITICS/01/29/bush.speech.txt.
91. See Press Conference by President Bush on 13th March 2002, at http://www.whitehouse.gov/news/releases/2002/03/20020313-8.html.
92. Gen. Myers Interview with CNN TV, 6th April 2002, US Department of Defense Website, at http://www.defenselink.mil/transcripts/2002/t04082002_t407genm.html.
93. Webster Griffin Tarpley, 9/11 *Synthetic Terror Made in USA* (Joshua Tree: Progressive Press, 2005); Albright sabotages extradition of bin Laden by Sudan (pp. 141–44); FBI told by Bush to back off bin Ladens (pp. 144–45); *Le Figaro*: Bin Laden treated at American Hospital [in Dubai], July 2001 (pp. 149–151).
94. Elias Davidsson, "Simple Math Demonstrates that the Official 9/11 Account Is a Fabrication," at http://www.aldeilis.net/aldeilis/index.php?option=content&task=view&id=440&Itemid=107.
95. At http://www.un.int/usa/99_077.htm.

96. See State Department terrorism statistics, at http://www.state.gov/s/ct/rls/pgtrpt/2003/33771.htm.
97. SC Resolution 1373 (2001) at http://www.un.org/News/Press/docs/2001/sc7158.doc.htm and Counter Terrorism Committee, at http://www.un.org/Docs/sc/committees/1373.
98. Security Council resolution 1456 (2003), Annex.
99. Ed Herman and David Peterson, "The Threat of Global State Terrorism: Retail versus Wholesale Terrorism," at http://zmag.org/Zmag/Articles/jan02herman.htm.
100. Mike Allen and Dana Priest, "Memo on Torture Draws Focus to Bush," *Washington Post* (9th June 2004), at http://www.washingtonpost.com/wp-dyn/articles/A26401-2004Jun8.html.
101. David Morgan, "US Has Sent up to 70 Terror Suspects to Egypt," Reuters, 15th May 2005, at http://news.yahoo.com/s/nm/egypt_usa_torture_dc; see also Jane Mayer, "Outsourcing Torture, the Secret History of America's 'Extraordinary Rendition' Program," *New Yorker* (14th February 2005), at http://www.newyorker.com/fact/content/?050214fa_fact6; Neil Mackay, "Torture Flights," *Sunday Herald* (Scotland, 16th October 2005), at http://www.sundayherald.com/52303.
102. Seven states and 378 local or county governments in the US have adopted resolutions opposing specific parts of the USA Patgriot Act, "that may infringe on important civil liberties . . . including presumption of innocence, due process, legal counsel and probable cause (and) protection from unreasonable searches and seizures." In "Some N.J. Towns, Counties Are Against Law," *Asbury Park Press* (21st May 2005), reported by Associated Press, at http://www.911citizenswatch.org/modules.php?op=modload&name=News&file=article&sid=548&mode=thread&order=0&thold=0.
103. Jonathan Turley, "Naked Power, Arbitrary Rule," *Los Angeles Times* (21st July 2003), at http://cscs.umich.edu/~crshalizi/sloth/2003-07-21.html.
104. See Executive Orders Issued by President Bush, web page of the White House, http://www.whitehouse.gov/news/orders.
105. "President Issues Military Order: Detention, Treatment, and Trial of Certain Non-Citizens in the War Against Terrorism," White House website, 13th November 2001, at http://www.whitehouse.gov/news/releases/2001/11/20011113-27.html.
106. The term "confiscate" is merely a euphemism for an act of outright theft.
107. Executive Order: Confiscating and Vesting Certain Iraqi Property, White House web page, 20th March 2003, at http://www.whitehouse.gov/news/releases/2003/03/20030320-10.html.
108. Ann W. O'Neill, "Secret Courts, Secret Dockets, Secret Arguments, Secret Imprisonments," *South Florida Sun-Sentinel* (8th January 2004), at http://www.unknownnews.net/040112secrets.html; also David M. Reutter and Paul Wright, "Secret Court Docket Practice Exposed," *Prison Legal News* (December 2003), at http://www.prisonlegalnews.org; and Bill Mears, "Court Declines Appeal on 9/11 Secrecy," CNN, 23rd February 2004, at http://edition.cnn.com/2004/LAW/02/23/scotus.terror.secrecy.
109. See Giles Tremlett, "Spain Tries Greenpeace Five," *Guardian* (11th May 2005); "Greenpeace Charged under Anti-terror Laws," 11th May 2005, at http://www.statewatch.org/news/2005/may/04greenpeace.htm.
110. U.S.–NATO Missions Annual Conference, Brussels, 19th January 2002: Senator Richard G. Lugar, "NATO's Role in the War on Terrorism."
111. Ian Macleod, *Ottawa Citizen* (December 11th 2004).

112 In a speech in his Sedgefield constituency. Source: *Guardian* (5th March 2004), http://politics.guardian.co.uk/iraq/story/0,12956,1162991,00.html.

113. Examples: "Al-Qaeda Nuclear Plans Confirmed," BBC, 16th November 2001; "Al Qaeda Documents Outline Serious Weapons Program," CNN, 25th January 2002; "Al-Qaeda 'Was Making Dirty Bomb'," BBC, 31st January 2003; Bill Gertz, "Reports Reveal Zarqawi Nuclear Threat," *Washington Times* (20th April 2005). None of these stories could be independently verified.

114. While the tangible effects of terrorism can be measured in terms of damage to material goods and direct harm to body and limb (and are objective indicator of harm) the psychological effects of terrorist acts cannot be attributed to the perpetrators. These are the result of media coverage of such acts.

115. Webpage of the US Department of State: http://www.state.gov/s/ct/rls/pgtrpt/2003/33771.htm.

116. National Center for Victims of Crime Website, at http://www.ncvc.org/ncvc/main.aspx?dbName=DocumentViewer&DocumentID=38716.

117. Webpage of the US Department of State: http://www.state.gov/s/ct/rls/pgtrpt/2003/33771.htm.

118. See above.

119. World Health Organization: Surviving the First Five Years of Life, at http://www.who.int/whr/2003/chapter1/en/index2.html.

120. A number of countries, particularly the United States and Israel, oppose the inclusion of 'state terrorism' into a draft Comprehensive Convention on International Terrorism proposed by India. See Siddharth Varadarajan, "UN Terror Draft to Oulaw Israeli Strikes," Time News Network, January 2002, at http://www.globalpolicy.org/wtc/un/2002/0130treaty.htm.

121. A particularly egregious case is that of the UN sanctions against Iraq which were intended to create hardship for the Iraqi population as a means of coercion and which caused the deaths of over half a million children. See writings on economic sanctions and the Iraq sanctions at http://www.aldeilis.net/aldeilis/index.php?option=content&task=view&id=226&Itemid=120.

122. This chapter was a paper presented by the author at the Sixteenth Congress of the International Association of Democratic Lawyers, Paris, 7/11 June 2005. The IADL is an NGO with Consultative Status at the ECOSOC and UNESCO. Revised in June 2006.

8

JFK and 9/11: Insights Gained from Understanding Both

Peter Dale Scott

In American history there are two types of event: ordinary events, which the information systems of the country can understand and establish, and deep events, or meta-events, which the information systems of the country cannot digest. If history is what is recorded, then meta-history is the sum of events which tend to be officially obscured or even suppressed in traditional books and media. Important recent examples include the political assassinations of the 1960s, Iran-Contra, and now 9/11.

The study of these meta-events has slowly become more respectable in the almost half-century since the JFK assassination. A major reason has been the emergence of the Internet and other forms of new media, where the same meta-events tend to get far more extensive treatment.[1] If the new media come in time to prevail over the priorities of the old, it is possible that we will see a paradigm shift with respect to what is appropriate for serious public discourse.

What I have learned over the years is that it is helpful to look at all these meta-events together. This is true for both external reasons (how the nation and its media handle meta-history) and for internal reasons (the content of meta-events themselves).

I am not here to talk about the external reasons, but they too are important. The press aversion to the facts of 9/11, the official 9/11 Commission and Report which perpetuate the original official misrepresentations, the astonishing malfunction of the FBI and other agencies—all these features of 9/11 will come as no surprise to those who have been studying JFK.

Instant Identification of the Culprits

History repeated itself in another 9/11 respect as well: the speedy identification of the alleged culprits.

In the case of Oswald, within fifteen minutes of the assassination and long before Oswald was picked up in the Texas Theater, they put out on the police network, and possibly other networks, a description of the killer—five foot ten, 165 pounds[2]—which exactly matched what was in his FBI file and in CIA documents about him.[3]

One problem was that this didn't match the actual height and weight of the man picked up and charged, which was five foot nine and 140 pounds.[4] The five-foot-ten-inch measurement was also suspect because it was attributed to Howard Brennan, who saw someone in the sixth floor window, but only from the waist up. Brennan subsequently failed to pick out Oswald in a police line-up.[5] So there is a question where the police were able to get that exact measurement of 5' 10", 165 pounds. It appears someone had already pre-decided who was going to be accused before the police found Oswald in the Texas Theater.

Meanwhile on 9/11 the FBI already had a list of alleged hijackers by 9:59 a.m. on September 11th, which was when the second tower collapsed.[6] 9:59 a.m. was at least four minutes before United Airlines Flight 93 had hit the ground. According to the 9/11 Report (which I don't believe) it was seven minutes before NORAD knew that Flight 93 had been hijacked.[7]

Even within the bureaucracy there were suspicions that the FBI was drawing on pre-9/11 files for its identifications.

> "I don't buy the idea that we didn't know what was coming," a former FBI official with extensive counter-terrorism experience has since said. "Within 24 hours [of the attack] the Bureau had about 20 people identified, and photos were sent out to the news media. Obviously this information was available in the files and somebody was sitting on it."[8]

Lt. Col. Anthony Shaffer of the Pentagon Able Danger program had a similar reaction:

> We were amazed at how quickly the FBI produced the name and pictures of all nineteen hijackers. But then again, we were surprised at how quickly they'd made the arrests after the first World Trade Center bombing. Only later did we find out that the FBI had been watching some of these people for months prior to both incidents."[9]

So it's worth thinking for a moment about the two events together. And consider also other meta-events in which the identity of the person who is ultimately going to be identified as the culprit is established at the very beginning, such as James Earl Ray (by means of the bag with the gun planted near his room).[10] In all these cases the culprit appears to have been pre-designated: it isn't elaborate investigative work after the meta-event that finds them, so much as following through on what has already been established, from the very beginning.

The Continuities of Meta-Events

By the internal reasons, I mean the overlap in the content of successive meta-events. I began to look at JFK and Watergate together because of Frank Sturgis, alias Fiorini, a minor figure in both.[11] Nixon, using the veiled threat that investigating Hunt would get into the "Bay of Pigs thing," coerced the CIA into ordering the FBI to suspend its investigation of the money trail in Mexico.[12] Later Haldeman, who transmitted the threat, presented the very credible hypothesis that Nixon was referring to the JFK assassination.[13]

My JFK-related studies of the CIA Mexico station have led me to some very interesting unanswered questions about Watergate. Why for example did FBI Director L. Patrick Gray suspend the questioning in Watergate of George Munro, the outside CIA officer responsible for the taping system which allegedly overheard Lee Harvey Oswald?[14]

The JFK-Watergate links I could pin down were anecdotal, almost coincidental. But when Iran-Contra came along, my knowledge of anti-Castro Cubans in 1963 supplied a more solid background for my chapters in the *Iran-Contra Connection*, and again in *Cocaine Politics*.[15]

Now we come to 9/11, and once again my years with JFK are helpful. Let me start with one common feature which I see at the very heart of understanding what Dick Cheney was doing on 11th September 2001.

Role of White House Communications Agency (WHCA) and the Secret Service

Research into the JFK assassination has helped me analyze what I consider to be a crucial unresolved question about 9/11: what time did Cheney arrive in the underground bunker beneath the White House?

Cheney himself first told Tim Russert on "Meet the Press" that it was before the Pentagon was hit, in other words, before 9:37 a.m.[16] This would have been in time for Cheney to give two important orders from the bunker: an order for all aircraft to land immediately at the nearest airport at 9:42,[17] and then, after consulting Bush, an important but disputed triple order (which according to Richard Clarke included a shoot-down order) at about 9:50.[18]

Then Cheney radically changed his story, to say that he arrived in the bunker twenty minutes later, "shortly before 10 a.m."[19] The 9/11 Report suppressed the first story and endorsed the second: "We have concluded, from the available evidence, that the Vice President arrived in the room shortly before 10:00, perhaps at 9:58."[20] David Ray Griffin has called this claim "an obvious lie."[21]

I now believe that Cheney did enter the room at this time, but that the Report is guilty of misrepresentation in the word "arrived." The easiest interpretation of the entire record is that indeed Cheney had first arrived a half hour or more earlier, before 9:37; and he then for some reason *returned* to the tunnel leading to the bunker, to have important phone calls with Donald Rumsfeld and the President, before coming back once more to the bunker at 9:58.

There is no record of these phone calls.[22] The easiest explanation why there is no record of the phone calls would be that Cheney wasn't in the bunker where people were taking notes and logs were being kept. He went to use a back channel from a secure phone somewhere else. And everyone agrees, even Cheney himself, that he used a secure phone in the tunnel at this time.[23]

This matter could be resolved by going to the records of the White House Communications Agency. They kept logs. The Secret Service also kept logs. And we have logs from that day that record phone calls at 9:15 a.m. and 9:20 a.m., and another phone call at 10:18 a.m.[24]

But Thomas Kean, the commission chairman, complained publicly that the logs were not complete.[25] We have in fact the equivalent of the notorious eighteen-minute gap which was discovered in the course of the Watergate investigation.[26] The 9/11 Commission does not present any records from the logs for the time of the phone call, either because they never saw them, possibly because the logs had been purged before they got to the commission, possibly because the commission purged them themselves. Or, and this is what I believe, because the phone in the tunnel was a back channel for which normal logs were not kept, possibly because it was a higher classification for the topic Cheney was discussing—Continuity of Government.

For the unrecorded phone calls resulted in a triple order covering three matters: 1) protection for Air Force One; 2) orders (the content of which is disputed) about planes, which may have involved the shoot-down order;

and 3) Continuity of Government.[27] "Continuity of Government" (COG) was a long-established plan, radically revised in the Reagan era, for a response to an emergency which among another things "set aside . . . constitutional and statutory requirements [and] established its own process for creating a new American president."[28] COG was partially implemented on 9/11, and in my next book I will argue that one consequence has been the barrage of recent orders, such as the suspension of habeas corpus, infringing on the traditional rule of law.[29]

Why would Cheney exit the bunker for these calls? Were they were so sensitive that he did not wish all those in the bunker to hear them? Or was their classification so high that most people in the bunker were not cleared to hear them? These were the two most important calls Cheney made that day. And yet, as the Report indicates, those taking notes in the bunker in the PEOC have no record of a call to Bush, and the Report has no record of Cheney's call with Rumsfeld either.[30]

In the tunnel Cheney was using a secure system of the White House Communications Agency (WHCA), operated in conjunction with the Secret Service. Thus in researching 9/11 I went to the WHCA website. I was startled to read there that "WHCA was also a key player in documenting the assassination of President Kennedy."[31] This statement raises the question of whom they documented it for; on the basis of my research, they didn't document it for the Warren Commission. As far as I know, the WHCA logs and transcripts were in fact withheld from the purview of the Warren Commission and subsequent public investigations, until a few minor logs and summary reports were released in December 1996 to the Assassination Records Review Board (ARRB).[32]

From these released logs and reports I learned that the main WHCA switchboard in Washington had no connection to Dallas at the time of the assassination. However a back channel was set up, through the Secret Service, of which the main WHCA switchboard was unaware.

> Direct communication set up immediately between Agent directly outside of emergency room [in Parkland Hospital] and Mr. Behn [Special Agent in Charge, White House Secret Service detail] in his office in Washington which became the Washington Command Post and clearing house.[33]

So it wasn't even a back channel back to the WHCA, but to the head of the Secret Service detail in his office in Washington, "which became the Washington Command Post and Clearing House."

What do we know of what happened at that Command Post on that day? Almost nothing. But the example of 9/11 suggests that that is where we should look to learn more about post-assassination JFK developments, such as the arrangements for the autopsy.

Furthermore, if we were ever to get the pre-assassination WHCA records on 22nd November 1963, we might learn more about why Secret Service Agent Winston Lawson, for example, stopped right in front of the Texas School Book Depository. This was where a man at this time was having a so-called epileptic fit, which led to the Dallas Police ordering a direct pathway for an ambulance to be opened to Parkland Hospital.[34] As a result, after the shooting of the President occurred, there was already an easy path opened for the President's car to go to Parkland. The road was open while access was blocked, not for the President but for the so-called epileptic. (When he got there, he got off the stretcher and turned out not to have had an epileptic fit at all.)[35]

I commend to the students of both these events, JFK and 9/11, the importance of these back channels on the days in question. The Commission's records are scheduled to be released in 2009,[36] at which point we should press for all back channel documents pertaining to Continuity of Government, COG. I believe these may tell us about warrant-less wiretapping, about the building of detention camps, and so on. I consider this to be a very important topic.[37]

Drugs, the JFK Assassination, and CIA Cuban Exiles

In *Deep Politics*, and especially *Deep Politics Two*, I discuss the importance of the Mexican drug traffic as a unifying factor in the JFK case. The Mexican drug traffic was connected to Jack Ruby, to the Mexican DFS which taped Oswald, to Richard Cain who involved himself in the JFK case, and to some of the Cubans with whom Lee Harvey Oswald was allegedly associated.[38] But a study of the Mexican drug traffic leads swiftly to the extraordinary protection which can be conferred by that traffic in the United States. It is a key, I have argued, to Jack Ruby's special status with the Dallas Police Department.[39]

The background of drugs in the JFK assassination is again emphasized, for different reasons, in two important new books, each of which supplements and reinforces the other. Lamar Waldron's new book, *Ultimate Sacrifice*, looks at the relation of the so-called French Connection to the mysterious Frenchman (either Jean Souêtre or Michel Victor Mertz) who was reportedly in Dallas November 22nd, 1963.[40] *Someone Would Have*

Talked, by Larry Hancock, looks in addition at drug connections in Central America and also Laos. In Laos two notorious veterans of the CIA's JM/WAVE station in Miami, David Morales and Carl Jenkins, both served as chief of the CIA base in Pakse, where opium and heroin from the CIA's Hmong army was trans-shipped to Vietnam.[41] (Morales has been linked in a number of books to the JFK assassination, and has recently been alleged to have attended the scene of the RFK assassination as well.)[42]

Carl Jenkins protégé Rafael Quintero subsequently became involved with Richard Secord in supporting Oliver North's drug-tainted Contra operations in Central America.[43] A key figure in this operation was fellow JM/WAVE Cuban exile Luis Posada Carriles. Posada was a former CIA terrorist wanted for crimes ranging from blowing up a Cubana airliner in 1976, to killing a tourist in Cuba in 1998, to a failed assassination attempt on Castro in 2000. Oliver North's Enterprise gave him a job at the Ilopango airbase in El Salvador, where, according to former DEA agent Celerino Castillo, two hangars were reserved for cocaine shipments.[44]

In the 1990s, according to the Mexican journal *Por Esto*, Posada Carriles was protected in Guatemala, Belize and Mexico by narco-traffickers in the Central American cartel headed by Otto Herrera García, an associate of the major Mexican trafficker Ismael Zambada. The State Department website says of Otto Herrera García: "In 2001, alone, his organization moved approximately twelve metric tons of cocaine, and may have the ability to smuggle as much as two tons of cocaine into the United States each month."[45]

Posada, a terrorist protected by a major drug trafficker, was smuggled into the US, and applied for political asylum. In August 2003, the Miami bureau of the FBI made the startling decision to close its case on Posada. Subsequently, according to the FBI, several boxes of evidence were removed from the bureau's evidence room. The agent responsible was a Cuban-American whose father came out of the Cuban exile network.[46]

Since then, in a change of heart, the Justice Department has reopened the case, by pursuing, not Posada, but the files of the *New York Times* reporter (Ann Louise Bardach) who interviewed him.[47] She fought back with a report on her problems in the *Washington Post*: "Justice Department . . . struck a plea deal for about two years in prison for Posada's comrades Santiago Alvarez and Osvaldo Mitat, who had been facing up to fifty years in prison for the illegal possession of hundreds of firearms."[48] Santiago Alvarez, formerly of Comandos L, is one of the Cuban terrorists who pledged participation in the Revolutionary Junta of Paulino Sierra Martinez, whose connection to the JFK assassination is discussed in books by Robert Blakey and myself.[49]

Drugs and al-Qaeda

How important were drugs in the financing al-Qaeda? There are two takes on this. The British Parliament was told on 4th October 2001, that "al Qaeda's activity includes substantial exploitation of the drug trade from Afghanistan."[50] But the 9/11 Commission went out of its way to say that

> While the drug trade was a source of income for the Taliban, it did not serve the same purpose for al Qaeda, and there is no reliable evidence that Bin Ladin was involved in or made his money through drug trafficking.[51]

This was after US Central Command reported that in December 2003 a dhow was intercepted near the Strait of Hormuz carrying almost two tons of hashish valued at up to ten million dollars. There were "clear ties" between the shipment and al-Qaeda, the Centcom statement said.[52]

The drug-trafficking Islamic Movement of Uzbekistan (IMU), like al-Qaeda a by-product of CIA-ISI plotting in the 1980s,[53] is said to have come "under the influence of the Taliban and Al Qaeda" after 1998.[54] And Ralf Mutschke, Assistant Director of Interpol, told the US Congress that "according to some estimations IMU may be responsible for seventy percent of the total amount of heroin and opium transiting through the area [of Central Asia]."[55] While such quantitative estimates remain uncertain, it is known that the IMU set up heroin labs in territories under its control.[56]

Loretta Napoleoni has argued that there is an Islamist drug route of al-Qaeda allies across North Central Asia, reaching from Tajikistan and Uzbekistan through Chechnya to Kosovo.[57] This leads us to the paradoxical fact that in 1988 Clinton came to the support of the al-Qaeda-backed Kosovo Liberation Army (KLA). He did so even though "In 1998, the U.S. State Department listed the KLA . . . as an international terrorist organization, saying it had bankrolled its operations with proceeds from the international heroin trade and from loans from known terrorists like Osama bin Laden."[58]

Soon *Mother Jones* reported that

> in the six months since Washington enthroned the Kosovo Liberation Army in that Yugoslav province, KLA-associated drug traffickers have cemented their influence and used their new status to increase heroin trafficking and forge links with other nationalist

> rebel groups and drug cartels. . . . According to recent DEA statistics, Afghan heroin accounted for almost twenty percent of the smack seized in th[e US]—nearly double the percentage taken four years earlier. Much of it is distributed by Kosovar Albanians.[59]

This leads in turn to the allegations of Sibel Edmonds, the Turkish-American former FBI translator, who has been prevented from speaking directly by an extraordinary court order,[60] but whose allegations have been summarized by Daniel Ellsberg:

> Al Qaeda, she's been saying to congress, according to these interviews, is financed 95 percent by drug money—drug traffic to which the US government shows a blind eye, has been ignoring, because it very heavily involves allies and assets of ours—such as Turkey, Kyrgyzstan, Tajikistan, Pakistan, Afghanistan—all the 'stans—in a drug traffic where the opium originates in Afghanistan, is processed in Turkey, and delivered to Europe where it furnishes 96 percent of Europe's heroin, by Albanians, either in Albania or Kosovo—Albanian Muslims in Kosovo—basically the KLA, the Kosovo Liberation Army which we backed heavily in that episode at the end of the century.
>
> In other words, the US is in effect, . . . permitting, or 'not acting against,' a heroin trade—which not only corrupts our cities and our city politics, AND our congress, as Sibel makes very specific—but is financing the terrorist organization that constitutes a genuine threat to us. And this seems to be a fact that is accepted by our top leaders, according to Sibel, for various geopolitical reasons, and for corrupt reasons as well. Sometimes things are simpler than they might appear—and they involve envelopes of cash. Sibel says that suitcases of cash have been delivered to the Speaker of the House, Dennis Hastert, at his home, near Chicago, from Turkish sources, knowing that a lot of that is drug money.[61]

In 2005 Sibel Edmonds's charges were partly aired in *Vanity Fair*. There it was revealed that Edmonds had had access to FBI wiretaps of conversations among members of the American-Turkish Council (ATC), about bribing elected US officials, and about "what sounded like references to large-scale drug shipments and other crimes."[62]

Sibel Edmonds's charges are so important that the traditional media, predictably, ignored them.[63] I'm drawing attention to Sibel Edmonds's claims here, not because I consider them proven, but because I consider a top priority of the new Democratic Congress should be to give her charges a proper investigation for the first time. These charges are not just pertinent to 9/11 alone, but to the whole fabric of how this country is run.

Sibel Edmonds is not alone in alleging a 9/11-drugs connection.[64] There was also another witness, Indira Singh, who said publicly when speaking about 9/11: "I was told that if I mentioned the money to the drugs around 9/11 that would be the end of me."[65]

One thing we can say with confidence: the flow of Afghan heroin west through Turkey is a problem that can be traced back to the CIA's complex involvement with a) Pakistan's ISI intelligence service, b) with the drug-linked Bank of Credit and Commerce International (BCCI), and c) with Islamist Afghan mujahedeen like the drug-trafficker Gulbuddin Hekmatyar in the 1980s.[66]

In fact the web of influence in America which Edmonds describes corresponds closely to BCCI's influence in the 1980s, when the head of BCCI used to boast to the leader of Pakistan about BCCI's role in getting aid for Pakistan approved by the US Congress.[67]

The ISI and its assets continued to be implicated in drug trafficking after the shutdown of BCCI in July 1991.

> In an unusually frank interview in September 1994—which he later denied—the former Pakistani prime minister, Nawaz Sharif, disclosed that General Aslam Beg, the army chief of staff, and the ISI boss [from 1990 to 1992], Lieutenant-General Asad Durrani, had [in early 1991] proposed raising money for covert foreign operations through large-scale drug deals. . . . The ISI's involvement in the Sikh separatist movement was recognized in a 1993 CIA report on Pakistan's drug trade, which stated the heroin was being used to fund its purchases of arms."[68]

Prominent in ISI's covert foreign operations at this time were the Arab Afghan terrorists supporting the drug trafficker Hekmatyar in Afghanistan, of whom I am about to say much more.

Double Agents: Oswald and Ali Mohamed

Among these Arab Afghan terrorists, the US Government had its own double agents, including a very important one, Ali Mohamed. Meanwhile, in *Deep Politics* I explored at some length the possibility that Lee Harvey Oswald was also, as Silvia Odio had heard, a possible "double agent . . . trying to infiltrate the Dallas Cuban refugee group."[69]

I went on in *Deep Politics* (written in 1992) to make observations about Oswald as a double agent, observations that I now consider applicable to 9/11:

> The preceding chapter considered the possibility that Oswald was associated with anti-Kennedy Cubans in order to investigate them on behalf of a federal agency. But we saw it alleged that Oswald was a double agent collaborating with some of these groups, either (as I suspect) because he or his handlers shared their goals [that is, anti-Kennedy goals], or possibly because he or his handlers had been "turned" by those they were supposed to investigate. Such a possibility was particularly likely with targets, like Alpha 66, about which the government itself was conflicted, of two minds.[70]

It is necessary to recall that Alpha 66 in early 1963 conducted a series of raids, not just against Cuba, but against Soviet ships in Cuba. It was obviously trying to shipwreck the US-Soviet understanding on Cuba, thus to torpedo the whole Kennedy policy of détente with the Soviet Union. Unambiguously the raids met with the total disapproval of Robert Kennedy's Justice Department (which cracked down on them and made a public announcement that they had to cease). At the same time there continued to be support for Alpha 66 from the CIA.[71]

Double agents frequently become the stars both of the groups they penetrate and the government agencies to whom they report. Some of the most violent and feared members of the IRA were in fact members of Britain's special forces, including John Joe Magee, billed as the IRA's "torturer-in-chief," according to Neil Mackay, Home Affairs Editor of the *Sunday Herald*.[72] "A former soldier who joined the Provisional IRA at army intelligence's request," the *Guardian* reported in 2002, said that both MI5 and the FBI were in on the act.[73]

In America there was the example of Gary Rowe, an FBI informant inside the Klan, who knew some of the same people as did Joseph Milteer, the white racist who accurately predicted the JFK assassination.[74] Rowe famously helped to convict those who were with him when civil rights worker Viola Liuzzo was murdered, but was never prosecuted for his other killings.[75] Diane McWhorter, whose father was in Rowe's Klan cell, later wrote that "Almost as soon as he [Rowe] infiltrated the organization, Klan violence in Birmingham flared, and would burn as long as he remained in town."[76]

Recently I have been writing about an analogous figure in al-Qaeda: Ali Mohamed, who was Washington's double agent inside al-Qaeda, and also a chief 9/11 plotter.[77] *Triple Cross*, a new book by Peter Lance, confirms that Ali Mohamed, one of al-Qaeda's top trainers in terrorism and how to hijack airplanes, was an informant for the FBI, an asset of the CIA, and for four years a member of the US Army.[78] This special status explains why one of his protégés, El Sayyid Nosair, was able to commit the first al-Qaeda crime in America, back in 1990, be caught along with his co-conspirators, and yet be dismissed by the police and FBI as (and these are actual quotes) a "lone deranged gunman" who "acted alone."[79]

In fact, the FBI was aware back in 1990 that Mohamed had engaged in terrorist training on Long Island; yet it acted to protect Mohamed from arrest, even after one of his trainees had moved beyond training to an actual assassination.[80] Three years later, in 1993, Mohamed was actually detained in Canada by the RCMP. But he gave the RCMP the telephone number of his FBI handler in San Francisco, and after a brief call the RCMP released him.[81] This enabled Mohamed to fly later in the year to Nairobi, and begin to organize the eventual al Qaeda attacks on the US embassies in Africa.

Mohamed's trainees were all members of the Al-Kifah Center in Brooklyn, which served as the main American recruiting center for the Makhtab-al-Khidimat, the "Services Center" network that after the Afghan war became known as al-Qaeda.[82] The Al-Kifah Center was headed in 1990 by the blind Egyptian Sheikh Omar Abdel Rahman, who like Ali Mohamed had been admitted to the United States despite being on a State Department Watch List.[83] As he had done earlier in Egypt, the sheikh "issued a fatwa in America that permitted his followers to rob banks and kill Jews."[84]

Ali Mohamed was training these Islamists to fight in Afghanistan. However the Soviets had totally withdrawn from Afghanistan by February 1989, and all of this training was going on in late 1989, at a time when the US government, to paraphrase what was just said about 1963, was of two minds about what to do in Afghanistan.

The CIA were backing Gulbuddin Hekmatyar, a major heroin trafficker with his own heroin labs, to get rid of the secular, anti-Islamist government in Kabul, which the Russians left behind.[85]

Meanwhile a State Department official, Edmund McWilliams, objected that "Pakistani intelligence and Hekmatyar were dangerous allies," and that the United States was making an important mistake by endorsing ISI's puppet Afghan interim government.[86] But Ali Mohamed's training, both in Afghanistan and later around New York, was precisely designed to strengthen the Arab Afghans in Brooklyn who were allied with Hekmatyar.[87]

Mohamed Ali's trainees became involved in terrorist activities in other parts of the world. One of them, Anas al-Liby, became a leader in a plot against Libyan president Mu'ammar Qadaffi. Anas al-Liby was later given political asylum in Great Britain, despite suspicions that he was a high-level al Qaeda operative.[88] As the French authors Brisard and Dasquié point out, Qadaffii's Libya in 1998 was the first government to ask Interpol to issue an arrest warrant for Osama bin Laden. They argue that Osama and al Qaeda elements were collaborating with the British MI5 in an anti-Gaddafi assassination plot.[89]

Another of Ali Mohamed's trainees, Clement Rodney Hampton-El, accepted money from the Saudi Embassy in Washington to recruit Muslim warriors for Bosnia.[90] He was also allowed to go to Fort Belvoir, where an Army major gave him a list of Muslims in the US Army whom he could recruit.[91] Fort Belvoir was the site of the Army's Land Information Warfare Activity (LIWA), whose Information Dominance Center was "full of army intelligence 'geeks' " targeting Islamic jihadists.[92]

Hampton-El's recruiting for Bosnia was part of a larger operation. Numbers of Arab Afghans were trained for Bosnia, and later for the Kosovo Liberation Army, by Ayman al-Zawahiri, the top associate of Osama bin Laden in al Qaeda, and also a close ally of his fellow Egyptian, Ali Mohamed.[93] (Ali Mohamed had sworn allegiance to al-Zawahiri in 1984 while still in Egypt, and he twice arranged for al-Zawahiri to come to stay with him in California for fund-raising purposes.)[94]

Meanwhile US intelligence veterans like Richard Secord helped bring Arab Afghans recruited by Hekmatyar to Azerbaijan, in order to consolidate a pro-western government there.[95] And in 1998 the US began bombing Kosovo in support of the Kosovo Liberation Army, some of whose cadres were both trained and supported in the field by al Qaeda's "Arab Afghans."[96]

So Ali Mohammad's activities intersected with US covert operations, and this fact appears to have earned him protection.[97] Jack Blum, former special investigator for the Senate Foreign Relations Committee, commented that

> One of the big problems here is that many suspects in the [1993] World Trade Center bombing were associated with the Mujahedeen. And there are components of our government that are ab-

> solutely disinterested in following that path because it leads back to people we supported in the Afghan war.[98]

What agency would have been interested in protecting Mohamed? The CIA claimed to have ceased using him as an operative back in 1984.[99] Yet in 1988 Ali Mohamed flew from Fort Bragg to Afghanistan and fought there, while he was on the US Army payroll. His commanding officer didn't like it, but Mohammad was apparently being directed by another agency.[100] Ten years later, in 1998, a confidential CIA internal survey concluded that it was "partly culpable" for the 1993 World Trade Center bombing, carried out by some of Ali Mohamed's trainees.[101]

After a plea bargain, Ali Mohamed eventually pleaded guilty in 2000 to having organized the bombings of US embassies in Africa, but as of 2006 he had still not yet been sentenced.[102]

The Cover-Up Modus Operandi: He "Acted Alone"

Unambiguously Mohamed's trainees became involved, almost immediately, in terrorism on US soil. In November 1990, three of Mohamed's trainees conspired together to kill Meir Kahane, the racist founder of the Jewish Defense League. The actual killer, El Sayyid Nosair, was caught by accident almost immediately; and by luck the police soon found his two co-conspirators, Mahmoud Abouhalima and Mohammed Salameh, waiting at Nosair's apartment. They found much more:

> There were formulas for bomb making, 1,440 rounds of ammunition, and manuals [supplied by Ali Mohamed] from the John F. Kennedy Special Warfare Center at Fort Bragg marked "Top Secret for Training," along with classified documents belonging to the U.S. Joint Chiefs of Staff. The police found maps and drawings of New York City landmarks like the Statue of Liberty, Times Square—and the World Trade Center. The forty-seven boxes of evidence they collected also included the collected sermons of blind Sheikh Omar, in which he exhorted his followers to "destroy the edifices of capitalism."[103]

All three had been trained by Ali Mohamed back in the late 1980s at a rifle range, where the FBI had photographed them, before terminating this surveillance in the fall of 1989.[104] The US Government was thus in an excellent position to arrest, indict, and convict all of the terrorists involved, including Mohamed.

Yet only hours after the killing, Joseph Borelli, Chief of NYPD detectives, struck a familiar American note and pronounced Nosair a "lone deranged gunman."[105] Some time later, he actually told the press that "There was nothing [at Nosair's house] that would stir your imagination . . . Nothing has transpired that changes our opinion that he acted alone."[106]

Borelli was not acting alone in this matter. His position was also that of the FBI, who said they too believed "that Mr. Nosair had acted alone in shooting Rabbi Kahane." "The bottom line is that we can't connect anyone else to the Kahane shooting," an FBI agent said."[107]

The initial reaction of the NYPD had been that Nosair was part of a conspiracy.[108] This impression was strengthened when a detective discovered that Nosair's car had been moved after Nosair was arrested. As a result, according to the District Attorney prosecutor on the case, William Greenbaum, "We sensed a much bigger conspiracy, and we were sure that more than one person was involved."[109]

How then to explain the ultimate assurances that Nosair was a lone assassin? John Miller, who went on to be the assistant director of public affairs for the FBI,[110] blamed the culture of the NYPD: "The prevailing theory in the NYPD was, 'Don't make waves.' . . . So in the Nosair case, when Chief Borelli turned a blind eye to the obvious, he was merely remaining true to the culture of the NYPD."[111] Miller's unlikely explanation suppressed the relevant fact that the FBI, and eventually the District Attorney's office which prosecuted the case, turned a blind eye to the obvious as well.

In the light of those forty-seven boxes of incriminating evidence, it is more likely that the US law-enforcement system has a cover-up modus operandi or MO for dealing with a suspect who is marginally attached to intelligence operations, covert operations, even controversial operations which are opposed by other elements of the US government. It is to tell the public (as they did earlier in the case of Oswald) that the suspect "acted alone."

In thus limiting the case, the police and FBI were in effect protecting Nosair's two Arab co-conspirators in the murder of a US citizen. Both of them were ultimately convicted in connection with the first WTC bombing, along with another Mohamed trainee, Nidal Ayyad. The 9/11 Report, summarizing the convictions of Salameh, Ayyad, Abouhalima, and the blind Sheikh for the WTC bombing and New York landmarks plots, called it "this superb investigative and prosecutorial effort."[112] It said nothing about the suppressed evidence found in Nosair's house, including "maps and drawings of New York City landmarks," which if pursued should have prevented both plots from developing.

And proper surveillance of this circle might have led investigators to the developing 9/11 plot as well. "Lance pinpoints how, in 1991, the FBI, knowing of a New Jersey mail box store with direct links to al-Qaeda, failed to keep it under watch. Just six years later, two of the 9/11 hijackers got their fake IDs at the same location."[113]

The cover-up MO here is relevant to what I said at the beginning. To end up having an unsolvable crime, one should pre-select a candidate or candidates who cannot be properly investigated. Thus the ideal pre-selected candidate will be one about whom the truth will never emerge, *because of the candidate's controversial involvement in previous covered-up operations*. This will ensure that an institutional cover-up, already in place, will be extended to cover the new crime, even if it is a major one.

Oswald was one such pre-selected candidate. Those conspiratorially involved with Ali Mohamed and with 9/11 would also seem to fit the same description. That is what struck me most when I went back to compare the two meta-events: the killings of Kennedy and of Meir Kahane. Both Oswald and Nosair were quickly declared "lone" assassins, to protect someone or something else.

I should make clear that with respect to 9/11, I have certain knowledge of only one fact: that there has been and continues to be a massive cover-up. I have not yet properly integrated the earlier cover-up in 1990 of Nosair's associates, including Ali Mohamed, into my theory of what happened in 2001. I do however believe that the earlier cover-up is a relevant fact which merits further investigation.

The similarity between the cover-up of Oswald in 1963 and Nosair in 1990 is striking. In both cases the truth about the predesignated culprit was unpursuable, because he was part of an operation too embarrassing to disclose. In the case of the Ali Mohamed trainees, this is a major scandal. These people could have been stopped back in 1990, and they weren't.

I conclude from this that it is a matter of paramount importance to learn more about these meta-events and their cover-ups. Because when we can understand what has happened before, we will be more able to deal with such a meta-event when it happens again. As I have said so many times, to understand any of these events in real depth, you have to look at what is on-going in all of them.

The traditional media seem determined, predictably, not to help in this matter. As I write this, six weeks after Lance's *Triple Cross* was released, Lexis Nexis records only one post-publication reference to it or to Ali Mohamed—the *Toronto Sun* of 19th November 2006.[114] But there is no lack of interest on the Internet, where as of this writing there are 43,600 hits on *Triple Cross*.)[115]

The gravity of the Ali Mohamed matter is compounded by the context of the drug traffic. To get to the level where we can cope and deal with these recurring problems in our country, we will have to understand the continuity, and deal with it every time it surfaces.

Because if we don't deal with it this time, and we probably won't, it will surface again.

WTC- 7 came down at 5:20 pm displaying all the characteristics of a classic controlled demolition: a complete and symmetrical collapse into its own "footprint" (foundation) at close to free-fall speed, even though it was not hit by any airplane, had no jet fuel-based fires, and appeared to be under no threat of collapse. Larry Silverstein, who had leased the Word Trade Center and had insured it for $3.5 billion agasint terrorist attacks just six weeks before 9/11 gave an interview during which he explained that he had told the "fire comander" that there had been so much death and destruction, perhaps the best thing to do would be to "pull it." He said they made the decision to "pull" and they both watched the building come down.

NOTES

1 Even the vocabularies of the old and new media diverge. A Lexis Nexis search in December 2006 for the word "parapolitics" in major newspapers yielded five entries, only two of them from the United States. The same search on Google yielded 86,100 hits. Meanings of "parapolitics": 1) "A system or practice of politics in which accountability is consciously diminished" (Peter Dale Scott, *The War Conspiracy* [New York: Bobbs Merrill, 1972], p. 171); and 2) The intellectual study of parapolitical interactions between public states and other forms of organized violence. See Robert Cribb and Peter Dale Scott, "Introduction," in Eric Wilson and Tim Lindsey, eds., *Government of the Shadows: Parapolitics and Criminal Sovereignty* (London: Pluto, 2007).

2. WR 5, 17 WH 397 (Transcript of Dallas Police Channel One, before 12:45 p.m., 22nd November 1963).

3. E.g. CIA Cable 74830 of 10th October 1963 to Mexico City, http://www.maryferrell.org/mffweb/archive/viewer/showDoc.do?docId=30335&relPageId=2; reproduced in John Newman, *Oswald and the CIA* (New York: Carroll and Graf, 1995), p. 512.

4. Manning Clements FBI FD-302 of 23rd November 1963; in Warren Report, p. 614.

5. WR 5; Sylvia Meagher, *Accessories After the Fact* (Mary Ferrell Foundation Press, 2006), pp. 10–13, 78n.

6. Richard A. Clarke, *Against All Enemies: Inside America's War on Terrorism* (New York: Simon and Schuster, 2004), 13–14.

7. 9/11 Commission Report, p. 30.

8. William Norman Grigg, "Did We Know What Was Coming?" *New American* (11th March 2002), http://www.thenewamerican.com/tna/2002/03-11-2002/vo18no05_didweknow.htm.

9. Peter Lance, *Triple Cross* (New York: HarperCollins, 2006), p. 383.

10. James W. Douglass, "The King Conspiracy Exposed in Memphis," in James DiEugenio and Lisa Pease, eds., *The Assassinations: Probe Magazine on JFK, MLK, RFK, and Malcolm X* (Los Angeles: Feral House, 2003), pp. 499–501.

11. Historically I was first drawn to this because in the news of the Watergate break-in in the *New York Times*, on June 17th 1972, which I remember quite vividly, there was Frank Sturgis, alias Frank Fiorini. I had already written about him in *The Dallas Conspiracy* a year before, because of his role in perpetuating false Oswald stories, what I now call Phase One Oswald stories, linking Oswald falsely to Cuba (Peter Dale Scott, Paul L. Hoch, and Russell Stetler, eds., *The Assassinations: Dallas and Beyond* [New York: Vintage, 1976], pp. 356, 360–62).

12. Fred Emery, *Watergate: The Corruption of American Politics and the Fall of Richard Nixon* (New York: Random House/Times Books, 1994), pp. 186–194.

13. Anthony Summers with Robbyn Swann, *The Arrogance of Power: The Secret World of Richard Nixon* (New York: Viking, 2000), pp. 198–99, 505.

14. Testimony of FBI Director L. Patrick Gray, *Senate Watergate Hearings*, Volume 9, p. 3456: "On my own initiative, I also ordered that George Munro, CIA station chief in Mexico City, not be interviewed." (Munro, a long-time CIA officer in Mexico City, was not the station chief.) Cf. Felt FBI Memo of 29th June 1972 to Bates, SAIC FBI

Washington Field Office. The reference to Munro is redacted in the Nedzi Watergate Hearing: U.S. Cong. House, Committee on Armed Services, *Inquiry into the Alleged Involvement of the Central Intelligence Agency in the Watergate and Ellsberg Matters*, Hearings, 94th Cong., 1st Sess., H.A.S.C. No. 94–4 (Washington: GPO, 1975), p. 220.

15. Jonathan Marshall, Peter Dale Scott, and Jane Hunter *The Iran-Contra Connection: Secret Teams and Covert Operations in the Reagan Era* (Boston: South End Press, 1987); Peter Dale Scott and Jonathan Marshall, *Cocaine Politics: The CIA, Drugs, and Armies in Central America* (Berkeley: University of California Press, 1998).
16. "The Vice President appears on Meet the Press with Tim Russert," 16th September 2001, http://www.whitehouse.gov/vicepresident/news-speeches/speeches/vp20010916.html: "I went down into what's call a PEOC, the Presidential Emergency Operations Center, . . . But when I arrived there within a short order, we had word the Pentagon's been hit." To minimize the issues in this chapter, I have accepted the Report's revised time for the hit (9:37 a.m.). The time for Flight 77's crash was originally announced as 9:45 a.m. (*New York Times*, 13th September 2001, A21).
17. *9/11 Report*, 29. The Report says that the order was given by FAA national operations manager Benedict Sliney (who was on his first day at the job). But a year earlier Mineta had testified to Congress (as he would later to the Commission) that he himself, from the PEOC, issued the order (U.S. Congress, Senate, Committee on Commerce, Statement by Norman Y. Mineta, Hearing on Federal Aviation Security Standards, 20th September 2001); cf. Dan Balz and Bob Woodward, *Washington Post*, 27th January 2002.
18. Clarke, *Against All Enemies*, p. 8; 9/11 Report, p. 38. The two accounts agree about Air Force One and COG, but not about the planes (Clarke: "tell the Pentagon they have authority from the President to shoot down hostile aircraft;" 9/11 Report: "The White House requested . . . a fighter combat air patrol over Washington, D.C.")
19. *Newsweek* (31st December 2001).
20. 9/11 Report, p. 40.
21. David Griffin, "9/11, the American Empire, and Common Moral Norms," in David Ray Griffin and Peter Dale Scott, eds., *9/11 and American Empire: Intellectuals Speak Out* (Northampton, Massachusetts: Olive Branch, 2006), p. 8; citing 9/11 Report, p. 40.
22. 9/11 Report, p. 41.
23. 9/11 Report, p. 40.
24. The Commission had phone log verification, from the Secure Switchboard Log, for Bush's call to Cheney at 9:15, and for an unimportant call made by the President about 9:20 to FBI Director Mueller (9/11 Report, p. 463, footnote 204: "White House record, Secure Switchboard Log, 11th September 2001 (call [about 9:20 a.m.] from Bush to [FBI Director] Mueller"). The Report cites the Secure Switchboard Log again for what they call a second "confirmation call at 10:18 a.m." For the two-minute "confirmation" call at 10:18, the Report cites a "White House record, Secure Switchboard Log, Sept. 11, 2001" (9/11 Report, p. 41, and footnote 221, p. 465).
25. Thomas Kean later complained that "The phone logs don't exist, because they evidently got so fouled up in communications that the phone logs have nothing. So that's the evidence we have." "There's no documentary evidence here," added Vice-Chairman Lee Hamilton. "The only evidence you have is the statements of

the president and vice president" (9/11 Commission, Hearing of 17th June 2004, http://www.9-11commission.gov/archive/hearing12/9-11Commission_Hearing_2004-06-17.pdf).

26. Emery, *Watergate*, pp. 414–18. There is an analogous JFK gap as well. "Most Americans have heard of the 'eighteen-minute gap' in a Nixon Presidential tape—the erasure was part of a cover-up for which Nixon was driven from office. But few know of the erasure of a 1963 conversation between President Lyndon Johnson and FBI Director J. Edgar Hoover, a call recorded less than twenty-four hours after the murder of President Kennedy. This new documentary short, The Fourteen Minute Gap, relates Rex Bradford's discovery of the erasure, initial denials by the LBJ Library, and his failed attempt to get the story into the national media" (Rex Bradford, "The Fourteen Minute Gap," http://www.maryferrell.org/wiki/index.php/The_Fourteen_Minute_Gap).
27. Clarke, *Against All Enemies*, p. 8; 9/11 Report, p. 38. The two accounts agree about Air Force One and COG, but not about the planes (Clarke: "tell the Pentagon they have authority from the President to shoot down hostile aircraft;" 9/11 Report: "The White House requested . . . a fighter combat air patrol over Washington, D.C.")
28. James Mann, *Rise of the Vulcans* (New York: Viking, 2004), pp. 138–145, 295–96. James Mann noted correctly that the original purpose of the plans was "in order to keep the federal government running during and after a nuclear war with the Soviet Union." He failed to mention that the planning eventually called for suspension of the Constitution, not just "after a nuclear war," but for any "national security emergency." This was defined in Executive Order 12656 of 1988 as: "any occurrence, including natural disaster, military attack, technological emergency, or other emergency, that seriously degrades or seriously threatens the national security of the United States" (Executive Order 12656 of 18th November 1988, 53 FR 47491, 3 CFR, 1988 Comp., p. 585; http://www.archives.gov/federal-register/codification/executive-order/12656.html).
29. Peter Dale Scott, *The Road to 9/11: Wealth, Empire, and the Future of America* (Berkeley: University of California Press, 2007, forthcoming), Chapter 14.
30. 9/11 Report, p. 41.
31. http://www.disa.mil/main/whca.html.
32. In the 1990s the AARB attempted to obtain from the WHCA the unedited original tapes of conversations from Air Force One on the return trip from Dallas, 22nd November 1963. (Edited and condensed versions of these tapes had been available since the 1970s from the LBJ Library in Austin.) The attempt was unsuccessful: "The Review Board's repeated written and oral inquiries of the White House Communications Agency did not bear fruit. The WHCA could not produce any records that illuminated the provenance of the edited tapes." See Assassinations Records Review Board, *Final Report*, Chapter 6, Part 1, 116, http://www.archives.gov/research/jfk/review-board/report/chapter-06-part1.pdf.
33. NARA Record 172-10001-10003 (22nd November 1963), WHCA statement, "Dallas."
34. Peter Dale Scott, *Deep Politics and the Death of JFK* (Berkeley: University of California Press, 1998), pp. 273–74, 277–78; quoting 23 WH 841, "cut all traffic for the ambulance going to Parkland."

35. Scott, *Deep Politics*, pp. 273–74, 277–78.
36. Supporting evidence for the 9/11 Report is scheduled for release on 2nd January 2009. See 9/11 Commission, *Media Advisory*, 20th August 2004, http://www.9-11commission.gov/press/pr_2004-08-20a.pdf; Thomas H., Kean, and Lee H. Hamilton, with Benjamin Rhodes, *Without Precedent: The Inside Story of the 9/11 Commission* (New York: Knopf, 2006), p. 312: "All of our records were transferred to the National Archives, with an agreement that they would be made public at the beginning of 2009."
37. Peter Dale Scott, "Homeland Security Contracts for Vast New Detention Camps," Pacific News Service, 8th February 2006, http://news.pacificnews.org/news/view_article.html?article_id=eed74d9d44c30493706fe03f4c9b3a77; *Project Censored 2007: The Top 25 Censored Stories* (New York: Seven Stories, 2006)
38. Peter Dale Scott, "Drugs, Parapolitics, and Mexico: The DFS, the Drug Traffic, and the United States," in Eric Wilson and Tim Lindsey, eds., *Government of the Shadows: Parapolitics and Criminal Sovereignty* (London: Pluto, 2007).
39. Peter Dale Scott, *Deep Politics and the Death of JFK* (Berkeley: University of California Press, 1998), pp. 70–71, 132, 136–38.
40. Lamar Waldron, with Thom Hartmann, *Ultimate Sacrifice* (New York: Carroll and Graf, 2006), pp. 74, 170.
41. Larry Hancock, *Someone Would Have Talked* (Southlake: JFK Lancer Publications, 2006), pp. 126, 135; cf. "Guns, Drugs, and the CIA," Frontline, PBS, 17th May 1988. Jenkins had earlier been attached to the CIA's drug-supported asset in Thailand, the Thai Border Police (p. 416).
42. Gaeton Fonzi, *The Last Investigation* (New York: Thunder's Mouth, pp. 380–390; Noel Twyman, *Bloody Treason: On Solving History's Greatest Murder Mystery: The Assassination of John F. Kennedy* (Rancho Santa Fe: Laurel, 1997), pp. 462–64 (JFK); *Guardian* (20th November 2006) (RFK).
43. *Final Report of the Independent Counsel for Iran-Contra Matters*, Chapter 14, http://www.fas.org/irp/offdocs/walsh/chap_14.htm.
44. Celerino Castillo III and Dave Harmon, *Powderburns: Cocaine, Contras, and the Drug War* (Oakville, Ontario: Mosaic, 1994), pp. 137–39.
45. http://www.state.gov/p/inl/narc/rewards/47900.htm.
46. Bardach, *Washington* Post (12th November 2006).
47. Bardach, *Washington Post* (12th November 2006).
48. Bardach, *Washington Post* (12th November 2006).
49. 10 HSCA 99-100; G. Robert Blakey and Richard Billings, *The Plot to Kill the President* (New York: Times Books, 1981), pp. 170–74; Scott, *Deep Politics*, pp. 89–91, 329–330, 371.
50. "Evidence Presented to the British Parliament, 4th October 2001," *Los Angeles Times*, 10/4/01. Cf. e.g. *Minneapolis Star-Tribune* (30th September 2001); *Asia Times* (8th December 2001); *New York Times* (4th October 2001; 11th October 2001); *San Francisco Chronicle* (4th October 2001). For further documentation, see Peter Dale Scott, *Drugs, Oil, and War*, pp. 32, 36.
51. 9/11 Report, p. 171. I find this statement one-sided and misleading, but less so than the opposite claim of Yossef Bodansky: "The annual income of the Taliban from the drug trade is estimated at $8 billion. Bin Laden administers and manages these

funds—laundering them through the Russian mafia . . . (Yossef Bodansky, *Bin Laden: The Man Who Declared War on America* [New York: Random House, 2001], p. 315).

52. "US 'seizes al-Qaeda drugs ship'," *BBC News* (19th December 2003).
53. Robert Dreyfuss, *Devil's Game: How the United States Helped Unleash Fundamentalist Islam* (New York: Holt, 2005), p. 287: "There is no question that the Casey-ISI actions aided the growth of a significant network of right-wing Islamist extremists [including] the Islamic Movement of Uzbekistan."
54. Rohan Gunaratna, *Inside Al Qaeda: Global Network of Terror* (New York: Columbia University Press, 2002), p. 170. Cf. *New York Times* (3rd May 2001): "There are sketchy but widely circulated stories that the [IMU] militants are trained by the Taliban and receive money from drug traffickers and from Osama bin Laden, the exiled Saudi accused of leading an international terrorist group." Cf. *Guardian* (17th May 2005): "Both the US and Britain link the IMU to al-Qaida, and the Afghan heroin trade."
55. "The Threat Posed by the Convergence of Organized Crime, Drugs Trafficking, and Terrorism," Written Testimony of Ralf Mutschke, Assistant Director, Criminal Intelligence Directorate, International Criminal Police Organization—Interpol General Secretariat, before a hearing of the Committee on the Judiciary, Subcommittee on Crime, 13th December 2000; http://judiciary.house.gov/Legacy/muts1213.htm.
56. *Wall Street Journal* (3rd May 2001).
57. Loretta Napoleoni, *Terror Incorporated: Tracing the Dollars behind the Terror Networks* (New York: Seven Stories, 2005), pp. 90–97: "[IMU leader] Namangiani's networks in Tajikistan and in Central Asia were used to smuggle opium from Afghanistan. It was partly thanks to Namangiani's contacts in Chechnya that heroin reached Europe" (p. 91); "It was thanks to the mediation of Chechen criminal groups that the KLA and the Albanian mafia managed to gain control of the transit of heroin in the Balkans" (p. 96).
58. "KLA Funding Tied To Heroin Profits," *Washington Times* (3rd May 1999).
59. Peter Klebnikov, "Heroin Heroes," *Mother Jones* (January–February 2001). I have written elsewhere of how what I called a meta-group affiliated with Adnan Khashoggi took advantage of the NATO bombing of Kosovo to consolidate the Kosovar drug route via Abkhazia (and Turkey). See "The Far West Drug Meta-Group: Part 1." Article for *Nexus: New Times Magazine* 13.3 (June–July 2006), pp. 25–31, 82, http://www.nexusmagazine.com/articles/DrugMetaGroup1.html. This version is without footnotes; go to "The Global Drug Meta-Group: Drugs, Managed Violence, and the Russian 9/11," *Lobster* (29th October 2005); http://lobster-magazine.co.uk/articles/global-drug.htm), for a footnoted version. In February 2006 a member of the meta-group confirmed part of my hypothesis: namely, that the so-called "Pristina dash" of Russian troops to seize Kosovo's main airport had been prepared for by his meta-group colleague Vladimir Filin (Anton Surikov, *Pravda-info* (8th February 2006); http://forum.msk.ru/material/power/7495.html; cf. http://www.left.ru/burtsev/ops/prishtina.phtml).
60. On 18th October 2002, Attorney General John Ashcroft invoked the State Secrets Privilege in order to prevent disclosure of the nature of Edmonds's work on the grounds that it would endanger national security.
61. Daniel Ellsberg with Kris Welch, KPFA, 26th August 2006; http://wotisitgood4.blogspot.com/2006/10/ellsberg-hastert-got-suitcases-of-al.html.

62. *Vanity Fair* (September 2005). According to the ATC web site, "As one of the leading business associations in the United States, the American-Turkish Council (ATC) is dedicated to effectively strengthening U.S.-Turkish relations through the promotion of commercial, defense, technology, and cultural relations. Its diverse membership includes *Fortune* 500, U.S., and Turkish companies, multinationals, nonprofit organizations, and individuals with an interest in U.S.-Turkish relations." It is thus comparable to the American Security Council, whose activities in 1963 are discussed in Scott, *Deep Politics*, p. 292.
63. In December 2006 a Lexis Nexis search of major newspapers for "Sibel Edmonds" and "drug" produced no relevant results. A similar search on Google yielded 99,100.
64. The most sensational charge of a direct 9/11-drug connection is made by Daniel Hopsicker in his self-published book *Welcome to Terrorland*. "Hopsicker is still researching the three Huffman-trained 9/11 pilots, who he says had financial, drug-trafficking and military intelligence ties to the U.S. government. He is developing suspicions that Atta and the entire school were involved with Osama bin Laden in heroin trafficking. Hopsicker reports that on 25th July 2000, the DEA in Orlando discovered more than 30 pounds of heroin inside a Learjet owned by Wally Hilliard, owner of Huffman Aviation. Earlier that month, on July 3rd, Atta and Marwan Al-Shehri had started flight lessons at Huffman. Hopsicker claims it's not a coincidence that Atta was allegedly importing heroin with Hilliard's help, selling Afghanistan's notorious opium and heroin to finance the Taliban. Hilliard would not be interviewed for this story. 'The apparatus that Osama bin Laden set into place along with the CIA back in the '80s, still exists,' Hopsicker says. 'The FBI is protecting an operation set in place back in the '80s . . . a money-laundering device to funnel money to the Afghan Mujahedeen and to flood this country with heroin'." Sander Hicks, *Long Island Press* (26th February 2004), http://www.911citizenswatch.org/modules.php?op=modload&name=News&file=article&sid=82). Hopsicker's charges are reported, but only minimally corroborated, in Sander Hicks, *The Big Wedding* (Vox Pop #2, 2005), pp. 31–39. Most other researchers, myself included, are looking for more independent corroboration.
65. Indira Singh testimony, 9/11 Citizen's Commission, p. 128; http://www.justicefor911.org/September-Hearings.doc. Indira Singh was a one-time senior employee of J.P. Morgan, who was fired after she shared her concerns about an Arab-financed contracting firm with her bank and the FBI.
66. Scott, *Drugs, Oil, and War*, pp. 27–58.
67. Peter Truell and Larry Gurwin, *False Profits: The Inside Story of BCCI, the World's Most Corrupt Financial Empire* (Boston: Houghton Mifflin, 1992), p. 132.
68. Michael Griffin, *Reaping the Whirlwind: The Taliban Movement in Afghanistan* (London: Pluto, 2001), pp. 149–150; *Washington Post* (12th September 1994), p. A13.
69. Scott, *Deep Politics and the Death of JFK*, p. 252; quoting Lucille Connell, p. 26 WH 738.
70. Scott, *Deep Politics and the Death of JFK*, p. 257.
71. Hinckle and Turner, *Deadly Deceits*, pp. 173–76. Cf. Hancock, *Someone Would Have Talked*, pp. 177–78.
72. *Sunday Herald* (15th December 2002); http://www.sundayherald.com/29997.

73. *Guardian* (6th July 2002).
74. Scott, *Deep Politics*, pp. 49–52.
75. Curt Gentry, *J. Edgar Hoover: The Man and the Secrets* (New York: Penguin, 1992), p. 585; cf. p. 484.
76. Diane McWhorter, *Carry Me Home: Birmingham, Alabama—The Climactic Battle of the Civil Rights Revolution* (New York: Simon and Schuster, 2001), p. 163.
77. Peter Dale Scott, "The Background of 9/11: Drugs, Oil, and US Covert Operations," in David Ray Griffin and Peter Dale Scott, eds., *9/11 and American Empire: Intellectuals Speak Out* (Northampton, Massachusetts: Olive Branch, 2006), pp. 73–78. For updates, see my website at http://socrates.berkeley.edu/~pdscott/q.html.
78. Lance, *Triple Cross*, p. xxvii, etc.
79. *Newsday* (8th November 1990); quoted in Peter Lance, *1000 Years for Revenge* (New York: Harper Collins, 2003), p. 35; *New York Times* (16th December 1990).
80. Lance, *1000 Years for Revenge*, pp. 29–37.
81. Lance, *Triple Cross*, pp. 123–25.
82. Robert Dreyfuss, *Devil's Game: How the United States Helped Unleash Fundamentalist Islam* (New York: Henry Holt, 2005), p. 278; John K. Cooley, *Unholy Wars: Afghanistan, America, and International Terrorism* (London: Pluto, 1999), pp. 87–88; Lance, *1000 Years for Revenge*, pp. 29–31; *Independent* (1st November 1998).
83. Rahman was issued two visas, one of them "by a CIA officer working undercover in the consular section of the American embassy in Sudan" (Peter L. Bergen, *Holy War, Inc.: Inside the Secret World of Osama bin Laden* [New York: Free Press, 2001], p. 67). FBI consultant Paul Williams writes that Ali Mohamed "settled in America on a visa program controlled by the CIA" (Paul L. Williams, *Al Qaeda: Brotherhood of Terror* [Upper Saddle River: Alpha/Pearson Education, 2002], p. 117). Others allegedly admitted, despite being on the State Department watch list, were Mohamed Atta and possibly Ayman al-Zawahiri (Nafeez Mosaddeq Ahmed, *The War on Truth: 9/11, Disinformation, and the Anatomy of Terrorism* [Northampton, Massachusetts: Olive Branch, 2005], pp. 46, 205).
84. Wright, *The Looming Tower*, p. 177.
85. Steve Coll, *Ghost Wars* (New York: Penguin, 2004), p. 195. In retrospect, the decision to back Hekmatyar against Najibullah appears to have been disastrous. As Ahmed Rashid predicted accurately in 1990, "If Afghanistan fragments into warlordism, the West can expect a flood of cheap heroin that will be impossible to stop . . . Afghanistan's President Najibullah has skillfully played on Western fears of a drugs epidemic by repeatedly offering co-operation with the DEA and other anti-narcotic agencies, but the West, which still insists on his downfall, has refused. If President [George Herbert Walker] Bush and Margaret Thatcher continue to reject a peace process, they must prepare for an invasion of Afghan-grown heroin in Washington and London" (Ahmed Rashid, "Afghanistan Heroin Set to Flood West," *Independent* (London, 25th May 1990): "In early 1988 the State Department negotiators had been preparing to accept an end to CIA assistance." They then reversed themselves and held out for a matching of Soviet and CIA support to the two factions. Apparently the policy shift was motivated by an unscripted remark by Reagan to a television interviewer (Coll, *Ghost Wars*, pp. 176–77).

86. Coll, *Ghost Wars*, p. 196; cf. Pp. 197-202; Barnett Rubin, *The Fragmentation of Afghanistan* (New Haven: Yale University Press, 2002), p. 251. McWilliams's argument found support among mid-level State Department officials in Washington; "Still, the more State Department officials mouthed the McWilliams line, the more Langley argued the contrary" (Coll, *Ghost Wars*, p. 197).
87. Cf. Lance, *Triple Cross*, pp. 20, 66.
88. Lance, *Triple Cross*, pp. 104–05. In May 2000 al-Liby's house in Britain was raided; and the police discovered an al-Qaeda terror manual which was largely written and translated by Ali Mohamed.
89. Brisard and Dasquié, *Forbidden Truth*, pp. 97–102, 155–59. A leader in the plot was Anas al-Liby, who was trained in terrorism by Ali Mohamed while Mohamed was still on the payroll of the US Army (Peter Lance, *Triple Cross*, p. 104; see also Chapter 9).
90. *United States v. Omar Ahmad Ali Abdel Rahman et al.*, Federal Court, SDNY, 15629-30, 15634-35, 15654, 15667-68, 15671, 15673; Kohlmann, *Al-Qaida's Jihad*, pp. 72–74; J.M. Berger, "Al Qaeda Recruited U.S. Servicemen: Testimony Links Plot To Saudi Gov't," Intelwire.com, http://intelwire.egoplex.com/hamptonel010604.html.
91. *United States v. Omar Ahmad Ali Abdel Rahman et al.*, Federal Court, SDNY, 15629-30, 15634-35, 15654, 15667-68, 15671, 15673; Kohlmann, *Al-Qaida's Jihad*, pp. 72–74; J.M. Berger, "Al Qaeda Recruited U.S. Servicemen: Testimony Links Plot To Saudi Gov't," Intelwire.com, http://intelwire.egoplex.com/hamptonel010604.html. In my talk, I said erroneously that Hampton-El was recruiting for Afghanistan.
92. Lance, *Triple Cross*, p. 331.
93. Marcia Christoff Kurop, "Al Qaeda's Balkan Links," *Wall Street Journal* (1st November 2001): "For the past ten years . . . Ayman al-Zawahiri has operated terrorist training camps [and] weapons of mass destruction factories throughout Albania, Kosovo, Macedonia, Bulgaria, Turkey and Bosnia."
94. Lance, *Triple Cross*, pp. 11, 194–98.
95. Peter Dale Scott, "The Background of 9/11: Drugs, Oil, and U.S. Covert Operations," in David Ray Griffin and Peter Dale Scott, eds., *9/11 and American Empire*, pp. 75–76.
96. Yossef Bodansky, *Bin Laden: The Man Who Declared War on America* (Roseville: Prima, 2001), pp. 298, 397–98.
97. Cf. Robert Friedman, *Village Voice* (30th March 1993): "In the aftermath of the bombing, many are wondering why there wasn't a comprehensive, wide-ranging investigation of Meir Kahane's murder. One possible explanation is offered by a counterterrorism expert for the FBI. At a meeting in a Denny's coffee shop in Los Angeles a week after the Kahane assassination, the 20-year veteran field agent met with one of his top undercover operatives, a burly 33-year-old FBI contract employee who had been a premier bomber for a domestic terrorist group before being 'turned' and becoming a government informant. 'Why aren't we going after the sheikh [Abdel Rahman]?' demanded the undercover man. 'It's hands-off,' answered the agent. 'Why?' asked the operative. 'It was no accident that the sheikh got a visa and that he's still in the country,' replied the agent, visibly upset. 'He's here under the banner of national security, the State Department, the NSA [National Security Agency], and the CIA.'"

98. Robert Friedman, *Village Voice* (30th March 1993).
99. Lance, *Triple Cross*, p. 16.
100. Lance, *Triple Cross*, p. 43: "Ali Mohamed defied his commanding officer and prepared to go [to Afghanistan] anyway. At that point, it seems clear that he was serving two sets of masters at Bragg."
101. Andrew Marshall, *Independent* (1st November 1998).
102. Lance, *Triple Cross*, pp. 3, 7. The CIA has shown through the years the lengths it will go to, to prevent having its sometime assets testify in open court. Cf. Scott and Marshall, *Cocaine Politics*, pp. 36; Peter Dale Scott**,** *Drugs, Contras and the CIA: Government Policies and the Cocaine Economy* (Los Angeles: From the Wilderness, 2000), pp. 39–40 and *passim*.
103. Lance, *1000 Years*, p. 34.
104. Lance, *1000 Years*, p. 31; Peter Lance, *Cover Up: What the Government Is Still Hiding about the War on Terror* (New York: HarperCollins, 2004), p. 25.
105. *Newsday* (8th November 1990); quoted in Lance, *1000 Years*, p. 35.
106. *New York Times* (8th November 1990); Robert I. Friedman, *Village Voice* (30th March 1993).
107. *New York Times* (16th December 1990).
108. "Nosair, the NYPD had already learned, had apparently not acted alone . . . Lieutenant Eddie Norris . . . seemed to be looking at a conspiracy involving three and possibly more assassins." John Miller and Michael Stone, with Chris Mitchell, *The Cell* (New York: Hyperion, 2003), p. 43.
109. Lance, *Triple Cross*, p. 59.
110. Lance, *Triple Cross*, p. 115.
111. Miller *et al.*, *The Cell*, pp. 44–45.
112. 9/11 Report, p. 72.
113. *Toronto Sun* (19th November 2006).
114. *New York Times* (28th August 2006) did cover, albeit disparagingly, an earlier National Geographic TV special in August 2006, which drew selectively from Lance's work.
115. The silence of the US press about *Triple Cross* was broken very slightly on 19th December 2006, with the following bland reference in the *New York Times* in the wake of the firing by News Corp of the book's publisher, Judith Regan: "Peter Lance, the author of 'Triple Cross,' an investigative work about the F.B.I. and the terror network of Osama Bin Laden, said Ms. Regan abandoned his book, released in late November, when the media storm erupted over the O. J. Simpson project, even canceling a scheduled interview with him on her own radio program."

9

Explaining the Inexplicable: Anatomy of an Atrocity

John McMurtry

The system works.

—US Secretary of Defense Donald Rumsfeld[1]

In May 2004, when undeniable pictures of tortures of Iraqi prisoners by US occupying forces were published, leading Americans and the international community were indignant. Yet no one in the media of record or anyone else in a position of public trust scrupled to observe what had started it all: the lawless US invasion of Iraq in March 2003, "the supreme crime " under international law, the crime which the judges at Nuremberg described as "only differing from other war crimes in that it contains within itself the accumulated evil of the whole."[2]

The torture was, as the judges at Nuremberg had foreseen, a predictable *consequence* of "the supreme crime." Yet all mention of the tortures in official culture remained disconnected from the cause.

It was reassuring that the international media had finally broadcast reports of crimes against humanity instead of ignoring them. But manichean slogans of "the Free World" versus "the Terrorists" remained decoupled from the criminality of the occupation itself. That the US focus of concern was "damage to America's image" indicated the nature of the problem. Although the Red Cross had reported that seventy to ninety percent of the torture victims were ordinary citizens picked up at random, this did not diminish cries for redirecting attention back to "the real danger, the terrorists endangering America." That the official Taguba Report itself was not permitted to question anyone above a part-time reserve-army woman officer (who was kept out of the interrogation room by US Defense Intelligence), was nowhere described as evidence of top-down control.[3] That the far worse crimes of maiming and killing defenseless Iraqi women and children by bombs were delinked from the torture regime inside the prisons indicated that the murderous blind eye was still closed.

Documented reports of criminal abuse of prisoners by US forces had been coming in to high command since the invasion of Afghanistan in 2001 with no decision to stop the routines.[4] "Stress positions," "humiliation," "use of [attack] dogs," "sleep deprivation," "subjection to noise," "prolonged isolation," "food and water deprivation," "restriction of toilet facilities," and "diet denial" were the generic orders.[5] Yet ever since 13th November 2001 shortly after 9/11, Presidential decree had unilaterally overridden the US-signed Geneva Convention of 1949 on the Treatment of Prisoners for the first time in its history. Anyone who objected was deemed to be "lending support to terrorists." The TV public itself daily watched prisoners—never charged or tried under any due process of law—hooded, shackled and limb-trussed. There were no visible questions asked about the brutality of the abuse, nor about the colonial occupation of the Cuban territory to perpetrate the crimes. What was central was "the torture scandal" and opinions on how to manage perception of it. Accordingly, "communist Cuba" was subjected to new and crippling sanctions for *its* "human rights abuses" as the state of siege by illegal US embargo and destabilizations was stepped up. The Orwellian set-points of meaning did not arouse media or expert questions.

Decoding the Compulsion to Disconnect

What could explain the systematic disconnect from reality with no consciousness of it? It was not confined to the US Right or even the US As the torture regime was exposed, the omnipresent liberal intellectual, Michael Ignatieff, urged fellow Canadians on public television to build up their military to join the US in enforcing "human rights" across the globe.[6] The disclosure of the videotaped Iraq tortures after years of lawless proscription was itself revealing of the selective mind-set at work. In fact, the story of US torture on *60 Minutes* in late April 2004 was a broadcast that had been held back for weeks because its pictures of torture by Americans were "not very patriotic" to show.[7] Only when "CBS heard that Seymour Hersh, working for the New Yorker" was planning to publish fresh photographs . . . and a damning report [by the army itself] . . . did the network decide to go ahead".[8] Until the reports came out elsewhere first, the facts could not be seen. In consensual closing of the doors of perception, the documented evidence was blocked out as non-existent.

Throughout, US concern remained narcissistic. "America is suffering a blow to its international image," the elite and the many regretted, with indifference to the fate of the victims about whom there was no further interest. The fatal pattern was overlooked that tells all—*that the US security state repudiates any law if it protects the lives of people outside itself.* Since "America's defense of its interests and investments" abroad entails the right to reject whatever is deemed inconsistent with it, it follows that its right is to act above the law. In the words of the US September 2002 National Security Strategy document: "We will take the actions necessary to ensure that our efforts to meet our global security commitments are not impaired by the potential for investigations, inquiry, or prosecution by the International Criminal Court (ICC), whose jurisdiction does not extend to Americans and which we do not accept."[9]

Not only immunity from international criminal law was thus assumed. Unilateral American repudiations of the Convention for the Prevention of the Crime of Genocide, the Kyoto Protocol, the Rights of Children, the Landmines Treaty, the Convention Against Racial Discrimination, the Comprehensive [Nuclear Bomb] Test Ban Treaty, the monitoring and testing requirements of the Chemical and Biological Weapons Treaties, the Covenant for Economic, Political and Cultural Rights of Nations, and the proposed Treaty on the Limitation of the Military Use of Outer Space all continued with no joining of the dots by expert commentary. What repels the pattern from view? Something deeper than class and faction is at work. A regime of meaning operates across classes and scientific disciplines themselves to disconnect the elements so that the whole cannot be seen. To be above the law—including laws applied by the US to prosecute others—was assumed by all as "America's leadership of the Free World." Silently, the impunity that once only God-Kings pretended to was internalized by other states and the UN itself as the regulating freedom of globalization.[10]

Exposure of the US torture regime in Afghanistan and Iraq left the impunity intact. The pictures made plausible denial impossible, but the criminal occupation of Iraq continued with renewed UN support on 8th June 2004. Only disconnected pieces were perceived. The "War on Terrorism" vindicated all. That the same justification was used decades earlier by the Third Reich was not observed, least of all by those invoking "appeasement of Hitler" as a justification to invade poor non-industrialized countries.[11] The comparison was unthinkable through America's lenses of self-conception which assumed itself as "the society of human rights."

Behind one corporation-friendly state was the precipitating Reichstag Fire of 27th February 1933 to declare war on all who stood in the way. Behind the successor war state was the destruction of the World Trade Center on 9/11 to allow the same in different degree. Both industrial super states were supported by familiar transnational corporations working both sides.[12] Both claimed "terrorism" by shadowy others as the ground of "self-defense" by emergency legislation and wars of invasion. But unlike the Reichstag Fire, 9/11 was advised as desirable before the event, by the Bush regime's own Project For A New American Century. To be exact, PNAC planned a "process of transformation" to achieve "full spectrum US dominance" across the world which was made contingent on "some catastrophic and catalyzing event—like a new Pearl Harbor" if the process was not to be a "long one."[13]

The wish of the men positioned to enable its fulfillment was duly granted within a year of Bush Jr's inauguration, on 11th September 2001. Well known former allies monitored around the clock fulfilled their long known declaration of intention to attack the World Trade Center.[14] One former US-financed agent, Omar Abdel Rahman, was specially experienced at the job, having masterminded the first attack on the WTC in 1993 before warning at his trial of another to come.[15] Another formerly assisted agent in Afghanistan, Osama bin Laden, who was US armed and supported to attack the Soviet-supported government of Afghanistan, was better known for the plan. When 9/11 happened, CIA Director George Tenet immediately attributed the attack to bin Laden, and referred to the US flight-trained Zacarias Moussaoui.[16] Still, any foreknowledge was ruled out as "conspiracy theory," and so the ruling mind-set stayed closed as "realistic" and "patriotic."

The facts of 9/11 which are disconnected from are now copiously documented.[17] But why and how these facts are ruled out by the masses and elites at the same time is *not explained*. The argument has been at the first-order level of the facts, not the lawlike operations *on* the facts by the collective thought-system that selects, ignores and reconnects them in new form—what I call the "regulating group-mind"(RGM).[18] Only when we understand this meta-level of *constructing the facts and their meaning in accordance with their conformity to and expression of a pre-existing structure of understanding* can we know what is going on or, more specifically, can we find our way out of the anomalies and disconnects of our era.

The Regulating Group-Mind: A Paradigm Example

Understanding of the RGM in the first instance proceeds by three basic principles of explanation:

1. Here is a "regulating group-mind" or socially regulating syntax of thought and judgment which
2. locks out all evidence against its assumptions; and
3. blinkers out the destructive effects which reveal its delusions.

Response to 9/11 and the 9/11 Wars are my central paradigm example of the operations of the RGM across classes and borders. Yet the RGM operates on every level, and explains also the paralysis of nations in responding effectively to planetary ecosystem collapse. The RGM may lie behind every systematic social pathology of our era. In each case, it blocks out facts and connections of life-and-death significance, and in each instance, its exclusion is a variation on one life-blind thought regime, the "shadow subject" of our era.

Received understanding of 9/11 is a turning-point instance of the operations of the ruling group-mind, but is selected for forefront attention because of its taboo hold against so much uncontested evidence and reason. Primary connections which are pre-empted on the most general plane are: (1) the policy declaration in 2000 by US national security planners in PNAC, which expressed the commitment to "full-spectrum dominance" by the US state across the world; (2) its expressed desire for a fast-track to this dominance rather than "a prolonged one"; and (3) the perfect consistency between this policy, what happened on 9/11, and what happened afterwards through the 9/11 Wars on Afghanistan and Iraq.

An acute example of blocking out the defining elements of this evident continuity of fact and meaning is that all US air defenses at the most central level were coincidentally down on 11th September 2001 in precise accord with (1), (2), and (3). This connection is as important and demonstrable as any could be for history, but it is nevertheless consistently excluded from the contents of consciousness in all public commentary, and even in Left discourse itself—the tip of the deeper disorder of the RGM that we do not yet suspect.[19] In fact, there was no attempt to achieve any US air-defense intervention with the rogue 9/11 planes until after two jumbo jets had hit different buildings of the World Trade Center in leisurely succession and a third plane or missile had hit a just-vacated wing of the Pentagon—all of this long after the four known and separately hijacked planes had rerouted and flown around unimpeded within the most heavily defended airspace in the world for well over an hour altogether with none disturbed by any sign of defense reaction until after all three buildings had been hit.[20]

That the US war state which then went into motion showed signs of long planning in each case was not perceived as significant,[21] nor was connection to the past statements proclaiming the purpose these plans sought to fulfill. All conformed to the taboo against joined meaning. There were many levels of the disconnect. Singly and together, they ruled out of view the evident through-line of events from the policy record prior to 9/11, to 9/11 itself, and then to "America at War" continuously since in enactment of the original policy plan.

Disconnect also ruled on the question of "terrorism" itself. Even as young Americans were killed in rising numbers in Iraq, while non-American families were terrorized across entire countries by the US invasions in violation of the most solemn law of nations, "terrorism" was perceived in all received discussion as solely the Other's affliction on the Free World and its allies. That in fact, on the contrary, virtually all the terrorization proceeded from the war-crimes, carpet bombings of societies, and systematic torturing of the legally innocent by the US in its "war against terror" was elided from consciousness. The legal definition of terrorism itself was excluded from expert discussion of it.[22] That "the central issue facing America and the world" was in these ways reversed in its meaning across cultures and classes was inexplicable when the majority had no interest in reproducing the inverted story as their own meaning. No received theory can explain such a phenomenon, yet there was an explanation. All the facts and connections were unthinkable within the *a priori* set-points of the reigning thought-system.

The connections across plan and fulfillment, cause and effect are not seen by the RGM *to the extent that they conflict with its deciding assumptions*. When one recognizes that each and all are consistent in expression of one regulating syntax of meaning, anomalies of 9/11 or ecological blindness are no longer anomalous. Since this "way of life" is presupposed by all its creatures as their own framework of cognition,[23] the problem is always with what does not conform to it, which is therefore perceived as subversive, irrational or the enemy. Variations on the terminology of abuse of those whose thought does not conform is the media commentator's principal poetic license and flair. Since the ruling group-mind always operates *a priori*, facts cannot dislodge what its categorial structure perceives and knows already. Thus no one in the international media noticed thirty-three months later in the most dramatic exposure of US defense intelligence cover-up and criminality in a generation—the "Iraq torture scandal"—that the clear connections between the master strategy minted before 9/11 and everything that had occurred since held intact with no movement to modification even *after* the exposures of the most brutal moral and political crimes.

The lead idea of a "catastrophic and catalyzing event" to expedite desired geostrategic control over vast regions of formerly public-owned oilfields which were no longer within or protected by the Soviet Union was simply not discussed. No one appeared to notice how amidst all the disasters of the Iraq occupation that the master strategy had strikingly achieved all of its declared pre-9/11 objectives. The through-line of meaning—seizure, control, and restructuring of the routes and sources of the vast and publicly owned oil resources of Central Asia ("the Afghanistan War") and the Middle East ("the Iraq War")—remained unseeable as the reason *for* 9/11. The RGM perceived, instead, "another historic step forward for freedom" and "a better world without Saddam's brutal regime." Diversion of thought to the designated enemy of the group is certainly an RGM operation of the greatest importance, perpetually disconnecting consciousness from unthinkable objects of attention. It precedes any conspiratorial concealment or ruling class manipulation because it is a preempting block by a collective regime of understanding. Since it vindicates the knowing group and its members in a manner on which all can agree whatever facts contradict their perceptions of self and other, its perception remains secure and consensual.

Not even "the international community" up in arms about the tortures seemed, therefore, to notice the dramatic reversals of fact and meaning. Rather, the tortures themselves were disconnected from their cause as strange anomalies. In return to consensual security, the assistance of "the international community" itself was increasingly called for by both contesting US political parties to sustain the criminally illegal occupations. Even former foes of the Iraq invasion, France and Russia included, did not publicly perceive the fact that it was "the supreme crime under international law," although that was the ultimate law governing the Security Council they sat on. Instead, the illegal war occupation was provided unanimous approval of the UN Security Council on 16th October 2003, and again on June 8th, 2004, with congratulations around the world for "the emerging consensus on Iraq."[24] The group-mind disconnect was now global.

Financial, logistical, and moral assistance for the now UN-approved occupation was accordingly demanded from "those concerned about the people of Iraq." "The full and free independence of Iraq" proclaimed for 30th June 2004 allowed, in fact, none.[25] No assured say or veto by US-appointed governors over the armed forces occupying the country was granted, and the agreed-upon choice by the UN envoy (Lakhdar Brahimi) of the Prime Minister (the anti-Saddam scientist, Hussein Shahristrani) was reversed. In his place, with none in the UN remembering the fact, a former killer for Saddam and then CIA-backed emigré (Iyad Allawi) was installed, representing an organization created by the CIA and Britain's MI6.[26] The ruling group-mind was a closed box with moving sides, but none within its consensus across parties and cultures publicly doubted or raised questions of the continuing war criminal occupation. It was now called "rebuilding free Iraq." The long promise of the White House of "complete and full handover of power" was perceived as discharged with no evident notice of the compounding disconnect from reality. The "new consensus on Iraq" left all armed force, control of the economy, privatization and financial planning in US control or that of its dependent appointees. Full approval by the UN Security Council was then duly granted "after disagreements were resolved by US flexibility."

A narrow epistemology variously rules across the new world order. The dominant conversation transpires within life-delinked co-ordinates, and the truth is what sells, with academic theories as all else.[27] It follows that problems are resolved by changing words and perceptions so that people buy into the story for sale. "Terrorists," for example, can only be those that resist occupation by "nations of the Free World," whether in Baghdad or the West Bank of Palestine. Even when the armed forces of Israel and the US murder resistance leaders at pleasure, blow up village houses and families, and continuously enforce a scene from Hell on civilian populations, none of this can qualify as "terrorist" to the ruling group-mind because this category admits only *non*-Free World others into it. Even inversion of the meaning of the term on whose behalf a "war without end" is fought cannot appear as an issue. For its consensual operations are prior to the reality it selects and excludes to understand. If the historical referent of "terrorism" is state attacks on civilians, this meaning too is blocked out of view prior to denial or affirmation. Consequently, laws for "counter-terrorism" are made across the world to meet "the international community's greatest threat." The problems which daily determine peoples' life or death are, accordingly, blinkered out *a priori*.

Life Consciousness versus the Shadow Subject

"Not for oil" was a wide public sentiment against the US-led invasion of Iraq, an historic uprising against the hold of the ruling group-mind by that opening of life consciousness which always leads the human condition. But not just Middle East oil was involved. Everything the people lived from was involved. In Iraq, the expropriation was planned, sudden and total, but only seen in glimpses. Publicly controlled banks, industrial infrastructures, electricity and water supplies, food production and delivery systems were all time-scheduled for dismantling, control and marketization by US-led and -subsidized corporations.[28] The full-spectrum confiscation was called the Comprehensive Privatization Plan, a history-turning document not commented upon in the media or parliaments. The Comprehensive Privatization Plan—itself a war crime not possible without 9/11 to realign global perception—was to be complemented by "forgiveness of Iraq's debt." Market liberation was not to be burdened with costs that public subsidies could pay. The system-deciding logic was consistent throughout, but its throughline of meaning was unthinkable to the acceptable parameters of discussion. Under terms to be specified by the International Monetary Fund, permanent debt service payments were set into motion, with publicly stripped conditions of existence for the Iraqi people to be specified by the usual IMF conditions of "economic stability and development." The latest market miracle was, in accordance with the ruling paradigm, expected with no economic planning required. Texas bank-owning James Baker III, the Bush Jr. point man for the stolen 2000 US election, was the same person selected to counsel agreement from European and Russian banks and officials for Iraq's "debt forgiveness."[29]

In market theory, the stage was set for what the 25th September 2003 *Economist* affirmed as "a capitalist dream." The pattern was familiar in outer fact, but its regulating logic was not. The pattern was as pure-type as it gets, and was proclaimed as "freedom" and "future prosperity." On the ground unseen through the ruling market prism, there was no limit to the market double take from the non-market world and confiscations of public wealth: first from American taxpayers to pay for the over $1-billion-a-day armed forces supplied and serviced by US multinational corporations in semi-monopoly or no-bid conditions which guaranteed super profits to be paid by the present and future common wealth of the public realm; and secondly, at a much higher rate, there was the systematic dispossession of the Iraqi and Central Asian peoples whose natural and built resources were systematically privatized by armed force for control by US-selected transnational corporations. Meanwhile the media daily limned denunciations of the "lawless violence" of armed resisters in approximately exact reproduction of the perceptions of the Palestinians by Israel, the ANC by South Africa, and the Kenyans by Britain half a century earlier. The ruling market group-mind reproduces through time with different names for its expressions. "Freedom," "development," and "civilization" are the known continuous advances, but always a more total corporate market on the ground is the systematic effect.

In fact, not even the opposing US presidential candidate, nor formerly opposed governments, nor the international press and academics once deviated from affirmation of Iraq's "liberation." It was a given of Free World discourse. The unanimity on the issue was not explainable by coercion, private profit, or conspiracy. A deeper order of determination governed throughout. The genocide of a socialist society was unspeakable to name, although what happened to Iraq, as the U.N. Coordinator of Humanitarian Aid, Denis Halliday, observed was "in keeping with the definition of genocide in the U.N. convention".[30] Instead, the group-mind knew that "Saddam Hussein was a brutal dictator who had to be replaced," and that his "invasion of Kuwait" in 1991, and then "Islamic terrorists' attack on America" in 2001, were the background causes of "Iraq's difficulties." That Saddam himself was paid, armed and directed by the US from obscurity into war against Iran and afterward until his 1991 invasion of Kuwait which was not opposed by the US until after it started, were facts that did not register through the chinks of the RGM; nor, more deeply, did the deaths of over 1,000,000 Iraqis since 1991 by US-led bombings, depleted uranium contamination, and sanctions against repairs of free public water and electricity systems paid for by still publicly owned oil.[31] All this was blocked out a priori by the market thought-system which ruled. And so clashing opinions, perpetual news, and academic detail work all moved within the reference points and coordinates of the one consensual program of perception and judgment. Isolated facts of mass death were reported from life-conscious medical witnesses at work behind the scenes, but they appeared and disappeared with no effect on the iron cage of understanding. What the group-mind knew, as it does in stadiums, squares and coliseums across millennia, was that the designated enemy must be overcome. All remain excited and united in group meaning that sees only itself, while reproduction of the group battles as the spectacles of history is perceived as higher meaning.

11th September 2001 fed perfectly into RGM escalation in place of historical learning.[32] It first made the invasion of Afghanistan an act of "necessary self-defense" against "terrorist training camps attacking the US," terrorist camps which were, like Saddam Hussein, financed, armed and directed by US intelligence forces from their inception.[33] Within two years, "America's New War" to invade and occupy Iraq by armed force in place of UN inspections was propelled by a new perception of "weapons of mass destruction threatening the world." No one in official culture connected the wars to the stated Project of America that preceded them, nor to the market epistemology for which the only truth is what sells. Least of all were the wars connected to global market growth—although all that occurred realized these directing principles on long and short-term planes of time. The shadow subject selected for and approved the new reality as necessary and good without the genocide of a people being seen.

In this way, Iraq was now "liberated by America" with an "absolutely convinced" Tony Blair and Bush leading history from their "cojones meeting"—"to do what I think is right".[34] Many critics read these leaders as merely self-serving liars. But there is a deeper order to their lies. The function of leadership of a group-mind is to exemplify its prejudices as militant certitudes. Thus even when the WMDs that justified the invasion of Iraq were nowhere to be found, the closed circle remained firm across parties and nations. The invasion that was illegal and failed as occupation had to continue if Iraq was to remain liberated. "We must hold the course," "win the peace," "not turn our backs," all agreed through the regulating lenses. New leadership would replace old, but the set-points of meaning and purpose were fixed. What is not recognized by the self-interest theory of motivation is that the regulating group-mind may override even the self-serving calculus of opportunistic state leaders. They go as sacrifices, or not, but the meta-program rules on. It is the shadow level of determination behind the eyes. The Iraq genocide is a symptom of the larger world crisis it propels. Until the deciding base is mutual life and life conditions, the vicious deciding circle remains closed.

The line between the group-mind and life consciousness is clear once seen. The RGM is disconnected from life co-ordinates of perception and decision by a self-referential value system. Life consciousness is oppositely regulated. It is aware of life requirements around it as its body of reference, with no a priori edge to identification. Its common life-ground is ultimately all the conditions required to take our next breath. The group-mind, in contrast, is enclosed within itself as on automatic pilot. It has many variations within our time and others, but *always refers attention back to its own regulating categories of meaning instead of the conditions of enabling life.* It may proclaim "the free market and democracy" and "the enemies of freedom," or "Allah's faithful" and "the unbelievers." No problem of life destruction can, in any case, register to a group-mind calculus because nothing of value exists beyond it. Externalities to its framework of judgment do not compute to it, and so its ruling metric becomes more formally fixed and life-blind the longer and wider it rules. Eventually, it blocks out any refutive feedback loop even at the level of breath itself—as the absurdly named "pro-life movement" of US market culture expresses in microcosm. From the standpoint of market set-points of mind, only atomic selves and pieces can be seen in reified abstractions from wider organic needs and interconnections.

At its most fateful, the ruling group-mind reproduces itself as the same even in the midst of the life-system collapse which its closure finally leads to—as with the Easter islanders, pre-Columbian Mesoamerican empires, the god-king Khmers—and the global market system today. The rigid reference body of decision and meaning fails to recognize or respond to the stripping and draw-down of life conditions which its command assumptions entail—much the same as a failed immune system at the cellular level.[35]

But who disagrees with the ruling frame of perception and understanding of the global corporate market? Who across the public platforms of the Free World imagines a life-coordinated economy? Who in US political life, or even in world governments or scholarly analyses, dissents from universal market supremacy with no alternative? The consequences of this preconscious absolutism may be to destroy whole societies or social infrastructures upon which hundreds of millions depend for their existence. Yet all proceeds in accordance with a set of ruling presuppositions which are closed to question. The systematic genocide of a region-leading economic order and its looted cradle of civilization as "liberation" is only a bounded exemplar of the thought system. From early geostrategic plan to destroyed health records, the life co-ordinates of the people being brought to market never counted. The decisions for their deliverance to "new freedom" were not an issue except for the marginalized.[36] The specter of the ruling subject behind was not exposed by anyone.

When the pictures of systematic hands-on torture emerged as public counter-evidence to the set-points of understanding Iraq's "liberation," the war-crime cause which "accumulates in itself all war crimes" remained unmentioned—as blocked out as the through-line of meaning of 9/11 preceding it. Deeper than the presidential cabal's operations lay the ruling meta-program in command across the ruler-ruled division. The group-mind that blinkers out whatever does not fit its organizing frame of meaning is strange to theory because it is housed across classes, countries and cultures by a cognitive regime which is not rooted in locale, practice, or productive prestige.[37] It structures the mind itself beneath professional and cultural variation from Rio de Janeiro to New York to Shanghai.[38] Not even psychiatry yet penetrates its disorder because it cannot speak from a couch. Marx, in turn, has reified its basic regulating principles as external economic "laws of motion" which cannot explain why people both identify with and reject them.

A micro-example of what Blake called "the mind-forged manacles" occurred immediately prior to the invasion of Iraq in clinical conditions. Their grip within and across societies and selves far from the theatre of war disclosed the transcendental set-points across borders. The public broadcasting producers of my own country, Canada—who are in the pay of no US multinational corporations and accept orders from no one outside—continuously produced their stories prior to 20th March, 2003 within the ruling line of "Saddam's dictatorship" and "the war against terror and weapons of mass destruction," even as the supreme crime of US military invasion remained unnamed, but proclaimed as "inevitably" unfolding. A silent clamp-down invisibly awaited anyone who called the assumed meaning into question. To test the hold of the ruling group-mind, I accepted an invitation onto CBC Sunday News to debate a well-known US geostrategic planner and co-manager of the Project for A New American Century, Thomas Donnelly, the Sunday before the US invasion of Iraq. I did not remain within the assumed parameters of discussion. I explained that the US was engaged in launching a criminal war against the Iraqi people, and continuing its genocidal destruction of the people's socialized infrastructures of water supplies, electricity, food distribution, and public healthcare and education. To the predictable group-mind reflex of "what about Saddam's brutal dictatorship" and "use of biological weapons against his own people," I observed US arming and support of Saddam and his regime in these actions from the beginning. I said Mr. Donnelly ought to be arrested under the relevant Canadian Criminal Code section, the Crimes Against Humanity Act, for counseling war crimes and crimes against humanity with no justification of self-defense, and in sabotage of ongoing and accurate UN weapons inspections. He responded with grimaces and slogans of praise for America's love of freedom since the "US liberation of Europe".

CBC management did not approve. The "arrest" phrase was deleted from the thirty-minute delayed broadcast. The research reporter who had arranged the debate would not return my inquiries on the debate's feedback, but would only refer to other matters, and was soon no longer on CBC Television's major public affairs program. The experimental as well as control conditions yielded a consistent result. Reality was blocked out a priori. Neither fact nor argument was relevant to or accommodated by the prior regulating framework of understanding. Far from the Washington political center and across an international border in a time of life-groundswell rising against the coming US invasion, the deep lines of disconnect were at work—the omnipresent on-off switches of the ruling group-mind. They work only so far as they are not seen. Their invisible lines of force are what make us "not know what is going on" even when the evidence shows mass murder and is known.

Understanding the 9/11 Wars

Long-time US National Security Committee adviser to the President, Zbigniew Brzezinski, wrote four years before 9/11 what inside US geostrategists were already thinking across Republican-Democrat divisions after the collapse of the Soviet Union: "[The United States needs] unhindered financial and economic access [to] Central Asia's natural resources," he advised, "[especially] the enormous economic prize of the natural oil and gas located in the region." But, he continued, it will be "difficult to fashion a consensus on foreign policy issues, except in the circumstances of a truly massive and widely perceived direct external threat."[39] That "truly massive and widely perceived threat" was provided by 9/11. What the former Democrat National Security Adviser to the President advocated in 1997, and what the Bush Presidency's Republican Project for a New American Century called for in 2000, thus formed across party divisions as a vector of the ruling market group-mind.

At the epicenter of this global market construction is the public and elite response *to* it: why such facts in clear through-line of purpose and effect have been silenced in public and media discussion. The consensus has crossed the poles of Left-Right division, with even Left institutions like Z-Net gatekeeping against the connected meaning.[40] The taboo against knowing the facts was encoded into the identity structure across ideological partitions. Any fact exposing the official story was a "conspiracy theory" or, to Z-Net, a "distraction." Given the known pre-9/11 search by US geostrategic planning for a publicly salable reason to invade central Asia and Iraq,

9/11's convenient occurrence was disconnected from what it provided the ideal pretext for—administration legitimation and militarily imposed new control over the world's main supplies of oil. Each war for seizure of oil source was, in turn, disconnected from the known plan to achieve it, and all was disconnected from the ecogenocidal pattern now in military motion as well. Why when the very major invasions of Afghanistan and Iraq to ensure this control occurred right after 9/11, the sole context within which these wars could be sold as defensive, did no US public figure, even the heroic Noam Chomsky, join the dots of the unfolding strategic plan? The answer is given by the evidence. A regime of consensual disconnect had formed with the overwhelming consensus blocking challenge to it. Even the most painstaking case *for* administration complicity in 9/11 featured an exonerating title.[41]

Political history since 9/11 deepened the mystery of the mind-lock whose wider meaning we investigate here. Despite a subsequent record of years of spectacular lying about Iraq by the Bush administration, still the mass media, foreign affairs correspondents and opposition critics blinkered out the accumulating further evidence for a strategically constructed 9/11 attack—for documented example, the anonymously blocked F.B.I. investigations before 9/11, the ignored intelligence warnings from many foreign state agencies beforehand, and the immediately prior visit to Washington of the CIA-advised Pakistani intelligence (ISI) paymaster of one of the lead hijackers.[42] Even the fixed reference points of physical science were ignored in understanding the steering event—most evidently, the massive steel infrastructure collapses whose instant fall from plane impacts alone, or none at all, contradicts the laws of engineering physics.[43] Here more paradigmatically than the unrecognized war crime itself, a structure of denial and projection somehow decoupled elite and public consciousness from the evidence. We know Church authorities would not look through Galileo's telescope to examine the astronomical facts, but in this case the ruling group-mind embraced entire societies, while the this-worldly evidence which it blacked out was against the interests of almost all of its community of thought. The consensual refusal to see beneath any known calculus of advantage or exchange was anomalous. Only group-mind operation provided an explanation.[44]

Given the Bush Jr. regime's non-stop blocking or attack-dog treatment of those suspicious of top-level inaction before 9/11—including the FBI Director of Anti-Terrorism, John O'Neill (who resigned in protest and then died in the World Trade Center as its chief of security), and later the Bush administration's own official chief adviser on counter-terrorism, Richard Clarke—what more evidence was required for thought to suspect a reason? How could the long prepared plans for invasion of Afghanistan and Iraq, which 9/11 alone justified, *not* be connected to the stand-down of defenses before it? What could explain why even the elites of America could accept that the "most crooked, lying group I've ever seen"—John Kerry's overheard aside about the string-pullers of the Bush Jr. administration—were somehow *not* in on what "all the buzz in Washington" was increasingly warned about prior to 9/11?[45] If , moreover, a number of prominent Americans followed the warnings not to be in the buildings or on the relevant flights on that day, and Bush himself was kept isolated by agenda and security managers from all commander response before and after the attack until after all the buildings had been hit, how could the US secret security command *not* be coordinated with the sustained failure of response? How, in overview, could such a *long chain of coincidences possibly occur by continuous chance?*

Everyone now has probably heard that known Al-Qaeda members were long left free to operate inside the US with even FBI investigations blocked by orders from above as they learned to fly, and that four American jumbo-jets were somehow successfully hijacked all at the same time with no security system successful against any member all the way through to the crashes. Once every one of the nineteen alleged hijackers was safely through the many gates of prevention and now untouched and in control of four commercial jumbo-jets simultaneously, the story goes, their hijacked airplane buses then flew around inside normally full US air-grids without any interruption for seventy-five minutes—the Air Force advertises a two-and-a-half-minute time from ground wheel to full throttle through the skies—free-winging about the most heavily watched and protected airspace in the world with military airports all around, and then, presto and telegenically, they skillfully crashed one hijacked jumbo-jet after another into central symbolic buildings of the US—while conveniently hitting the recently de-occupied portion of the Pentagon. "Bring 'em on!" can almost be heard through the smoke of the blown-up buildings. The increasingly despised Bush administration whose Inauguration Parade had been unprecedentedly egg-pelted and chased off the central streets of Washington had good reason to want the change of enemy that would entirely reverse their fortunes. Consider the notorious secret command co-ordination which is everywhere at work in the US national security state. Then think through the multi-level and inconceivable failures of preventative procedures on every level and at every gate from immigration to flight control to Defense Intelligence and the CIA—all "coincidentally" coming together to permit the total throughline past all stops to a simultaneously filmed, released and broadcast "Attack on America!"—with all the names of the guilty dead hijackers immediately known, although there was no evidence from the burnt-out wreckage. It was sold and exported across oceans where it could not be checked.

The many close relatives and associates of the man accused, Osama bin Laden, were then immediately exempted by White House fiat from any standard questions of their knowledge of the accused mastermind, escorted in security-cleared planes when no one else in America was allowed to fly, and deposited in safe houses in the desert kingdom of Saudi Arabia where no investigative questions were permitted. The documented details will not be repeated here, but they are impressively massive in confirming, and none disconfirming, the long open pathway to the attacks and a continuing consistent stand-down of investigation since. When all of this faultless sequence of coincidence working continuously in one direction and in favor of one vast payoff matrix was followed, in turn, by a stonewalling of questions by everyone at the top on whose watch 9/11 occurred, still no public questions arose. Everything before 9/11 and after it that bridged the forbidden meaning across it was disconnected from the event. When such a chain of coinciding actions and reactions all consistent with one explanation alone is so systematically blocked out by all around and delinked at every joint, there has been a shut-down of reason that needs to be *explained*. That is our purpose here—to analyze 9/11 and the 9/11 Wars as a paradigm illustration of the ruling group-mind at work, and to explain how these phenomena connect as unthinkable expressions of one regulating meta-program—the "shadow subject" of the global market thought-system.

If one remembers the record of sacrifices of countless thousands of people to covert geopolitical strategies of which the US corporate security state is long known to approve, sometimes millions of people at a time on false pretexts—as in Indonesia and Vietnam—what could block the meaning here after 9/11? Why would everyday and elite perception assume that the Bush Jr. strategic cabal—who arranged the usurpation of the US presidency and then waged a mass-murderous war by false pretext led by many of the very same leading officials who presided over death-squads and criminal secret deals destroying countless lives in prior Republican administrations—would be above allowing 9/11 when it gave them and US corporate empire unprecedented new domestic and foreign powers? What would have been done *differently* any step of the way had all been strategically planned? The real difficulty here is to find compelling evidence *against* this hypothesis—for example, *some* loss or harm to *any* of the Bush executives who reaped such vast rewards by the show attack. There is no such exculpating evidence.

In place of contra-indicative evidence, the ruling assumption is that "they could never do such a thing"—an expression of the wider religion of America analyzed ahead. In the background of history, the motivations for murderous crimes by state leaders against their own citizens are familiar enough, the warp and woof of supreme power. Making others terrified is the logic of control within the framing game of the regulating group-mind across its variations. All Henry II required to murder the Archbishop of Canterbury was a question in front of those who served him. So why would distinctively power-corrupted men facing the biggest early presidential popularity slide in polling history and enmeshment in the greatest electoral and business frauds in all US history, and a sliding market recession after the stock market meltdown which their criminally fraudulent chief financer led, just turn away from letting a planned option scenario which would save them go ahead? Would there not have to be a group delusion, perhaps operating across the individuals themselves, to make all the normal questions unthinkable even as their accumulating collapse on all fronts was reversed overnight into public adulation and near absolute power?

Just such a structure of delusion may be provided by the deification of the President bearing America's "manifest destiny to save the fallen world by her God-given power."[46] Certainly, implication of "the President of the United States of America" in the terrorist attack would unbearably contradict ruling assumption. A murderous complicity to gain cabal and nation-state world command would hardly fit the ruling religion of America's self-conception as God-blessed and inspired in her "shining city on the hill." So which goes, the faith in America's greatness and goodness in the world, or the facts which disclose the opposite at the very top? At some point, the systematic block against reality discloses to us the demonstrable *zone of the unthinkable*—the defining limit of the group-mind.[47]

"Conspiracy theory" is the stigma term to fence off the taboo zone, just as "communist" once was to alternatives to the American way. Few ask, "Do you prefer *coincidence theory?*" If they did, the term of abuse would change—perhaps to "anti-American" or "terrorist." By one invalidating predicate or another, the unthinkable is blocked out *a priori*. But would it not be perfectly *rational* in the market logic of calculated risk for this regime's top-secret planners and their principals to exploit the greatest opportunity of history to establish their planned "full spectrum dominance" if they were positioned to allow it on fast track? Would not the managed risk of being able to control investigations for the next four years and to denounce any accuser as "unpatriotic" and "betraying America at war" not be worth the chance in the ruling market calculus? Why would this once-in-a-lifetime opportunity *not* have been considered as an option when mass-kill nuclear-attack options have long been a daily fare of US national security analysis? Would it not, in fact, be *irrational* from the strategic wargaming standpoint to forfeit an unprecedentedly great payoff matrix to save fewer lives than three months of US traffic accidents?

These were chief executives trained to seize every opportunity for self and corporate gain managing at the geostrategic level in which the most ruthless decision scenarios are produced by which millions die. Was there anything in the known record to indicate any aversion of any of them to self-maximizing rationality at these levels? Bear in mind more US soldiers were killed or maimed within months by the Iraq occupation itself than American civilians on 9/11. Recall as well Rumsfeld's response to innocent women and children slaughtered by American bombs: "Stuff happens".[48] Even outside the *Realpolitik* of world empire, the corporate market calculus is seldom deterred by "externalities" of others' deaths, and these were all corporate CEOs of the most aggressive kind. Why, then, would they be so "soft" as to fear taking far bigger pay-offs for their own group and US global empire? The regulating group-mind of the global corporate market selects towards allowing 9/11, not against it. So why would this known calculus in US security as well as CEO circles be ruled out as unthinkable in *understanding* 9/11?

There's a deeper general operation at work here than "the catalyzing event" of 9/11 itself. This is the regulating market structure of consciousness that selects what facts are seen and not seen in accordance with whether it pays off to risk-takers and "feels good" to consumers. This calculus operates altogether independently of whether the object of desire is "true" or not, or life-serving rather than deadly, these concepts being foreign to the market paradigm. The deciding question is: "Can we sell it? Will they buy it?" Fear is the undertow hook—Do I look right? Am I safe?, but desire is its expression. Both moments join in the one episteme that all assume. Buying and selling is "market freedom," "our way of life." "Finding new wealth and markets" is the necessity of growth. Understanding the market value system and epistemology is how we come to understand the fear and aggression of 9/11 and the 9/11 Wars.

Certainly all prefer the pleasant certitudes that "America leads the Free World," and that its President or secret intelligence apparatus "could not possibly" exploit the planning and execution of such a crime as occurred on America's soil on 9/11 and afterwards. Yet the Bush administration's chief executives counseled or endorsed prior Republican President Reagan's presiding over the smuggling of cocaine into the US to addict inner city Americans so as to illegally finance war crimes against Nicaragua, and before that the arming of the mullah dictatorship of Iran so that it held onto American hostages long enough for the election to be lost by "the human rights presidency of Jimmy Carter" to, revealingly, the "anti-terrorist" Reagan regime. The reason why such connections to past practices are lost to view is that they are ruled out *a priori* by the ruling group-mind. So long as there is no operational failure, there is no problem to see.

When Ronald Reagan was provided with the pomp of national sainthood after he fortuitously expired in May 2004 at the height of disquiet about the US torture regime in Iraq, we were reminded of his ultimate legacy. *"He made us feel good again."* "Feeling good" is the folksy correlative of "utility function" and "welfare" in the neo-classical market calculus. It is what the Constitution's "pursuit of happiness" has come to mean through the market prism. That is why the public identification with Ronald Reagan was so deep, whatever his falsehoods and war crimes. Behind him was the same group-mind as behind Bush junior twenty years later. In the continuity of history, corporate CEOs like Baker, Cheney, Rumsfeld and trans-administration bureaucrats like Elliott Abrams and Paul Wolfowitz bridged the generational turn to market and military absolutism as America's post-Vietnam triumph. "We will make America great again".

Yet life consciousness exceeds the bounds of the prison within. The marginalized ask questions. They do not block out the facts that administration people stole the 2000 presidential election by overriding legal voting procedures, rode on Enron jets and its criminal financing to get there, and were on the watch on 9/11. They know that this cabal succeeded in blocking Congressional access to even official records of national energy policy secretly advised by the same Enron executives. If they succeeded in cover-up there, why not here? So those not constrained within the ruling thought-system ask, why would anyone believe this group is above permitting 9/11 to gain vast powers? "You are the Haves, and the Have Mores. You are my base," is Bush Junior's known salute to those who take the most.

Why, then, has the most elementary query after any crime—*cui bono?* (who benefits?)—been suspended from question about 9/11? When the most self-evident line of thought has been blinkered out across a people, only an a priori thought system can account for it. As with other great problems of our era, the group-mind disconnects by *stopping thought before it arises.*

That is why in all the public fixation on 9/11, the interests served by its occurrence were, otherwise inexplicably, not related to explanation of it. These payoffs, unprecedented in any presidency in the history of the Republic, provide guidance in the taboo zone of the unthinkable. Since their pre-emption from public discussion in North America discloses critical tension at the heart of America between its patriotic identity and its market presuppositions, these interests of private capital, military empire and cabal power secured by 9/11 need to be identified. They include open access to the world's formerly untouchable and greatest wealth resources, new command position over public financing for subordinate militaries and police apparatuses not only in the US but across the globe, privatization of the world's richest publicly owned and state-controlled oilfields and the social infrastructures they support, new declared right to suspend the historical basis of rule by law, habeas corpus, to protect the reigning order against subversion, legitimation of a president who lost the election until illegal mass invalidation of votes by Bush state officials and a stacked supreme court illegally confiscated votes in the thousands in Florida and overturned the state's vote-recount laws, public diversion from the regime's known corrupt support and energy policy determination by the most criminally fraudulent corporate leadership in American history, unprecedented new powers for price leveraging of oil supplies and military services for a "war without end," new police powers across borders to imprison without right of legal defense any one deemed to obstruct an international trade and investment meeting, and—at the crest of glory instead of ignominy—unlimited new rights of men with draft-dodging pasts to command everyone else with fawning media attention.[49]

The problem of the collectively unthinkable runs deep into the psyche. "I can't believe . . ." is the sign pointing back to the mind-block behind it. Even media consumers' insatiable desire to know the dark secrets of the famous is here quieted. The sentiment shared among all who acquiesce that "the President could not possibly have been involved in 9/11" was, by its own description, disconnected from the issues of fact or truth. Throughout, one defining operation of the ruling group-mind in all its forms prevailed. *The reference points of meaning were pegged beneath consciousness by determining pre-*

suppositions which organize understanding to conform to them, and to screen out all that does not. These on-off switches of the group-mind are not natural drives or conscious instincts of survival, but ruling assumptions which structure the heart and senses as well as thought-system which selects, organizes, and reinforces the felt sides of being. Once these set-points of consciousness are fixed by dividing lines of war, a fateful consequence follows. Their closure of prejudice-set *absolutely disconnects* feeling and awareness from facts and relations which conflict with the anchoring assumptions. In response to the extreme pressures of forcing reality to conform to manufactured delusions, the group and its members become increasingly submerged within a pre-conscious field of hysteria, denials and projections. In the case of 9/11 and the 9/11 Wars, the shadow subject of the ruling group-mind and its executive vector propelled two war criminal invasions of other societies and police-state laws across the world in under three years.

We can see, if we do not turn away, the monstrous pattern across pretexts and wars—the global market group-mind harnessed to the American military juggernaut and a bottomless consumer maw that only desires more.[50] All serve one transnational regime—the globalizing, US-led corporate market that occupies within and without with no limit of growth or barrier of life need. Its system-deciding program is based in a presupposed economic paradigm centuries old that has become hardened into perceived laws of nature. With no limit of rule and war fever as the mega-machine's moving passion across borders, the regulating program becomes mechanically homicidal. The atomized masses of America and global corporate market expansion are made one in a salvational fantasy of triumphing over the Enemy. At the same time, disconnection of all attention from the failing conditions of human existence follows by displacement. Market "externalities" become "collateral damages" by war as well.

At the regulating center rules the group-mind's meta-program, by which individual experience and perception themselves are preconsciously organized. It is "the moral compass" that Republican operators invoke, in terms of which coherence and meaning are found in whatever is selected by the lead vector of the ruling group-mind to war upon next. Here the system-decider is consistent across aggressions, but not acknowledged because of its inhuman meaning. What is selected to remove or destroy always advances the global corporate market *over formerly independent and self-organizing forms of life*, however false the justifications or defenseless the victims in the way might be. This too is a testable empirical generalization. The goal is proclaimed as "freedom" and "prosperity" through group-mind lenses, but the process is structured throughout by command assumptions beneath negotiation. In reality, one form of Other to the Free World is selected for attack and appropriation—any autonomous, public or civil commons sector that can be privatized for profit, and any individuals, movements or societies obstructing the conversion. When the moving line of global marketization is by "peaceful means," it is by strategic electoral marketing. When the appropriation is by armed force, it must be preceded by a *casus belli*—which was 9/11's function.

The Regulating Principles of Market War and Peace

Since all within the mind frame of the ruling group-mind agree by assumption on what "freedom," "growth," and "future prosperity" mean, the only question left is how to get there. Constructed pretext and the doomsday bombing of innocent poor peoples are the extremist recourse through the twentieth century. 9/11 fits with a larger tradition, but for the first time promises "a market war everywhere and without end." Beneath the surface logic of "conspiracy to rule the world"—revealingly projected onto "World Communism" in the previous period—lies a core mode of aggression. It too is unthinkable within the RGM, but its deepest line of advance is *to negate all life limits as they arise*—the shadow meaning of "global market freedom".

What can never be recognized by the regulating market group-mind is the systemically life-destructive effects of its limitless expansion—which must be continuous and maximal by its own internal logic. That's why the ultimately carcinogenic nature of this process is never penetrated even by those who, like the Club of Rome, sense a cancer at work.[51] They cannot connect it back to the logic of the global market because this would contradict the ultimate assumption of the ruling thought-system—that market growth is permanently necessary and good. Only "growth" without mention of capitalism or the market can be bad. Thus, the growth of the populations of the non-consuming poor must be the problem. "Anti-growth" perspective thus becomes another variation on the ruling mind-set. Social scientists in general express another variation on the same underlying meta-program of thought—assuming or reifying market growth as akin to natural laws. What increasingly follows from this ruling thought structure—the system-decider of the whole—is evident for the world to see—extinction spasms, climate destabilization, forest and fish stock draw-downs, polluted waters, and unbreathable urban air in cumulative escalation. But here too, *the coherent connection of structural cause to structural effect is unthinkable to the set-points of the regulating group-mind.*

What then, more exactly, is this "ruling thought-system"—or, more elliptically, "dominant paradigm"—which structures perception, understanding and decision across the global market? It is the ruling algorithm formalized by Command Assumptions 1–15 ahead. These decisive assumptions are generic and assumed rather than demonstrated, and together they regulate—consciously or preconsciously—the social perception, understanding and judgement of the market RGM across individuals and cultures at both cognitive and affective levels. The foundational thought-system of (1) to (15) operates more or less automatically, and thus forms the shadow identity structure of the peoples of the Free World in the "era of globalization".[52]

While these commanding presuppositions are entirely human in construction, they appear as the external structure of necessity to which "all must adapt to survive." It's not an exaggeration to say that all of planetary existence is now included as an actual or potential object of these "laws of motion of the economy," from the genes of first people's seeds to the ocean floors and the skies above. America's military supremacy across the borders of the world is the high-tech investment vector and enforcement arm of the ever expanding "global market process." By its limitless "growth" and "globalization"—concepts which unwittingly disclose the totalitarian nature of the system—all conditions of life are progressively converted into its subservient functions as the meaning of "development," "progress" and "civilization." The 9/11 Wars are the militant forward edge of this global corporate-market march, and its meta-program moves mechanically on all fronts. But every step expresses a system-deciding logic which is the ultimately deciding order of determination.

Trade, investment and political-legal treaties have been the system's mode of transnational advance since 1988, with thousands of articles of prescription codified in such administrative instruments as NAFTA and the WTO which are armored against any elected legislature debate by their international treaty form. Media and infotainment programs of every kind are its communications relations for the public and legislators, with only a very few ever reading their contents. But behind and governing all levels of the global system is the invisibly regulating market syntax of judgement which silently selects and excludes what elites and populations think, decide and expect throughout.[53] Its format crosses divisions of persons and cultures as the intersubjective "internal" order of the global meta-program, and can be tested for its hold by any state-level policy or decision in "the Free World." Although it exerts its own lines of force as the bounds and rules of social and especially elite consciousness, it is presupposed beneath debate as the non-negotiable givens of it.

Since few in the market sciences or philosophies penetrate their own parameters of discussion, and since the atomic methods of each block out *a priori* any awareness of a group-mind, they remain oblivious to this deeper level of meaning and determination. When it is exposed even in part by ground-breaking conception, its meaning is ignored or attacked—including, revealingly, by the famous originator of the concept of "paradigm revolution"itself.[54] In such ways, it has become silently obligatory in economic and related sciences to deny or foreclose any social reality but self-maximizing individuals in aggregates connected by social science statistics or paradigm models, but never a "regulating group-mind" or "collective thought-system." The first rule of any RGM is that it cannot examine itself. Methodological preemption is the ultimate level of closure against self-recognition.

The on-off switches of the regulating group-mind ramify up and down the hierarchy of power and across social issues. Thus just as "more government" or "socialism" are standard group-mind labels to block out reason on public-sector formations,[55] so in the 9/11 turn, one stigma phrase, "conspiracy theory," hypnotized populations into a set-point of compliance. Complex systems do not continue intact unless all their sub-systems collaborate. With the media as the speech and sign system of the regulating group-mind, the "9/11 attack on America" permitted what was impossible before it. It allowed an illegitimate administration to transmute into America's patriotic champion at war—above accountability and the rule of law. "Defending America from another terrorist attack" became a political blank check for corporate corruption of government expenditures with impunity, war criminal acts and threats across the Islamic and alternative third world, and attacks on civil rights and commons at home. Nothing was fated, but all was undertaken as if it was. "Necessity" prefaced every turn to an ever more totalitarian rule of the unchallenged meta-program.

"Counter-Terrorism" and "the theater of war" were assumed to be "national security" while social organization to protect and enable citizen life from threats on it could not compute through the regulating categories of meaning. What could also not be seen from the ruling group standpoint was that the shadowy terrorists used the same homicidal methods in dispossessed microcosm as the US armed forces did in billion-dollar-a-day macrocosm. What neither side's standpoint could see was that *each required the other as demonic Enemy for every step of the "war" strengthening the terror capacities and performances of each in different degrees.* That's why, at the preconscious level, the war was declared to have no end. The logic was catastrophic and self-propelling at escalating levels, but inaccessible to comprehension by the mechanisms of the RGM, a derangement of many variations. Thus every escalation predictably increased the terror on the ground in proportion to the war against it which justified, in turn, ever more vigilance and funds ahead of all else as "the only way to eliminate the scourge of terrorism."

The group-mind by definition compulsively blinkers out its effects the more they are the opposite of declared objectives, as with the "more global market growth" war on nature to "enable better environmental protection." Leaders and followers continue in the same spirals in accordance with the same command assumptions, and the only general constant of outcome once its natural limits have been reached is more life and life condition destruction by the meta-program. The movement from ruling group-mind to cultural insanity is thus traveled with ever more certitude of conviction and unthinkability of alternative.

In fact, terrorist-transfixed consciousness crossed elite and party divisions from 9/11 to the next election, with the opposing 2004 Democratic platform emerging to frame humanity's condition amidst increasing ecological and majority-world meltdown as "The Post-9/11 World" in which the anti-terrorist measures, technologies, inspections, controls and laws already in place were "not nearly enough"[56] The costs for America and the world were far deeper and wider than the narcissism of small differences on the stage. All joined in round-the-clock proclamations of the "war against terror" while, hardly seen, the devastating pollution and destruction of the planet's conditions of life proceeded at ever higher levels. "Higher growth" and "more market spending" remained assumed as the natural condition of survival, and more of both were generated by the war without end. That life growth and well-being were, in fact, being confiscated for more peoples and ecosystems was "out of touch with reality" through the lenses of the ruling group-mind. Reversal operations by consensual assumptions are the RGM's reproductive cycle. The shadow on the wall grew all the while greater. The alternative super-power looming on the horizon, China, multiplied the US's monetized growth rates and escalated destructions of nature and rural livelihoods as a "new market miracle," now presided over by the Communist Party.

In this way, the world's increasingly deadly environmental and social problems were resolved by being both compounded and blinkered out. The global-market crusades led the dimly known and ancient path of collective insanity, but at a world level of destruction—blocking the systemic causes from view by methodological avoidance and repudiation of "negative thinking," while stepping up the life-world devastation as "necessary market growth." The public sectors whose collective actions could alone meet the problems of the failing global market paradigm were, at the same time, drained by the military costs of over a billion-dollars-a-day on US-led market wars and simultaneous multi-hundred-billions of tax-cuts to the wealthy. All proceeded in accordance with the regulating market principles, but the deadly effects could not be seen through its categories of judgement. Instead, market panaceas were now proposed for the war-devastated Middle East which lacked even intact public water systems. The United Nations Development Program itself—the leader in promoting a Human Development Index with basic life co-ordinates—switched into line and stepped to the same drum-beat as the world market crusades. It co-sponsored a US-circulated plan for "G8-Greater-Middle-East Partnership" to prescribe the universal market solution—"an economic transformation similar in magnitude to that undertaken by the formerly communist countries of Central and Eastern Europe." Improved life means or livelihoods were not included in this "market transformation," nor any address of their decline in "the formerly communist countries of Central and Eastern Europe" by reduced nutrition of the majority, defunding of free education and health-care provision, and radically new insecurity of livelihood for workers and pensioners. These were unseen or accepted as "natural consequences of market reforms." Attention focused instead on the new market miracle of "micro-finance" at hand. "A mere $100 million a year for five years will lift 1.2 million entrepreneurs (750,000 of them women) out of poverty through $400 loans to each"[57] As elsewhere, there was no relationship between problem and solution, nor any connection of understanding to the life-system problems involved. Disconnect was again consensual.

In accordance with the locked-in assumptions, nations competed against nations in producing market commodities at low cost for the prosperity of all—thus privatizing, defunding and deregulating public sectors, life-protective standards, and civil commons evolved over generations so as to "achieve market efficiencies and growth." The One Panacea was assumed by all as Economic Law—from the British Labour government to Putin's Russia to the post-Apartheid African National Congress. It followed that the panacea be applied to the bombed-out Middle East as well. That it had failed everywhere else on life measures was of no moment to the regulating structure of understanding. Resistance arose at the margins in many forms, but no "security measure" was taken that did not project the terror onto resisters as justification for more of the same. US government "bioterrorist initiatives" exemplified in microcosm the "public health in reverse"[58] That the "terrorist threat" which spread terror everywhere was global market totalization *itself* was inconceivable to the group-mind. Even as "the greatest armed forces in history" invaded, bombed and tortured across the heartlands of the ancient Middle East and Central Asia, all terrorism was necessarily by the Other from which the armed resistance still came.

Many thinking people penetrated to the geostrategic pattern at work, but not to the regulating group-mind prejudices behind it that crossed continents and selected for every decision. The final system-decider was not perceived any more than a computer program is conscious of itself. "Terrorism" instead of "communism" was the changing designator of system Enemy, but what was, in fact, attacked everywhere was any social formation blocking access to the last great frontiers for global market pricing, exploitation and control—far beyond Islamic societies to the commons of space and the thinking mind itself.[59] Conversely, what was selected with no limit of funding for its feeding cycles were the US-armed and "security" forces and its allied ancillary operations in other nations, along with free infrastructures, tax holidays and increasing automatic subsidies for successful transnational corporations "attracted to more cost-effective investment conditions."

In the historical background, David Rockefeller long ago expressed in simple terms the lead vectors of the world system in the post-national future. "A supernational sovereignty of an intellectual elite and world bankers," he advised in a leak from the June 1991 Bildersberg annual meeting," is surely preferable to the national autodetermination practiced in past centuries." The steering mechanism of mind-and-money that Rockefeller and the Bildersberg meeting shared was also borne by the directing centers of the main political parties, careerist and entrepreneur academics, the corporate press, and leading-brand political classes across the world. The ideal was largely in place so far as all nations had accepted IMF conditions as their financial frameworks for privatization, de-regulation, defunding of public sectors, homogenous-export economies, and open borders to transnational corporate commodities. These were the heady realms of "neo-classical theory" and "financialization." In the more enthusiastic foreground of market worship, tens of millions of poorer and working-class devotees paid to pray for the profit returns of God's grace, and the most devout awaited Armageddon and the Rapture to come. The group-mind only prevails by having many levels of certitude and devotion.

For market science itself, the magic of the invisible hand infallibly transfigured the limitless desires of market selves into "the public welfare"—the meaning of the First Theorem of Welfare Economics, the mathematical ideal of market theory which deduces that purely self-seeking market agents will necessarily produce a providential outcome of "the public welfare."[60]

But a ruling group-mind requires the zeal of the private imaginary too. This was the American Dream which moved its creatures as the shining light of the market soul, the dream that "anyone can get rich," as Ronald Reagan put it in the language of Everyman. The 9/11 turn to war across the Middle East, Baghdad, and Mongol Asia was thus launched in a moral universe in which the intersection of divine plan and history was already set. America, God's contemporary chosen nation with all the world as its Canaan, moved rapidly on the ground to fulfil its grand mission: to liberate peoples everywhere to the promised land of "market freedom and democracy." The material meaning—full-spectrum US military and corporate dominance of every asset perceived necessary with no outer or inner perimeter to the right of invasion by financial or armed means to secure it—was "the last best hope of humankind." As the intellectual elite agreed, only a Leviathan can keep order, and only money provides a medium of value that allows commensurable objects to be measured.[61]

The conversion of all life organisation and conditions into commodities to mediate money sequences in perpetual increase was not a problem that was seen by neo-classical economics or political science because it was already known to be the nature of the real world. Thus ever more of Earth existence was converted into variations of "market growth," from privatized water systems across the world to the engineered chemicals and genes of future frankenfoods and obesity, from the oilfields of poor countries to virgin air and cyberspace".[62] Peoples variously rebelled against the instances—in Cochabamba, the Niger Delta, the European food market, and the anti-Star Wars movement—but the ruling shadow subject, the deciding market group-mind, was not conscious of any meaning beyond itself. "Grow or die" was the motto of reproduction and increase, the new evolutionary mechanism on earth, with money demand, not life need, as the finally regulating value command. Accordingly, only more market money transactions for priced commodities computed as "development" or "well-being." Since life itself did not count in the ruling metric, its degradation and destruction did not register in National Accounts.

The problem of corporate market corruption of the social order was evident in its germinal state to Abraham Lincoln over a century ago. Lincoln privately warned of a problem whose name is unspoken in economics texts. "As a result of the war," Lincoln warned, "corporations have been enthroned and an era of corruption in high places will follow, and the money power of the country will endeavour to prolong its reign until all wealth is aggregated in a few hands and the Republic is destroyed".[63] Lincoln was duly assassinated within a few months, by the "lone assassin" central to American mythology. US corporate rule has since been instituted across the world and triumphalist over all alternatives, destabilizing and invading wherever there is room for more "freedom" and "development" for money-sequencing operations which all peoples compete to enlarge. The 9/11 Wars have been a turning-point symptom in this meta-pattern of modern history, but the rigid set-points of the regulating thought system command from behind throughout. Corporate oligopoly that overrides all life limits follows deductively from the market thought regime.[64] As long as no public authority recognizes the bearings of shared life co-ordinates, and charters its "corporate citizens" accordingly, there is only more systematic life destruction by the imperatives of the system whose metric disregards life-despoiling effects as "externalities".[65]

The "soulless mega-machine," in Lewis Mumford's phrase, is not dependent on this or that US administration, but each helps to determine the extent to which its prescriptions rapaciously invade and transmute life-systems. The Bush Jr. administration has wherever possible bypassed or repudiated limiting domestic and international laws as expression of "our freedom." Academic report of his own convictions confirm an exemplary creature of the ruling group-mind.[66] Regulating the larger global market before and after his regime, however, are command assumptions in terms of which all decisions are made by its bearers—the thought infrastructure of "the Free World." These regulating principles are, in turn, *preconsciously life-blind*. That is, they are not altered by nor sensitive to any facts of life loss, however systemic. Only price signals can register to the ruling calculus, which is indifferent to life requirements unless controlled by non-market values. This life-blind calculus is perceived, however, as "scientific rigor" which is much prized. From the Thatcher-Reagan turn on, its command prescriptions escalated as the One True Faith of our era. As in former times, the assumptions of a ruling Invisible Hand steer the group-mind. But the providence of the Market is not doubted even by Science.

Understood within the larger reference body of history, the meta program which regulates the perception and understanding of our epoch was formally born in 1776, the year of Adam Smith's first testament, *An Inquiry Into the Nature and Causes of the Wealth of Nations* and the year of the American Revolution across the Atlantic Ocean. Its ruling presuppositions form the framing metaphysic of market monotheism and, ultimately, the 9/11 Wars which are its New Crusades, where armed invasion is again the corporate market's moving line of world expansion. Since the end of the opposing superpower system in 1991, its global paradigm has been internalized as the consensual structure of acceptable perception. It has become the "no-alternative" determiner of social meaning to which all official cultures across the world—except the "Axis of Evil"—tacitly conform; and to which every ruling political party defers as the silent first condition of contesting national elections. Elections themselves, in turn, have morphed into marketing competitions between advertised brand products, yet are assumed as the only kind of democracy and freedom that exists.

The fall of the Soviet state, we might say, was the rebirth of the market group-mind as not only having "no alternative" anywhere, but "the end of history." 9/11 marked a second and less visible turning-point towards universal corporate-market rule. That is, it legitimated as "self-defense" pre-emptive armed attack on any movement or force that was opposed, whether unarmed "violence-threatening protestors" in domestic public spaces, or "suspected terrorists" in civilian populations of the militarily occupied world. Behind all the variations of times and conditions, one unexamined reference body of thought ruled as the set-points of human freedom and well-being. Its inner logic determined every step of the post-1988 global market crusades, first by transnational trade and investment treaty-fiats inalterable by elected legislatures, and secondly by the machinery of war since September 11th, 2001. What before 9/11 was a world becoming aware of the life-despoiling mechanics of the global corporate system and its one-sided decrees binding societies to its agenda became, after 9/11, a monoculture of "the war against terrorism." Disconnection from every real problem which humanity faces of collapsing life-support systems was in this way licensed as a global as well as patriotic necessity.

We need to keep in mind here a forgotten fact—that it was one month before 9/11 in Genoa, Italy, that the greatest international demonstration ever (over five hundred thousand people) mobilized against the global market's rule by treaty edicts and binding prescriptions on societies which recognised only corporate investor rights. In harbinger of the post-9/11 days to come, warplanes flew overhead to intimidate the demonstrators, and police beat hundreds while they slept as "terrorists."[67] 9/11 stopped the citizen tide of growing protests overnight, and set in motion legal changes across nations to imprison as "terrorists" anyone who "obstructed" by labor strike, demonstration or bodily obstruction of vehicles any "international meeting," such as the "anti-globalization protests" which had been increasingly arising prior to 9/11.[68]

In short, 9/11 served an unspoken function of world-historical importance. It war-drummed off the world stage all protests against the globalizing corporate market, and liberated corporate states to proceed without "obstacles to trade and investment" presented by people and societies.[69] The Iraq invasion was a demonstration to the larger global community of US supreme power ready to override borders by force of arms as it willed after 9/11—its "credibility to the world." Behind the universal demand of "free markets and democracy," the right to make war on whatever did not concede to the prescribed formulas was asserted. The subject which ultimately ruled within and across elites and peoples was not led by, but led the possessing classes, the armies and state executives. The regulating sovereign was a meta-program, and all official culture conformed to its command assumptions as revealed laws of nature. Beneath learned awareness, it was a total metaphysical, epistemological, and moral system, more absolutist in social prescription than the Universal Church Militant of medieval times. All was perceived, understood and prescribed through a prism of assumptions and received truths. We can unpack the layers of this "regime within" by a fifteen-step algorithm of principle-sets interlocked as one organizing, generic thought-system. Its inner logic of command is what we refer to as "the regulating market group-mind":

1. Pursuit of maximal monetary assets and commodities for oneself is:

   i: natural for humans, however this natural fact may be denied,

   ii: rational in all places and times, and

   iii: necessary for all social progress and development;

2. There is no rightful limit on capital and commodity accumulation or inequality, nor any social or human right to redistribution, by natural laws of property right and economic development;

3. Freedom to buy and sell in self-maximizing transactions of money and priced commodities is the proven basis of all economic efficiency, and there is no outer limit to this system's rightful globalization;
4. The market's money-price system always optimally allocates resources and distributes goods and services in every society to ensure the best of all possible worlds in that society as well as globally;
5. Competitive money-profit maximization by investors is the engine of all economic and social advance, and must be liberated from state regulation or "monopoly" public ownership to preserve and advance social and economic progress;
6. Government intervention in self-regulating market competition is only justified if required for market security and growth, but is "dictatorial" by any violation of "free market flows of commodities and capital";
7. Individual consumer desires are permanently increasing and unlimited, and everyone everywhere wants more commodities to satisfy them as their primary choice and freedom in the world;
8. Every consumer good people need or want must be produced and distributed by the market in proportion to the "effective demand" for it, that is, the possession of sufficient money to pay as the economy's selector of fitness to survive;
9. The public interest and human welfare can only be achieved and developed by market competition of producers and sellers because it alone provides incentives for labor, cost efficiencies and technological innovations which are the bases of the wealth of nations, freedom and human well-being:
10. Market growth is therefore always beneficial with no limit to its conversion of planetary and human life-organization into more market activities, more commodities for consumers, and more investment profits for successful firms in the limitless expansion of "development," "progress" and "civilization";
11. Protection of domestic production is the disastrous policy of "protectionism," although subsidization of leading transnational enterprises is sometimes necessary in the "new competitive reality" of the global market;

12. Whatever facts of life disaster (such as mass loss of livelihood and environmental pollution) may seem to contradict the necessity and validity of market principles (1) through (11), they are only correctable by more rigorous understanding and application of market principles;

13. If the "creative destruction" by global capitalism destroys ancient settings and ways of life, these are unavoidable costs of development and progress which the market necessitates, and can only be properly solved by "substitute technologies" and "market price mechanisms" as distinguished from "dictatorial state prohibitions" and "socialist slavery";

14. Individuals, groups or governments which doubt or criticize:

    i: the supremacy of the market system,

    ii: the inherent efficiency of its production and distribution of goods, or
    iii: the freedom of its agents thereby reject "the free market and democracy";

15. Any and all societies, parties or governments which cling to or seek any alternative of economic organization are necessarily "irrational" or "despotic," and must be overcome to defend the Free World, including by armed force wherever necessary.

These covert commands of world rule form the "regulating market group-mind" to which published thought and speech in the global market normally conforms, and to which governments defer to survive in "the new reality." Together they constitute a system-deciding algorithm of how to live for "free peoples." Since "the overwhelming majority of people agree," whether by tacit agreement or militant prescription, the universally binding system is not perceived as binding or prescriptive, but as "natural" and "necessary." In theory and representation, the words "corporation," "transnational corporations" and "corporate power"—which denote the actually ruling mechanisms of power—are unspoken in all official and economic literature because they signify the earthly reality that the ruling group-mind is structured to block out. On the ground, the ruling thought-system is increasingly expressed by the competitively expanding rule of the global corporate market restructuring all fields of human and natural being as "market growth" which all agree is necessary and good.

A simple question tests the hold of this regulating group-mind as an absolutist and universal thought regime. What government, mass medium or neo-classical economist does *not* conform to each and all of (1) to (15) in speech and judgement? Some US administrations may be described as more extreme than others in the use of armed force against non-market uprisings and societies, but which if any of these principles is overtly violated by any government or even opposition in "the Free World"? Who in public life acknowledges that any society may hold to or pursue any *other* path? The debate is preconsciously limited to narrow parameters within which the market's tolerance is normally confined. The limits of debate and criticism are set by the assumption that any alternative system is inherently inferior or evil, with any socialist formation, in particular, requiring "economic restructuring" to "join the community of free nations." Beneath observation, no market principle rules out the armed invasion of any non-market society or development that does *not* conform. All market precepts have selected for "market expansion" as desirable and inevitable since its genocides of the first peoples began over five centuries ago. That "tolerance" is universally supposed by intellectuals as the lead virtue of the "free market" discloses the preconscious hold of its prejudice-set. The command principles of social life reproduction have become as inviolable as their own prescriptions once were to the former Universal Church.

The Market Rationality of the 9/11 Attack on America

To understand our problem at the site of a current taboo zone of thought, we may ask: how would the US executive construction of 9/11 itself violate any *market* principle? Or, more directly, what in market logic or value-set does not affirm its consequences of market growth and globalization? The answer may be that the sacrifice of 2,700 lives on 9/11 was too great to be countenanced by any sane mind. Yet this answer fails to recognize that the only cost recognised by the market calculus is a cost to business. All other costs are, accordingly, classified as "negative externalities." Human or natural life loss therefore do not compute in any market theorem. Only the incomes of market agents count to its metric of value. This is not polemic. It is the defining meta-principle of the market thought system, but unthinkable insofar as it conflicts with deeper intuitions of life value in itself.[70]

The money costs of an act of terrorism are also excluded under rules of insurance exemption, and so are borne by victims and the public purse. In further fact relevant to market gains and losses, the US market was in a deep slide prior to 11th September 2001—largely due to the burst speculative bubble which Bush Jr.'s own chief electoral financier, Ken Lay of

Enron, helped to lead. 9/11 then stimulated massive new state spending on construction, military purchases, and a war that alone added an estimated $100 billion a year to a billion-dollar-a-day military budget. This infusion of public wealth into "the war against terrorism"—after a short stock-market dip—propelled a US market recovery within two months. All along, the pre-9/11 recession was perceived as "another terrible blow to America from the 9/11 terrorist attack." This reversal of facts followed from regulating market lenses. That is to say, and the claim can be tested, any facts which do not fit market presuppositions are adjusted so that they do. This is a continuous process of adapting facts to the ruling paradigm, as opposed to adjusting the ruling paradigm to accommodate the facts. It is another indicator of the dominant paradigm's cumulative collapse as a coherent thought system.[71]

The market meta-program also favors 9/11 by seeking its market-growth consequences as primary imperative—not just market growth out of recession by an infusion of investment and demand by military and related spending, but more deeply, *by the destruction of a non-market society and consequent access to its assets* (which in this case may have exceeded in value all energy assets held in the industrial Free World). Such an outcome is the maximum good conceivable through market sets-points of valuation, and accordingly steers geopolitical strategy of market states as a given of payoff options.[72] On the level of theory, only necessary and beneficent effects can be seen. On the level of liberal democratic sentiment, "removing a brutal dictator for a free market economy and democratic process" is an a priori good of the highest order. As understood from this multi-level calculus of the market thought regime, even 2,700 people killed in the World Trade Center is not an issue to detain the tough-minded. In principle, as we know, deaths do not compute to market yardsticks of value except as lost incomes. On the geostrategic plane of the world's super state, the issue is clearer still. Decision here, the record shows, is perfectly indifferent to loss of life so far as it directly or indirectly advances US investment interests and military control to defend them.[73]

If overthrow of a non-market dictatorship blocking access to the global market's most precious and increasingly scarce wealth is maximally good to the ruling value-set, then nothing that goes wrong can countervail these asset gains from its standpoint. Optimal states of expectation—as subsequent history confirms—thus predictably followed in train after the invasion of Iraq in March 2003. Liberty and economic development were invariably perceived through the prism of market judgement: extension of more efficient market relations of production and distribution to the locked-in resources and peoples involved; new private capital formations and freedoms; opportunities for spectacular market growth where before there was none; relief of consumers from inefficient Arab monopoly of oil; a competitive price system to properly deploy and allocate resources instead of an "Islamic or socialist prison" keeping the people in "backward dependency on handouts and subsidies"; and "historic new vistas for foreign capital and local entrepreneurs to lead both Afghan and Iraqi societies out of the dark ages to development and freedom." Annunciations of "the first Islamic market miracle" were on the lips of market believers before the electricity was back on.

In short, *market magical thinking* prevailed in accord with the principles of the regulating market group-mind even in the face of mass homicidal consequences. Expected "optimums" and "miracles" were known to follow from society's conversion to market laws. The invasion itself was understood in terms of these expectations from starting plan on through successive disasters of occupation. Yet no one appeared to connect back to the set-points of the market paradigm which generated the illusions. Why would this be? The market prejudice-set *explains* what nothing else can: that there was no US post-invasion plan to rebuild an economy shattered by two US saturation bombings and twelve years of US-enforced sanctions, no plan—as distinguished from no-bid contracts to favored corporations—to rebuild the destroyed life infrastructure that had killed over five hundred thousand children. There was, in fact, no social plan at all *because* this was not in accord with the ruling assumptions of the market thought-system.

In ascendant market logic—as F.A. Hayek and his disciple, Margaret Thatcher proclaimed from before the beginning of the neo-classical revival—"economic planning is serfdom," or, more metaphysically, "there is no such thing as society; there are only consumers and firms." Market-state "liberation" was, in Iraq or elsewhere, thus certain to bring new freedom and prosperity to a "long-shackled command economy." If 9/11 would lead to such beneficent consequences once the opportunity was seized, and this optimal expectation followed from the ruling principles, then why would it be *wrong* for a risk-taking leadership to "allow its great challenge and incomparable opportunities"? New freedoms for foreign investment and for individuals to produce, to exchange and to compete were known beforehand to ensure economic well-being for all—even after Moscow and Kabul had quickly became unliveable by the same formulae, and even after Iraq's infrastructures had also been bombed and embargoed into genocidal devastation. If all that could be seen through the market prism was good news, why not here? "Shock and awe" on the geopolitical front, "shock treatment" on the domestic front. Each was "necessary for market restructuring" and "society's freedom and development." The invasion of Iraq was the reproduction in macrocosm of what was already known in national microcosm: privatization of a "failing state enterprise," with the "necessary sacrifices" of people's livelihoods on a corresponding scale.

The metaphysical assumptions at work disclose a systematic disconnect from life reality. When Assistant Secretary of Defense Paul Wolfowitz expected flowers of welcome thrown in the streets in a Paris-like welcome of the liberators, he was expressing the ruling market group-mind of which he was a lead creature. He was not alone in his structure of thinking. Almost no one in the official world has proposed another path than "necessary sacrifices" for redemption by "market structural adjustments and society-wide reforms" over 20 years. Thus the complete incapacity of the market-state invaders of Iraq to provide even collective security from attack, or the most basic infrastructures of water and electricity, let alone food and employment or healthcare or education—was not anywhere related to *the ruling economic paradigm in terms of whose magical thinking one disaster after another had happened across borders and continents for 20 years—from Argentina to Russia to Indonesia.*[74] The promised land was built *a priori* into the ruling model, but even *after* decades of disaster the transition was assumed as "inevitable" and with "no alternative." No one thought to ask: Could any mumming of slogans and life destruction from the Dark Ages rival this mass-sacrifice regime as deliverance?

No one on stage, including even Left commentators, seemed to question the claim that "we liberated Iraq."[75] The hold of the regulating market group-mind across factions and disagreements remained fixed, the unseen common ground of the "stay in Iraq" imperative intractably assumed across competing US party establishments through every disaster of support and policy. The fact that Iraqi society had long led the region in health indicators prior to the US invasions, and was now, in looted ruins, chorally proclaimed "liberated" disclosed the collective mental disorder. But none connected the effects back to their causal structure.

The market value-set, in fact, selected towards every step from 9/11 on. "Selling the goods" has many meanings. The deepest prejudice of the market meta-program underneath its apparently scientific mathematical notations is that *it conceives all that exists in terms of money inputs, throughputs and outputs in ratios of minimum cost and maximum revenue or commodities for private busi-*

ness or consumers. For the regulating thought-system, these money sequences are laws of nature and reality, and societies either "adapt" to them or do not survive. There is nothing in its calculus, therefore, to deter rather than to favor any life destruction that yields awesome market opportunities, including an occasional terrorist spectacle. To track the program here is unthinkable, but advisable. It reveals the warp of the regulating paradigm itself. The concept of "necessary sacrifices" for tradeoffs between increased market returns and lost livelihoods and lives is known well, but is suspended, along with other questions, in understanding 9/11. If the market calculus does not compute life lost or gained but only priceable assets and gains, while its national-security calculus does not recognize law as binding on actions "to protect US interests and investments abroad," then why *not* let the attack come to secure both? If the most systemic and global life destructions of our time, including ecological collapse and the obesity-malnutrition outcome, can continue to escalate even after the consequences are known with only denials or fig-leaves in response, then why not 9/11 and a far bigger pay-off matrix? The truth is that no market principle rules out any of these horrific consequences, and all select towards them.

The US geopolitical calculus is based on defense of US corporate market interests, present and future, and there are, as we know, few or no US-recognized constraints of law on "national security" matters and reasons. If 9/11 was planned by a former leading ally of US national security planners, Osama bin Laden, and then enacted by the "moral equivalents of the founding fathers," as sanctified US President Reagan called the Taliban and their allies in their US-armed war against yet another secular socialist government, why would it not have been *also* game-planned in the normal way as an option scenario? We need to bear in mind here that all economic and armed-force strategic planning pivots around the "pay-off matrix" of decisions. This is the meaning of "rationality" for all of the interlocked market thought-systems, including major areas of moral and political philosophy (for example the self-maximizing contractarian model in both of these fields). We need also to understand that the strategy frameworks of this "rationality" are military in prototype and development, and are the logical core of economic theory as well as military strategy since 1950.[76] We need then to recognize that the unthinkable is the standardly desired zone of effective strategy in both military and market thought-systems.

Since the very conceptual frameworks of market and military sciences have been increasingly coextensive at the US leading edge since the Second Great War, why would we expect them to be suspended *only here*?[77]

Why would this scenario already repeatedly anticipated *not* have been gamed when long-term market treasure and US military rights across the Middle East and Central Asia were at stake? The pay-off matrix to the principals and financers of the Bush Jr. administration of the 9/11 turn has been explained above, along with the wider payoffs to US global market empire and its most precious resource. This pay-off set also grows greater the more "the war on terror" appropriates public resources and attention to enrich and empower the same military, oil and corporate-state interests. At the same time, the military-industrial complex of the US, NATO, Middle East and world markets become more interlocked and mutually profitable across continents the more this system is positioned for new pathways of expansion. The peerlessly lucrative exchange corridors of Saudi oil money for US arms and world oil price-setting itself are just two key elements. 9/11 and the 9/11 Wars, in short, enable favorable payoff options on all fronts at the maximizing margins. In light of these history-determining pathways of decision, we may see how the regulating market thought-system increasingly articulates itself through human actors as the "shadow subject" behind every preference, policy and self-maximizing choice.

To lose the golden opportunity to achieve fast-track US "full-spectrum dominance" and maximal self-profit at the same time would, therefore, not make sense within the parameters of the ruling order of rationality and value. It would forfeit vast increase in domestic and world right to command, the unpopular Bush regime's gain of legitimacy as a war presidency, and new control over the greatest regional resource of global market assets in US history. Cost-benefit analysis beforehand, then, would rationally expect asset gains of unprecedented magnitude, with minimal prospective losses. In strategic terms, the decision path and outcomes were irresistibly attractive. In historical terms, 9/11 spurred the 9/11 Wars which, in fact, expanded US-led market control over former great obstacles of alien borders, Islamic culture, and barriers to control of the world's greatest natural riches on the basis of completely predictable military dominance. From the standpoint of the market and military calculus, in sum, 9/11 propelled every step of a process culminating in a super-maximizing pay-off matrix. It would be irrational to think that such calculations were inaccessible to those whose motive, purpose and training is to deduce them.[78] Conversely, nothing else but 9/11 (or its like) could have enabled any one of these priority objectives to be achieved in this time frame- as prior strategic policy formation was clear in recognizing. The hidden system decider throughout, the market-military calculus, forms a consistent explanatory through-line to the present that explains what is otherwise multiply anomalous.

Yet there is another plane of "moral compass" which needs to fix on 9/11 and the 9/11 Wars to "capture hearts and minds" for the mass support within America which would be required to sustain such a revolutionary strategic path in the face of predictable domestic and foreign opposition to the lack of demonstrated cause—"the religious-moral factor" to be analyzed ahead. Technically, the background variables are all favorable for execution of the strategic option that yields maximum payoffs to US domination. Global market operations present no obstacles for whoever plans the hijack logistics, and assist every step required. Effectively anonymous bank-laundered money accounts are daily and profitably processed by market agents in accordance with the instructions of principals, for example, by delegating functions unconnected with each other and through proxies of instruction. As well, the rule of international and national criminal law does not bind al Qaeda and has been publicly repudiated by the Bush Jr. administration as inapplicable to Americans, while US national law has never led to impeachment of a "President at War." The family of bin Laden was not even questioned. Desired delivery of market goods with payment in cash on time can always be fast-track and secretive by at least Swiss bank conduits, and so market money demand and mutually profitable exchanges can traverse most of the necessary conditions—including paying for services to well-placed positions for turning the other way at undetectable moments of the exactly timed sequencing. It is a matter of record that market transactions allow for anything that conforms to the relations of price, profit and exchange: slavery, mass murder, buying of politicians and warlords, trafficking in deadly commodities in mass volumes, and pay-offs to government and military functionaries. There is no limit even within scholastic market axioms.

As is well known, there were even escalated put options on airline stock before 9/11 in evident foreknowledge of the fall of airlines stocks from the hijacks, and no arrests were made. I will not try to repeat here all the evidence of foreknowledge which are already documented. But covert operations at the political level were needed to execute the transnational through-line of strategic war actions *after* 9/11 with public support. The mistake, which Ground Zero institutionalizes, is to disconnect 9/11 from what preceded and followed it. But if we consider the historical continuum as it in fact occurred, the connections are restored. One level of explanation remains, however, to understand the logic of the public *political passion* that could have embraced the official story of 9/11 and 9/11 Wars with no kickback of delegitimization. Here as well, a life-blind thought system regulated beneath the actors' consciousness of it, the ruling group-mind at the level of patriotic identity.

The Religion and Group-Mind of America Behind the US War State

Nothing else but a profound wellspring of ready emotional identification could have motivated a collective mind-block in America against the most elementary forensic questions on this administration's official story of 9/11, and then overwhelming approval of war criminal invasion of two other societies en route to or on vast oil reserves, the second society with no remotely demonstrated connection to the 9/11 attack. For ordinary people as well as elected legislators to remain silent or enthusiastically support such an historical sequence of events, something more than market motivation is required to explain the phenomenon. Here explanation must move to another plane, that of what may be called "the religion of America." On this plane of *verstehen*, understanding from the inside, the ruling group-mind is transparent. It centers on "the President of the United States" as one and identical with "America" and its "divinely ordained mission to liberate humankind".[79] In fact, operationally, "the President" means the US national security apparatus and its infotainment feeding system to the US and world media. From this hallowed pulpit of both sacred and secular power, a currently dominant faction, the rulers of the party in office, propagates the good news of the collective faith and supreme power of which the US presidency is "the highest office on earth." On the everyday level, the instant culture of endless market miracles and wonders holds all classes in a mesmerism of the expectant present moment.[80] The ultimate moment of the religion of America is the "clear and present danger" of the Enemy, in struggle against which American heroes are made. It is in such clarion moments that the quintessential operations of the group-mind of America are most clearly evident.

To put the matter in wider terms, the religion of America propels and legitimates the wider global market crusade with America as the world's savior state—"the leader of the Free World," serving "a higher destiny" to liberate all peoples. This is the spiritual *point d'honneur* of the ruling group-mind across borders, and it is what appeals directly to the hearts and minds of Americans, their "loyal allies," and free market believers in general. One sees and hears this collective self-worship proclaimed around the clock even in other countries thousands of miles away. "This great country of ours," "the greatest country in the world," "the leader of freedom-loving peoples everywhere," "the last best hope of humankind" are choral epithets of America's self-description widely carried by others as political and economic fact. "The idea of America," echoes the subdued John Kerry at the height of his campaign to dislodge a "polar opposite" George Bush as President, "is, I think proudly and chauvinistically, the best idea we've developed in this world."[81] The concept of America as an "idea" with no base or qualifier discloses the nature of the reference body which the ruling group-mind adopts as its ultimate value and meaning. It is by definition delinked from the life-ground.

The self-conception of America as supreme on earth in matters of significance is obligatory in public policy formation and expression of acceptable opinion in America. Famous "anti-foundationalist," Richard Rorty, for example, propagates the meaning of "American democracy" and "the human rights society" as given without any thought of contrary fact to his assumptions occurring once throughout an indefatigable corpus of cynicism about truth.[82] There are many variations of expression on the American group-mind. It rules outside America in the dominant idea that the US is "the undisputed leader of the Free World," "the leader of democracy and freedom," and "the world's overwhelmingly supreme power," standard givens of Western press discussion. The contradictory meanings of these epithets are not seen, in predictable conformity to the ruling group-mind. When demonstrators do call these meanings into public question on the streets in foreign nations, they are typically surrounded and attacked by their own countrymen in riot gear as "anti-American." No one I know within America or even outside it yet observes this phenomenon as indicative of an absolutist world religion backed by armed might. Yet America's certitudes of higher being, supreme power and benevolence of will are daily incanted as articles of public faith. None may be doubted without accusations of treason.[83]

Such a religion is idolatrous in principle, but this meaning is not possible to recognize from its standpoint. If it is at the same time propelled by a conviction of overriding natural right, and has mass-homicidal weapons to execute its convictions, then no limit appears to exist to inhibit the destruction of what opposes it. Indeed, natural limits of world ecosystems themselves are overridden freely and the most extreme inequality is assumed as a title of America's greatness.[84] In this way, the Invisible Hand comes to work on both economic and political planes as "globalization" and "freedom." America's market God is at the same time a fiercely jealous God that tolerates no alternative. That a "competitive" and "tolerant" order simultaneously prohibits any opposition to itself is not perceived as contradictory for it follows predictably from the first principles of the RGM. A fateful set of historical consequences proceeds from this closure to critical feedback. If the religion of America legitimates limitless money-sequence growth from the US corporate center to marketize all that exists as the meaning of "America's leadership of the Free World," then it follows that US market assumptions are converted into acts of war against all opposition or obstacles to its higher mission.

"In God we trust" is appropriately the sustaining certitude of a money-sequence economy reorganizing and conquering the world as "our freedom".[85] At the center, the chosen feel and see inside the ruling circle as US—"our own group," in the words of the academic guru of the US national security cabal, Leo Strauss.[86] This invisibly deciding group, us as US, has an invisible center like the market's invisible hand, but rules the chaos of competing national selves at the global political level. Yet it too is a corporate negotiation and price system—pressuring and buying others in voluntary exchanges at a self-advantage, with armed threat for non-compliance with the given corporate market order.[87] The logic of the market group-mind rules all the way up and down. "The value of a person is his price," says Hobbes. The will to stand against this equation is revolution, suggests Marx. There is no in-between for the religion of America.[88]

Any alternative is known *a priori* as an act of enmity to the faith. Within this regulating mind-frame, the meaning of "democracy" is not, as Lincoln or Jefferson thought, self-government by the people. It is a *process of locating group-mind preferences that the ruling group shares with a dominant voting bloc of America by continuous polls of opinion to select and market brand products which can best sell.* This is the political process that crystallizes the group-mind as a ruling force. Elections test the competing products, what is meant by "democracy" in this thought system, but the material condition of success is always corporate financial and media support (with unusual exceptions destabilized and overthrown by the same instruments combined with US state covert actions).[89] Here as well, there are two planes of the ruling order of meaning and decision, the economic and the political. Both are regulated across party oppositions by an interlocked set of absolutes which favor or exclude this or that candidate or policy in a continuous winnowing process. The regulating absolutes are pre-reflective, non-negotiable, and together constitute the ruling group-mind as a structure of understanding and judgement across parties, with the Command Assumptions 1–15 above as the generic market frame of mind. Yet the "room between" their poles of possibility may be of momentous importance—not only because a corporate market order may be fascist as well as quasi-social-democratic, but because the latter possibility may raise givens of the group-mind to consciousness, question and modification. This progressive social option was chosen in response to structural market unemployment—now called "natural unemployment"—to which the "Keynesian" public-investment solution responded until the Thatcher-Reagan counter-revolution against the welfare state and Vietnam defeat.

In all, the group-mind religion of America has remained relatively constant over generations with a more extremist fundamentalism coming increasingly to rule since this post-Vietnam counter-revolution. The ultimate command assumptions at work comprise the patriotic level of the ruling market group-mind which motivate its lead national vector. They are never systematically stated, but are more a primitive grammar of belief that is uncodified. Nevertheless, we can formulate their ultimately governing presuppositions as a regulating set of principles operating "on top of" the general market principles defined by (1) to (15) above. Each and all of these deciding presuppositions of the collective faith of the world's market leader can, like our previous principles, be tested by seeking to find exceptions—for example, one national political leader in the US who transgresses or challenges any of them. Here we find the political completion of "the ruling group-mind of America" as the global market's supreme power—*the shadow subject of America behind its media, military and financial selectors on the ground, and what enforces market principles as universal across the world.* These command assumptions of the nation constitute the bare subject-predicate system of "the world's sole superpower," or the inner identity of the US which leads the market meta-program as its supreme ruler on earth. The silently regulating givens of (1) to (6) below determine all acceptable public thought in America, including by state-secret policy formation:

1. America is the moving line of goodness and freedom in the world; therefore

2. All who oppose America are the enemy and evil; therefore

3. The free and the good of America must triumph over the evil enemy to protect the world; therefore

4. America's armed forces abroad must be supreme to prevail over threats to itself and the Free World; therefore

5. America is the Free World's Commander-in-Chief and Armed Forces abroad, which must achieve what (1)–(4) require by force of arms as necessary; therefore, by transitivity,
6. America cannot in principle commit crimes or wrongs against others in defending itself and the Free World.

These regulating givens of the group-mind of America form the inner algorithm of its own distinctive religion and morality, as well as of its politics and geostrategic planning. Through their internalization by acculturation, the governing elite and the masses become one and arrive together at the narcissist center for everything, America itself. US culture is, accordingly, always Americans beholding themselves in one or other mode, the religion of self-adoration which crosses parties and factions and whose criterion of goodness is aggregate sales. Anything which challenges this common ground challenges the US and, consequently, the identity structure of each within the circle of "our own group," an elastic line which may include Bandar Bush, but citizens are its normal outer bound. If sales and group-mind assumptions conflict, as with Michael Moore's documentary, *Fahrenheit 9/11*, which calls into question the identification of America with its war President, then it is predictable from the ruling group-mind of America that the sales venues of the offending market product will be blocked at every level so far as possible *within the limits of the American market itself.* When the religions of the Market and of America are in conflict instead of, as normal, two aspects of the One, a new dynamic of self-recognition becomes possible.

Yet normally while more and more others who are not believers in the religion of America may be enraged at lawless US-led destruction of people's life conditions or planetary life-organization itself, a reverse operation occurs within the American group-mind to invalidate all opposition and opposing facts as "anti-American" or "hatred of America." This emergent correlative of anti-Semitism joins the ideologies of the Chosen People of past and present.[90]

Yet once unmarginizable criticisms come from within America at the same time—as with the Vietnam and Iraq wars—then a space for public thought opens beyond the closed limits of the ruling group-mind. Here as well lie progressive possibilities for change in the group-mind itself, for example, de-identification of the war President with America or, more deeply, distinction between "loving America" and acquiescence in the group-mind assumptions above. Within the closure of the religion of America, however, it is predictably unthinkable within its thought-system to accept connections and facts that indicate that the Presidency of the United States of America would permit a mass-homicidal attack to occur on America—an unbearable contradiction within the binding faith for most.[91] Yet here too, though with more difficulty since there are no pictures to register the facts in the American mind, one can never rule out movement beyond the command assumptions by evolved social intelligence. It is also possible, on the other hand, that the "rational" perspective analyzed in the previous section finds *no contradiction between the ruling assumptions above and selection of an option scenario that maximizes America's payoff matrix by allowing 9/11 to occur.* Here it would simply be a matter of having to dissemble the plan to the masses and "soft" politicians—as Leo Strauss and the strategic thinking community in general recommend—so as to "achieve great objectives" that others' limited understanding cannot rise to.

The group-mind admits of many possibilities, but only holds so far as its assumptions are not laid bare and opened to question. There are many intelligent dissenters from the religion of America, but they can be easily recognized and are accordingly marginalized—for example, the many Americans who think their president led a war criminal invasion or had foreknowledge of the 9/11 plan. They are thus predictably attacked for betrayal of America and/or lunacy by those who are creatures of the ruling group-mind. This is a time-honored operation. Nothing is fixed, but so long as its assumed absolutes rule *a priori*, they are law-like in their hold, especially in the face of the evil Other which defines the Self-Group. Without acceptance of the primary Enemy as the defining Other of the US, there is a crisis of group-mind identity. America requires this determination by negation to sustain its closure to reality.

Such a crisis in the religion of America—the problem of no Other to define US after the fall of "the evil empire"—was resolved by 9/11. The secular world which expected an age of peace with no evil superpower left did not recognize the necessity of a diabolic Other to justify America's command leadership of the Free World. A "war without end" against the "enemy of international terrorism" sustained this ruling identity. Without it, America's society of market selves was without evangelical solidarity in armed force, and without legitimacy of its vast post-Cold War military expenditures. The group-mind and its Other unite different levels of the working whole as their system-decider at all levels of confrontation.

Yet the religion of America does not, revealingly, require a transcendental God ruling above it. With or without invocation of a traditional

God, the narcissist self-center can only go one place, back to itself as good and triumphant, and those who oppose it as evil. This metaphysic does not require a religious dualism in the normal sense. Leo Strauss and Ayn Rand, for example, are not theists, but are more absolutist prophets of the market gospel and the religion of America than native-born Americans. The duality of God (Self) and Devil (Other) only requires the Market and the Nation as Supreme to provide group worship with its armed incarnation in this world. Reverence for pure selfishness of the individual or group—which Strauss and Rand respectively advocate—is more militant with *nothing above* the self or group.

Clinically, psychiatry knows the disorder of narcissism well. It observes the defining propensities of autosuggestive hysteria and disconnection from reality, apt descriptors for daily television on "America at war against terrorism." But the unifying disorder is writ within and across the group-mind so it cannot be apprehended from outside its own field of meaning. When narcissism becomes psychopathic, the *Diagnostic and Statistical Manual of Mental Disorders* explains, further and more disturbing properties of mental disorder are revealed. The self lies glibly, manipulates others, is parasitic, and denies all responsibility for destructive actions. The clinical definitions of the narcissistic psychopath and the market religion of America correlate too perfectly to ignore. They are as microcosm to macrocosm, ego to group-mind, but the shadow subject is not seen. For the first rule of any group-mind is that it cannot adopt itself as an object of critical reflection. This is the distinguishing nature of its self-referential circle, and its consequent life-blindness.

This syntax of the American group-mind has been the propelling center of the global market religion since 1991, and more unilaterally since 11th September 2001. The Invisible Hand's chosen nation is America, and the US President is the Market God's Supreme CEO on earth. All the principles of one monotheistic construction overlap in one global subject bearing them, "the Free World," of which America is the centre, the leader and the supreme power. The regulating logic is evident once seen, but as psychiatry has long observed, the unconscious may be fanatically compulsive when *not* seen. *The meta-theme is old. An all-powerful, all-knowing and jealous Supreme Power rules the world to realise the group's worldly desires in accordance with an invisible design.* "The Almighty's gift of freedom to the world which America has the obligation to spread" is a current positive mode of expression of this regulating article of faith. "You are either with us or for the terrorists" is its meaning as a life-and-death ultimatum.

We know of the pre-Reformation Islam that is the current Other of the market thought-system, but we do not know the self-worship of the Market and America which is its Western mirror image. The intelligent certainly sense the fanatic logic in US witch-hunts of Un-Americans, vast prisons of the poor doing no offense to any person, tens of millions malnourished and without healthcare in the world's wealthiest market, and—most fatefully for the rest of the world—endless US threats and wars against societies not following the ruling corporate-market order. But we do not yet penetrate the market religion of America behind the symptoms. Again, the regulating logic is evident across phenomena once seen. Yet since the market's invisible laws and commands are infallible and above reproach, the transcendental set-points of Providence on earth, it is apostasy to penetrate the veil. Few thinkers dare to. Thus America bears this ruling group-mind into unending war against whatever-is-not-it with "the support of the Free World".[92] The Religion of the Market and of America are thus one—the Invisible Hand and the World Superpower united in leading the world to perpetual and universal growth and triumph over the Enemy to Progress and Freedom. 9/11 and the 9/11 Wars are the global market's new Sword, but none read the crystallizing shadow subject behind the transient events and actors.

From the standpoint of the market religion of America, 9/11 was a clarion call. America's universal mission of freedom on earth and its natural right to rule the world as "defense" became luminously clear through the regulating prism. The underlying metaphysic of supreme identity was consistently confirmed by US leaders' political speeches and policies across Party oppositions, with the Kerry candidacy of the Democrats in 2004 providing further evidence of the shared ruling assumptions beneath attack ads. The same logic of US supremacy and global market rule was the shadow script for contending opponents throughout.[93] No ally disagreed either with the commanding presuppositions. No line was drawn on America's claim to world leadership, freedom's representation on earth, or right to root out all other societies' weapons which might deter the US from invading it, and certainly no one questioned the transnational corporate market order. It was heretical, as France saw, even to disagree at the UN about the US right to invade another sovereign society even in the midst of U.N. inspections.

Yet a puzzle arises as to how the collectivity of the market religion of America can arise among economic self-maximizers for whom only more money for oneself counts as real value. In the words of America's most famous contemporary legal intelligence, lawyer Johnnie Cochran, "the color of justice is green".[94] How can such a nation come together as "the leader of the Free World," "America one and undivided"? What *joins* the members of the unifying religion at the center of their being to unleash them into willing attack on whatever does not conform? Here we move to a deeper, primeval assumption propelling the US war state. The inner meaning of this will can be found as a general principle in Hobbes' *Leviathan* and in the canonical contractarian political philosophies after him such as John Locke's *Second Treatise on Government*: "the right of nature" to kill another to secure self and property before this authority is transferred to a sovereign state.[95] Yet something more primitive forms the shadow subject of America as a people from its comparatively recent beginnings in other nations' wilderness continent which was already occupied by tens of millions of people, something ready to strike as self-definition against the great powers of the unknown land, against the "red tribes and savages" attacking over centuries, against foreign kingly rule from an island its people left to be free, against "European empires meddling in the Americas," and—on a century later through America's technological miracles in conquering a vast nature indifferent to its goals, beyond the Great Depression and War in which "America saved Europe and humanity from the Nazis"—down to the Cold War triumph over "Soviet enslavement and communism" to, finally, America's last great test and vindication as "history's greatest nation." "The Attack on America on 9/11" was, we might say, a third-millennium call to America's known mission in the moral universe. "America's moral compass" and the "Almighty's destiny" pointed clearly to the launch of the "American Century"—to unleash the one and only superpower to a climactic world crusade across the former Babylonian empire to Central Asia and the borders of India "bringing liberty to the world." Let the dark forces come. We and God shall prevail in the empire of the good and the free.[96]

The identity that binds a great nation operates on two levels, the religio-millennarian vision as well as the market's price system. But the *differentia specifica* that distinguishes American culture at both micro and macro levels is what all must have and be willing to use to have liberty in and out of America—money and the gun. Money is the medium of all the market's gains and losses, and no more needs to be said of it here. But the power to kill—symbolized by the gun in all its multiplicity of forms and extensions in America and as America abroad—is more distinctive of the US as a nation, and more revealing of the character structure behind the 9/11

Wars. Deep in the American psyche, the fear turning back to conquer the Other which is always perceived to threaten it, lies the self's final definer in a world of dark forces waiting to attack. At bottom, it may be said to be the deciding will of the group-mind of America: *"I can kill, therefore I am."*

Where is this equation not the propelling determiner of America's historic identity across races and ethnic identities, past and present, and in the 9/11-era operations across the world? The power to kill the other bridges self-assertion across image and reality, law-abiding patriots and gangsters, the good and the bad alike. It is all, in the end, that the market self unmoored from the larger community can ultimately count on in the Hobbesian world of each against all where "the restless desire for power after power ceaseth only in death." It is, we might say, the beast at the core of the group-mind of America, the fascinator and repeller of hearts and minds, the abyss across which the US Leviathan stretches in a world without a covenant.

"I can kill, therefore I am" is a logic that goes back to before Hegel's master-slave dialectic glorified it as the transcendental source of self and philosophy. Before and after, it haunts the modern Anglo-American projection of the barbarous "State of Nature" prior to its civilization by Social Contracts (which express the market thought system at another level, in just-so pure theories of justice and morality). After the 9/11 attack on the US, the meaning of "we can kill, therefore we are" was reborn as the patriotic will. Yet even after 9/11, the heroic stature of America calls itself into question when the killing of the Other is by industrial bombs falling eyeless from the sky on poor populations and their basic means of continuing life without disease and death. Although all that may matter to this moral universe is to show "We are Number 1 in the world" and "only the free market can provide freedom and democracy," still the saturation bombing of a defenseless and impoverished people provokes uprising beneath the group-mind regulators of meaning. The life of humanity refuses the offer that can't be refused. Even though there is almost no popular form of American culture that does not bear the undertow meaning of the master longing—from hunting other creatures to kill them, to the mock murders of wrestle-mania and video-games of shooting others in droves, to the kill-'em language of America's favorite sports and the pervasive violent entertainments on living-room screens, to the government of the most populous state by a movie robo-killer—still, something snaps out of the field of group-mind submersion. It may take a generation to unfold—but the end is already written on the mind-lock that cannot tell the difference between the life and death of others.[97]

At bottom lies the unseen equation of US armed force to America itself. If America is at war in "a war without end," then the equation rules out its life modes of peace. No received economic metric can see this problem, let alone measure it. Market growth is the only metric of social health visible through the regulating market prism. With no social life but consuming market selves against the Enemy, "we can kill therefore we are" becomes the American collectivity which is nowhere else allowed to exist. The armed force of the US is in unobserved fact the only collectivity willingly funded by taxpayers since tax-cut government began. All other pooled resources for nation-state action are "socialism" to the group-mind. In the only national collectivity supported, the *esprit de corps* of America becomes beneath understanding the boot-camp and the killing fields of others. "We can kill, therefore we are" joins market selves in a thousand points of light. The sky-lighting bombings are "our credibility in the world".[98]

This is why the Democratic Party, otherwise unaccountably, abdicated from its responsibility to oppose once the parameters of the "war against terrorism" began, affirming with "no daylight between us" the criminal invasions of other societies, the emptying of the US Treasury, the systematic abridgement of legal rights, and the waiving of environmental laws for the military.[99] Society-staggering increases of public expenditure on weapons of mass destruction displaced vital life needs on every level. Disconnect ruled from the heart and mind. It was Un-American to oppose.[100] When a people are incarcerated within their group-mind, more paralyzed than 1930s Germans in their dread of being named "unpatriotic," the war cannot stop. That is why it was essential that the war began: to render armed seizure and control of other societies' lands and wealth as America's natural right. It was not by accident that Hobbesian theory was dominant in America's intellectual elite. Underneath detection, a moving spring of self-defense as armed invasion was accepted as given.[101]

No cause other than the 9/11 attack could have incited American legislators to sacrifice their constituents' tax-dollars in the long-term trillions, the lives of other Americans, and the reputation of America in the world, as US security geostrategists from both parties recognized beforehand. Without an attack on America, unilateral armed-force invasions of distant societies were wars that could not be sold "after Vietnam." 9/11 reversed the tide of a generation. Beneath all the surface phenomena of party politics and competing media and opinions ruled the Market Religion of America for which the globe was its resource basin and labor pool, its land of milk and honey of the Promised Land of three millennia later. The historical subject now was the ruling market group-mind, and its commanding assumptions were the set-points for every decision. That the accumulating effects in the larger world of global market expansion beyond all barriers were the ozone layer shredding, oceans rising, and environmental indicators in precipitous decline could not register through the regulating framework of meaning.[102] All that was externality to the ruling calculus. Conflicting interests of party, class and ethnos merged as the propelling consensus of the life-blind.

At the middle and working class levels, "we love America" was the shared self-image of citizens. Since "patriotic Americans" all loved America, and America was "our men and women serving in our armed forces abroad," they could no longer distinguish their beloved country from the crimes of the national security state. The deployments of armed terror, mass disinformation, secret narco-links and political bribery and coercion at every level were denied, necessary, anomalous, or exceptions.[103] The monstrous equations were assumed *as* America which "must be defended against her enemies." Those who oppose America are "anti-American." The victims are the enemy. War crimes are "collateral damages." One absurd equation builds onto another as a paranoid mass cult called "patriotism," but all proceeds in accordance with the shadow subject of the ruling group-mind.

It's certainly true that there are market-class biases to the effects. The resources of the poor are expropriated for transnational market profit and consumption, while the US Treasury itself is structurally adjusted to a wide-mouth siphon to the rich for "market investment and growth." But the class bias of the payoffs do not explain the all-class affirmation of the silently deciding assumptions that select and exclude towards every decision, trend and outcome. Only what fights back is perceived by the US and the Free World as a problem to be overcome, and only military and market plans are selected for resolved collective action. Global trade edicts, IMF market-restructuring and—after 9/11—direct military invasions follow from the global market meta-program, the sole meanings of "development," "defense" and "security" which make sense to the regulating thought regime. The geostrategic hinge on which all turns is 9/11—both the karmic blow-back and the launching site of "the war without end." It is the unseen synecdoche of implosion of a life-disconnected empire. Beyond its group-mind rule opens the horizon of the life economy alternative.[10]

Notes

1. Press Conference, May 3rd, 2004.
2. See http://www.crimesofwar.org/thebook/crimes-against-peace.html
3. Reserve officer Brigadier-General Janet Karpinski revealingly reported after "the torture scandal" had disappeared from the headlines that she was a "scapegoat," and that the man who the US Defense Department replaced her with, Jeffrey Miller, relocated from the Guantanamo prison in Cuba operating outside the Geneva Conventions, advised: "They're like dogs. If you don't treat them like dogs, you'll lose control" (CNN, June 15th, a clip not repeated).
4. The torture began as routine as soon as the invasion of Afghanistan occurred with all of the methods exposed in Iraq only three years later used primarily on ordinary people picked up at random. "The torture was in many ways worse," observed the Human Rights Watch in the area, "not operated even nominally in accordance with the Geneva Conventions—the whole system operates outside the rule of law." The Independent Human Rights Commission set up in June 2002 by the European Union "Bonn agreement" concurred: "From those who are talking about human rights and democracy, it is a great shock" (Duncan Campbell, "America's Afghan Gulag," Guardian Weekly, 2nd–8th July 2004, pp. 15–16). Over two years before, a press report had revealed that prisoners had been held in inhuman conditions at the US Bagram airbase in Afghanistan with fatalities from the criminal abuse (Dana Priest and Barton Gellman, "US Decries Abuse, but Defends Interrogations," Washington Post, 26th December 2002).
5. See, for example, John Stanton, "The Practices of Torture," Global Outlook, Summer 2004, p. 26.
6. Michael Ignatieff earlier described the US in the New York Times Magazine as a "global hegemony whose grace notes are free markets, human rights and democracy enforced by the most awesome military power the world has ever known" (cited by Gilbert Achcar, "Greater Middle East: The US plan," Le Monde Diplomatique, June 2004, p. 6). As we will see ahead from its regulating assumptions, Ignatieff, "a human rights specialist," expresses the ruling group-mind well in a faux-cosmopolitan varient.
7. Ignacio Ramone, "'Torture in a Good Cause'," Le Monde Diplomatique, June 2004, p. 1.
8. Quoted by Ramone, ibid.
9. Cited by Nicola Short, "The Challenges of Bush's Foreign Policy," Science for Peace Bulletin, May 2004, p. 2.
10. US Ambassador to Iraq, John Negroponte, for example, is described by UN Secretary-General, Kofi Annan, as "an outstanding professional, a great diplomat, and a wonderful ambassador here" (Robin Wright and Colum Lynch, "Tough road ahead for Negroponte," Washington Post/Guardian Weekly, April 29th–May 5th, 2004, p. 29). Negroponte first presided over the funneling of weapons, money and political support to war criminal attacks on Nicaragua as ambassador to Honduras from 1981 to 1985, and then led the US at the United Nations Security Council when it perpetrated "the supreme crime under international law" by directly invading Iraq in 2003

while UN arms inspections were proceeding. (Annan was UN Secretary-General at the time.)

11. See, for example, William Shirer's classic, The Rise and Fall of the Third Reich (Greenwich: Simon and Shuster,1960), pp. 453–54., 792–93). The German commander-in-chief's words were almost exactly the same as the American's almost seventy years later: "We have no interest in oppressing other people—He has led a reign of terror—[with] a tremendous military arsenal—It is intolerable for a great power to remain a passive onlooker" (CCPA Monitor, April 2003, p. 9).
12. In 1933, President Roosevelt's US Ambassador to Germany, William Dodd, said: "A clique of US industrialists is hell-bent to bring a fascist state to supplant our democratic government and is working closely with the fascist regime in Germany" (Richard Sanders, Facing the Corporate Roots of American Fascism (Ottawa: Coalition to Oppose the Arms Trade, 2004), p. 3. President George Bush Jr. may be understood from a biographical standpoint as carrying on a family tradition originating with his paternal great-grandfather and grandfather, George Herbert Walker Bush and Prescott Bush, who were investigated by the Roosevelt government for collaboration with the Nazis, Prescott Bush as a primary financial operative in the banking structure of the Nazi war machine (see Webster Tarpley and Anton Chaitkin, "Bush Family Ties to Nazi Germany—the Legacy of Prescott Herbert Bush," Global Outlook, Summer–Fall, 2003, p. 54). Transnational corporations which armed, equipped and financed the Nazis also included major subsidiary operations of General Motors, Ford, IBM, Dupont, IT&T and Standard Oil (now Exxon).
13. See http://www.newamericancentury.org/. The exact quotation from PNAC is (emphasis added): "Further, the process of transformation, even if it brings revolutionary change, is likely to be a long one, absent some catastrophic and catalyzing event—like a new Pearl Harbor".
14. Despite claimed surprise by George Bush and Condoleezza Rice at the mode of the 9/11 attacks, a simulated plane attack on the Pentagon was conducted long before as a "Mass Casualty Exercise" on 24th–26th October 2001 (Michel Chossudovsky, "The Pentagon Simulated a Scenario of an Actual Terrorist Attack Ten Months before 9/11," Global Outlook, Summer 2004, p. 36.)
15. See notes 40 and 41 ahead for sources of documentation of these and other facts referred to through this analysis which are neither widely reported nor connected, but are screened out by the operations of what is analyzed in this study as "the regulating market group-mind."
16. An exact account runs as follows: "Tenet told Boren that he feared Bin Laden was about to try something big, and that people underestimated 'the capabilities and the reach' of what al-Qaida was 'putting together.' What Tenet didn't tell Boren, [Washington Post journalist Bob] Woodward said, is that the CIA had intercepted a flurry of communications over the summer of 2001 suggesting that something 'spectacular' was imminent. As the two men talked, Tenet's security guards approached their table and told Tenet that there was a 'serious problem'. . . the World Trade Center had been attacked. . . According to Woodward, Tenet then turned to Boren and said: 'This has bin Laden all over it.' But before Tenet left the table, Woodward said he made one more comment—a reference to Zacarias Moussaoui—that suggested that the CIA Director's prescience may have fallen short when it came to preventing

the attacks. 'I wonder,' Tenet said, 'if it has anything to do with this guy taking pilot training'." <archive.salon.com/politics/war_room>.

17. See note 42.
18. I distinguish the concept of "group-mind" from the related, but circumscribed micro-concept of "groupthink" associated with the work of Irving L. Janis, Groupthink: Psychological Studies of Policy Decisions (Boston: Houghton-Mifflin, 1972). Janis proposes a model for a "defective" decision outcome by a small, isolated group of homogenous and cohesive members in a stress situation (for instance US national security decisions such as the US Bay of Pigs invasion of Cuba). While there are common operations at work here—principally, moral certitude of cause, stereotyping of opposition, and collective rationalization—"groupthink" in the committee sense is an exact micro-symptom of the much deeper and wider structure of group delusion of "the group-mind." The group-mind, in turn, is constituted by unexamined a priori principles regulating everyday and elite consciousness via a normative syntax of perception, understanding and judgement which is presupposed across individual and cultural divisions. The top-level, secret and ultimately failed decisions which Janis and co-researchers examine are, I contend, downstream expressions of a more systematic cultural disorder—just as a criminal war of aggression is the downstream effect of a social regime of thought that selects for and approves it, and blocks out any criterion of value other than operational failure. Janis's model itself symptomizes the problem of the RGM by selecting for case study only what fails operationally, thus excepting ecogenocides themselves if there is no failure to operationalize the desired objective.
19. "The tacit dimension" of cognition pioneered by Michael Polanyi (The Tacit Dimension, New York: Doubleday, 1967) is solely constructive, never systematically misleading. Polanyi characterizes the meaning and operations of the tacit dimensions as: "we know more than we can say." So his inquiry does not address the "regulating group mind" investigated here.
20. Barrie Zwicker, a long-time national reporter and broadcaster in Canada, was the first to publicly document, establish, and broadcast the facts of the "stand-down" of central air defenses in the US on 11th September 2001 in "The Great Deception: What Really Happened on 9/11" (Mediafile, Vision TV Insight, 21st and 28th January 2002, www.visiontv.ca), with no rebutting evidence countering his nationally broadcast two-part documentary since). Years later, on June 17th, 2004, CNN broadcast an isolated exchange between the FAA (US Federal Aviation Administration) and NORAD (North American Aerospace Defense Command) which relayed the emergency message of hijacked planes and the requirement to "scramble" intercepting military aircraft. The NORAD respondent replied: "Gee I don't know—," and when a response was demanded rejoined, "Everybody's just left the room." The first question is, How did this blocking happen? The second is, Why would a mere fragment of its meaning appear only three years after the fact with no media investigation or explanation of such a hot fact of news.
21. It has become publicly well known that Bush Jr. had been pressing intelligence personnel for reasons to attack Iraq since he entered the White House, but less well known that five days after 9/11 an "unidentified Pentagon spokesman" reported to the Gainesville Sun: "We've been planning this war [against Afghanistan] for the last

three years." (I am indebted to Bruce Gagnon, Co-ordinator of the Global Network Against Weapons and Nuclear Power in Space for this report <http://www.space-4peace.org>).

22. Terrorism is defined by the standard world insurance clause to exclude liability as: "an ideologically motivated act or acts including but not limited to the use of force or threat of violence or force, committed by or on behalf of any groups for the purpose of . . . instilling fear in the public or a section of the public." So far as I know, no one has applied this definition of terrorism to the daily acts of the US and Israel in countries they illegally occupy, although these actions fit the legally binding definition.
23. A revealing case of the "creature" mind is US National Security Advisor to the Bush Jr. Administration, Condoleezza Rice, as she is described by her former Professor of Political Science at Denver University, Alan Gilbert.(I am indebted to G.A. Cohen for sending me this account). Gilbert pays full credit to her all-round "capacities to excel," but concludes from such decisions as her demand that the illegally ousted and US-kidnapped Jean-Bertrand Aristide, President of Haiti, be prohibited any residence in the West Indies, that "she is lost in her performance" ("The performer lost in her performance," Salon Magazine, April 9th, 2004). This account does not explain the evil actions of the lead-vector role she fills, whereas the group-mind regulating it does.
24. "The new flexibility of the US on working with international partners" was featured in the world press across continents. That the social infrastructure of Iraq was destroyed, over one million of its people dead from US-led invasions and embargoes, and its possibility of a secular socialist future eradicated were not problems that registered for the UN Security Council which, in quintessential expression of RGM determination, voted unanimously to approve the continuing US occupation.
25. As the eminent Jonathan Schell points out from study of the administration's own statements, "the new 'sovereign' Iraq will not: possess authority over either American forces or its own; be able to pass legislation; control its own news media; make decisions about the economy of the country" (Jonathan Schell, "Politicizing the War," TomDispatch, May 28th, 2004). These facts did not deter the world's media and experts of record from continuously wondering how "Iraq's new sovereignty" would play out in faithful reproduction of the false RGM premise as true.
26. Julian Borger, "The CIA Finally Gets Its Man," Guardian Weekly, June 4th–10th, p. 9.
27. For example, the universally valid "ideal speech situation" imagined by Jürgen Habermas is a specially market-friendly theory by a priori ruling out critical engagement with the "self-regulating" market order as a problem, and by never addressing life purpose or reality outside the what and how of communication as ideally conceived (Jürgen Habermas, Theory of Communicative Action, Volumes 1 and 2 (Boston: Beacon, 1984). The reality of life conditions and needs outside the circle of words can never compute if they are not reference points of the talk. With no reference body of life co-ordinates to anchor or test the meaning of words and words about words, even unanimous and unforced agreement can accept cumulative ecogenocide outside of its community of discussion, as it does in fact today.
28. The "Comprehensive Privatization Plan for Iraq" was issued by a 101-page US State Department document prescribing the total revolution of privatization and deregu-

lation. (Liam Lacey interview with Greg Palast, CCPA Monitor, December–January 2004, pp. 18–19).

29. US decrees in Iraq explicitly connected its control over Iraq's resources to the right to self-defense of the United States in such forms as Executive Order 130303 (italics added): "The threat of attachment or judicial process against the [US-controlled] Development Fund for Iraq, Iraqi petroleum and petroleum products, and interests therein constitutes an unusual threat to the national security and foreign policy of the United States" (Ibrahim Warde, "Iraq: A License to Loot the Land," Le Monde Diplomatique, May 2004, p. 2). Observe how the US here not only institutes its right to war-criminal expropriation of control over and right to Iraq's oil as the law of Iraq (itself a war crime under law), but defines any "judicial process "against this criminal expropriation of possession as "an unusual threat to the national security of the US." Here we see an assumption of lawless power that first puts itself above the law, and then treats as a cause of war any lawful recourse against its criminal actions. Our account of the "religion of America" ahead explains the logic of the group-mind which produces such policy decisions as acceptable and accepted.
30. Denis Halliday, "The UN Failed the Iraqi People," Global Outlook, Winter 2004, p. 48.
31. The facts of Kuwait's slant-drilling into Iraq's oilfields from its artificially created oil-state were not observed, although the US green-light to Saddam to invade and the concocted atrocity story of "babies in incubators cut off from electricity by Saddam's armed forces"(a story arranged by a US advertising firm working with the daughter of the Kuwait Ambassador to Washington) were ephemerally reported before disappearing to restore the normality of group-mind perception.
32. Postmodern ideology preconsciously affirms this arrest of historical learning on another level of global market "liberation," the level of theoretical alibi. It repels all bases of co-operative subjecthood, decidable life facts, unity of understanding and history itself which might ground market-system critique and constructive alternative. See, for example, Jeffery Noonan, Critical Humanism and the Politics of Difference (Montreal: McGill-Queen's University Press, 2002).
33. See, for example, Nafeez Ahmed, Behind the War on Terror: Western Secret Strategy and the Struggle for Iraq (Gabriola Is: New Society Publishers, 2003).
34. Bush Jr. asserted his "cojones"in unison with war poodle Blair: "I was going to act. And if it cost the presidency, I fully realized that" (William Hamilton, "Bush Ordered Secrecy on War Plans, Book Claims," Washington Post/Guardian Weekly, April 22nd–28th, 2004, p. 30).
35. For systematic development of this analogue, see John McMurtry, The Cancer Stage of Capitalism (London: Pluto, 1999).
36. "The sites targeted for looting and burning [,—the] Ministry of Planning, Information, and Health[,] support the speculation that a concerted attempt has been made to destroy crucial data . . . [while] there was heavy guarding of Oil and Interior Ministries by US tanks and soldiers. . . The data from pre-Gulf War health records is critical to establish a baseline showing increases in post-Gulf War levels of cancers and birth defects in Iraq . . . [from] the direct bombing of cities with 'depleted' uranium weapons" ("Press Release by Association of Humanitarian Lawyers," UN

NGO, 25th April 2003). "Major funds to restore food and relief supplies to the Iraqi people" amounted to 21cents (U.S) per capita per day for the "emergency period."

37. Thus Pierre Bordieu's concept of "habitus" cannot explain the phenomenon of the regulating group-mind because "habitus" is always rooted in practice or locale. Nor can the concept of "hegemony" of Antonio Gramsci because it is grounded in productive class membership.
38. Thus legendary socialist and worker leader of Brazil, President Lula da Silva, leading a delegation of 450 people, met with Communist Party officials in China in the first week of June 2004 to further "Brazil's success in locking into Chinese markets" by mass supply of soybeans grown from a fifty-percent increase in burnt-out and clearcut Amazon rainforests ("from 30 to 60 million hectares under agriculture"), while China simultaneously planned to remove three hundred million people from their ancestral rural lands to the mega-cities of China (AP News Service, 4th June 2004). The global market formula is in such ways universalized as "progress and development" by the leading heirs of socialism and communism.
39. Zbigniew Brzezinski, The Grand Chessboard: American Primacy and Its Geostrategic Imperatives (New York: Basic Books,1997), pp. 124, 211.
40. At the behest of American friends who were disquieted by the belittling dismissal by editor Michael Albert and Z-Net regulars of allegations of administration foreknowledge of 9/11, I wrote a reply as a Z-Net Commentary on 22 May 2002 whose introductory overview read: "The most telling documented evidence has been altogether ignored, and not a jot of counter-evidence has been thought necessary to disconfirm the foreknowledge hypothesis. Instead we are once more treated to name-calling with no refutive substance." Michael Albert kindly published and replied to my article, but did not engage any fact or argument of my reply. Michael Albert's general argument (and Noam Chomsky's with whom he has elsewhere shared authorship of the position) is that "institutional analysis" must eschew particularist "conspiracy theory." While I sympathize with this method, I note that 9/11 denial is itself an institution, and is based on a deeper and comprehensive institution, the market group-mind.
41. David Ray Griffin, The New Pearl Harbor features a title which repeats George Bush Jr's own words to describe 9/11, and simultaneously relates it to an event in 1941 which precipitated the US declaration of war on fascism, not a justification for constructing it. In such ways, even the best critical exposé of the domestically constructed terror attack must compare it to an exonerating opposite event (against the Nazis and Japan over Pearl Harbor) to lead past the blinkers of the group-mind censor.
42. Documentation for this and subsequent facts I report ahead about the construction of the 9/11 attack can be found in Nafeez Ahmed, The War On Freedom: How and Why America Was Attacked (Joshua Tree: Tree of Life, 2002), Michel Chossudovsky, War and Globalization: The Truth Behind 9/11 (Canada: Global Outlook, 2002), Thierry Maysson, 9/11: The Big Lie (London: Carnot, 2002; translation of L'Effroyable Imposture, Paris: Carnot, 2002), and—in definitive summary—David Ray Griffin, The New Pearl Harbor. Paul Thompson, "September 11: Minute By Minute," Center for Co-operative Research (www.cooperativeresearch.org) provides exact time co-ordinates of the event and response to it.

43. I am indebted to Professor John Valleau, Chemical Physics Theory Group, University of Toronto, for drawing my attention to this scientific anomaly of the plane-impact causal sequence. No. 7 building of the World Trade Center, which was hit by no plane, was also coincidentally "pulled" (demolished) on 11TH September 2001. A single source of the physics analyses of the World Trade Center building collapses is available at <911review.org>. The extreme anomalies of energy transformations from the plane impacts reported in the official story, such as the complete pulverization of the building concrete and wide dissipation as smoke, has led to the hypothesis of demolition-wiring of the buildings beforehand. No official investigation has been done of these striking scientific anomalies.
44. Even Michael Moore's famous documentary, Fahrenheit 9/11, was refused contracted US distribution by the Disney Corporation and otherwise blocked and attacked although its attention was centered on the long-term Bush-bin Laden business affiliations and mutual profits by their families from the 9/11 Wars as well as Vice-President Cheney's Halliburton Corporation and the Wall Street Carlyle Group in which Bush Sr. and James Baker are invested. These interests in war-profiteering are understood here as collateral re-enforcers of the regulating market group-mind whose rule, as Moore's documentary confirms, is internalized by the poor and the enlisted as their own set-points of emotional identification and aggression.
45. See also note 14.
46. The American people's tradition of self-conception as God's chosen people on earth to possess, as Israel did, the lands and wealth of others "as far as the eye can see," with force of arms as providential instrument, is a guiding thread of vision through US genocides and wars for over two centuries. David Noble of York University tracks this theme in his The Promised Land (2005), which bridges from Abraham in Genesis to the Bush Jr. Administration. As Lyman Beecher puts it in 1835 (cited in Noble): "If this nation is, in the providence of God, to lead the way in the moral and political emancipation of the world, it is time she understood her high calling, and were harnessed for the work," to which Albert Beveridge adds, "God marked the American people as the chosen nation to finally lead in the regeneration of the world." We will see ahead the place of this thinking in the "religion of America." Here we observe that security in such a vision is incompatible with any facts that tell against it.
47. Sigmund Freud engages the problem of the group-mind in the form of crowds as analyzed by his contemporary, G. Le Bon in Psychologie des Foules (1895), and observes: "In groups the most contradictory ideas can exist side by side and tolerate each other, without any conflict arising from the logical contradiction between them" (Sigmund Freud, Volume 12, Civilization, Society and Religion [London: Penguin, 1991], p.106.) Freud's famous model is the primeval group herd with individual libidinous ties to the group leader. Neither Freud nor Le Bon, however, recognize the group-mind as a normalized cognitive frame of mind regulating everyday perception, understanding, and self-identity independently of any crowd presence or direct ties to a leader.
48. "'We went out of the house [after a village wedding party sleepers had been bombed by US planes at 3 A.M.] and the American soldiers started to shoot us. They were shooting low on the ground and targeting us one by one," she said. She ran with her

youngest child in her arms and her two young boys, Alei and Hamza close behind. . . then her two boys lay dead. . . A doctor in the nearest hospital, in a-Qaim, told the Guardian last week that the dead included eleven women and fourteen children. . . The US military on Monday continued to insist that its operation had been properly targeted" (Rory McCarthy, "Wedding Party Attack Kills 42," Guardian Weekly, 28th May–3 June 2004, p. 11).

49. Gregory Palast, The Best Democracy that Money Can Buy (London: Pluto, 2002) most systematically exposes the facts of the corrupt election and policy behavior of the Bush Jr. administration before and since 9/11. The nature of the police-state legislation outside of the US since 9/11 is most economically explained by the Canadian Association of University Teachers in "Civil Liberties, Human Rights and Canada's Security Legislation" (Ottawa: CAUT/ACPPU, 2004).
50. An examination of "real-time war as pop culture" is provided by Paul Rutherford, Weapons of Mass Persuasion (Toronto: University of Toronto Press, 2004).
51. For analysis of the global system as an increasingly carcinogenic disorder on the social level of life organization, see my The Cancer Stage of Capitalism.
52. For systematic obfuscation by scholarship of the "market mind" so as to preconsciously or otherwise remove any disquieting trace of the life-blind logic explained ahead, see Jerry Z. Muller's, The Mind and the Market (New York: Random House, 2002).
53. The choice-path structure towards the 9/11 Wars is explained by the ruling market group-mind, but only as one set of dramatic expressions of it. An exact account of its phenomena if not of its inner logic is provided by Mark Blyth in Great Transformations (New York: Cambridge University Press, 2002). He explains how "business repertoires" of thought and action "which resonate with the core identities" of businessmen preceded revolutionary policy attacks on public sectors to dismantle them across the world in the 1980s and 1990s with no compelling economic evidence to justify them. "Absent the transformative effect of such ideas on agents' perceptions of their self-interest and the policy choices of the heirs of embedded liberalism make no sense," Blyth concludes (p. 269). While Blyth provides masterful evidence for the phenomena and expressions of what I define as "the regulating group-mind," his concept of it as the expressed "ideas" of the business classmisses the deeper and wider syntax of social perception and judgment at work.
54. In his Foreword to the definitive but ignored work of Ludwik Fleck (Foreword, 1976, to Ludwik Fleck, Genesis and Development of a Scientific Fact (Chicago: University of Chicago Press, 1834–35/1979), pp. ix–x), the celebrated Thomas Kuhn dismisses Fleck's idea of a "collective mind" as "vaguely repulsive," "an hypostasized fiction," a "damaging metaphor," and "intrinsically misleading." He provides, however, no argument or evidence for his dismissal. I interpret his abhorrence as itself a paradigm example of the "regulating group-mind," in this case the dominant "market group-mind," which cannot conceive of a collective thought system because its method stops at individual agents and aggregates in exchange relations. Pre-emption of any alternative conception, however compelling, follows—here by abusive characterizations with no scientific justification thought necessary. In this way, a preconscious taboo forms at the level of philosophy of science itself, blocking out reasoned reflection a priori even in critical paradigm research.

55. A perfect example of how this group-mind operation deterred 1984 presidential candidate, Walter Mondale, from an "industrial strategy" which would have distinguished his campaign from the "free market worship" behind the sputtering Reagan campaign, is provided by Mark Blyth, ibid, pp. 192–94.
56. These were the highlights of the "opposing" program proclaimed by the Democratic National Convention in July 2004. I am indebted for its contents to an active Convention attendant, Eileen Dannemann, Director of the National Coalition of Organized Women. A committee proposal at the Democratic Party Convention for a new Department of Peace was rejected, in predictable accordance with the "religion of America" explained in the next section.
57. Gilbert Achcar, "Greater Middle East: The US plan," Le Monde Diplomatique, April 2004, p. 6. Bilateral trade treaties with the US, "free trade zones," and membership in the WTO were other market remedies proposed by the UNDP in collaboration with the US and the Arab Fund for Social and Economic Development (Afsed). That none of the latter "market transformations" had worked in achieving greater life security, or more basic needs fulfillment, or better education and cultural opportunity, for any society in market-reformed "Central and East Europe" did not compute to the group-mind which now regulated official thought across the former East bloc and the Islamic world as magically "transformative" to the better whatever the contrary evidence.
58. Hillel W. Cohen, Robert M. Gould et al., "Bioterrorism Initiatives: Public Health in Reverse?"American Journal of Public Health, November 1999, p.1629–630.
59. "If the universities are to be businesses, then let us have fair trade between them," says Professor Emeritus John Tiffin, who is co-author of The Global Virtual University (London: Routledge, 2004), confidently expressing the market group-mind at work inside higher education itself. Tiffin dismisses objections to the marketization of higher research and education as a "brand issue," thereby preconsciously ruling out the nature of education as free and informed critical inquiry not dependent on any private interest for its inquiries.
60. Paul Samuelson asks, "What does this all mean?." In accordance with the formulae of neo-classical economics, he answers on behalf of the First Theorem of Welfare Economics by assuming that although the First Theorem of Welfare Economics has no proven applicability to any actual economy or problem while at the same time ruling out all "externalities" like pollution, unemployment and malnutrition, it shows that , "even the best planner cannot come along with an ingenious reorganization scheme and find a solution superior to the competitive marketplace" (Paul Samuelson and William D Norhaus, Economics (New York: McGraw-Hill, 1992). In this way, the leading liberal neoclassical economist of the era expressed the a priori market group-mind at the level of theory, as did the title of his canonical text which preempted all alternative conceptions of economics as inconceivable.
61. Neo-classical economics can only quantify across incommensurable factors and interpersonal differences by the homogenous unit of money which eliminates all differences in a common metric of measurement. But this gain in simplicity must necessarily repress all differences and values that are not representable as money quantities—such as human life itself. When I posed this problem to Yale economist John Roemer, who styles himself a "non-bullshit Marxist," he advised others at the

table that "John is against science." The occasion of this discussion was in New Haven after a Yale University Conference in Honor of G.A. Cohen on his Sixtieth Birthday on 10th May 2001.

62. The Project for the New American Century (PNAC) thus headlines the US geo-strategic plan to be followed by its armed force deployments as "CONTROL THE NEW INTERNATIONAL COMMONS OF SPACE AND CYBERSPACE," explaining that its text shows how to (I quote) "pave the way for the . . . to control [and] determine the future shape of international politics here on earth."
63. November 21st 1864 Letter to Colonel William Elkins, cited by Emmanuel Hertz, Abraham Lincoln: A New Portrait, Volume 2 (New York: Liveright, 1931), p. 954.
64. See the fifteen-step "global market algorithm" ahead.
65. The exact normative and constitutional nature of this public accountability is spelled out in John McMurtry, Value Wars: The Global Market versus the Life Economy (London: Pluto, 2002).
66. Harvard Professor of International Business, Yoshi Tsurumi, recalls Bush Jr. as a student: "I still vividly remember him. In my class, he declared that 'people are poor because they are lazy'. He was opposed to labor unions, social security, environmental protection, Medicare, and public schools. To him, the anti-trust watchdogs, the Federal Trade Commission and the Securities Exchange Commission were unnecessary hindrances to 'free market competition'" <www.glocom.orgopinions/essays/20040301_tsurumi_president>.
67. The facts took until 2004 to come out. "According to a magistrates investigation, the police improvised lies to justify a blood-soaked raid at the Diaz school, which was used by protestors as a headquarters" in Genoa in 2001. "The raid, which left dozens injured after being kicked, punched and beaten with batons, raised an international outcry" until 9/11 displaced it from the news. The police at the G8 Summit "planted petrol bombs at the protestors' headquarters, and falsely accused them of stabbing a police officer" (Rory Carroll, "Italian Police Framed G8 Protestors," Guardian, 22nd June 2004).
68. See"Civil Liberties, Human Rights and Canada's Security Legislation" (Ottawa: CAUT/ACPPU, 2004). In the case of faraway India of entirely different culture and history, the same logic of legislation to rule out public protest under the same concept, here the "Prevention of Terrorism Act," was imposed by the "liberalizing" Bharatiya Janata Party (BJP) regime, a Hindu fundamentalist party, but no less regulated by the global market meta-program operating across East and West cultural divisions and right-wing-liberal oppositions.
69. A public demonstration against the Free Trade Agreement of the Americas ministerial meetings in Miami in November 2004 was thus "attacked by thousands of militarized police in full riot gear including electrified shields, tanks, automatic and) semi-automatic weapons, tear gas, concussion grenades [and] rubber bullets" which resulted in "more than 100 protesters treated for injuries, 12 hospitalized, and 250 arrested. . . . Miami police chief John Timoney was quoted by papers as saying: 'We're locking them up. We'll try to do as many arrests as we can" (Jennifer Van Bergen for the Lawyers Guild, 26th November 2004). Miami police were provided with $8.5 million of "anti-terrorist funds" by the Bush administration, in return for

which the Mayor of Miami described the treatment of anti-FTAA protesters as "a model for homeland security."

70. Neo-classical economics is entirely derived from models of non-living systems, dominantly those studied by classical mechanics and in extremum principles of calculation. The unobserved result is the a priori exclusion of life-organization co-ordinates from the calculus. For example, the standard texts of neoclassical economics do not include or discuss any concept relating to what is required for humans to stay healthy and alive because money-demand, not life need, is the sole criterion of a consumer good and of the consumer entitled to it.
71. Reason would posit a hypothesis, and look for evidence to disconfirm as well as confirm it. With 9/11 thought, as well as market thought in general, the conclusion is assumed as true, while disconfirming facts are ruled out of view.
72. Hence months after the invasion of Iraq, Deputy Secretary of Defense, Paul Wolfowitz, made the famous remark in the August 2003 edition of Vanity Fair: "We had no choice . . . Iraq was swimming in a sea of oil."
73. As Chomsky's work demonstrates in rich detail—for which he is called a "fanatic" out of print by fellow academics—for example, Richard Rorty and Jay Newman—whose own published work, ironically, features disquisitions on "tolerance." Here we see the reverse operations of the market group-mind at work even in the minds of professional philosophers arguing against group dogma.
74. Joseph Stiglitz, Globalization and Its Discontents (New York: Norton, 2002) penetrates the structure of delusion at work in the IMF, but seldom confronts the defining principles of the regulating market program as such. His comment regarding the failures of IMF Structural Adjustment Programs across the world—"the IMF simply assumed that markets arise quickly to meet every need" (p. 55)—applies in general.
75. These were the words of David Korn of The Nation arguing against the administration's Iraq policies on CNN on June 2nd, 2004.
76. The definitive study of the military-market-machine interlock of contemporary economic theory is provided in detail by Joseph Mirowski, Machine Dreams: Economics Becomes a Cyborg Science (Cambridge: Cambridge University Press, 2002).
77. For an anatomy of the theoretical axes of market science, technology and war as a unified meta-system, see Value Wars, ibid, pp. 198–220.
78. For the most detailed, critically informed and leading account of the inner sanctum of US military-economic strategic analysis as well as the automaton rationality of contemporary economic theory in particular, see Machine Dreams.
79. We should bear in mind here that when a US Federal Appeals Court in San Francisco found in favor of a suit brought against the post-1954 inclusion of "under God' in the Pledge of Allegiance as an unconstitutional abridgement of the separation of church and state, the US Congress condemned the decision, the US Senate voted unanimously for a resolution against it, and all senators and congressmen together gathered on the steps of the Capitol building to recite in unison the Pledge with "under God" in it, followed by God Bless America. (I am indebted to David Noble's manuscript, The Promised Land, for this account). In this revealing event, we meet the group-mind of America in collective sing-song across elected politicians of opposing parties.

80. Secretary of State Colin Powell's words are worth reporting here, explaining his place as chief foreign minister in the decision to mount the US war-criminal attack of Iraq in 2001: "He would not intrude on that most private of presidential spaces—where a president made decisions of war and peace—unless he was invited" (cited by Bob Woodward, Plan of Attack (New York: Simon and Shuster, 2004). Only a sacred space could rule out discussion of an issue of the most profound public international importance in relation to which Secretary Powell was appointed as the lead public servant. Here we see how the religion of America, which is analyzed ahead, regulates thought at the highest level of responsibility so as to produce pious incoherence.
81. Glenn Kessler, "Kerry: Democracy Can Wait," Guardian Weekly, 4th–10th June 2004, p. 7.
82. See, for example, Richard Rorty, "Human Rights, Rationality, and Sentimentality" in Stephen Shute and Susan Hurley, eds., On Human Rights: The Oxford Amnesty Lectures (New York: Basic Books, 1993). Here the "neo-pragmatist" Rorty condescends in certitude of premise he elsewhere ubiquitously calls into question: "We in the safe, rich, democracies feel about the Serbian torturers and rapists as they feel about their Muslim victims. They are more like animals than like us" (p. 126). Rorty expresses a representative assumption of America's superiority in human rights prior to the exposure of a transnational US torture regime in Afghanistan, Iraq, and occupied Cuba as well as official repudiation of the Geneva Conventions forbidding torture. Yet the long prior record of US military, prison and covert torture across the world and poorer American populations, including by state-of-the-art instruction at the School of the Americas which has trained torturers for Latin America and other regions over decades, is also blinkered out by Rorty as non-existent, whatever the documented facts. His cognitive block against evidence disconfirming the central assumptions of the group-mind does not, however, pose a problem to his intellectual followers across the globe.
83. One should distinguish between the religion of the Market and of America, but they are complementary as the Invisible Hand and its Incarnation. In each case, the monotheist properties of supreme power, benevolence of will and infallibility are assumed as given.
84. Consider George Kennan's often cited post-War declaration of US right whose logic is not deviated from today: "We have about fifty percent of the world's wealth, but only six percent of its population. . . .Our real task in the coming period is to devise a pattern of relationships which will permit us to maintain this position of disparity without positive detriment to our national security." What has changed other than the numbers since Kennan's policy statement is that the separation between Church and State has dissolved in the imperial religion of America.
85. "In God We Trust" has been on US coinage a longer time, but the words, "under God," were only inserted into the American Pledge of Allegiance at the height of "the Red Scare" in the 1950s. In contrast, the American constitution intentionally excludes any reference to a higher power so as to institute constitutionally the separation of Church and State. Susan Jacoby, A History of American Secularism (New York: Holt, 2004). The religion of America is a long construction which peaks in the post-911 era.

86. Leo Strauss, Natural Right and History (Chicago: University of Chicago Press, 1953), pp. 98–9.
87. As numerous US intelligence agents have reported, including when I was Chair of Jurists at the War Crimes and Crimes Against Humanity Tribunal at the Alternative World Summit in Toronto in 1989, US dollars in large amounts are regularly deployed in the field as a standard price and exchange mechanism for purchasing local power-holders, such as the warlords in Afghanistan after the US invasion of 2001, and generals of Saddam's armed forces in the US of Iraq in 2003. The invisible hand of the market which regulates market supply by market demand is here reproduced at the political level with senior government and military figures also selling as commodities for whatever price the market is willing to pay. As in the formal market, armed force backs the security of the exchange and the working order of its transactions and contracted deliveries of goods. Incorruptibility of public servants in evolved societies, conversely, eliminates the market in public representatives—a level of civilization not comprehended by market principles.
88. Any other alternative is "communist" or other evil by definition, even if only minimal life-security is sought by poor non-industrialized people aspiring beyond the status of beasts of burden ("donkeys" in US-supported Nicaraguan President Somoza's terms before his 1979 overthrow by the "Communist" Sandinistas). Somoza, as virtually all other such market-state dictators, functioned to ensure primary commodities to US-located transnational corporations and kingly privileges for his group—an arrangement conceptualized as "an ally of the US" or, at the other pole of representation, "a military dictatorship," but in neither case with any linkage back to corporate market function. As the beloved "Great Communicator" said to the heroic rag-poor Sandinistas—with no loss of public support for his "very popular presidency"—there was only one US condition for a cessation of financed "Contra" war crimes against Nicaraguan society's main harbor and medical clinics. "Just say Uncle," he chortled. In such ways, the meaning of the world perceived through the lenses of the ruling group-mind becomes entertaining and a preference of American consumer desire.
89. Exceptions indicate the rule—for example, Salvador Allende's winning Socialist Party before the US-supported military coup d'état in 1973, and Hugo Chavez's winning candidacy for President in Venezuela from 1999 to 2004 (which featured a non-stop but unsuccessful US-supported campaign to unseat his elected government by armed coup d'état and other means). Jean Aristide's late 1990s electoral rise in Haiti and subsequent fall in 2004 was also an exception, but was marked by the usual US financial, corporate media, and proxy-armed-force selectors against elected government not conforming to RGM expectations.
90. Thus US media opinion leader, George F. Will, infers that anyone who criticizes the state of Israel's policies—as with those in a European Union poll who ranked Israel and the US as "the greatest threat to world peace"—is "anti-Semitic." Since, he further infers, it is only "the left" who criticize Israel, then "the left is reduced to adapting that perennial of the right, anti-Semitism." Therefore, "the left" produces "a new twist to its recipe for salvation through elimination" (George F. Will, "The left's latest radical chic: anti-Semitism" (Washington Post, 4th March 2004). Will, a former professor of Political Science at the University of Toronto, exhibits the ruling group-mind's operations of reversal and projection in quintessential expression with

none recognizing the moral syntax generating the deranged meaning, but hundreds of media reproducing it as expert commentary.

91. This is why even a sophisticated expensive magazine like Vanity Fair, featuring a market tone of worldly pleasure and ironic superiority in a few articles sprinkled amidst advertisements for expensive products, was obliged to mock as otherworldly ravings the hypothesis of strategic foreknowledge of 9/11 (Rich Cohen, "Welcome to the Conspiracy," Vanity Fair, May 2004, pp. 138–154). The group-mind operation was familiar. Belittle the hypothesis as blaming mysterious Others (the "Illuminati," "the Jews") for an event in which fabled meanings are involved ("the Holy Grail," "the Great Pyramids"), with the incoherence of the journalists' account projected onto the hypothesis itself. A key fact which is inexplicable is then buried within the text—in this case, the meeting, which is not disputed, of "the head of Pakistani's intelligence [Gen. Mahmoud Ahmad] with top White House officials before the attacks" while "instruct[ing] Umar Sheikh to wire $100,000 to the lead hijacker, Mohammed Atta"—to prove report "balance." That no engagement with the facts or connections is once required to invalidate the counter-RGM explanation is unlikely to be noted by the reader. In this way, innoculation against the facts is achieved without meeting them.

92. A major challenge to America's perceived role of "leadership of the Free World" arose with its internationally unpopular invasion of Iraq in 2003, and thus a significant possibility of pathway out of ruling group-mind assumptions was presented. Those who came to perceive "an error," however, were regulated by the same generic assumptions as those they criticized, thus remaining within the confines of the ruling group-mind. Only failure to succeed operationally in armed invasion and occupation raised doubts. The destruction of another social order that worked demonstrably better than market neighbors for the life prospects of the working majority thus remained assumed as "liberation." America could only "save Iraq" and "American credibility" by succeeding operationally in the war-criminal occupation. In this way, the system-deciding imperative of market growth and globalization remains on track through every violation of individual and social life as "liberation," however genocidal under law. Disconnect ruled a priori.

93. "The single greatest threat we face in the world today," said John Kerry as the polar icecaps melted and extinctions were a thousand times their evolutionary background rate, "is a terrorist armed with nuclear weapons" (John Kerry, Palm Beach, 27th May 2004 Press Conference to launch eleven-day foreign policy tour). The fixation on foreign terrorists expressed the deep consensus across the opposing sides of the divided nation as the given on which discussion was based. Senator Kerry, it followed also from the common group-mind, presupposed that the US had the right to enter other societies at will, and seize all materials it deemed as a threat such as perceived "bomb-making materials." . . . "Here's what we must do: The first step is to safeguard [sic] all bomb-making materials worldwide [while the US itself renounces international treaties against nuclear testing, proliferation and first use]. That means making sure we know where they are, and then locking them up [under US control] and securing them wherever they are [thereby prescriptively allowing any override of other countries sovereignty and right to defend themselves versus US attack]." One meta-program, analyzed here as "the religion of America," was the common syntax

of understanding and judgement beneath what was called "the polarized presidential election."

94. CNN, 10th June 2004. The disconnect between ego-greed content and high moral ground of proclamation is not observed, but follows from the market logic of the Invisible Hand regulating the individual market greed of each into the freedom and welfare of all as an a priori law of neo-classical economics. See note 60 above on the First Theorem of Welfare Economics.
95. The right to kill the violator of one's property is a baseline "Right" and "Law of Nature" for John Locke in his canonical Second Treatise on Government, and that which is delegated by Social Contract to the State to execute on the individual's behalf to protect and punish offenders against private property, the latter for Locke being the cornerstone of all society and state legitimacy.
96. If one dissects the Bush Jr. administration's selections and inventions of facts to justify and pursue its war from 2000 on, one discovers that no regulating principle of the market religion of America is called into question even by rising opposition criticism and demands for alternatives. Thus in the factually accurate and detailed account by Vanity Fair in May 2004 (pp. 228–244, 281–294), the difference between the Bush regime and its opponents was on the extent to which data was fabricated for official promulgation (all, in fact, repeated with passion at the televised UN Security Council by the administration "statesman," Colin Powell), the failure of the occupation on the ground (never recognized as a war crime), and lack of international support for the supreme crime under international law. Former Democratic Secretary of State Madeleine Albright expressed her difference with the Bush regime on the basis of the same religion of America, with proposed US global rule and supreme power as the very given objectives on which both the criticism and the alternative were based. "Multilateralism," she advised, "is a way to maximize [US] power" (p. 293).
97. It follows from this group mind-set that the deaths of Iraqi civilians in the Iraq occupation would not be tracked or reported, as then occurred in fact.
98. The US National Anthem's references to the explosion and delivery of lethal industrial weapons—"the rocket's red glare, bombs bursting in air"—are no longer anomalous once we penetrate the primeval level of the religion of America.
99. The National Defense Authorization Act of September 2002 exempted the armed forces from the existing Endangered Species Act and Migratory Birds Act and use of depleted uranium, recognized as "ecological warfare " under Protocol 1 of the Geneva Conventions (added after the Vietnam War). Depleted-uranium weaponry not only continued to be developed and used in grave risk and harm to Iraqi civilians (as well as Bosnians and Afghanis) and US soldiers themselves, but to the world's other species. "The Pentagon as I write," adds Michele Landsberg, "is seeking new exemptions from environmental laws that govern hazardous wastes, toxic clean-up, and air quality, as well as those protecting wildlife habitat, whales and other marine animals" ("Precious environment is another casualty of war," Toronto Star, 23rd March 2003, p. A2).
100. Justice Department guidelines to airport security officers, for example, identify "Greens as likely terrorists," reports Douglas Stuber, formerly the leader of Ralph Nader's Green Party presidential campaign (Frederick Sweet, "Green Party 'Terrorists'," Intervention Magazine 6, January 2004.

101. Its unspoken meaning was extortionate, but inaccessible to RGM perception: "Our defense is defending you from us."
102. A graphic simple profile of the cumulative effects of uninhibited industrial and consumption growth is provided by the following general facts: (1) "The burning of fossil fuels has almost quintupled since 1950"; (2) "The consumption of fresh water has almost doubled since 1960"; (3) "The marine catch has increased fourfold"; (4) "Wood consumption is now 40% higher than 25 years ago" (Jack Manno, Privileged Goods: Commoditization and Its Impact on Environment and Society [London: Lewis, 2000], p. 3). The rate of increase of consumption, pollution, degradation and exhaustion as systemic effects of (1) to (4) has not slowed since in any of these spheres of the planetary life-ground, but has grown; while the overall contribution of the US military, the world's largest polluter and environmental destroyer (by design, but not reported by Manno or other environmental analysts) has steeply increased (mainly by the 9/11 Wars and skyrocketing US military expenditures; see note 77 above).
103. See, for example, Noam Chomsky, Hegemony or Survival: America's Quest for Global Dominance (New York: Holt, 2004).

NOTE: This paper was originally presented to the International Citizens's Inquiry into 9/11, Convocation Hall, University of Toronto, May 30th, 2004, and has undergone major development for publication here.

Among the effects brought about by the source of energy used to destroy the Word Trade Center were around 1,400 "toasted" cars, some of which were in parking lots (above), others from a half-mile to as much as a mile-and-a-half away (over). This appears inexplicable if only conventional modes of demolition were involved.

Some "toasted" cars were strewn across FDR Drive *(top and middle), while others—mangled like beer cans—were on the streets of lower* Manhattan *(bottom).*

EPILOGUE

Conspiracy and Closed Minds on 9/11

Morgan Reynolds

While more Americans doubt the 9/11 story every week, evidence abounds that many have a mental block against rational examination of the evidence. The possibility that it was an inside job is a non-starter for them. Programmed "cut outs" ensure that 9/11 doubts are consigned to the "conspiracy" closet.

Last June I was explaining the fuss over my 9/11 article to a family member who shall remain anonymous, and he interrupted and said, "I don't want to talk about it." Millions join him in that sentiment. By implication they might as well say "I'd rather cling to the official 9/11 myth," or "If mass murderers run free, I'm fine with that," or "If 9/11 was an inside job, then I'm ruled by monsters and I might have to do something about it. I'd rather watch Paris Hilton."

American Exceptionalism

Where does this passive attitude come from? Causes are many but American indoctrination has two sides that figure very prominently in the explanation:

- Belief in "American Exceptionalism"
- Disbelief in Political Conspiracies

The first belief massages the American ego: we are heroes, always the good guys in history, and we can trust our government to be the same. The second steers us clear of subversive theories and thwarts connecting the dots. American exceptionalism is "Civics 101, the Disneyfication of U.S. history," the "We're so good" formula of "those stupid romances commonly called history." Like no other nation in history, we are an unparalleled success, or so we are told. With American self-esteem unrivalled, denial about 9/11 is hardly surprising. Conventional wisdom, in effect, says

> Yes, criminal gangs have ruled in other nations from time to time, perhaps always, but it has never happened here and cannot happen here. Evidence to the contrary is bogus, I do not have to even look at it. For one thing, I vote. We are the world's greatest duh-mocracy. In fact, I voted for Bush-Cheney (or that other Skull-and-Bones candidate from Yale, I forget). I am fully invested with this regime and I'm not a criminal or traitor, so Bush-Cheney must not be either. After all, we the people are the government. Criminals and traitors do not even look like us: they look like Arabs, Germans, Japanese, Chinese.

The second belief holds that conspiracy theories are simply no more than a symptom of a mental disease. Such infantile beliefs stem from delusion and paranoia, not objective reality. On its face, it is preposterous to believe that the U.S. government would attack its own people. History is about accidents, bungling, lone nuts, chaos and coincidence, not planning or cause-and-effect, execution and cover-ups.

"False Flag" Terrorism

Americans know a great deal that just is not so. The hidden history of false-flag terrorism is key, followed by trained aversion to conspiracy. When bad things happen on a large scale, chances are that an important group of people wanted them to happen and made them happen.

Governments throughout history have provoked or staged attacks on their own people to serve the powers behind the throne ("the money power"), glorify themselves, engage in vast government spending, reward friends, exert domestic control, stimulate the juices of war, annex neighbors and pursue vast geo-strategic rearrangements (including the "global domination project"). A few examples:

- Nero burned Rome to blame the Christians (A.D. 64)
- The U.S. provoked Mexican-American war (1846)
- The U.S.S. Maine sinking (1898)
- The S.S. Lusitania sinking (1915)
- The Reichstag fire (1933)
- Hitler's staged attack on the Gleiwitz radio station (1939)
- The "surprise attack" at Pearl Harbor (1941)
- The Bay of Pigs conspiracy (1961)

- Operation Northwoods (1962)
- LBJ's Gulf of Tonkin conspiracy (1964)
- The Kuwait baby incubator hoax (1991)
- The yellow cake and WMD scams (2002)

Ruthless though plotters be, the basic principle "is as mundane as insurance fraud," observes Webster G. Tarpley, author of *9/11: Synthetic Terror* (2005), and nicely illustrated with the obscure hoax that started World War II. Hitler wanted to invade Poland but knew the German majority did not support war, so a group of hapless German convicts was dressed up in Polish army uniforms, marched to the Gleiwitz radio station, machine gunned to death, arranged as if storming the building, and Nazi agents read an anti-German statement in Polish declaring Polish forces had invaded Gleiwitz and taken over the radio station. With this farce and related border stunts, Hitler invaded Poland the next day, 1 September 1939. "Wag the dog" anyone?

Mistakes about Conspiracies

Many Americans know that the JFK, RFK, MLK and other assassinations were inside jobs, and that Nixon's Watergate and Reagan's Iran-Contra are proven conspiracies with criminal convictions. Blatant government murder of U.S. citizens occurred at Waco, Ruby Ridge and the Oklahoma City bombing. Yet some would still argue that the scale of 9/11 was too big to be an inside job because it would involve so many people. Someone would surely squeal and we would hear about it, goes the argument, and that has not happened.

JFK's triangulation murder involved hundreds and nobody "ratted" that out in any substantial way, although Jack Ruby was close before he was found dead in his cell. Dozens of deaths surrounded the case. Here's how large, inside conspiracies work:

- Conspiracies—partnerships in crime—are common: a corner drug deal is a conspiracy and one in four federal prosecutions include conspiracy charges.
- At the maximum, hundreds rather than thousands probably were necessary to carry out the 9/11 psychological operation.
- Many conspirators are ideologues committed to the idea that the 9/11 hoax would serve the interests of the nation. Worthy ends

justify murderous means to this crowd. The human cost of 9/11 turned out to be "only" a month's highway fatality toll and served the magnificent ends of starting a global war on terror, two invasions and more to come, billions more in defense spending, torture, new agencies, "Patriot" controls, domestic spying, enormous new contracts, more debt and many other attractive consequences.

- Many participants are cunning sociopaths (amoral) with the mindset of stone cold killers. They wear a suit or military uniform but have no respect for the lives of the "little people." They are ruthless, witness the fool in the White House: "But all in all, it's been a fabulous year for Laura and me," a tone-deaf president declared in a December 2001 interview.
- Only the trustworthy are at the center of the hub-spoke-and-wheel compartmentalization necessary in a complex conspiracy. Only the arrogant few at the hub know the big picture before hand.
- The most secretive regime in US history puts a huge premium on personal loyalty and gets it.
- Most participants did not know before it happened how "over-the-top" the Twin Tower demolitions were going to be. The job may even have been contracted out ("outsourced") to ruthless foreigners. Once done, it's too late to get out.
- Any participant would hesitate to squeal after the event because, at the minimum, disbelief, disgrace and grief would follow. The major media, inside 9/11 from the start, could always discredit squealers, if that were to become necessary.
- Risk-taking behavior is always greater in groups than for lone individuals (Psychology 101).
- Once involved in the plot, everyone is "in for good.'
- Conspirators face no threat of arrest, prosecution and punishment by the government's justice system, a proven fact since government and media obstructed and trashed New Orleans district attorney Jim Garrison's JFK investigation and prosecution.
- Controllers discipline participants through billions of dollars in black budgets and drug money, death threats, assassination and blackmail.

- Blatant and repeated resistance against truthful investigations, aided by obstruction of justice and abetted by media silence, prove that there is a lot to hide.

Consider one control technique among many: a very high CIA official died a few years ago and on good authority I know that he had a "24/7" CIA presence to protect against a deathbed confession in front of hospice personnel. "I'm not into conspiracy theories," says filmmaker Michael Moore, "only those that are true."

Unjustifiable Disbelief

The fundamental difficulty is not really disbelief about the ability to keep conspiracy secrets but disbelief that U.S. government officials would really collaborate in attacking America and take 3,000 innocent lives at the World Trade Center. But this is naïve.

First, government is an instrument of social compulsion. Organized force is what government does. The belief that soft-hearted people rise to the top in government is akin to the belief that softies were whipping-masters on slave plantations.

Second, setting WTC bombs could very easily have been contracted out to Mossad, otherwise known as "executioner to the world." Killing? It's what we do (because this is "life or death for Israel," blah, blah).

Third, people are taught that they control their government and live in a democracy. But all governments are run by insiders, usually permanent and dominated by their paymasters. Whenever policy or personnel really matter, international bankers call the tune for modern governments daily dependent on them for new loans and refinance of the old. These financiers look out for themselves and believe in a New World Order, a one-government world, and have no allegiance to America or its founding principles.

Fourth, the U.S. military oath requires an oath-taker to "support and defend the Constitution of the United States against all enemies, foreign and domestic." The enemy within the gate is the major threat today, whether it is called by the name "conspiracy" or not, not the enemy outside.

Skepticism about conspiracy, small or large, is beside the point in the case of 9/11 because the official Osama-and-Nineteen-Young-Arabs (ONYA) conspiracy tale is so farcical and impossible. Nearly everyone in America has easy access to the internet and hundreds of websites expose the 9/11 fraud. The analysis is out there and in a few dozen books, although the mainstream media ignores it all.

Only government could have pulled off a psy-op this big, not a rag-tag band of Arab incompetents without visible means of support, who were repeatedly running afoul of law enforcement in the field. All other intelligence services and governments know the real story about who did 9/11.

It is like an elephant in the living room, studiously ignored by insiders who keep quiet about it. After thorough exposure via the Downing Street memo and other conclusive evidence about the Bush-Cheney lies to justify invading Iraq, it takes a lot to remain ignorant about 9/11. This is no longer about a conspiracy that is too large to work. Ignorance increasingly has to be willful.

According to one engineering study, the support columns "shredded" the 100-ton airliner, which virtually "disappeared." Not only was the damage consistent with a much smaller aircraft or missile, but the engineers ommited the massive engines from their analysis. This exemplifies the quality of much of the official evidence.

Petition to the Congress of the United States

Scholars for 9/11 Truth

TO THE MEMBERS OF THE HOUSE OF REPRESENTATIVES AND OF THE SENATE OF THE UNITED STATES OF AMERICA:*

PLEASE TAKE NOTICE THAT,

On Behalf of the People of the United States of America, the Undersigned Scholars for 9/11 Truth Hereby Petitions for, and hereby demands, Release of the Following kinds of documents, video and films, and physical evidence to the public for study by experts and scholars investigating the events of 9/11:

1. Immediate release of the full Pentagon surveillance tapes, of which five frames (only) have been released via the official ASCE report, as Judicial Watch has also requested. We further demand release of the video tape seized by FBI agents minutes after the Pentagon hit, from the fuel service station near the Pentagon, as well as any other videotape which shows the 9/11 strike on the Pentagon.

See

http://news.nationalgeographic.com/news/2001/12/1211_wirepentagon.html

http://www.defenselink.mil/releases/2000/b05012000_bt218-00.html

http://www.defenselink.mil/news/May2000/20005022a.jpg

http://perso.wanadoo.fr/jpdesm/pentagon/pages-en/fct-videos.html

2. Immediate release of 6,899 photographs and 6,977 segments of video footage held by NIST, largely from private photographers, regarding the collapses of WTC buildings on 9/11/2001 (NIST, 2005, p. 81). In particular, all footage relating to the collapse of WTC 7 (including shots before, during and after the collapse) must be released immediately, without waiting for the NIST report on WTC 7, which is long overdue and may be prolonged indefinitely.

3. An explanation from Vice President Richard Cheney regarding the "orders" described by Secretary of Transportation Norman Mineta in his testimony before The 9/11 Commission. Secretary Mineta stated that while in an underground bunker at the White House, he watched Vice President Cheney castigate a young officer for asking, as a plane drew closer and closer to the Pentagon, "Do the orders still stand?" The officer should be identified and allowed to testify at a deposition under oath.

See http://www.911truthmovement.org/video/hamilton_win.wmv

4. The documents generated by Vice President Cheney's energy task force have been kept from the public. A court case brought forth a few maps that display oil fields in the Middle East. We hereby put Congress on notice that there is probable cause with regard to criminal activities by the Cheney Energy Task Force involving a criminal conspiracy to launch illegal wars and/or terrorist activities. We therefore demand that Energy Task Force document that comprise, discuss, or refer to plans to invade the Middle East, including Iran, and Venezuela or other sovereign nations be released immediately.

See Cheney v. District Court 542 U.S. 367 (2004) and United States v. Nixon 418 U.S. 683 (1974).

http://www.worldnetdaily.com/news/article.asp?ARTICLE_ID=33642

5. Audio tapes of interviews with air traffic controllers on-duty on 9/11 were intentionally destroyed by crushing the cassette by hand, cutting the tape into little pieces, and then dropping the pieces in different trash cans around the building. We demand an explanation for this destruction of evidence and ask that the possible existence of other copies of such tapes or perhaps of written transcripts of the interviews be pursued. All air traf-

fic controllers on-duty on 9/11 should be allowed to testify during a public forum under oath.

See http://query.nytimes.com/gst/abstract.html?res=F0091FFE3C580C748CDDAC0894DC404482&incamp=archive:search?

http://web.archive.org/web/20040509021515/http://www.suntimes.com/output/terror/cst-nws-tape07.html

6. The Secret Service, which is highly trained to protect the President from danger and to move him to a secure location in the event of a threat, breached its own standard procedures by allowing President Bush to remain at a public location for 25 minutes after it was known that the nation was under attack. All Secret Service personnel who were at Booker Elementary School with President Bush on 9/11 should be required to testify in public and under oath about these events.

See http://abcnews.go.com/Politics/story?id=121331&page=1

http://www.whatreallyhappened.com/IMAGES/feral_press_9-10.gif

http://www.whatreallyhappened.com/bushbook.mov

7. On the morning of 9/11, some five "war games" or "terror drills" were being conducted by U.S. defense agencies, including one "live fly" exercise employing aircraft. These drills reportedly included the injection of false radar blips onto the screens of air traffic controllers. In addition, the government was running a simulation of a plane crashing into a building the morning of 9/11. Who was in charge of coordinating these war games and terror drills? Who had the ability to issues orders in relation to their conduct? On which screens were "false radar blips" inserted? When did such false injects commence? When were they purged from the controllers' screens? What was the effect of these activities on standard procedures for interdicting hijacked aircraft?

See http://www.911readingroom.org/bib/whole_document.php?article_id=92

http://www.fromthewilderness.com/free/ww3/031505_mckinney_transcript.shtml

http://www.spiegltech.com/media/McKinney2.rm (6 minutes, 12 seconds into the video)

http://www.boston.com/news/packages/sept11/anniversary/wire_stories/0903_plane_exercise.htm

8. It has been reported that the FBI long ago found three of four "black boxes" from the two airplanes which hit the Twin Towers, yet has consistently denied that they were ever found. Their data would be of the greatest importance to understanding the events of 9/11. This matter must be investigated and the data they provide released to the public.

See http://www.pnionline.com/dnblog/extra/archives/001139.html

http://www.counterpunch.org/lindorff12202005.html

For each of the four sites under investigation, the 9/11 Commission reported that two Boeing 757s, and two Boeing 767s (FAA, Part 121, airliners) owned by United Airlines and American Airlines were hijacked by novice pilots and were subsequently crashed, resulting in an unimaginable loss of life. Approximately 3,000 people died the morning of 9/11 as the direct result of these officially reported hijackings and subsequent crashes.

These four scheduled airliners were reported to have carried a total of 266 passengers and crew members, which, under FAA and NTSB regulations, demands a comprehensive investigation of the primary and contributing causes of each. In the case of suspected criminal foul play, the NTSB would normally assign the lead investigative role to the FBI, with assistance of investigators from the NTSB and FAA. A comprehensive investigation of each aircraft crash is not a regulatory option: they would have been mandatory. Therefore, we demand public release of each comprehensive crash investigation report, including access to all physical evidence that was required to have been collected and secured at a suitable facility. Such evidence should have included a large assortment of indestructible parts, including landing gears, surface actuators, engines, black boxes, and so on. The serialized parts would be invaluable in identifying each aircraft and, contrary to some reports, could not have "vaporized" upon impact.

Considering the enormous loss of life and financial collateral damage, if no crash investigations were conducted, who made the decision to disregard the FAA, Part 121, regulatory requirement? In the absence of the Part 121 investigation reports, the identity of the responsible authorities who made the decision not to investigate must be released, and they should be made immediately available for deposition under oath.

9. In the weeks before 9/11, the US Stock market showed rather high levels of activity on companies that would subsequently be affected by the attacks. The afternoon before the attack, alarm bells were sounding over trading patterns in stock options. A jump in United Air Lines some 90 times (not 90 percent) above normal between September 6 and September 10, for example, and 285 times higher than average the Thursday before the attack, have been reported. A jump in American Airlines put options 60 times (not 60 percent) above normal the day before the attacks has also been reported. No similar trading occurred on any other airlines appear to have occurred.

Between September 6-10, 2001, the Chicago Board Options Exchange saw suspicious trading on Merrill Lynch and Morgan Stanley, two of the largest WTC tenants. An average of 3,053 put options in Merrill Lynch were bought between Sept. 6-10, compared to an average of 252 in the previous week. Merrill Lynch, another WTC tenant, saw 12,215 put options bought between Sept. 7-10, whereas the previous days had seen averages of 212 contracts a day. According to Dylan Ratigan of Bloomberg News: "This would be the most extraordinary coincidence in the history of mankind, if it was a coincidence. This could very well be insider trading at the worst, most horrific, most evil use you've ever seen in your entire life. It's absolutely unprecedented."

On September 18, 2001, the BBC reported: "American authorities are investigating unusually large numbers of shares in airlines, insurance companies and arms manufacturers that were sold off in the days and weeks before the attacks. They believe that the sales were by people who knew about the impending disaster". According to the London Independent, October 10, 2001: "To the embarrassment of investigators, it has also emerged that the firm used to buy many of the 'put' options—where a trader, in effect, bets on a share price fall—on United Airlines stock was headed until 1998 by 'Buzzy' Krongard, now executive director of the CIA."

See http://news.bbc.co.uk/1/hi/uk/1549909.stm

http://news.independent.co.uk/business/news/story.jsp?story=99402

The 9/11 Commission, after looking into the pre-9/11 stock trades, never denied their unusual nature. Instead, the Commission declared that al-Qaeda did not conduct the trades, and asked no further questions.

http://www.amazon.com/gp/product/1566565847/qid=1120623441/sr=8-1/ref=pd_bbs_ur_1/103-8086269-4513445?n=507846&s=books&v=glance

Who, if not al-Qaeda, performed the incriminating trades? This information exists, it can be easily obtained, and it needs to be made public. Moreover, illegal money transfers may have been processed through computers housed at the World Trade Center shortly before planes crashed into the Twin Towers on 9/11. We demand a disclosure of the source of the put options and that this whole sordid affair receive a complete and public investigation.

See http://www.rediff.com/money/2001/dec/17wtc.htm

http://archives.cnn.com/2001/TECH/industry/12/20/wtc.harddrives.idg/

10. Eyewitness testimony and a substantiating photographic record suggest that a large sample of slag from the World Trade Center is being held at Hangar 17 of the John F. Kennedy International Airport in New York City. Access to the slag sample should be made available to appropriate physicists in order to conduct non-destructive X-ray Fluorescence tests and other forms of examination, which should reveal evidence of the cause of the collapse of the Twin Towers. Based on these tests, we further demand two small samples (about the size of a fist) be extracted from this large piece for further scientific analysis.

See http://911proof.com/resources/Slag+Sample.gif

11. Release of a complete inventory of the plane wreckage and debris from flights 11, 77, 93 or 175 or any other aircraft that crashed or was destroyed on September 11, 2001, including, but not limited to:

(a) the location (whether warehouses or otherwise) of all such items;

(b) a catalog of photographs and videotapes taken of any and all such items; and

(c) a list of all tests and examinations concerning any and all such items, including reports of such tests or examinations.

12. Release of a complete inventory of any steel, other metal or other material from the World Trade Centers, including, but not limited to:

(a) the location (whether warehouses or otherwise) of all such items;

(b) a catalog of photographs and videotapes taken of any and all such items; and

(c) a list of all tests and examinations concerning any and all such items, including reports of such tests or examinations.

On behalf of the People of the United States of America, we demand that the cover-up in this case end and that the kinds of documents, video and films, and physical evidence described above be provided to the public for experts and scholars to evaluate and assess in their efforts to expose falsehoods and reveal truths about events on 9/11.

FOR THE SOCIETY:

James H. Fetzer, Ph.D.
Founder and Co-Chair
Scholars for 9/11 Truth

Steven E. Jones, Ph.D.
Co-Chair
Scholars for 9/11 Truth

7 March 2006

*An online version of this petition -- with clickable links -- may be viewed here: http://st911.org/petition

NOTE:
The online version is also available at http://www.thepetitionsite.com/takeaction/929981172?ltl=1141667399

According to the government, the Twin Towers—not to mention WTC-3, WTC-4, WTC-5, and WTC-6—were destroyed by the combined effects of aircraft impacts and jet-fuel based fires, which weakened the steel and brought a "pancake" collapse. As Paul Craig Roberts has oberved, the official account suffers from "a massive energy deficit." So whom should we believe? The administration or our lying eyes?

Appendix

Selected Press Releases

Scholars Affirm Cheney Complicity in 9/11

Duluth, MN (PRWEB) March 12, 2006—A society of experts and scholars contends that the prosecution of Zacarias Moussaoui—for willfully concealing advance knowledge of the events of 9/11—has the status of a Soviet-style "show trial" and functions as a diversion from the real culprits. The nonpartisan group, Scholars for 9/11 Truth, asserts that the evidence implicating Vice President Dick Cheney of that very offense is more obvious and compelling. If they are even remotely correct, then the alleged terrorists appear to have been cast in the role of "patsies."

The experts base their conclusion on testimony presented to the 9/11 Commission by U.S. Secretary of Transportation Norman Mineta on May 23, 2003, which was omitted from its final report, and on related events at the Pentagon. Members of the society will present their findings during a press conference to be held at 1 PM on Tuesday at the United States Courthouse in Alexandria, VA, the location of a trial to determine whether Moussaoui, who is called "the 20th hijacker", should serve a life term or receive the death sentence.

"Mineta's testimony is devastating," observed James H. Fetzer, Ph.D., McKnight Professor at the University of Minnesota. Fetzer is the founder and co-chair of the scholars' society, which recently joined with Judicial Watch in calling for release of documents, films and videos, and physical evidence withheld from the public by the administration. "It pulls the plug on the Commission's contention there was no advance warning that the Pentagon was going to be hit."

According to Secretary Mineta's testimony, which is in the public domain, when he (Mineta) arrived at an underground bunker at the White House (known as the Presidential Emergency Operations Center), the Vice President was in charge. "During the time that the airplane was coming in to the Pentagon", he stated, "there was a young man who would come in and say to the Vice President, 'The plane is 50 miles out.' 'The plane is 30 miles out.'

"And when it got down to, 'The plane is 10 miles out,'" Mineta continued, "the young man also said to the Vice President, 'Do the orders still stand?' And the Vice President turned and whipped his neck around and said, 'Of course the orders still stand. Have you heard anything to the contrary?'" One way to construe these remarks could be that the orders were to shoot down the plane.

The scholars suggest that that is an implausible interpretation. The Pentagon, they observe, may be the most heavily defended building in the world. If the orders had been to "shoot it down," then no doubt it would have been shot down. Moreover, there would have been no apparent reason for the young man to have expressed concern over whether or not "the orders still stand." Shooting it down, under the circumstances, would have been the thing to do.

"The only reasonable interpretation of the orders," Fetzer observed, "is that the incoming aircraft should not be shot down, which would have been an obvious source of anxiety for an aide. Since it contradicts the official story about the Pentagon," he added, "it had to be suppressed and was not even included in The 9/11 Commission Report." And other scholars, including Professor David Ray Griffin of Claremont Graduate University, have drawn the same conclusion.

Philip J. Berg, Esq., Former Deputy Attorney General of Pennsylvania and a past candidate for Governor, Lt. Governor, and U.S. Senate from Pennsylvania, who is a member of Scholars for 9/11 Truth, added, "Those who made it happen were obviously in the position to know that it was going to happen and therefore could have sounded a warning alarm. The case against Cheney is more powerful than the case against Moussaoui.

No one is more culpable than the perpetrators. If Moussaoui deserves the death penalty, what does our Vice President deserve?"

Berg also represents William Rodriguez, a WTC witness, in a RICO lawsuit against officials in the administration for complicity in the events of 9/11. Other members of the society include Robert Bowman, head of the "Star Wars" program in both Democratic and Republican administrations; Morgan Reynolds, former Chief Economist for the Department of Labor in the Bush administration; Andreas von Buelow, former assistant defense minister of Germany; and Griffin, a noted theologian and author of The 9/11 Commission Report: Omissions and Distortions.

Members of the society point to other indications of advance knowledge, which include volumes of put-options placed by betting that the stock value of United and American Airlines would drop. The SEC has detailed information about those who placed the options, which it has not released to the public. "Time and time again," Fetzer remarked, "evidence that would expose the official account to be a deception and a hoax intended to manipulate the nation has been concealed."

According to Fetzer, experts in the society of scholars, including pilots and aeronautical engineers, physicists and mechanical engineers, have established that flying these planes would have been beyond the "hijackers" capabilities, that it would have been virtually impossible for cell phone calls to have been placed during those flights, and that even the Saudi Arabian Embassy has long confirmed that several of the accused "hijackers" did not die on 9/11.

"It does not take rocket science to infer that, if these guys were killed in the crash of these aircraft, then they cannot be alive and well and living in Saudi Arabia," he remarked, "yet the FBI has not bothered to revise its list of suspects." Other studies available on the society's web site at www.911Scholars.org indicate that the passenger manifests for the four flights did not include the names of the hijackers nor were autopsies conducted on them.

"A growing body of evidence supports the inference that these 19 men were patsies for forces within the United States government," Fetzer concluded. "This trial appears to be yet one more illustration of Karl Rove's policy of 'creating our own reality' to serve the political goals of the administration, even when it comes at the cost of the lives and the security of the American people. The idea that Bush is 'the security president' is just a cruel joke!"

Scholars Call Moussaoui Trial a "Charade"

Washington, DC (PRWEB) April 22, 2006—The trial holding Zacarias Moussaoui responsible for the horrors of 9/11 has all the marks of a political charade, according to Scholars for 9/11 Truth, a society of experts devoted to exposing falsehoods and establishing truths about the events of that day. "Even the most basic elements of due process have been violated," according to James H. Fetzer, its founder and co-chair, "by failing to prove that the accused had anything to do with 9/11. What we are seeing here tends to substantiate Charlie Sheen's allegations."

Fetzer insists there has been a clever ruse to confuse the jury by using a confession to one plot as though it were evidence of complicity in another. As The New York Times (April 27, 2005) reported, Moussaoui "confessed" to having been involved in a plot to fly a plane into the White House to free Sheik Omar Abdel Rahman, who is serving a life sentence for terrorist acts. He denied that he was part of the 9/11 attacks in New York City and Washington, D.C.

A Judicial "Shell Game"

The mentally unstable Moussaoui has now "confessed" that he and shoe-bomber Richard Reid were going to hijack a fifth aircraft and fly it into the White House, which was not the plot of which he was convicted. The Scholars believe government prosecutors have been playing a deceptive "shell game" by tying him to 9/11. Even the FBI has expressed doubts about Moussaoui's new version of events, since Reid left a will naming Moussaoui as his beneficiary, which was very odd if they were going to participate in a suicide mission together.

The government claims Moussaoui should be put to death for failing to report everything he knew about 9/11, which it claims would have saved lives. "This is blatantly unconstitutional," says 9/11 Truth Scholar

Webster Tarpley. "Under the Fifth Amendment to the US Constitution, nobody can be prosecuted for a failure to incriminate themselves.'"

"This entire trial has been a farce," says Fetzer, a professor of philosophy at the University of Minnesota. "Government prosecutors have contaminated witnesses, elicited testimony they cannot corroborate, and—according to multiple reports—even forced Moussaoui to wear a 'stun belt'. 50,000 volts should be enough to keep anyone from straying from the script," he said. "It is very difficult to imagine how testimony taken under duress is admissible."

The 9/11 Truth Movement

The fast-growing, over 200-member strong society is only the tip of an iceberg of a "9/11 Truth" movement which has produced dozens of books and scores of websites assailing the official version of 9/11. According to those involved, it's an uphill battle. John Leonard, a member of S9/11T and the publisher of several books on 9/11, including one by Webster Tarpley, insists that at least one basic element of the "9/11 Truth" idea can be conveyed in less than a minute, but he finds most Americans have psychological barriers to it.

"When we hit a fact that contradicts our world view, we usually pause, rationalize it and keep going. But sometimes we stumble onto something and want to dig deeper. That's where 9/11 researchers get started." Psychologists describe the resistance to ideas that threaten our sense of security as "cognitive dissonance", which can occur when, for example, a mother discovers evidence her husband has been molesting their daughter.

To demonstrate his position, Leonard asks people to consider three points: First, as the video-clip on this page (wtc7.gif) reveals, when WTC-7, a 47- story building that was not hit by any airplane, collapsed at 5:20 PM on 9/11, it displayed all of the signs of a controlled demolition, including sudden and complete collapse at virtually the rate of free fall into its own footprint, precisely as old casinos and hotels are brought down in Las Vegas.

Second, the collapse of WTC-7 is not even mentioned in The 9/11 Commission Report and has yet to be explained by the government. When Steven Jones, professor of physics at BYU, wanted the video of the collapse played on Tucker Carlson's MSNBC program, only a single frame was shown, which is typical of the attention it has drawn from the national media.

Third, for WTC-7 to be brought down by controlled demolition implies the existence of previously positioned explosives. That raises the possibility there were previously positioned explosives in WTC-1 and WTC-2 as well. Jones' own physics research, archived on the Scholar's web site at www.911Scholars.org, suggests that all three must have been brought down by controlled demolition.

Appeals to Fabricated Evidence

The most stunning example of government mendacity in the Moussaoui trial, Fetzer explains, came with the inflammatory recordings, allegedly the last moments of Flight 93, which went down in Pennsylvania. "Not only should they not have been admitted into evidence," he said, "but Allen Green has noted that much of the conversation is from the passenger cabin—which would not have been picked up by the cockpit voice recorder, even through an open door. Yet the cockpit door was supposed to be closed before it was finally broken open using a drink cart."

Another blunder was noted by a Muslim member of S9/11T. The last words of the "hijackers" on the tape are "Allah is great! (Allahu akbar!"). Muhammad Columbo says, "The last words of a Muslim cannot be these! They are used in the call to prayer, or in an attack at war. On the moment of death, a Muslim must confirm that "There is but one God, Allah, and that Mohammed is his prophet!" The government's own evidence proves either the tapes or the Muslims are fake.

Fetzer has also been struck by the use of phrases that appear to come from Hollywood scripts. "It's not enough that he talks about "making his day" as though he were a fan of Dirty Harry, but he also parodies "Born in the USA" with his rendition of "Burn in the USA" and has described his trial as a 'cyberlynching'. We are so used to movies that we may not notice this is supposed to be real life, where this trial appears to be following a script.

Patsies and Moles

Another perception of the events taking place in Alexandria, VA, comes from Webster Tarpley. "Moussaoui represents the classic case of the patsy - part double agent consciously working for the government, part psychotic, part fanatic, part dupe," Tarpley observes. "His lawyers tried to save him by suggesting he is a delusional paranoid schizophrenic, and this may be accurate."

"Like shoe bomber Richard Reid, Moussaoui is a product of Finsbury mosque in London, long notorious as a British intelligence recruiting center for expendable patsies...." In his book, "9/11: Synthetic Terror," Tarpley explains that, "Again and again, terrorist groups with US-UK backing have intervened against progressive nationalists in the Arab world, in favor of fundamentalists."

Of "false-flag" operations (a term from sailing ship days, when a war could be begun by raising an enemy flag and attacking one's own side), Tarpley observes, "The patsies ultimately have three vital functions. The first is that they have to be noticed. They must attract lots and lots of attention. They may issue raving statements." That description does seem to fit Moussaoui.

Secondly, they must stay out of jail, not to carry out the terrorist attack—that is a job for the professionals—but only to be blamed for it. Keeping them out of jail is a job for "the moles."

After the terror act is complete, the moles turn on the patsies and destroy them. In this case, the situation may be more complex, since Moussaoui has expressed the belief that he is going to be pardoned by President Bush, possibly in exchange for Americans captured in the war in Iraq.

Painwashing and Propaganda

On March 21, 2006, CBS reported the prosecutors' allegation that Moussaoui's lies to FBI agent Harry Samit had prevented the FBI from thwarting or at least minimizing the 9/11 attacks. Samit himself, however, in one of the most embarrassing twists of the trial with regard to the government's case, testified that he had already "warned higher-ups and others in the government at least 70 times that Moussaoui was a terrorist."

This nullifies the entire prosecution, Fetzer observes. "Ignoring five or six reports of this kind might reflect incompetence. Twenty or thirty, criminal neglect. But ignoring 70 reports has to be a matter of deliberate policy." Samit's testimony proves that, even if Moussaoui had come forward to incriminate himself in a plot in which he was not involved, it would not have helped. "Which means," Fetzer adds, "that this trial is simply an exercise in propaganda."

Jerry Mazza, Online Journal (April 14, 2006), has described the trial as a "painwashing," which he defines as repeating the same painful stories over and over again until the audience's resistance to questioning their authenticity is overcome. Leonard adds, "9/11 was what Pavlov called 'traumatic conditioning,' a way of reversing your normal characteristics by deep shock."

"If our findings are correct," Fetzer observed, "then the American government has been using acts of violence to instill fear into the American people in order to manipulate us for political purposes. That, however, is the definition of 'terrorism'; which means that the American government has been practicing terrorism on the American people. That may be difficult for many Americans to accept, but the evidence is clear and compelling. Charlie Sheen was right!"

Osama Tape Appears to be Fake, Experts Conclude

Duluth, MN (PRWEB) 28 May 2006— The latest audio tape attributed to Osama bin Laden appears to be one more installment in a succession of evidence fabricated by the US government to deceive the American people, according to Scholars for 9/11 Truth. "This tape is only the latest in a series of fabrications intended to mislead the American people," said James H. Fetzer, the society's founder. "The closer we get to revealing he truth about 9/11, the more furiously the government fights to conceal it!" He said members of Scholars and other experts had detected evidence of fakery.

In this new recording, a voice attributed to Osama bin Laden asserts that Zacarias Moussaoui was not involved in 9/11, which he knew to be the case because he had personally assigned the 19 hijackers involved in those events. The Osama of this tape thereby implicitly confesses his responsibility for orchestrating the attacks. However, in a tape released on December 27, 2001, the authenticity of which is not in doubt, Osama denied having had anything to do with 9/11. "Moreover," Fetzer added, "some of the 19 hijackers he 'personally assigned' have turned up alive and well."

To be sure, this new tape is not the first one in which bin Laden appears to take responsibility for the attacks. As David Ray Griffin, a prominent member of Scholars, points out, "The Osama on the video tape that appeared on December 13, 2001, confessed to planning the 9/11 attacks. But he is far darker and much heavier than the real Osama bin Laden. People can see the difference by looking up 'The Fake bin Laden Video Tape' on google."

Griffin's point is supported by a work-in-progress by members of Scholars for 9/11 Truth, which appears on its web site under the heading, "9/11: Have we been lied to?" It offers evidence of fakery in some of the videos based upon various physical properties of the figures that are presumed to be Osama, pointing out that there are differences in the ears, cheeks, eyebrows, length of the nose and shape of the nostrils. "The use of computer analysis can 'fine tune' these questions of facial characteristics," Fetzer said, "but the gross differences already show they are not the same."

Content Inconsistencies

"Another problem with the video of December 13, 2001," Griffin pointed out, "was that its stocky bin Laden praised two of the alleged hijackers, Wail M. Al-Shehri and Salem al-Hazmi, by name, and yet both the London Telegraph and the Saudi embassy reported several days after 9/11 that al-Hazmi was still alive and working in Saudi Arabia. Given the fact that the earlier video in which Osama confessed was clearly a fake, we should be suspicious of this latest apparent confession."

A professor at Duke, Bruce Lawrence, who has published Messages to the World: The Statements of Osama bin Laden, expressed profound skepticism about a tape that was released January 17, 2006, in a report that appeared two days later. "There's nothing in this from the Koran," Lawrence said. "He's, by his own standards, a faithful Muslim who quotes scripture in defense of his actions. There's no quotation from the Koran in the excerpts we got, no reference to specific events, no reference to past atrocities." Lawrence also observed the tape ran only 10 minutes, whereas the shortest previous tape, at 18 minutes, was nearly twice as long.

Fetzer noted that many of the same anomalous properties are found in the latest tape. "Compared to Osama's past performances," he observed, "this message is too short, too direct, and full of falsehoods. It was even described on CBS News by Bob Schieffer as 'almost American'." A translation of the text of the tape has also been released by IntelCenter, a private company that does contract work for the US government. "I suppose

I would be accused of being a 'conspiracy theorist' to suggest there is any connection," Fetzer added.

Authentic Voice/Fake Content

Informed that Reuters news agency has reported confirmation that the voice on the tape is indeed that of Osama bin Laden, Fetzer replied, "The fact that the voice is his does not prove that the tape is authentic. We have had phony tapes before using voices that were authentic. Mark Bingham, a passenger on Flight 93, is supposed to have called his mother and said, 'Hi, Mom, this is Mark Bingham!' His mother confirmed it was his voice, but does anyone seriously believe that Mark Bingham would have used his last name in identifying himself to his mother?"

Griffin agreed, adding, "Back in 1999, William Arkin published an article entitled, 'When Seeing and Hearing isn't Believing' (which can also be accessed on google). Describing the new technology of 'voice morphing' (or 'voice synthesizing'), Arkin explained that, if audio technicians have a recording of your voice, then they can create a tape in which your voice—your authentic voice!—says anything they wish."

In a press release on April 22, 2006, the Scholars observed that a tape played at the trail of Zacarias Moussaoui included discussion among the passengers about using a drink cart to break down the cabin door alleged to have been picked up on a cockpit voice recorder, which does not record conversations in the passenger cabin. "This is not the first and certainly will not be the last time that the American government plays the American people for suckers," Fetzer said.

"We have just acquired new evidence that the Pentagon video tapes were processed and manipulated in an apparent effort to distort or conceal what happened there on 9/11," Fetzer observed. "Apparently, whenever the government feels the need to bolster the official myth about 9/11, it simply fabricates a new tape! Anybody who wants to keep score should visit our web site."

Scholars for 9/11 Truth is a non-partisan society of experts and scholars dedicated to exposing falsehoods and establishing truths about the events of 9/11. It maintains a web site at www.911Scholars.org, where it archives its studies, documents, records and evidence.

Documentary support for the conclusions reported here may be found at the Scholars for 9/11 Truth web site at www.911Scholars.org.

Index

L

M

N

O

P